MEDIA, CHILDREN, AND THE FAMILY
SOCIAL SCIENTIFIC, PSYCHODYNAMIC, AND CLINICAL PERSPECTIVES

MEDIA, CHILDREN, AND THE FAMILY
SOCIAL SCIENTIFIC, PSYCHODYNAMIC, AND CLINICAL PERSPECTIVES

Edited by

Dolf Zillmann
Jennings Bryant
University of Alabama

Aletha C. Huston
University of Kansas

LEA LAWRENCE ERLBAUM ASSOCIATES, PUBLISHERS
1994   Hillsdale, New Jersey   Hove, UK

Lawrence Erlbaum Associates, Inc., Publishers
365 Broadway
Hillsdale, New Jersey 07642

Library of Congress Cataloging-in-Publication Data
Media, children, and the family : social scientific, psychodynamic, and
    clinical perspectives / edited by Dolf Zillmann, Jennings Bryant,
    Aletha C. Huston.
        p.   cm.
    Includes bibliographical references and index.
    ISBN 0-8058-1210-5 (alk. paper). — ISBN 0-8058-1415-9 (pbk. :
alk. paper)
    1. Mass media — Social aspects — Congresses.   2. Mass media and the
family — Congresses.   3. Mass media and children — Congresses.
4. Television broadcasting — Social aspects — Congresses.
5. Pornography — Social aspects — Congresses.   I. Zillmann, Dolf.
II. Bryant, Jennings.   III. Huston, Aletha C.
HM258.M3743   1994
302.23 — dc20   93-40758
                                                                              CIP

Books published by Lawrence Erlbaum Associates are printed on acid-free
paper, and their bindings are chosen for strength and durability.

Printed in the United States of America
10   9   8   7   6   5   4   3   2

CONTENTS

v

PREFACE

The weather in Pittsburgh during November 9 to 11, 1990, was uncommonly gloomy. Fog, rain, wind, and cold chilled to the bone those who dared to venture outdoors. The atmosphere inside the Green Tree Marriott was considerably different, however, as a small group of scholars meeting therein generated enough heat and light to warm and illuminate several hotels.

The locus of the intellectual combustion process was an assemblage of scholars brought together by National Family Foundation President Barbara Hattemer to share findings and insights on the effects of media on children and family. The kindling that created an occasional hot flame was *diversity*. Not only did the participants reflect widely divergent political orientations and value systems, but they represented three distinct domains of inquiry into human motivation and behavior: social scientific, psychodynamic (or psychoanalytical), and clinical practice. Representatives from these three areas rarely speak to each other, much less listen. Yet Barbara Hattemer recognized that each of these three domains was privy to important evidence and insights that needed to transcend epistemological and methodological boundaries if understanding of the topic was to improve dramatically. For her awareness of and appreciation for diverse research traditions and for her dedication to theoretical and practical integration, we are exceedingly grateful. Moreover, we want to express our gratitude to Barbara Hattemer for the grace and finesse she so consistently demonstrated in organizing and moderating the conference.

The conference was such a success that the editors of this volume wanted to extend the conversation—at a later time and to a wider audience. Accordingly, we invited a select group of conference presenters to reflect further on their topic areas, to assimilate ideas garnered from other conference participants, and to package their ideas as chapters in this book. We asked the authors not to stop with a summary of findings but to lend additional distinction to the book by applying the "binoculars" of their particular perspective and by offering suggestions as to the implications of their findings. We hope readers of this volume will learn as much as we have from exposure to scholars with diverse perspectives and ways of knowing.

The contents of this volume have been organized into six parts. Part I, "Media and the Family," contains five chapters concerned with some of the broader issues and integrative themes in this area. The initial chapter, "Media Influence, Public Policy, and the Family," written by the volume editors, attempts to provide a foundation for the rest of the book by offering a treatment of several of the concepts that undergird the study of media, family, and children. Additionally, several critical interrelationships between scholarly inquiry, public policy, and media practices and performance are explored.

A second foundation chapter by Margaret Andreasen, entitled "Patterns of Family Life and Television Consumption From 1945 to the 1990s," provides valuable and frequently illuminating normative data that serve to anchor many of the later discussions in the book. Andreasen also includes several suggestions for changes that need to be made by media, families, and researchers if we are to improve the operation of media and the functioning of families in modern society.

Many of the criticisms and concerns with television and family values that have received attention in the popular press stem from the way families are presented in media fare and how media family members act and interact. In "Family Images and Family Actions as Presented in the Media: Where We've Been and What We've Found," Thomas Skill presents the findings of several systematic content analyses of family life as exhibited in American mass media. Some of his conclusions may be surprising.

Alison Alexander moves the discussion from media content to media effects. In "The Effect of Media on Family Interaction," she first reviews options regarding the kinds of effects that television can be expected to have on family interaction and succinctly summarizes the research evidence supporting these various positions. A major contribution of this chapter is that it offers a rethinking of the theoretical perspectives from which research in family and media may best be conducted.

One of the most productive new methodologies for examining the role of media in contemporary family life is the Experience Sampling Method (ESM). Robert Kubey briefly reviews contributions of that research tradition in "Media Implications for the Quality of Family Life." His analysis of the implications of the research findings from ESM and other methodologies used to assess media effects provides stimulating reading.

Part II is entitled "Developmental and Educational Implications." The first chapter is Aletha Huston and John Wright's "Educating Children With Television: The Forms of the Medium." One contribution of this chapter is a discussion of the effects of television's formal features on children's intellectual activities, with particular attention paid to forms used in educational television. Another is an explanation of ways television can be used as an ally of parents, rather than as an enemy.

A different tack on the benefits media can have is taken by Ernest Allen of the National Center for Missing and Exploited Children, who notes in "Strategies for the 1990s: Using the Media for Good" that "the media can be the best friend the parents of a missing child may have." This chapter provides a practitioner's perspective and a valuable case study of educational and prosocial benefits of judicious public communication campaigns. The suggestions for future strategies for prosocial media use proffer ideas that are a radical departure from orthodoxy.

A second case study of effective prosocial media use is contained in Dorothy Singer and Jerome Singer's chapter, "Evaluating the Classroom Viewing of a Television Series: 'Degrassi Junior High'." Systematic evaluations of the effects of targeted, prosocial television programs are too rare. The study reported in this chapter provides a useful model for how to conduct such media evaluation research. It also offers insights into the effects targeted media content can have on adolescents' attitudes and behaviors.

To see how psychodynamic perspectives can differ markedly from social scientific and clinical perspectives on media effects, one has only to compare Charles Ashbach's chapter with the others in this part. In "Media Influences and Personality Development: The Inner Image and the Outer World," Ashbach provides quite an inventory of the "profound changes in the mind, behavior, and personality" that television purportedly causes for children and adolescents.

The third part of this volume is devoted to essays on the perennially hot topic of "Effects of Violence and Horror." In "Televison, Films, and the Emotional Life of Children," Andre Derdeyn and Jeffrey Turley provide a clinical psychodynamic perspective on the functions and effects of horror films. The chapter is anchored by a case study of the meaning of a horror film for a troubled boy and the use of the film in his psychotherapy.

In "Confronting Children's Fright Responses to Mass Media," Joanne Cantor summarizes the results of a systematic research program on the effects on children of watching television shows and films that depict danger, injury, bizarre images, and terror-stricken victims. A valuable contribution of this chapter is that it offers a set of broad generalizations that emanate from her research program.

The past three decades have yielded a vast amount of research into the effects of television on viewer aggression. In "Television and Aggression: Recent Developments in Research and Theory," Russell Geen draws on research in three traditions to answer two questions: (a) Is watching violence presented on television associated with increased aggression in the viewer? (b) When observation of violence is followed by aggression, what intervening processes connect the two?

Part IV, "Sexual Content and Family Context," examines sexual thema in mainstram media and their effects. In the first chapter, Bradley Greenberg presents a summary of "Content Trends in Media Sex." Six different forms of media content are systematically examined: music videos, X-rated videos, daytime soaps, prime-time commercial network television, magazines, and movies.

The other chapter in this part considers the effects of watching a great deal of sexually oriented television programming. In "Effects of Massive Exposure to Sexually Oriented Prime-Time Television Programming on Adolescents' Moral Judgment," Jennings Bryant and Steven Rockwell present the results of three experimental studies that, in combination, attempt to address two questions: (a) Can the sexually oriented messages of primetime entertainment fare change teenagers' moral judgment? (b) What factors, if any, can mediate any media effects on teenagers' moral judgment?

Part V examines "Effects of Erotica and Pornography," a topic so volatile that it spawned commissions and task forces all over the globe during the past decade. Dolf Zillmann's "Erotica and Family Values" sets the stage for debate on this topic with its introducory statement: "The values manifest in erotic entertainment are on a collision course with those pertaining to family as the most fundamental social institution in society." The chapter contains a systematic conceptualization and explication of this claim.

In "Pornography and Sexual Callousness: The Perceptual and Behavioral Consequences of Exposure to Pornography," Jim Weaver summarizes research on the content characteristics of contemporary pornography and synthesizes much of the extant research evidence on the effects of pornography consumption. His conclusions suggest several areas of consensus, and he notes some strong implications.

One distinguishing feature of Victor Cline's chapter, "Pornography Effects: Empirical and Clinical Evidence," is that it really does integrate clinical and empirical social scientific perspectives. The blending of detailed examples from clinical practice with more objective findings from empirical research offers revealing insights into the uses and effects of pornography.

"Addiction" is frequently mentioned as an effect of exposure to pornography, but seldom has it been the subject of systematic treatment. Douglas Reed tackles this issue "head on" in "Pornography Addiction and Compulsive Sexual Behavior." Research evidence from medical and social scientific literatures is integrated into this clinically based treatment of a frequently overlooked media effect.

Although fairly common in medical research, systematic reviews that treat in the aggregate studies on the same topic are still rare in most areas of social scientific inquiry. In "A Systematic Review of the Effects of Aggressive and Nonaggressive Pornography," John Lyons, Rachel Anderson, and David Larson indicate the benefits of applying this approach to the study of the impact of pornography. Their review of 81 experimental studies indicates substantial concensus that exposure to pornography does have negative effects in several areas.

The final part is "Social Awareness and Public Policy." Judith Reisman's chapter on "Child Pornography in Erotic Magazines, Social Awareness, and Self-Censorship" is multidimensional. At one level is a report of a major content analysis, funded by the U.S. Department of Justice, of child pornography in three "soft core" magazines. At another level, two provocative subtexts reveal: (a) surprising responses to the reports of this content analysis, and (b) empirical assessments of industry self-censorship after these reports were circulated.

In the concluding chapter, Robert Showers examines "Research, Public Policy, and Law: Combination for Change." Historically, social scientific research findings have very rarely translated into changes in public policy and law. Showers indicates that pornography research may become a major exception to this rule. He concludes that researchers, lawyers, and policy makers must meet the challenges of integrating research, public policy, and law if America's children are to thrive in healthy families in the future.

One of the goals of the conference that birthed this book was consensus building in the area of media and family. From examining the findings and insights of a very diverse group of scholars, it seems to the editors that consensus building in several areas is a distinct possibility. We hope that this volume becomes instrumental to this end.

Jennings Bryant
Dolf Zillmann
Aletha C. Huston

Part I

MEDIA AND THE FAMILY

1

MEDIA INFLUENCE, PUBLIC POLICY, AND THE FAMILY

Aletha C. Huston
University of Kansas

Dolf Zillmann
Jennings Bryant
University of Alabama

Mass media are an integral part of virtually every society on the globe. Almost all children born in the United States in the 1990s will live in a home with at least one television set from Day 1 onward. Most children will have ready access to multiple television sets, many television channels, videotapes, videogames, computer games, magazines, books, audiotapes, and disks.

Mass media are distinct from other potential socializing institutions (e.g., schools, religious institutions) in several important ways: (a) Children's primary contact with them occurs informally as part of the home and family environment rather than in structured settings and activities; (b) with some important exceptions, the contents of mass media are not planned or designed to educate, to enhance development, or to socialize children into the mores of their culture. Instead, media are often designed for entertainment or attracting audiences to advertisements; messages are conveyed but are incidental to the purposes of the producers; (c) children's exposure to mass media begins in infancy. Long before most children enter any formal educational setting, they have watched hundreds of hours of television, and some of them have also had extensive contact with books and other media.

There is a widespread tendency to blame media for every social ill from declining academic skills among schoolchildren to the decay of morality in social conduct. A more muted, but continuing, theme extols the benefits conferred on society by mass media—instant information about world events, educational programming, and locating America's most wanted criminals. In order to make a responsible assessment of these claims, we need to define *media*.

WHAT ARE MEDIA?

When people refer to "media" in these contexts, they usually mean television, although popular music lyrics have generated their share of social criticism. Television is certainly the predominant mass medium in the sense that it occupies an enormous number of hours for people of all ages and is a central part of home life for many people throughout the world. However, "television" is a constantly changing medium because of new technologies and new systems of production and distribution. Cable and satellite broadcasting systems enable many viewers to have access to large numbers of channels, many of which are concentrated on particular audiences or types of programming (e.g., sports, news, children, languages other than English). Videotapes and players are available in every super-market, and the great majority of American homes contain a VCR. Remote controls are now routine equipment for television sets and VCRs, allowing viewers to shift readily and often among programs, to play tapes on fast forward and reverse, and so on. Computer technology has made possible computer games, videogames, and interactive activities with video images and sounds (Dorr & Kunkel, 1990).

The rapid dissemination of these technological changes has directly affected children and families in their home environments. The media environment in the average home in every industrialized country in the world was dramatically different in 1990 than in 1980.

Changing social mores and public policy have also led to changes in media content on conventional broadcast outlets (e.g., network television). With federal deregulation in the early 1980s came a reduction in the already small number of educational programs for children on commercial televi-sion and an increase in advertising to children (Condry, Bence, & Scheibe, 1988; Kerkman, Kunkel, Huston, Wright, & Pinon, 1990). There was little change in violence, but increasingly explicit sexual content.

Any discussion of the role of media in the lives of children and families must take account of the fact that *media* represent a moving target. The term encompasses many forms of communication that have undergone rapid changes during the years since World War II and will continue to do so.

The Family Concept

Society's view of the family—what it is and what it ought to be—makes "family" as much a moving target as the media. The traditional conceptualization of the so-called nuclear family stipulates cohabitation by a man and a woman who are joined in marriage and who raise their own genetic offspring together. The only universally tolerated deviation from this model concerns the children's genetic origin. The married couple is deemed entitled to care for children other than their own progeny and to assimilate them into the family unit.

This conceptualization of family has been severely challenged and drastically revised in recent years (Ahrons & Rodgers, 1987). Single-parent families, often but not necessarily residues of the nuclear family, have been growing in numbers and have gained general acceptance as nontransitory, permanent institutions of child nurturance. Moreover, in granting family status to cohabitational parent–child arrangements, the requirement of marital status for parents, single or otherwise, has been largely abandoned. Although not legally recognized in most locales, same-gender parenting by a couple is de facto accepted. Extended and multigeneration households and communal arrangements of adults with children, mostly composed of single parents and their progeny, are also accepted family forms.

In light of such changes it would seem prudent to abandon the idealized, narrow conceptualization of family in favor of a family concept capable of accommodating existing realities. For our purposes here, we can define family as cohabitational arrangements of adults and children in which the adults assume legal responsibility for the welfare and maturation of the children. This definition accommodates the nuclear family as much as alternative family forms of the present and future.

Media and Children

Children are a special audience (Dorr, 1986). Because of cognitive immaturity, they are generally assumed to be more vulnerable than adults to negative influences of television content (e.g., violence, pornography) and to the persuasive messages of advertising. Television is a particularly appealing medium to young children in part because many of its images and modes of representation are readily understood; it does not require the child to learn a complicated system of decoding as reading does, for example. As a result, it has enormous potential for contributing to children's development through educational and prosocial programming. Television specializes in stories and fantasy that may play a major role in personality development. The chapters in this book include psychoanalytic (Ashbach;

Derdeyn), clinical (Cline; Reed) and cognitive developmental (Alexander; Bryant & Rockwell; Cantor; Huston & Wright; Singer & Singer) perspectives on how children use and interpret what they see on television in both beneficial and detrimental ways.

Although some may disagree about how television affects children, no one disputes that they watch it a great deal. A conservative estimate is that the average child watches about 3 hours a day (Huston et al., 1992). Viewing time increases during the preschool years, drops a little around age 6 due to school entry, increases until late childhood, then drops again in adolescence.

The effects of viewing depend largely on the types of programs watched and the individual abilities and personality dispositions of the viewer. The chapters in this book offer a sample, by no means complete, of both positive and negative effects including education, prosocial behavior, coping with fear, personality development, violence, and pornography. In each domain, it is clear that children's responses to television content depend on cognitive developmental levels, personal dispositions, and the environmental context of viewing. For example, preschool children are frightened by different types of content than are older children; moreover, the same content may create nightmares for one child and be the source of coping skills for another. Several papers concentrate on negative effects of sexual content, but there is as yet little investigation of how media can (or do) contribute in a healthy way to children's learning about sex (cf. Roberts, 1982).

Media and the Family

Children's use of media is socialized primarily in the family (cf. Bryant, 1990). Television is an integral part of family life. Viewing occurs primarily with other family members, especially for young children. For example, in one longitudinal study, more than 70% of the time that 3- to 7-year-old children spent watching general audience programming occurred with a parent (St. Peters, Fitch, Huston, Wright, & Eakins, 1991). Moreover, television habits are formed early. The amount of television viewed is quite stable from age 3 onward, probably because it depends on family patterns that do not change readily (Huston, Wright, Rice, Kerkman, & St. Peters, 1990).

Social critics often berate parents for failing to regulate their children's television viewing. It is true that most parents exercise little control over the amount or kind of television their children watch. When they do regulate, they typically do so on the basis of program content rather than overall time. When parents encourage particular types of programs or exercise restrictions, there is some impact on their children's viewing. However, parental example is probably the most important way in which parents influence their children's television uses and abuses of television (St. Peters et al., 1991). Not only do parents provide a model of how to use television, but, because television is viewed in a communal part of the home (e.g., the living room, family room), children are exposed to what their parents watch simply by virtue of living in the same household.

Parents may also moderate or counteract the influences of television content on their children, once that content is viewed. Numerous studies indicate that adult discussion and explanation of content helps children to comprehend messages and increases the amount learned from educational programs. When parents and children discuss value issues raised by television (e.g., the justification for aggression), it is likely that children will be less influenced by negative content than when the television experience is unmediated (Desmond, Singer, & Singer, 1990; Wright, St. Peters, & Huston, 1990).

Television may also affect the family as a group – the ways they spend their time and the nature of their interactions with one another (Bryant, 1990). Families are often shown on television. Content analyses of their interactions help to understand the kinds of models portrayed (Skill, this volume). It is likely that families adopt some of the patterns they see on television, or that they consider those patterns normative. If the patterns involve hostile humor, lack of caring, or weak discipline, some people would argue that imitation would have negative effects on healthy family functioning. On the other hand, overly idealized patterns of family relationships could set a standard against which most real families compare poorly. Some critics have argued, for instance, that the Huxtable parents in the Cosby Show are unrealistically able to devote time and attention to their children in the midst of busy careers. Several of these possibilities are considered in the chapters in this book and in some earlier work (e.g., Brown & Bryant, 1990), but data are scant. The effects of family portrayals on viewers' behaviors and expectations are important topics for future research.

Television effects on the family go beyond program content to impacts of the medium itself on patterns of family life, time spent together, and outside activities (Robinson, 1990). Participant observations have shown that television has many functions in families, ranging from determining schedules to defining what is "right" (Lull, 1990). The demands of the medium, regardless of content, can affect the types of interactions among family members. For instance, parents and children tend to talk less to one another when viewing television than in other activities, but they are often in close physical proximity (e.g., touching, hugging; Wright et al., 1990). Once again, the research in this area is sparse and needs expansion.

Clinical Implications

Clinicians often encounter "effects" of television, movies, or other mass media in clients' fantasies and actions. Several chapters in this volume discuss the contributions of sexual media content to behavior disorders for both children and adults (Cline; Reed). Videotapes, some cable channels, and magazines have made hardcore pornography much more readily available to children growing up in the 1980s than in earlier decades (Huston et al., 1992). Clinicians and others have expressed considerable concern about the effects of pornography on children's and adults' views of "normal" sex, attitudes about sexual violence, and proneness to deviant sexual behavior.

Children are also the subjects in some pornographic films and magazines; campaigns against showing children or "pseudo-children" (adults dressed in childish costumes) did have some success by the end of the decade (Reisman, this volume). Children who participate in pornographic media are often sexually abused as well, a phenomenon that clinicians need to address (Silbert, 1989).

Television can also be used in prevention and treatment of emotional disturbance. Programs dealing with feelings, prosocial behavior, sensitivity to others, and coping with social problems have demonstrated effects on children's positive social development. One of the first and best documented is "Mr. Rogers' Neighborhood," a program for preschoolers that emphasizes the basic goodness and individuality of each human being (Stein & Friedrich, 1975). In the present volume, positive effects of "Degrassi Junior High," a program for young adolescents, are demonstrated (Singer & Singer). Clinicians can help parents and children select programs that are planned to deal with social and emotional issues in constructive ways.

Fears can also be dealt with through television. For example, well-designed films about surgery, going to the dentist, and the like can help reduce children's fears of such procedures. Cantor's work (this volume) includes a number of suggestions for ways in which parents and children can cope with fear-provoking content on television. A case study of a young boy (Derdyn, this volume) illustrates how a child's fascination with horror films can be used to good advantage in treatment.

Public Policy

Children and families live in a media environment that is not of their own making. They can select from what is available, but they do not have many opportunities to increase or change the menu. Decisions about production and distribution of most mass media are made by private corporations. In this country, because of the First Amendment to the Constitution, those decisions are protected from government interference except in unusual circumstances. The voice of the ordinary citizen, therefore, can be heard through nongovernmental advocacy and through carefully delimited public policies.

Broadcast television is subject to federal regulation through the Communications Act of 1934 establishing that the airwaves belong to the public. Stations must be licensed, and they are required to serve "the public interest, convenience, and necessity." Although this requirement has led to minimal regulation of any kind, it has been used to promote particular categories of programming. The Children's Educational Television Act of 1990, for example, established a requirement that each station must serve the informational and educational needs of children (cf. Huston, Watkins, & Kunkel, 1989). At this writing, there is little evidence of enthusiastic enforcement or effects on programming.

Efforts to restrict or prohibit certain kinds of content by government action are unlikely to succeed because they encounter problems of definition, diversity of opinion, and conflicts with basic principles of free expression. Advertising to children was restricted by the 1990 legislation, but program content (e.g., violence, sex) raises other issues. First, there is considerable disagreement even among communication specialists about how to define such content. Second, there are diverse values and opinions about what is "harmful" or objectionable. Finally, many people believe that the goal of achieving a reduction in objectionable content is not worth the loss of free expression required to regulate content.

Policy gets made and changed by executive action as well as by legislation. Agencies charged with enforcing the law can pursue their task vigorously or not at all. In the process, they often make policy as well as implementing it. One example is the concerted campaign by the Justice Department in the 1980s to eliminate child pornography and obscenity. They assembled and publicized casual and selected observations as well as research evidence about negative effects of pornography; they conducted federal initiatives and training for local prosecutors around the country; and they sought and received both legislative and judicial actions supporting their position (Showers, this volume).

Government funding is probably the most effective means of expanding the menu of media offerings. Public television was established in the late 1960s to supply quality informational programming for children and adults because this type of programming did not arise spontaneously in the commercial marketplace. Funds for public television were drastically reduced in the 1980s, and the number of educational programs produced for children declined accordingly. A newly established National Endowment for Children's Educational Television is charged to fund production of educational programs. Although its funds are relatively small, it is one means by which public policy can improve media offerings.

Goals of Media: Entertainment Versus Education

The educators' dilemma with television and other mass media fare derives from the simple fact that the media are commercial enterprises whose goal of profit maximization is served well by entertainment and poorly by educational efforts. This situation is unlikely to change, and one must accept the prospect that advertiser-supported media will remain partial to entertainment — with little, if any, educational strings attached.

The indicated struggle is apparent in the renewed controversy over children's television programming. The regulatory intervention manifest in the Children's Educational Television Act of 1990 has thus far failed to instill or restore educational responsibilities in broadcasters. Programming has continued to be educationally uninspiring. Its main objective remains to make largely moronic material more engaging to children, attracting and holding them to the screen for good ratings and revenue.

A major reason for the limited success of the 1990 act has been the lack of enforcement by an FCC that has been committed to minimal regulation for some years. The attempt to infuse educational responsibility through legislation has thus far prompted broadcasters, now required to prove to the Federal Communication Commission that their programming serves the "educational and informational needs" of children, to become excessively imaginative, if not plainly deceitful, in defending their products. In license-renewal applications, they claim that these products have cultural integrity. For instance, "Bucky O'Hare," a program without notable merit to educators, is said to deal with issues of social consciousness and responsibility as central themes because "good-doer Bucky fights off the evil toads" (Waters, 1992, p. 88).

On occasion, the industry's unwillingness to serve educational objectives surfaces in blatant fashion. The head of children's programming at CBS, Judy Price, expressed her concern about low ratings and the potential loss of money by suggesting that educational programming has no appeal to children. "If broccoli is the only thing on a kid's plate, that does not mean that he's going to eat it." And she defends what broadcasters' practice by insinuating a lack of consensus for educational efforts: "Who's to say what's appropriate for our young" (Waters, 1992, p. 88)?

Needless to say, in the commercial media world of today and tomorrow, a nurturant diet will not be the only item on the menu. Any such diet will, in fact, have to compete against the lure of a great variety of cheap sugar candy. High-quality, entertaining educational efforts are expensive and time-consuming to produce. When educational efforts through television collide with cheaply made entertainment and its arsenal of bells and whistles, the competition for audiences is fierce. At one level, it appears that entertainment surely will triumph in this battle (Wakshlag, 1985; Wakshlag, Day, & Zillmann, 1981). On the other hand, Saturday morning programming has experienced a drastic loss of audiences in the last several years, whereas children's cable channels have increased their audiences with programming that is more varied (Dorr & Kunkel, 1990).

Parental guidance and supervision in program choice may solve this problem to some extent. Assertive, maturing children will eventually succeed, however, in making their own choices, so parents cannot be expected to be the gatekeepers. This is particularly likely under the increasingly typical conditions of television consumption by children: with their own set in the privacy of their own room (Andreason, this volume).

The issue of educational merit has been raised for children's programming. Raising this issue for adult programming, even for programs addressing adolescents, seems ludicrous. In the United States we have grown accustomed to the idea that the commercial mass media, in pursuit of their own economic best interest, serve up entertainment first and foremost. Any educational purpose is secondary. Although the broadcast media are obligated to operate "in the public interest," the combination of a poor definition of such interest, a commitment to free speech, and an inability to prove compellingly that in particular cases public interest is violated make it seem absurd to expect genuine public education from the mass media. Noncommercial alternatives, supported by the public, are those burdened with the responsible and deliberate transmission of the cultural heritage—that is, with a specifically informational and educational mission. The media market forces again a competition between educationally ambitious and entertainment programming, with entertainment likely to win out easily.

In adult programming, then, entertainment rules supreme, with concern for the public's curiosity and the industry's pocket books, but without responsibility for consequences of consumption. The television screen is the grand fantasy maker—without liability for the aftermath. It is this implicit, yet absolute, refusal to assume any responsibility for social influences that many scholars dealing with the societal impact of the media find difficult to accept.

At the heart of this controversy is the media's preoccupation with violence and sexuality. Images of violence abound in programs for children, adolescents, and adults alike (Gerbner, Gross, Morgan, & Signorielli, 1986). Sexual imagery is similarly ubiquitous in these programs (Greenberg, this volume). The display of such images has apparent entertainment value. But not too many have suggested that prolonged consumption of material laden with portrayals of excessive violence or uncurtailed sexuality aids the emotional development of children and adolescents or consolidates the maturity of adults. On the contrary, research on media effects has shown such material to have nonimmediate consequences that benefit neither the individual consumer nor society at large.

Much research suggests adverse effects of the prevalence of violence on children and adults. Children may be disturbed and suffer setbacks in their emotional maturation (Cantor, this volume). Adults may come to misjudge the danger posed by social environments and develop apprehensions about being victimized (Gerbner et al., 1986; Zillmann & Wakshlag, 1985). Children and adolescents may adopt violent behaviors as a means of solving social conflict (Bandura, 1986; Huesmann & Eron, 1986), and adults' propensity for violent action may be enhanced in a great variety of circumstances (Geen, this volume).

The Television Violence Act of 1990, sponsored by Senator Paul Simon of Illinois, is based on the merits of the indicated media-violence research. It threatened legislative intervention in case self-regulation fails. Under such pressure, the major networks (ABC, CBS, NBC) recently adopted stringent violence-curtailing guidelines. They are, among others: Gratuitous or excessive depictions of violence, or redundant violence shown solely for its own sake, are not acceptable; programs should not depict violence as glamorous, nor as an acceptable solution to human conflict; depictions of violence may not be used to shock or stimulate the audience; scenes showing excessive gore, pain, or physical suffering are not acceptable.

The guidelines are, in fact, so stringent that their rigorous application lacks any credibility. The stipulation that violence shall not be used to shock or stimulate, for example, would seem to preclude the airing of horror movies generally. Is this likely to happen in the fierce competition of the networks with cable television and video rentals? It seems more likely that the networks will defy the agreed-upon guidelines the way they defied the Children's Educational Television Act.

Although the likelihood of children's exposure to suggestive or explicit portrayals of sexual behaviors is steadily growing, nothing is known about likely developmental consequences of such early exposure. Regarding adolescents, their natural curiosity about sexual matters is exploited by a wealth of teenyporn creations that ridicule sexual inexperience and glorify sexual callousness (Greenberg, this volume). Given the threat of the AIDS epidemic, such entertainment exploitation defines a dubious formula for sexual socialization, and it shows once more the unwillingness of the media to assume any responsibility for likely consequences of their money-making ventures.

The scarcity of data concerning the impact of suggestive erotica on children and adolescents contrasts sharply with the wealth of information on the consequences of exposure to hardcore pornography (Cline; Lyons, Anderson, & Larson; Reed; Weaver; Zillmann; all this volume). Demonstrated effects range from increased sexual callousness toward women to heightened self-perceived rape proclivity and from diminished empathy with the plight of rape victims to eroding beliefs in the family as a viable and desirable societal institution.

Erotica are, no doubt, big business (Hebditch & Anning, 1988; Weaver, this volume), and it is understandable that programmers find it difficult, apparently impossible, to resist the prospect of easy money. No wonder, then, that obstacles were eliminated and the way paved for half-way respectable erotica on the screen at home. What used to be unimaginable broadcast material became common fare within a few years. Screen voyeurism was born and became respectable (Leland, 1992). Esteemed entertainment stars now avail themselves to "show everything," thereby abolishing the distinction between pornography and more ambitious drama. The conventions of drama are changing before our eyes, leading to the expectation that in the near future several episodes of explicitly portrayed sexual behaviors, with the already common portrayal of frequent acts of excessively brutal violence, will be normative for dramatic productions (Zillmann, 1992b).

It would seem fair to credit the entertainment consumer with some responsibility for these changes. The commercial media, after all, only provide what the public values enough to spend money on. If the attainment of gratification through erotic entertainment were without cost in socially reproached and disallowed behaviors, the commercial exploitation of potentially prurient interest would generate little controversy. Ample research shows, however, that such cost does accrue to pornography (Marshall, Laws, & Barbaree, 1990; Zillmann & Bryant, 1989b). It is the prevention and elimination of that cost that is at issue.

How to Stem the Tide?

Can the apparent gap between realities of entertainment and visions of an informational–educational function of the mass media be bridged? Can education and entertainment be merged?

In a limited way it can. In children's educational television, for instance, such a merger was attempted and proved successful. The formula of the Children's Television Workshop, offering education in a playful amusing frame, attracts children to the screen that less entertaining programming does not (Bryant, Zillmann, & Brown, 1983; Lesser, 1974). In-school instructional television uses a variety of entertaining formats to teach math, history, and current events. In particular, the involvement of humor has been shown to have beneficial effects on both attraction to the screen and information acquisition (Zillmann & Bryant, 1989a). This entertainment strategy proved less useful in educational efforts with adults, however (Zillmann & Bryant, 1983). On the other hand, there is no reason to make educational efforts listless and drab when the material lends itself to being presented in an entertaining, more pleasant fashion (Bryant & Zillmann, 1989).

There also is the possibility of education through entertainment. Fiction undoubtedly educates. It informs about lifestyles, social conventions, and mores as well as about court procedures, board meetings, and dangers in dark alleys (Mendelsohn, 1966) — although not necessarily with great accuracy. Fiction also carries prosocial messages. For instance, in soaps, sitcoms, and action drama, few leading characters smoke these days; and many display a strong interest in good health by working out and eating right. Additionally, with the exception of alcohol, drug use is usually branded as inappropriate, stupid, dangerous, and plain bad. Recent erotica seek to promote condom use by having actors about to portray casual sex point to the irresponsibility of unprotected intercourse. Interestingly, by including such prosocial messages, the programmers show their conviction that erotica are capable of influencing people — which they vehemently deny for pornography at large.

It would be premature, however, to infer, on the basis of such tidbits of meritorious educational effort in entertaining fare, that commercially sponsored media, with just a little organized prodding, could be turned into an educational vehicle for the good of society. It must be recognized that entertainment does not, and never will, concentrate on the normative. The common case is known, dull, and boring. It is the uncommon, the extreme, the bizarre that captures the imagination of those seeking to be well entertained. It is what does not happen in one's family that intrigues. The unusual, be it violent or sexual, is more interesting and exciting than the usual. Entertainment embraces this premise and consequently is partial to the uncommon — the uncommonly bad and evil, the unusually violent and erotic, the exceptionally sad and desperate, and the extraordinarily fortunate and glorious. Given this consumer-imposed partiality of entertaining story telling in the broadest sense, entertainment cannot possibly be held to a veridical portrayal of social reality.

Furthermore, it must be recognized that the mass media are businesses seeking to maximize profits. This objective is rarely served by informational and educational efforts toward the common good, and media institutions understandably turn defensive, if not hostile, when reminded of obligations to serve the public interest.

Is legislative curtailment of the distribution of harmful material the answer? Or legislative imposition to disseminate educationally superior information? The latter may have a better chance than the former, but only if it is vigorously enforced (Huston et al., 1989). At the adult level, prosocial campaigns, such as information about measures to curb the spread of AIDS, may be legislated on occasion. However, it is difficult to see how socially beneficial formulae for entertainment could ever be broadly prescribed in a free-speech culture with free media markets.

This applies even more to any legislative effort at preventing the distribution of material deemed offensive or harmful. The offensive and obscene is claimed to be protected. In discussing pornography, Marjorie Hines of the ACLU (Rather, 1992) put it succinctly: "There should be no law punishing or suppressing sexually explicit expression, no matter how tasteless, offensive, or . . . vile." Some would go farther and protect free expression even in cases of demonstrable social harm. The demonstration of harm from messages is not easily achieved, however. Leaders and citizens alike seem to embrace the folk wisdom expressed in "Sticks and stones can break my bones, but words will never hurt me."

To date, the social sciences have largely failed to convince leaders and legislators that particular mass-media messages may cause measurable harm and ultimately be in the public disinterest. The methods currently extant in the social sciences seem incapable of incontrovertible "proof" of harm from consumption of specific media-disseminated messages (Huesmann, Eron, Berkowitz, & Chaffee, 1992; Zillmann, 1992a). Moreover, social scientists disagree. In discussing the effects of media violence, critics have raised the criteria for acceptable proof beyond those characterizing the social sciences in general (e.g., Freedman, 1992; Milavsky, Stipp, Kessler, & Rubens, 1982). By making the most of some inconsistencies in the findings, inconsistencies that are to be found in all research endeavors, they have created the impression that social scientists are in irreconcilable disagreement and lack reliable answers. Similarly, the literature on pornography has been interpreted by many as showing negative effects of sexual portrayals, especially when combined with violence. But not everyone agrees that harm has been demonstrated (e.g., Branningan & Goldenberg, 1987; Donnerstein, Linz, & Penrod, 1987). Under these circumstances it is difficult, indeed, to imagine that firm measures to prevent harm could ever be taken on the basis of research findings.

Such uncertainty is exacerbated by the argument that rapidly developing new communication technologies, which soon will place production and distribution capabilities into every home, will render any legislative attempt at curtailing harmful material meaningless and futile.

A good many media scholars have taken the position that audiences need to be prepared for a media world without restrictions. Efforts toward media literacy and the teaching of critical viewing skills (Brown, 1991; Corteen & Williams, 1986; Dorr, Graves, & Phelps, 1980) imply that harmful materials, likely to be encountered, are to be avoided or, if that fails, to be reinterpreted so as to render them innocuous. These preparatory educational efforts presume a rather mature media consumer, but it might prove illusory to expect viewers to turn down the lure of erotic and violent fare and to exercise choices in accordance with cultured taste. More illusory yet might be to expect them to avert influences that presently are only poorly understood.

Meanwhile, researchers will continue to try to demonstrate benefit or harm from particular media offerings, making the demonstrations as compelling as the development of science at this time allows. The resulting information undoubtedly will be used to bring pressures to bear on the industry to broadcast beneficial material and curtail practices that constitute a disservice to the public. If such pressures are to succeed, they must come from the public as much as from legislative bodies; and in order to make this possible, the public must be appraised of pertinent research demonstrations. They must also have the support of governmental policy makers who, in turn, influence regulatory agencies. It is hoped that this volume will contribute, in a minor yet appreciable way, to informing the public about the effects of the media, especially the entertainment media, on children and adults in the families that nurture these children. Perhaps, by creating an awareness of these effects, it could also foster a rethinking of the truism that "words (and images) will never hurt me." An ounce of prevention is better, after all, than a pound of medicine after the damage has been done.

REFERENCES

Ahrons, C. R., & Rodgers, R. (1987). *Divorced families: A multidisciplinary view*. New York: Norton.

Bandura, A. (1986). *Social foundations of thought and action: A social cognitive theory*. Englewood Cliffs, NJ: Prentice-Hall.

Brannigan, A., & Goldenberg, S. (1987). The study of aggressive pornography: The vicissitudes of relevance. *Critical Studies in Mass Communication, 4*, 262–283.

Brown, J. A. (1991). *Television "critical viewing skills" education: Major media literacy projects in the United States and selected countries*. Hillsdale, NJ: Lawrence Erlbaum Associates.

Brown, D., & Bryant, J. (1990). Effects of television on family values and selected attitudes and behaviors. In J. Bryant (Ed.), *Television and the American family* (pp. 253–274). Hillsdale, NJ: Lawrence Erlbaum Associates.

Bryant, J. (Ed.). (1990). *Television and the American family*. Hillsdale, NJ: Lawrence Erlbaum Associates.

Bryant, J., Zillmann, D., & Brown, D. (1983). Entertainment features in children's educational television: Effects on attention and information acquisition. In J. Bryant & D. Anderson (Eds.), *Children's understanding of television* (pp. 221–240). New York: Academic Press.

Bryant, J., & Zillmann, D. (1989). Using humor to promote learning in the classroom. In P. E. McGhee (Ed.), *Humor and children's development: A guide to practical applications* (pp. 49–78). New York: Haworth Press.

Condry, J., Bence, P., & Scheibe, C. (1988). The non-program content of children's television. *Journal of Broadcasting & Electronic Media, 32*, 255–270.

Corteen, R., & Williams, T. (1986). Television and reading skills. In T. M. Williams (Ed.), *The impact of television: A natural experiment in three communities* (pp. 39–86). New York: Academic Press.

Desmond, R. J., Singer, J. L., & Singer, D. G. (1990). Family mediation: Parental communication patterns and the influences of television on children. In J. Bryant (Ed.), *Television and the American family* (pp. 293–310). Hillsdale, NJ: Lawrence Erlbaum Associates.

Donnerstein, E., Linz, D., & Penrod, S. (1987). *The question of pornography: Research findings and policy implications.* New York: Free Press.

Dorr, A. (1986). *Television and children: A special medium for a special audience.* Beverly Hills, CA: Sage.

Dorr, A., Graves, S., & Phelps, E. (1980). Television literacy for the young child. *Journal of Communication, 30*, 71–83.

Dorr, A., & Kunkel, D. (1990). Children and the media environment: Change and constancy amid change. *Communication Research, 17*, 5–25.

Freedman, J. L. (1992). Television violence and aggression: What psychologists should tell the public. In P. Suedfeld & P. E. Tetlock (Eds.), *Psychology and social policy* (pp. 179–189). New York: Hemisphere.

Gerbner, G., Gross, L., Morgan, M., & Signorielli, N. (1986). Living with television: The dynamics of the cultivation process. In J. Bryant & D. Zillmann (Eds.), *Perspectives on media effects* (pp. 17–40). Hillsdale, NJ: Lawrence Erlbaum Associates.

Hebditch, D., & Anning, N. (1988). *Porn gold: Inside the pornography business.* London: Faber & Faber.

Huesmann, L. R., & Eron, L. E. (Eds.). (1986). *Television and the aggressive child: A cross-national comparison.* Hillsdale, NJ: Lawrence Erlbaum Associates.

Huesmann, L. R., Eron, L. D., Berkowitz, L., & Chaffee, S. (1992). The effects of television violence on aggression: A reply to a skeptic. In P. S. Suedfeld & P. E. Tetlock (Eds.), *Psychology and social policy* (pp. 191–200). New York: Hemisphere.

Huston, A. C., Donnerstein, E., Fairchild, H., Feshbach, N., Katz, P., Murray, J., Rubinstein, E., Wilcox, B., & Zuckerman, D. (1992). *Big world, small screen: The role of television in American society.* Lincoln: University of Nebraska Press.

Huston, A. C., Watkins, B. A., & Kunkel, D. (1989). Public policy and children's television. *American Psychologist, 44*, 424–433.

Huston, A. C., Wright, J. C., Rice, M. L., Kerkman, D., & St. Peters, M. (1990). The development of television viewing patterns in early childhood: A longitudinal investigation. *Developmental Psychology, 26*, 409–420.

Kerkman, D. D., Kunkel, D., Huston, A. C., Wright, J. C., & Pinon, M. (1990). Children's television programming and the "free market" solution. *Journalism Quarterly, 67*(1), 147–156.

Leland, J. (1992, November 2). The selling of sex. *Newsweek*, pp. 94–96, 101–103.

Lesser, G. S. (1974). *Children and television: Lessons from Sesame Street.* New York: Vintage.

Lull, J. (1990). Families' social uses of television as extensions of the household. In J. Bryant (Ed.), *Television and the American family* (pp. 59–72). Hillsdale, NJ: Lawrence Erlbaum Associates.

Marshall, W. L., Laws, D. R., & Barbaree, H. E. (Eds.). (1990). *Handbook of sexual assault: Issues, theories, and treatment of the offender.* New York: Plenum Press.

Mendelsohn, H. (1966). *Mass entertainment*. New Haven, CT: College & University Press.

Milavsky, J. R., Stipp, H. H., Kessler, R. C., & Rubens, W. S. (1982). *Television and aggression: A panel study*. New York: Academic Press.

Rather, D. (Host). (1992, November 18). *Porn in the USA*. CBS News: 48 Hours.

Roberts, E. J. (1982). Television and sexual learning in childhood. In D. Pearl, L. Bouthilet, & J. Lazar (Eds.), *Television and behavior: Ten years of scientific progress and implications for the eighties* (pp. 209-223). Washington, DC: U.S. Government Printing Office.

Robinson, J. P. (1990). Television's effects on families' use of time. In J. Bryant (Ed.), *Television and the American family* (pp. 195-210). Hillsdale, NJ: Lawrence Erlbaum Associates.

Silbert, M. H. (1989). The effects on juveniles of being used for pornography and prostitution. In D. Zillmann & J. Bryant (Eds.), *Pornography: Research advances and policy considerations* (pp. 215-234). Hillsdale, NJ: Lawrence Erlbaum Associates.

St. Peters, M., Fitch, M., Huston, A. C., & Wright, J. C., & Eakins, D. (1991). Television and families: What do young children watch with their parents? *Child Development, 62*, 1409-1423.

Stein, A. H., & Friedrich, L. K. (1975). The impact of television on children and youth. In E. M. Hetherington (Ed.), *Review of child development research* (Vol. 5, pp. 183-256). Chicago: University of Chicago Press.

Waters, H. F. (1992, November 30). On kid TV, Ploys R Us. *Newsweek*, pp. 88-89.

Wakshlag, J. (1985). Selective exposure to educational television. In D. Zillmann & J. Bryant (Eds.), *Selective exposure to communication* (pp. 191-201). Hillsdale, NJ: Lawrence Erlbaum Associates.

Wakshlag, J. J., Day, K. D., & Zillmann, D. (1981). Selective exposure to educational television programs as a function of differently paced humorous inserts. *Journal of Educational Psychology, 73*, 27-32.

Wright, J. C., St. Peters, M., & Huston, A. C. (1990). Family television use and its relation to children's cognitive skills and social behavior. In J. Bryant (Ed.), *Television and the American family* (pp. 227-252). Hillsdale, NJ: Lawrence Erlbaum Associates.

Zillmann, D. (1992a). Pornography research, social advocacy, and public policy. In P. Suedfeld & P. E. Tetlock (Eds.), *Psychology and social policy* (pp. 165-178). New York: Hemisphere.

Zillmann, D. (1992b). Weniger Pruederie und mehr Sex: Zukunftstendenzen in der amerikanischen Unterhaltung. *Bertelsmann Briefe, 128*, 69-73.

Zillmann, D., & Bryant, J. (1983). Uses and effects of humor in educational ventures. In P. E. McGhee & J. H. Goldstein (Eds.), *Handbook of humor research: Vol. 2. Applied studies* (pp. 173-193). New York: Springer-Verlag.

Zillmann, D., & Bryant, J. (1989a). Guidelines for the effective use of humor in children's educational television programs. In P. E. McGhee (Ed.), *Humor and children's development: A guide to practical applications* (pp. 201-221). New York: Haworth Press.

Zillmann, D., & Bryant, J. (Eds.). (1989b). *Pornography: Research advances and policy considerations*. Hillsdale, NJ: Lawrence Erlbaum Associates.

Zillmann, D., & Wakshlag, J. (1985). Fear of victimization and the appeal of crime drama. In D. Zillmann & J. Bryant (Eds.), *Selective exposure to communication* (pp. 141-156). Hillsdale, NJ: Lawrence Erlbaum Associates.

2

Patterns of Family Life and Television Consumption From 1945 to the 1990s

Margaret S. Andreasen
University of Wisconsin-Madison

Since the 1940s, family structure and function have probably undergone more profound and rapid revisions than during all the remainder of American history. Family values, lifestyles, use of discretionary time, and reliance on technological sophistication have all been affected, in some cases transformed, by the events of the last half century. And television as a medium has developed both technically and programatically during the same period. Thus, all the variables in the "family's-use-of-television" dynamic have changed individually and in relation to one another.

Using the methodology of the historian, and at times that of the cultural archeologist, I begin this chapter with a few assumptions: (a) family television consumption takes place within the context of family life and needs to be understood within the context of the family system; (b) both family function and the development of television technology occur within an historical, cause-and-effect driven social universe; and (c) our procedures for monitoring social and technological changes in relation to one another are suspect if not out and out haphazard. Additionally, because other chapters in this volume discuss specific television program content and its effects, I omit analysis of those topics and focus instead on technology development, family change since the advent of television, and media consumption behavior.

To learn about family life in years past, we are dependent on domestic artifacts, media chronicles, historical records, and published surveys. Unfortunately, many of the documents as well as census data that might provide some insight into family structure do not treat the family as the unit of analysis. Instead, the "household" is the focal unit. Although at times family groups and householders at particular addresses may coincide, we cannot count on such coincidence.

Moreover, there is and has been much confusion about the very definition of the family. As Jan Trost (1990) observed: "Evidently no one 'knows' what a family is; our perspectives vary to such a degree that to claim to know what a family is shows a lack of knowledge" (p. 442). Whereas we may attribute this confusion to the current multiplicity of American lifestyles, the surge in numbers of single-parented families, divorced and remarried spouses, split and reconstituted or "blended" families, increasing frequency of heterosexual or homosexual couples living together as "domestic partners," the problem of definition is not unique to the present. During a national conference on family life convened in 1948, participants struggled to find consensus on a definition of the family, only to conclude with the acknowledgment that "the most useful definition of a family for one analyst is not the most useful for another" (U.S. Bureau of the Census, 1948, p. 2). Without the same consensual definition over time, we cannot be certain that a family is a family is a family.

To be sure, some of the disagreement regarding definition emanates from the varied modes of viewing and handling data dictated by the many scholarly disciplines concerned with the realities of family life. But it is likely that the heterogeneity of the American social fabric and the absence of a clearly defined family teleology are also reflected in the lack of consensus.

THE FAMILY BEFORE TELEVISION

Regardless of definitional confusion, census data regarding marriage, divorce, birth, and employment do provide a profile of changes in family life. These, in turn, can be correlated with trends in the broader social milieu as well as with the advent of television. What these data make clear is that the American family seemed to be in trouble *before* television was widely adopted.

Although a number of young people did marry during World War II, many couples postponed marriage until the end of the war. Between 1944 and 1948 the number of marriages reached an all-time high, peaking in 1947 at about 200 marriages per 1,000 women 15 to 44 years of age. The same period saw a peak in the divorce rate with approximately 27 divorces occurring in 1946 for every 100 marriages taking place (Stencel, 1979). Although the divorce rate had been climbing steadily in this country since the late 19th century and there had been a similar though smaller peaking in conjunction with the end of World War I, the sudden increase worried many (see Fig. 2.1). While scholars convened at national meetings to explore ways of buttressing the family and family values, the popular press, especially traditional women's magazines, carried prohome, promarriage, antidivorce messages (Andreasen, 1990). By 1950 the divorce rate had dropped away from its post-World War II peak, and the 1950s were characterized by both a stabilized divorce rate and a rapidly rising birth rate. This was the era of the family and the child, and the dawn of television in the home.

It is important to note, however, that in spite of the contemporary tendency to view family life in the 1950s as cohesive and secure, this paradigm applied to only a portion of U.S. society. One quarter of the U.S. population was poor in the 1950s; more than 60% of those over age 65 lived

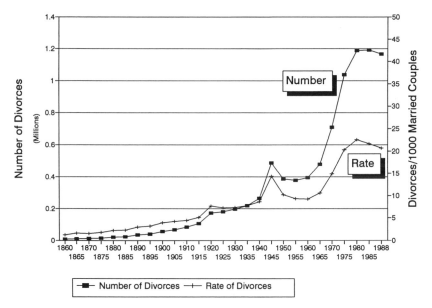

FIG. 2.1. Divorces from 1860 to 1988. Data for years 1860–1955 from Jacobson (1959, p. 90); for years 1960 and 1965 from U.S. Bureau of the Census (1991, p. 86); for years 1970 to 1988, from U.S. Bureau of the Census (1992, p. 90).

in poverty, and even though we may think of this period as pro-child, the decade ended with one third of America's children living in poverty (Coontz, 1992).

The thriving U.S. family, moreover, may have owed more to a set of economic circumstances than to high moral character. As historian Stephanie Coontz (1992) observed, some Americans' personal savings during World War II were high; real wages increased during the 1950s more than they had during the previous half century; and the U.S. government generously underwrote home loans, higher education, and inexpensive energy. Whereas these benefits enhanced the family's sense of security, Coontz attributed to them other effects as well: "These expectations encouraged early marriage, early childbearing, expansion of consumer debt, and residential patterns that required long commutes to work—all patterns that would become highly problematic by the 1970s . . ." (p. 29). Thus even without television, families in the 1950s may have set the stage for familial and social problems later in the century.

The Edenic Family in the Golden Age of Television

Television, however, diffused very rapidly. Present in only 9% of American homes in 1950, by 1960, 87.1% of households contained television sets (see Table 2.1). The average time spent viewing television lengthened from 4 hours and 35 minutes in 1950 to 5 hours and 6 minutes in 1960 (see Table 2.2). Although we have no way of measuring all the effects that television had on family life in the 1950s, a number of studies from that period suggests two conclusions: first, that most people believed that television was having a salutary effect on the family; and, second, that the television set was exogenous to family life. It was, in effect, a toy, a spectacle, an entertainment that family members, friends, and neighbors enjoyed together. Two thirds of the individuals surveyed in a Princeton University study reported in *Television Magazine* in 1949 (Siepmann, 1950) said that "it was their frank opinion that TV served to bring all of the family closer together . . ." and that it kept "the children home more" (p. 342). Bogart (1972) reported the results of several studies showing that families who owned televisions spent more time at home than they had prior to ownership and than families that did not own televisions.

Can we conclude then that television builds cohesive family structures? Siepmann (1950) was suspicious of such an assumption. Believing that silent co-viewing did not build relationships, he noted that "maybe it will take more than television to make a home into a family" (p. 342). And even the early days of television saw some solitary viewing (Bogart, 1972).

Whereas the level of concern about the effects of television on children

TABLE 2.1
Households with Television Receivers 1946–1990

Year	Households with Sets (1,000s)	% of Households with Sets
1946	8	.02
1947	14	.04
1948	172	.4
1949	940	2.3
1950	3,875	9.0
1951	10,320	23.5
1952	15,300	34.2
1953	20,400	44.7
1954	26,000	55.7
1955	30,700	64.5
1956	34,900	71.8
1957	38,900	78.6
1958	41,920	83.2
1959	43,950	85.9
1960	45,750	87.1
1961	47,200	88.8
1962	48,855	90.0
1963	50,300	91.3
1964	51,600	92.3
1965	52,700	92.6
1966	53,850	93.0
1967	55,130	93.6
1968	56,670	94.6
1969	58,250	95.0
1970	58,500	95.3
1971	60,100	95.5
1972	62,100	95.8
1973	64,800	96.4
1974	66,200	96.9
1975	68,500	97.1
1976	69,600	97.4
1977	71,200	97.4
1978	72,900	97.6
1979	74,500	97.7
1980	76,300	97.9
1981	79,900	98.0
1982	81,500	98.1
1983	83,300	98.1
1984	83,800	98.1
1985	84,900	98.1
1986	85,900	98.1
1987	87,400	98.1
1988	89,000	98.1
1989	90,000	98.2
1990	92,000	98.2
1991	93,000	NA

Sources: Data for years 1946–1950 are from Sterling and Haight (1978, p. 372). Data for subsequent years through 1987 are from Television Bureau of Advertising (1988, p. 3). Data from 1988 to 1991 are from the U. S. Bureau of the Census (1992, p. 551).

TABLE 2.2
Time Spent Viewing Television Per TV Household Per Day

Year	Avg. Time Per Day
1950	4 hours 35 min.
1951	4 hours 43 min.
1952	4 hours 49 min.
1953	4 hours 40 min.
1954	4 hours 46 min.
1955	4 hours 51 min.
1956	5 hours 1 min.
1957	5 hours 9 min.
1958	5 hours 5 min.
1959	5 hours 2 min.
1960	5 hours 6 min.
1961	5 hours 7 min.
1962	5 hours 6 min.
1963	5 hours 11 min.
1964	5 hours 25 min.
1965	5 hours 29 min.
1966	5 hours 32 min.
1967	5 hours 42 min.
1968	5 hours 46 min.
1969	5 hours 50 min.
1970	5 hours 56 min.
1971	6 hours 2 min.
1972	6 hours 12 min.
1973	6 hours 15 min.
1974	6 hours 14 min.
1975	6 hours 7 min.
1976	6 hours 18 min.
1977	6 hours 10 min.
1978	6 hours 17 min.
1979	6 hours 28 min.
1980	6 hours 36 min.
1981	6 hours 45 min.
1981-82	6 hours 48 min.
1982-83	6 hours 55 min.
1983-84	7 hours 8 min.
1984-85	7 hours 7 min.
1985-86	7 hours 10 min.
1986-87	7 hours 5 min.
1987-88	6 hours 59 min.
1988-89	7 hours 2 min.
1989-90	4 hours 6 min.
1990-91	4 hours 2 min.

Sources: A. C. Nielsen Co., annual averages for 1950 through
1981. Data for 1981–1982 through 1988–1989 from *Nielsen Report
on Television 1990* (1990, p. 6). Data for 1989–1990 and 1990–1991
from "Television Audience 1991" (1992, p. 12).

has been great, the attention paid to the effects on the family unit has been less evident. Early concerns about the medium regarding children were prompted by both program content and the concomitants of consumption behavior. Program content analyses revealed, for example, that children were exposed to many images of violence (Schramm, Lyle, & Parker, 1961). Apart from this potentially negative modeling effect, television viewing displaced time from homework, household chores, reading activities, and ordinary conversation among family members. Yet we cannot generalize about "effects on all children"; research has led us instead to *some* conclusions about *some* children under *some* circumstances *some* of the time. It is even more difficult to generalize about effects on entire families.

Learning theorists suggest that we learn from having behavior modeled for us, from having our notions reinforced or negated by others or by mass media, and from social interaction (McLeod & Brown, 1976; McLeod & O'Keefe, 1972). It seems that certain societal trends and values during the 1950s and 1960s could have accorded television both heightened modeling and reinforcement effects on family life. These trends include the "scientification" of America: increasing reliance on technology, scientific and engineering achievement, and experts who have the answers. Progress and modernity invalidated "old wives' tales" and family remedies for emotional as well as physical problems. Whereas Americans' actual knowledge of science was probably limited, respect for scientists and technical experts was high. Doctors and hospitals had made childbirth safer than in home delivery and had also taken the matter out of the hands of family members. DuPont was bringing America "better things for better living through chemistry" — nylon, teflon, dacron, orlon, and a broad range of plastics that celebrated modernity and the scientist's ingenuity. Confidence in men in white coats was abundant and remained so for some time. Whereas the National Opinion Research Center Poll revealed that in 1983 41% of a random sample had high confidence in scientists, in 1966, 72% of respondents had claimed such confidence (Scientists' Institute, 1984). The 1950s and 1960s were decades when the credibility of scientific authority encouraged familial reliance on expert advice. And television made great use of "experts" who promoted specific brands of aspirin, the efficacy of particular soap products, and even a brand of cigarettes that doctors preferred. The self-confidence of a young mother could well have been insufficient to challenge the wisdom of the technocrats and that of the poseurs using television channels to hawk material progress.

Vulnerability to media authorities probably also was heightened by the mobile circumstances of many families. The post-World War II landscape saw dramatic changes: The building of highways and burgeoning sales of automobiles made suburban life possible and attractive. Young upward-bound families were among those most likely to be physically mobile. In

1947, only 44% of household heads were living in the same abode they had occupied in 1940 (U.S. Bureau of the Census, 1948). By 1953, 20% of Americans lived in suburbs, and within the suburbs themselves the turnover could be very high. Areas around New York and Los Angeles, for example, saw new families moving into 40% of the houses each year (Hine, 1986). Physically distant from the support of extended family and surrounded by temporary neighbors, young families were not likely to find models for family living and reinforcement for traditional values in the places their parents had found them — close to home in a caring community. Under such circumstances, media models and advice could provide support. Women's magazines were, and continue to be, repositories of expert solutions to the problems of daily life (Andreasen & Steeves, 1983). Whereas the actual value of this advice has been questioned — some critics arguing that it merely undermined a woman's confidence and made her dependent on the periodicals — magazines succeeded and sold because they frequently anticipated a woman's information needs. *Good Housekeeping*, for example, in 1951 added to its sections on child rearing, needle crafts, foods, and home decorating a new feature on woman and the automobile. The suburban wife was given hints on what to do when the car began to skid, and on how to look neat and chic when behind the wheel. A few years later when car-pooling women had presumably mastered the machine, this section was dropped from the magazine.

Most surveys indicate that satisfaction with family life was strong during the 1950s; children and family life were high priorities (Hine, 1986). Television families mimicked, or perhaps modeled, this idyllic life. Small town and suburban neighborhoods served as the backdrop for lighthearted family shananigans, and children's minor misadventures occurred to demonstrate that father or Donna Stone did know best. Although the families were almost universally nuclear, White, middle, or upper middle class, living without television, and purged of all that was sick or old or unattractive, families without other norms in safe and secluded suburbs or small towns could well have admired this pallid standard. Middle-class families, for the most part, consumed these programs together, first in the living room and then in the room designated for television viewing — the family room, which women's magazines helped the mother of the family arrange and decorate (Hine, 1986; Wright, 1950).

Although there were occasional squabbles about which program to watch, these were generally peacefully resolved and even those whose preference lost in the family conflict remained to view the winning program (Bogart, 1972). But in making adjustments to television viewing, family life underwent a number of changes. Dinner conversation was often sacrificed to viewing, with 44% of families in one 1952 study reporting that they regularly ate in sight of the television set (Stewart, 1952). Although family members might watch the same program, they did not necessarily eat the same dinner at the same table. With the advent of the frozen TV dinner and the TV tray, it was possible for individual family members to have the dinner of their choice and to eat it without actually looking at another family member. No more cajoling junior to finish his spinach with the threat of no dessert should he refuse. Junior could choose a dinner tray without the offending vegetable. Even the food component of the meal experience no longer had to be shared.

Other family practices were altered as well. Families with television sets went to bed later than formerly; they slept less (Bogart, 1972) and conversed less, even though they spent more time in actual proximity (McDonagh, 1950; Stewart, 1952). Television at this point seems to be playing a role in the structuring of family rules and rituals, and as such its exogenous status in relation to the family system grows questionable. To the extent that the social functions it performed were integrated into the family system, television was endogenous to that system.

The Multiset Household

As television became a fixture in increasing numbers of homes, the industry realized the market would soon be saturated. Manufacturers adopted two standard strategies for dealing with what would otherwise mean the end of sales: (a) They developed new and improved models that made already purchased models obsolete (UNESCO, 1953); (b) they designed in the mid-1950s the portable, in other words "personal," television set. As sets with larger screens, color, and remote control came on the market, however, their purchase did not eliminate earlier sets from the home. The net effect was the development of multitelevision-set households (see Table 2.3). The set first purchased or the smaller set or the set less attractive for other reasons often became the children's unit and under some circum- stances the children's babysitter (Steiner, 1963). Although as early as 1951, four television owners out of five acknowledged having viewed an entire program alone (Bogart, 1972), the concern for adult isolation was probably less serious than that directed at children, who were regarded as more vulnerable to negative influences. Yet the family's "best set" was likely to draw all family members together for shared viewing (Bower, 1973). By 1981 parents and children were spending one fourth of their total time together in front of the television set (Timmer, Eccles, & O'Brien, 1985). It may be, however, that the desire to view the "best set" (i.e., individual hedonism, not familial cohesiveness) accounts for this togetherness.

In addition to the impetus to individual viewing provided by a growing number of television sets, from 1.4 in 1970 to 2.1 sets per household in 1990

TABLE 2.3
Color Television, Multiple-Set, and Remote Control Ownership

Date	% of TV House-holds with Color TV	% with Multisets	% with Remote Control
1955		4	
1960		12	
1965	7	22	
1970	41	35	
1975	74	43	
1980	83	50	
1985	91	57	29
1990	98	65	77
1991	98	64	78
1992	99	65	84

Source: Data from "Television Audience 1991" (1992, p. 2).

(U.S. Bureau of the Census, 1992, p. 551), two technological developments widely disseminated in the 1980s could further diminish the lustre of the one "best set." They are the proliferation of more narrowly targeted cable channels—now with an average of 35.6 channels available per household (See Table 2.4)—and the omnipresence of the remote control device that facilitates easy channel switching on the part of the family member who controls the device (see Table 2.3). Whereas it is likely that situation comedies on network television will appeal to a broad family audience, it is less likely that all family members will enjoy ESPN (the sports channel), C-SPAN (governmental affairs programming), or MTV (music videos). Moreover, it is probably easier to tolerate a single unchosen program than it is to endure another family member's frequent and remotely controlled swing through all television offerings currently being broadcast. Older and female viewers are particularly put off by such channel switching (Ainslie, 1988). Both of these technologies are likely to enhance individual viewing at

TABLE 2.4
Percent Share of Television Households Receiving Television Channels

Year	Number of Channels						
	1–6	7–10	11–14	15–19	20–29	30+	Ave. #
1985	8%	17%	25%	15%	16%	19%	18.8
1987	7%	14%	20%	13%	15%	31%	22.4
1989	7%	13%	12%	9%	8%	51%	30.5
1991	5%	10%	10%	8%	6%	61%	35.6

Sources: Data for 1985–1989 from Nielsen Report on Television 1990 (1990, p. 2); data for 1991 are from "Television Audience 1991" (1992, p. 9).

the expense of family or group viewing, and thereby to foster solitary consumption of the medium.

The New Family: Utilitarian Individualism Versus Traditionalism

By 1970, the child-centered lifestyle and family values of the 1950s and 1960s had garnered results, not always those desired or predicted by the parents of those children. During the 1970s a survey showed two basic types of family systems: the traditional family and "the new breed" (Yankelovich, Skelly, & White, Inc., 1977). Whereas both types espoused the values of marriage, religion, and saving money, the latter found hard work and financial security less attractive than patriotism and success. New-breed parents, representing 43% of all parents in 1977, also differed from the traditionalists in being self-oriented and unwilling to sacrifice for their children; believing children should not be pushed but should make their own decisions; questioning authority; believing boys and girls should be raised alike; and in regarding the having of children as an option, not a social responsibility. College students' personal values reflected the adoption of some "new-breed" assumptions. In identifying their very important personal values, students ranked self-fulfillment and education above family, and well above hard work and having children.

The family system, moreover, had to adapt to some significant scientific, economic, and social phenomena in the 1960s and 1970s. The development of the birth control pill, greater sexual freedom for women as well as men, the adoption by many states of no-fault divorce laws, rapidly rising divorce rates, rising fertility rates for unmarried women, economic pressures on women to work outside the home, higher levels of education for women and a concomitant desire for self-fulfillment in the work environment, and the glorification of material goods and their consumption appear to be indicators of a popular adherence to utilitarian individualism.

Yet this individualism was neither really new in American life, nor was it probably very utilitarian. Labeling "the corporate model of family endeavor" as now "defunct" (p. 455), Schwartz (1987) viewed the change as evolutionary and inevitable: "One might hypothesize that the traditional family was undermined with the founding of this country on the principle of enlightened self-interest. And when that principle actually came to be extended to all citizens in practice, not just theory, it was inevitable that the family, a group that must necessarily compromise some members' interests for the good of the whole, would change dramatically" (p. 446).

And that change has occurred. Only 28% of American families conform to the nuclear ideal of the 1950s (Fowles, 1988). Observing the magnitude of the change, Hine (1986) noted that in the 1950s people

> confidently projected the American family—Mom, Dad, Junior and Sis— unchanged, centuries into the future, spinning through the galaxies in starbound station wagons. And today, Mom and Dad are divorced, the factory where Dad worked has moved to Taiwan, Sis is a corporate vice president, Junior is gay, and Mom's a Moonie. The American Way of Life has shattered into a bewildering array of "lifestyles," which offer greater freedom but not the security that one is doing the normal thing. (p. 177)

Although we might attribute a decline in reported happiness with family life to an uncertainty about "doing the normal thing," it is clear that families of whatever structure are facing stresses not evident in the 1950s. Surveys conducted in the 1970s and 1980s reveal that married couples with children living at home were less happy than couples without children in the household, that lower levels of global happiness and satisfaction correlate with having children in the household, and that the birth of a child correlates with a reported decline in the perceived quality of most marriages (Belsky & Rovine, 1990; Glenn & McLanahan, 1981).

The stress that post-1950 families felt and continue to feel, however, may have been exacerbated by the very thing that many believe has accounted for the U.S. family's strength—its self-reliance. Achieving this ideal generally required long working hours and reduced discretionary time. But when familial self-reliance was also associated with a lack of buttressing connections to the greater community, the family was extremely vulnerable to being overburdened by social as well as economic and emotional expectations. With the "growth of family privacy as an ideal," Coontz found "private family relations more problematic than ever" (p. 121). Strong "family-first" values, she said, can discourage the meeting of social or emotional needs through nonfamilial associations, and ironically, "the obvious next step, of course, is that if I am not perfectly happy, it's my family's fault" (p. 120). Thus, family-first values that socially and emotionally isolate family members from other societal units, Coontz contended, set the stage for familial discontent.

The American Family Today

We may disagree about what families are and about what life purpose is appropriate for families, but probably we would agree that the *telos* historically accorded American families—"to grow new people and to further the growth" of members of the family system (Satir, 1972, p. 113)— has in some cases been abandoned or has been sufficiently overwhelmed by social and personal constraints so as to be inoperable. In addition to survey measures revealing low levels of affective well-being, we have demographic and social data that suggest that nurturing human growth is an unlikely if not impossible task for many contemporary families.

When we examine the scope of social malaise, we see that the family is not the only American institution that has suffered during the last few decades. We have experienced a decline in governmental, legal, and economic institutions as well. Our manufacturing base has been eroded, and labor unions are shadows of their former selves. Nor have we seen the kind of improvement in health care that a nation with our technological and economic resources might have expected to achieve. It is probably important, then, to see changes in the family as part of an overall societal shift that encompasses new and confusing gender roles, growing technological sophistication, and an encouragement of individual self-fulfillment through entrepreneurial enterprise and the consumption of material goods. Television, as well as the personal stereo, personal calculator, personal computer, single-serving gourmet frozen dinner, two-car household, and dual-controlled electric blanket, developed in and gave impetus to these trends. And just as ignoring these trends is impossible, so also single-mindedly "putting family first" will not undo them.

It is also unlikely that television or any other mass medium can solve the social, economic, and emotional problems confronting families or eliminate the profoundly stressful environments many families face. Nor, as this history reveals, can television on its own be held responsible for the splintering of families in the first place. Research data that are presented in this volume, however, show that television viewing can have negative and/or positive effects on individuals and families. Specific program content can reinforce particular data processing patterns, materialistic and consumption values, negative emotions, and aggressive behavior. The household viewing experience, which may isolate and at least physically separate family members from one another as each consumes and absorbs a set of images and jargon not to be shared with other family members, may deprive the family of a common parlance and reduce intrafamily communication. But we cannot reincarnate ourselves in Notel, that pretelevision Canadian community described by Tannis MacBeth Williams (1986). Given the fact, however, that television plays a prominent role in the household and the family system, we might do well to acknowledge its status at the start and then try to determine how the medium might best function within the system.

A Modest Proposal for Modest Change in Industry Practice

Whereas we expect private enterprise to do environmental, social, and economic impact studies before establishing specific industries, bus routes, or waste collection sites in our neighborhoods, we make no demands on the television industry to analyze either the societal or familial impact of what it brings into our living rooms. To be sure, this is no easy task. We cannot be sure about the precise effect of a given program on even a narrow age cohort of children, let alone on all children or on various combinations of adults and children. And the family today takes many forms. It is projected that by the year 2000, half of all American families will be stepfamilies; in 1987 Wald had already delineated 32 categories of stepfamilies (cited in Collins, 1987). In spite of the multiplicity of family structures and values, the television industry could, as a first step, fund the evaluation of programs for their most likely effects on the implementation of a general family teleology, for their perspectives regarding human development, and for their impact on family members' feelings of cooperation, adaptability, and cohesiveness, qualities Olson and McCubbin (1983) identified as characteristic of families who survive stress. Although such evaluations would not keep a program off the air, they might help families make choices about what to watch and would perhaps encourage discussion of family values within the context of the program.

We also need industry funding for more research on the effects of viewing environments, on how the viewing experience is mediated by contextual variables such as the combinations of family members present, the time of day when the program is viewed, the formality or informality of the room, the volume at which the program is monitored, the growing use of remote control devices and, most important, on how family rules interact with program and family audience composition to mediate the television experience.

But the consequences of particular programs or specific environments may indeed be inconsequential when compared with the potential effects of the superhighway of electronic messages that will enter homes via television screens during the next decade. A confluence of technologies—the digitalizing and compressed storage of audio and video communication, fiber optic wiring, computer controlled switching and patching mechanisms— will expand the frequency and the potency of video intrusion into the home. Telephone, computer and video technocrats are coordinating efforts to provide U.S. families with 500 or more channel options before the end of the century. Time Warner is already providing 150 channels to households in Queens, and Tele-Communications, Inc. will market in the spring of 1994 a cable decoder capable of providing access to 540 channels (Elmer-Dewitt, 1993). What content all of these channels will carry is still a matter of speculation, but it is fair to conclude that the profit motive will prevail. As commercial communication satellites beam myriad messages to the planet they orbit, families may indeed find themselves on the receiving end of the actualized motto one global satellite system, PanAmSat, celebrates: "Free Enterprise in Space" ("PanAmSat Goes Global," 1993, p. 41).

How that free enterprise will affect society is a matter of much debate: What will "a fragmented and TV-anesthetized society . . . do with 100 − or 500 − offerings" (Elmer-Dewitt, 1993, p. 52)? Yet little attention has been given to this electronic explosion's impact on the family. When many of the new channels are shopping networks facilitating purchase at the push of a button, when "smart television sets" collect and reveal to us at the end of a work day only the news we are personally interested in, or when voice activated remote control devices respond to four family members' vocalized sets of directions, will it even be possible for television viewing to be a shared family experience? This is a question that the industry has ignored, and one to which a nation concerned about the welfare of families must have an answer.

Given that there will be a plethora of channels, at the very least one of them should be an industry funded outlet promoting media literacy. This video service could serve as an antidote to the medium's current "entertainment" perspective of itself offered in televised video schedules, promotions of upcoming programs, and features emphasizing the glamour of actors or video settings. In addition to presenting in lay terms research data about effects of the electronic information highway on families and the greater society, such a video service could analyze the production costs, techniques, and appeal strategies associated with commercials and children's programming; the agenda setting of news organizations; the accuracy of politicians' charges and commercial claims; the authenticity of family portraits and familial behavior; sponsors' goals for specific programs; producers' goals for individual programs; audience targeting strategies, and so on. This television-news service would, in other words, provide all the television information families and consumers need to be television literate and defensive. Although a broad popular audience for such a service would not be expected, it would be a valuable resource for both the public and the media. One could imagine, for example, media reporters, particularly print reporters, monitoring it much the way that science reporters monitor the *New England Journal of Medicine*. Major stories would then be carried by all media.

A Modest Proposal for Modest Changes in Family Behavior

Most studies that examine children's television consumption and parents' estimates of that television viewing reveal that there is significant disagreement between the children's and parents' assessments. Such a discrepancy suggests family rules about the medium are either unclear or unenforced. When family rules regarding any other aspect of the system are not clearly articulated or are inconsistently enforced, the family system relies on hidden rules, avoidance, and passive aggressive behaviors to keep the system going. Family communication and healthy family functioning are the casualties, however, of these endeavors. It is important to communicate clearly and frequently about how television functions and how it is to be used within the family context. Children too young to engage in such discussion may nevertheless benefit from it indirectly because they will have the implementation of those rules modeled for them by older family members.

Second, even if working mothers and too-busy fathers have no time to co-view with children, it would be wise to try to monitor what children watch and the amount of time spent at television viewing. The best predictor that children will avoid delinquency is parental monitoring — asking children what they are doing, with whom, and when. Both of these recommendations also foster the kind of social interaction that can mediate some of the potentially negative impact of antisocial or antifamily television content.

And last, to counter the passivity that Kubey and Csikszentmihalyi (1990) have found associated with heavy television viewing, families might actively seek balance in their lives, both in the media resources they choose and in the allocation of sufficient time to nonsedentary and nonviewing familial activities. How might we create such balance in what may seem to be a world gone mad? We need help, and we have needed it for a long time. A researcher observed in testimony before a Congressional Committee: "We need studies which would result in ideas as to how the average family can create an atmosphere which will compete with television. The difficulty of these problems should not be underrated." The speaker was Paul Lazarsfeld, and he was testifying before the Kefaufer Committee investigating juvenile delinquency and the effects of television in 1955.

A Not-So-Modest Proposal for Researchers

Clearly, the research that would be done today could be far more sophisticated than whatever might have been attempted in Lazarsfeld's day. Yet even today what probably is required to acquire a knowledge base that takes into account a sufficient number of variables to be useful is a major interdisciplinary study. If researchers in child and adult development, family health, family communication, family values, social change, cognitive and affective responses to environmental circumstances as well as to video messages, and media effects could develop a coordinated research agenda focused on the impact of media on the family and then collaborate in its implemenation, they might accomplish what Lazarsfeld called for in 1955: "detailed and large-scale studies of what actually goes on in the home." A well-planned and coordinated effort would probably do more to help families, whatever their structure, find their way to balanced and healthy lives in the age of television than could any single-discipline study. This volume may be the beginning of such an endeavor.

REFERENCES

Ainslie, P. (1988, September). Confronting a nation of grazers. *CHANNELS: The Business of Communication*, pp. 54–57.

Andreasen, M. S. (1990). Evolution in the family's use of television. In J. Bryant (Ed.), *Television and the American family* (pp. 3–55). Hillsdale, NJ: Lawrence Erlbaum Associates.

Andreasen, M. S., & Steeves, H. L. (1983). Employed women's assertiveness and openness as shown in magazine use. *Journalism Quarterly, 60,* 449–457.

Belsky, J., & Rovine, M. (1990). Patterns of marital change across the transition to parenthood; pregnancy to three years postpartum. *Journal of Marriage and the Family, 52*(1), 5–19.

Bogart, L. (1972). *The age of television* (3rd ed.). New York: Frederick Ungar.

Bower, R. T. (1973). *Television and the public.* New York: Holt, Rinehart & Winston.

Collins, G. (1987, September 24). 80's stepfamilies: Forming new ties. *The New York Times,* pp. 21–22.

Coontz, S. (1992). *The way we never were: American families and the nostalgia trap.* New York: Basic Books.

Elmer-Dewitt, P. (1993, April 12). Take a trip into the future on the electronic superhighway. *Time,* pp. 50–55.

Fowles, J. (1988). Forum: The 1950s revisited, coming soon: More men than women. *The New York Times,* Section F, p. 3.

Glenn, N. D., & McLanahan, S. (1981). The effects of offspring in the psychological well-being of older adults. *Journal of Marriage and the Family, 43,* 409–421.

Hine, T. (1986). *Populuxe.* New York: Knopf.

Jacobson, P. H. (1959). *American marriage and divorce.* New York: Rinehart.

Kubey, R., & Csikszentmihalyi, M. (1990). *Television and the quality of life: How viewing shapes everyday experience.* Hillsdale, NJ: Lawrence Erlbaum Associates.

Lazarsfeld, P. F. (1955). Why so little known about the effects of television on children and what can be done? *The Public Opinion Quarterly, 19*(3), 243–251.

McDonagh, E. C. (1950). Television and the family. *Sociology and Social Research, 35*(2), 113–122.

McLeod, J., & Brown, J. D. (1976). The family environment and adolescent television use. In R. Brown (Ed.), *Children and television* (pp. 199–233). London: Collier–Macmillan.

McLeod, J., & O'Keefe, G. J. (1972). The socialization perspective and communication behavior. In F. G. Kline & P. J. Tichenor (Eds.), *Current perspectives in mass communication research.* (pp. 121–168). Beverly Hills, CA: Sage.

Nielsen report on television. (1990). Northbrook, IL: A. C. Nielsen.

Nielsen station index: U.S. television household estimates. (1988). Northbrook, IL: A. C. Nielsen.

Nielsen station index: U.S. television household estimates. (1989). Northbrook, IL: A. C. Nielsen.

Olson, D. H., & McCubbin, H. (1983). *Families: What makes them work*. Beverly Hills, CA: Sage.

PanAmSat goes global. (1993, April 19). *Broadcasting and Cable, 123*(16), 41.

Satir, V. (1972). *Peoplemaking*. Palo Alto, CA: Science & Behavior.

Schramm, W. L., Lyle, J., & Parker, E. B. (1961). *Television in the lives of our children*. Stanford, CA: Stanford University Press.

Schwartz, P. (1987). The family as a changed institution. *Journal of Family Issues, 8*, 455–459.

Scientists Institute for Public Information. (1984). *Credibility and the media: Roundtable discussion*. New York: Touche Ross.

Siepmann, C. A. (1950). *Radio, television and society*. New York: Oxford Press.

Steiner, G. (1963). *The people look at television*. New York: Knopf.

Stencel, S. (1979). *Editorial research reports on changing American family*. Washington, DC: Congressional Quarterly.

Sterling, C. H., & Haight, T. R. (1978). *The mass media: Aspen Institute guide to communication trends*. New York: Praeger.

Stewart, R. F. (1952). *The social impact of television on Atlanta households*. Atlanta: Emory University, Division of Journalism.

Television audience 1991. (1992). Northbrook, IL: Nielsen Media Research.

Television Bureau of Advertising, Inc. (1988, March). *Trends in television*. New York: Author.

Timmer, S. G., Eccles, J., & O'Brien, K. (1985). How children use time. In F. G. Juster & F. P. Stafford (Eds.), *Time, goods and well-being* (pp. 352–382). Ann Arbor: University of Michigan Institute for Social Research.

Trost, J. (1990). Do we mean the same by the concept of the family? *Communication Research, 17*(4), 431–443.

United Nations Educational, Scientific and Cultural Organization. (1953). *Television: A world survey*. Paris: Author.

U.S. Bureau of the Census. (1991). *Statistical abstract of the United States: 1991*. Washington, DC: U.S. Government Printing Office.

U.S. Bureau of the Census. (1992). *Statistical abstract of the United States: 1992*. Washington, DC: U.S. Government Printing Office.

U.S. Bureau of the Census with the National Office of Vital Statistics. (1948). *The American Family: A Factual Background* (Report of Interagency Committee on Background Materials, National Conference on Family Life). Washington, DC: U.S. Government Printing Office.

William, F. M. (1986). *The impact of television: A natural experiment in three communities*. Orlando, FL: Academic Press.

Wright, R. E. (1950, June). The newest idea in home planning is a family room. *Better Homes and Gardens*, pp. 64–65.

Yankelovich, Skelly, & White, Inc. (1977). *The General Mills American family report 1976–1977: Raising children in a changing society*. Minneapolis: General Mills.

3

FAMILY IMAGES AND FAMILY ACTIONS AS PRESENTED IN THE MEDIA: WHERE WE'VE BEEN AND WHAT WE'VE FOUND

Thomas Skill
University of Dayton

The "legacy of fear"—that sometimes real, most times imagined, power of the media—has been with us since the first day that we discovered how to send messages beyond the range of our voices and reach of our arms. The public concern reflected in this legacy of fear has been primarily focused on the effects that media may have on children. The 13 separate investigations known as the Payne Fund Studies (Charters, 1933) were motivated by a public concern regarding the influence of motion pictures on young people. Although some of the investigations by today's standard hardly measure up, their contributions to the public discussion, understanding, and policy formation at the time were quite significant. Exploring the content of the media as a first stage in the evaluation of its potential impact has been and remains a fundamental step in virtually every sizable investigation (Schramm, Lyle, & Parker, 1961). Whereas the intervening years of the 1940s to the 1960s expanded our methodological repertoire and theoretical understanding of the media, it was the violent events of the 1960s that once again fueled the legacy of fear. The Media Task Force Report, *Violence & the Media* (Baker & Ball, 1969), and The Surgeon General Report, *Television and Social Behavior* (Comstock & Rubinstein, 1972) each reflects public concern over the impact of the media.

Although the family has always been connected to media research because of its central role with children, the family was not a primary concern with regard to its presence in the media until the 1970s. The interior world of the family was no match for the external concerns of violence, sex, alcohol, delinquency, and the like. However, the perspectives provided in the NIMH report on *Television and Behavior* (McLeod, Fitzpatrick, Glynn, & Fallis, 1982) gave new impetus to the study of interpersonal behaviors, particularly in the family context.

At the time of the latter review, the extant research literature on manifest content of television was rather extensive, but investigations into the latent content were extremely limited. McLeod et al. (1982) stated: "Little attention has been paid to the content of the shows, particularly the interpersonal behaviors of television characters in their interactions. Curiously, although communication is universally acknowledged as an obvious and vital part of actual family life, televised family communication and interpersonal behavior have not been systematically examined" (p. 280). The second half of the 1980s has produced a wealth of research in this area.

CONTEMPORARY FAMILY CONTENT STUDIES

Among the earliest investigations of family interaction on primetime television was an exploratory study by Fisher (1974), who conducted a content analysis of marital and familial role behaviors of husband–father and wife–mother characters in commercial network television programs for a 1-week period. His findings indicated that parental and spousal relationships tended to be rather conflict free, and that emphasis was on affectionate and altruistic concern for one's spouse and children. Other findings revealed a general absence of violent or disruptive behaviors among family members, little concern for matters such as family finances and household chores, and few problems with the children.

Long and Simon (1974) explored patterns of interaction between men and women in a sample of prime-time television programs. Their findings revealed that men are more likely to be dominant (control, influence, pressure, dictate, lead, direct) than women. This study also indicated that, across family contexts in situation comedies, patterns of interaction between men and women are the most equal with regard to dominant behavior traits.

In a study of prime-time dramatic programs conducted by Manes and Melnyk (1974), it was found that women who were full-time homemakers were more likely to have successful marriages than those women who worked at careers outside the home.

McNeil (1975) content analyzed the character roles, marital, and parental status, and character relationships of some 243 males and females across 43 programs in March of 1973. Major findings indicated women characters were more closely allied with marital and parental themes than are men. Men continued to be portrayed as the primary bread winners in the family, outpacing women by almost 4:1. Marital and family relationships comprised 41% of the interactions by women and only 18% for men. Sixty-four percent of female characters' activities were focused on home–family–personal relationships as opposed to 32% for males. Overall, the findings indicated that females were fewer in number and more narrowly focused on family and personal issues.

In a 1977 U.S. Civil Rights Commission report, *Window Dressing on the Set*, based on data from the Cultural Indicators Research Project at the University of Pennsylvania, a sample of over 5,000 characters from prime time and children's Saturday dramatic programs were analyzed in terms of demographic composition, parental status, and perceived "goodness." The major findings of relevance to family life were that nearly 70% of the White males and 75% of the non-White males were not portrayed as husbands. Women, on the other hand were found to be portrayed as wives in over 50% of the cases if they were White; and in 45% of the cases of they were non-White. Overall, only 6.8% of the characters in the study were portrayed as having children.

THE DECADE OF THE 1980s: FAMILY AND TV RESEARCH FLOURISHES

Gerbner, Gross, Morgan, and Signorielli (1980), in their report to the 1980 White House Conference on the Family, indicated that mediated images of family life tend to be rather conventional and narrow in scope and very possibly a cause for concern to those involved in family policy:

> As the mass media have come to absorb many socializing functions of the family, they have offered us images of the family which may act as touchstones by which we gauge our experiences. The seductively realistic portrayals of family life in the media may be the basis for our most common and pervasive conceptions and beliefs about what is natural and what is right. (p.3)

This study revealed that images of home and family along with presentations of close personal relationships between men and women are the two themes that appear most frequently in primetime network television. During the period 1969 through 1978, over 80% of all prime-time programs emphasized these two themes in their storylines. Gerbner and his colleagues reported that home, family, and romance are important components of the way characters are portrayed, and that these presentations are, for the most part, traditional and stereotypical. Females' characters are cast into these roles more frequently than males'. With regard to the presentation of marital status, females were more likely to be explicitly shown as married. From 1969 to 1979, only 9.2% of the female characters could not be coded for marital status—45.2% were not married, and 45.6% were married or formerly married. In contrast, fully 24.3% of males' characters were not classifiable in terms of marital status, with 45.3% not married, and only 30.4% married or formerly married.

Signorielli (1982), using the same Cultural Indicators data base, studied the portrayal of married, formerly married, and single characters in primetime network television dramas. The findings revealed that men outnumbered women by three to one, and that women were more often portrayed as married and located in a home or family setting. Themes of home, family, marriage, and romance were seen as the domain of females. Married females were least likely to be involved in violence and usually did not have an occupation. It was also found that single characters were portrayed in the most positive light with the smallest frequency of conflict. They were presented as gainfully employed, more powerful, and most likely to appear in a variety of settings. Overall, television seems to cultivate the impression that marriage is a rather neutral and safe state of existence. Married women, however, were presented as least able to succeed at blending both career and family, a problem almost never encountered by males. Married men are not immune to television's distortion of marriage. When compared to single men, married males were seen as somewhat less powerful and less important.

The work of Greenberg, Buerkel-Rothfuss, Neuendorf, and Atkin (1980); Greenberg, Hines, Buerkel-Rothfuss, and Atkin (1980); and Greenberg and Neuendorf (1980) represents the first programmatic effort to catalog the latent content of families on prime-time television. Utilizing a modified version of Borke's (1967) instrument for systematic measurement of family interaction, these investigations sought to examine family-role behavior in terms of directionality of communications (going toward, going against, going away) coupled with a finer measure of "mode" for each direction (i.e., opposing, attacking, withdrawing, supporting, directing, etc.).

The findings indicated that offering information was the single most frequent act, followed by seeking information. Parents were most likely to give directions and children were least likely to do so. Supportive behaviors were most likely to originate with parents and spouses. Sons and brothers were least likely to demonstrate these behaviors. Children were found to seek support most often. Conflict in prime-time programs presented from 1975 to 1977 was most likely to occur among spouses and brothers. However, in the 1977–1978 season, conflict was found to be more evenly distributed across family roles. In a separate analysis of Black families, conflict was found to be more prevalent than among White families, with siblings and wives accounting for the greater portion of that conflict. Overall, affiliative acts were eight times more frequent than conflictual acts.

Shaner (1982) conducted a descriptive study of parental empathy and family-role interactions across a sample of situation comedies, action dramas, and soap operas. The findings indicated that characters in situation comedies exhibited higher levels of parental empathy than did characters in soap operas or action dramas. Overall, presentation of family life beyond the nuclear family was extremely infrequent, and the husband and wife relationship in the nuclear family situation was highly stereotyped; finding the husband most often in the instrumental role and the wife in the expressive role. Children in this analysis were found to be very precocious. They rarely behaved in accordance with the developmental stages of childhood. Showing concern and organizing were primary interaction roles for parents, and seeking support, attention, and gratification were primary interaction roles for children.

Glennon and Butsch (1982) asserted that "the television family, far from being simply a curious entertainment device, is connected to the ways in which family life operates in the real world" (p. 264). This study focused primarily on the social class elements of television's families, finding a dichotomy of portrayals: If the family was working class, the father and husband was generally seen as "inept, dumb or bumbling" (p. 267). However, if the family portrayed was middle class, then the viewer would find a rather competent father and husband in an "idealized picture of family life." It was concluded that "these idealized pictures may raise expectations about parent and child relations that are not realizable and can lead one to question one's own family adequacy" (p. 270).

In a related study that explored the relationship between social class and happiness across TV families, Thomas and Callahan (1982) examined primetime programs over a 3-year period beginning in 1978. Results indicate that "for the families portrayed on television, money clearly does not buy happiness and that, in fact, relative poverty does" (p. 186). Other aspects of this study revealed important information about the differences in family portrayals. Family sympathy, a measure of unity, and agreement among family members involved in a problem revealed that 88% of the middle-class families were rated good-to-high, whereas only 22% of the upper-class families exhibited good-to-high levels of sympathy. Helpfulness of characters within each family also indicated a strong negative relationship. Forty percent of the working-class family members were seen as "helpful," with 19% of the upper-middle and only 8% of the upper-class families rated as such. It was concluded that families of lower socioeconomic status have stronger and more harmonious interpersonal relationships, are likely to have more members with pleasant and agreeable personalities, demonstrate greater levels of good will toward each other, and have better problem resolutions than families with higher socioeconomic status.

Sweeper (1984) content analyzed 93 episodes of family comedy–drama series for the period 1970 to 1980. The focus of the investigation was the comparison of portrayal characteristics of Black and White families. The findings of this study indicated that members of Black families were more likely to come from broken homes than were White family members. Consequently, more Black households were headed by single females. Educational achievement and occupational status was lower for Black family members. When compared to White males, Black men were depicted as more hostile, vain, pompous, self-centered, and unreliable. Black mothers were more likely to be portrayed as obese or fat, whereas White mothers were seen as shapely or average. Overall, when compared to White families, interactions among Black family members were more conflictual, particularly among opposite-sex siblings.

Dail and Way (1985) content analyzed parental role behaviors, child-rearing patterns, and child responses to those roles and patterns in 44 family-oriented prime-time episodes airing in November and December of 1982. Across the 30 hours of programs, they observed 955 parental role behaviors, 833 child-rearing patterns, with 820 and 508 child responses to those roles and patterns. They reported that TV fathers were somewhat more active as parents than were the mothers, and that both mothers and fathers were portrayed in traditional ways, despite the greater presence of nontraditional family structures. In studying parental roles, these researchers employed a three-way category system: instrumental, expressive, or neutral. Instrumental role behaviors involved primary decision making by the parent. Expressive role behaviors were the nurturing and supportive parental behaviors. Neutral role behaviors were directions to the child that were in the form of a request or command on a neutral subject.

Dail and Way (1985) also found that fathers were more likely than mothers to display instrumental behaviors (33% for fathers and 27% for mothers), and mothers were more likely to display expressive behaviors (49% for the mothers vs. 39% for fathers). Neutral role behaviors accounted for 28% of the fathers and 24% of the mothers' responses. Overall, expressive parental role behaviors were the most frequent, accounting for 43% of all the behaviors.

The authors used a four-category system to analyze child-rearing patterns: authoritarian, authoritative, permissive, and neutral. The authoritarian pattern involved firm rules and enforcement in a demanding fashion with negative sanctions. Fathers used this pattern in 29% of the interactions and mothers, 20%. The authoritative child-rearing pattern was one that encouraged discussion with the child, displayed flexibility, and encouraged individuality in the child. Fathers employed this strategy in 47% of the interactions and mothers, 55%. The permissive pattern was defined as allowing the child to be annoying; the parent avoided confrontations and was largely nondirective. Fathers were found to use this pattern in 3% of their interactions and mothers, 1%. Neutral patterns were defined as comments not intended to be directive. Father accounted for 21% of these and mothers, 24%. Overall, fathers accounted for nearly 60% of the child-rearing behaviors in this study, leaving mothers with just over 40%. The child responses to patterns of child rearing were coded as either positive or negative responses. Nearly 87% of the responses by children were coded as positive, leaving just over 14% as negative responses.

Akins (1986) conducted a comparative analysis of family lifestyles and interactions across two sets of 30 commercial network television programs. One set was developed and aired in the 1960s, the other in the 1980s. The study examined television programs featuring a family with at least one preadolescent child. This investigation focused on the portrayals of family lifestyle and interpersonal interactions that may serve as possible models for children. The data were analyzed across two program eras in order to determine if, and to what extent, content themes and interaction patterns of family members had changed during the past 20 years. The findings indicated that children in the 1980's programs both initiated more interactions and exhibited more numerous interactions with their parents than children in the 1960's programs. Family members were found to be more supportive and more likely to show concern for each other in the 1980's programs. Conversely, family members in the 1980's shows were also more likely to evade, ignore, withdraw, and oppose one another than were families in the 1960's shows. Similarly, children in the 1980's programs were more likely to both seek information and initiate conflict with adults than children in the 1960's program. Family members in the 1980's programs exhibited more overt love and caring toward each other, but males in both the 1960's and 1980's shows were portrayed as more interactive than females. Whereas children's interests were portrayed in similar ways across the two programming eras, the concerns, problems, and program themes encountered by children in the 1980's shows were presented as more complex and adultlike than in the 1960's shows.

Selnow (1986) explored the nature of problem solving as presented on prime-time television and found that 88.7% of the subplots identified had clear, unambiguous resolutions. The data indicate that 43.3% of the problems were resolved in a confrontational manner (aggressive, verbal aggressive, or assertive strategies). However, 57% were found to be nonaggressive, and of those 18.5% of the problems were resolved by mutual agreement. The "rules" by which problems were resolved does suggest a prosocial emphasis. Nearly 85% of the problems were solved by truth and honesty, hard work, ingenuity, or good will. In terms of types of problems, women dealt with a majority of the romantic problems and men tended to employ the more aggressive solutions.

Skill, Robinson, and Wallace (1987) systematically analyzed, over a 6-year period (1979–1985), the range and extent of family-life configurations in prime-time television across conventional and nonconventional types of portrayals. The findings revealed that prime-time network television tends to reinforce conservative to moderate models of family life. Over 65% of all families presented were found to be conventional in configuration (oriented toward the nuclear family unit). It was also found that the nonstandard interpretations of family were highly diverse in their configurations and, for the most part, comfortably framed in the less threatening comedic form.

Larson (1989) looked at the nature of sibling relationships in a sample of nine episodes each of "The Cosby Show," "Family Ties," and "Growing Pains." Over 1,300 behaviors were coded for positive or negative direction (supportive or conflictual) and for function of the behavior (identification, regulation, or direct services). Overall, Larson found that 58% of the behavior among siblings was positive in direction, but, when analyzed by show, sibling interaction on "Growing Pains" was significantly less positive (43.5%) than on "The Cosby Show" (64.4%) and "Family Ties" (62.8%).

In terms of behavior functions, Larson's study indicates that the most frequently performed function was direct services (62.6%). This behavior involved giving information, negotiating arrangements, bargaining for favors, and threatening actions. Across all programs, 26.1% of these actions were negative in direction. Regulation was the next most common functional behavior among siblings. This was the "sounding board" function whereby siblings seek advice from one another. The data in this study indicate that over 80% of these behaviors were negative in direction. Identification behaviors, which essentially represent bonding among siblings, were positive in direction in over 90% of the coded interactions. However, only 5.8% of the behaviors recorded in this study were classified as identification.

Larson further explored the interaction between sibling dyads and found that older sister–younger brother dyads were significantly more supportive than younger sister–older brother dyads. There were no significant differences between same-gender dyads when comparing brothers to sisters. Larson indicated that, whereas the overall image of sibling behaviors are positive, many aspects of their behavior are clearly unsupportive – particularly in the area of regulation behaviors.

Skill, Wallace, and Cassata (1990) studied patterns of interpersonal conflict escalation and resolution across family configurations and roles in prime-time network television. This study provides important insight into the nature and range of conflict escalation and resolution models and strategies that are available to the viewing audience.

A sample of 21 prime-time episodes were coded using Raush, Barry, Hertel, and Swain's (1974) "A coding Scheme for Interpersonal Conflict." The data were analyzed across family roles (father, wife, brother, etc.) by family configuration type (intact, nonintact, or mixed).

Major findings in this investigation revealed that conflict-resolving acts occurred almost twice as often as conflict-escalating acts. Intact families were least likely to engage in conflict escalation and mixed families were most likely. Brothers in all family settings were most likely to escalate conflict. Mothers in intact families were the single group most likely to engage in conflict-resolving behaviors and least likely to escalate conflict. Parents and children across all family types tended to display respect and concern for one another. When problems did arise, it occurred most often between fathers and daughters. Although mixed families and brothers tended to present rather conflictual models, the state of family relationships on television, for the most part, can be characterized as more healthy than conventional wisdom suggests. Whereas many models for escalating conflict exist, models of conflict resolution are dominant – and the strategies available to the audience for resolving conflicts are rather diverse.

Comstock and Strzyzewski (1990) analyzed 29 hours of televised interactions across 41 prime-time network programs. This study examined conflict, jealousy, envy, and rivalry in family interactions. The data indicate that over 30% of the conflict situations involved parents and children, 19% involved spouses, 13% involved siblings. Integrative strategies, considered to be a constructive form of conflict because it promotes relational growth and maintenance, were employed most often by mothers and sons. Distributive strategies, considered a destructive form, were most often employed by siblings and spouses. The authors concluded that family conflict and the expression of jealousy occur frequently on prime-time television, but that these portrayals are not predominantly antisocial.

In a related investigation, Skill and Wallace (1990) explored the frequency and distribution of assertive power, conformity, and rejection behaviors in prime-time families. The sample for this study consisted of 21 episodes across 18 different programs in which one or more family groups served as the primary story vehicle. The interactions of family members were analyzed by family role (mother, son, sister, etc.) and by family type (intact, nonintact, and mixed configurations). Assertive power had five possible manifestations: reward, coercive, legitimate, reference, and expert. This investigation explored the extent to which family members employed one of the five types of power strategies, yielded to the power of others (conformity behaviors), rejected others' attempts to use power (rejection), or engaged in none of the previous behaviors (neutral). More than 2,000 communicative acts were identified in this study, and the findings indicated that intact families engaged in the fewest assertive power and rejection acts of all family types, and the most conformity acts. In terms of models of family life for the audience, the use of power in this study tended to be more positive than negative. Intact families, for the most part, used power in a compassionate fashion. Nonintact families followed closely, whereas mixed families (programs with both intact and nonintact families as primary story vehicles) were most likely to employ abusive forms of power such as coercion. The data overall suggested that models of family interaction on prime-time television tend to be rather diverse and for the most part tempered with a sincere concern for the members of their respective families.

FAMILY AND TELEVISION: WHERE DOES THE CONTENT LEAD US?

The emerging image of the fictionally presented family in television suggests the following:

1. Overall, the family is presented on television as a diverse and complex entity. All forms of family are presented, but the intact family remains dominate.

2. Data suggest that the role portrayals within family groups may favor traditional concepts of gender-role behaviors. Female characters are more likely than male characters to be linked to marital or family situations.

3. Interaction among family members is mostly cooperative and helpful. Conflict exists as a central part of most every family, but in most cases the conflict is handled in a healthy manner.

4. Children in families tend to be very precocious. Fathers tend to occupy the instrumental role, whereas mothers tend to exhibit more expressive behaviors.

5. Middle-class families tend to have parents that fit the "Ideal" role model. Working-class fathers tend to be presented as less vital.

6. Family happiness tends to be disconnected from financial status. Family unity tends to increase for middle-class families and decease for wealthy families.

7. Sibling relationships tend to be less harmonious than relationships with other family members. Brothers tend to escalate conflict more often than any other family member.

8. The overall use of power by families appears to be mostly positive and reasonable. The theme of concern and respect tends to resonate within the family unit.

Areas for further investigation with regard to family portrayals:

1. Outcome data in most content studies are weak. We need to more fully map the consequences of interaction behaviors if we desire to develop more useful inventories of social learning and/or social comparison models.

2. Sibling relationships keep turning up as negative role models. This is an area that requires further investigation, both in terms of what the consequences of those interactions are (do parents on TV correct these behaviors?) and what the perception of the audience is with regard to those behaviors (are viewers processing those behaviors?).

3. Future content studies need to address not only the outcome of behaviors but also the diversity of viewing options. Network television no longer represents the vast majority of television viewing in the United States. Program offerings from many sources have fragmented the national audience. Family images consist of current first-run programs and a great number of recycled images from 10, 20, and even 30 years ago. How has this fragmentation and diversification impacted the concept of "television families"?

4. Satires of family life on television need to be considered in context — are the "The Simpsons" and "Married With Children" viewed with the same perspective as "The Cosby Show" or "Growing Pains"? How are those viewing experiences different? The content in this situation may get in the way of the meaning.

CONCLUSION

The media, commercial television in particular, do provide a diverse range of family images. The data from study after study suggest that good and bad images appear frequently in most programs. However, behaviors that are affirmative continue to dominate the screen and will likely resonate most intensely among the audience. Even in the worst of those depictions, a wealth of information and vicarious experience is conveyed. Actions elicit reactions, interactions escalate into conflict, destructive and constructive patterns of behavior are established, and the consequences of one's actions are realized.

The challenges that regularly confront members of these mediated families may be narrowly conceived or superficially developed, and the resolutions frequently may appear as too simple, too easy, or just too fast. In some cases, those challenges may inappropriately fade into the background as other more pressing story elements emerge. But, as in life, most families muddle through—they sometimes deal rather responsibly with a challenge or problem, they occasionally avoid them, they may even run from them or deny that they even exist, and sometimes the problem is overmanaged. And there are those rare times when the problem is not resolved and the family attempts to cope. As families grapple with their challenges, there are moments of awkwardness and moments of eloquence, but in the end the essential message is clear: Family is important and each member has a stake in its survival.

Although the social sciences have not as yet been able to fully articulate the range and extent of the influences that these mediated messages have on the audience, there are those in the industry who have little doubt about the impact. In a 1988 interview, Gary David Goldberg, executive producer of "Family Ties," recounted a conversation that took place with Brandon Tartikoff during the development of the "Family Ties" series. Tartikoff explained to Goldberg that there are three essential elements necessary for a family show to be successful on network television (Hirsh, 1988): "The audience has to want to be part of that family. The audience has to see themselves in that family. And, the audience has to begin to want to watch because they think they can learn to be a better family." Goldberg summarized what he thought made "Family Ties" resonate so effectively with the audience: "I think a good 'Family Ties' episode will some how shine a little bit of light on what it means to be part of a family in America today . . . and take a step toward saying 'families matter, it's the most important relationship you'll ever have.' "

The evidence regarding the images of family life in the media, both anecdotal and empirical, seems to suggest that this institution has fared far better than most others in the symbolic world of the media. Certainly there are those families that are dysfunctional, and there are many models of behavior in all families that are undesirable. But the symbolic power of family images most distinctly rests in those families and those behaviors that emphasize the importance, centrality, worth, and joy of family life. Few episodes of any program leave the viewer questioning the value of the institution of family. In contrast, most other institutions as depicted in the media have serious, if not fatal, flaws. Education, health, justice, religion, and government are frequently seen as dysfunctional and fundamentally corrupt. With the sole exception of the satire, "Married with Children," redeeming internal qualities do exist, in varying degrees, within all families. Reconciliation and preservation undergird the closing themes of most every episode.

Two essential questions regarding mediated images of families remain unresolved: (a) Has the media, through its symbolical interpretation of families and family life, enhanced or detracted from the institution of family? And (b) has the media contributed to the perceived decline of family cohesion or has the media facilitated the strengthening of this fundamental social group? The answers to these questions depend largely on how one defines and evaluates the concept of family. As research on these issues pushes forward, the challenges for those in the family policy arena continue to mount.

REFERENCES

Akins, G. (1986). An analysis of family interaction styles as portrayed on television. *Dissertation Abstracts International, 47,* 2013A.

Baker, R., & Ball, S. (Eds.). (1969). *Violence and the media.* Washington, DC: U.S. Government Printing Office.

Borke, H. (1967). The communication of intent: A systematic approach to the observation of family interaction. *Human Relations, 20,* 13–28.

Charters, W. W. (1933). *Motion pictures and youth: A summary.* New York: MacMillan.

Comstock, G. A., & Rubinstein, E. A. (Eds.). (1972). *Television and social behavior.* Washington, DC: U.S. Government Printing Office.

Comstock, J., & Strzyzewski, K. (1990) Interpersonal interaction on television: Family conflict and jealously on primetime. *Journal of Broadcasting & Electronic Media, 34*(3), 263–282.

Dail, P. W., & Way, W. L. (1985). What do parents observe about parenting from prime-time television? *Family Relations, 34,* 491–499.

Fisher, C. (1974). Marital and familial roles on television: An exploratory sociological analysis. *Dissertation Abstracts International, 35,* 599A.

Gerbner, G., Gross, L., Morgan, M., & Signorielli, N. (1980). *Media and the family: Images and impact.* Washington, DC: White House Conference on the Family, National Research Forum on Family Issues. (ERIC Document Reproduction Service No. ED 198 919)

Glennon, L., & Butsch, R. (1982). The family as portrayed on television 1946–1978. In D. Pearl, L. Bouthilet, & J. Lazar (Eds.), *Television and behavior: Ten years of scientific progress and implications for the eighties, Vol. II: Technical reviews* (DHHS Publication No. ADM 82–1196, pp. 264–271). Washington, DC: U.S. Government Printing Office.

Greenberg, B., Buerkel-Rothfuss, N., Neuendorf, K., & Atkin, C. (1980). Three seasons of television family role interactions. In B. S. Greenberg (Ed.), *Life on television* (pp. 161–172). Norwood, NJ: Ablex.

Greenberg, B., Hines, M., Buerkel-Rothfuss, N., & Atkin, C. (1980). Family role structures and interactions on commercial television. In B. S. Greenberg (Ed.), *Life on television* (pp 149–160). Norwood, NJ: Ablex.

Greenberg, B., & Neuendorf, K. (1980). Black family interactions on television. In B. S. Greenberg (Ed.), *Life on television* (pp. 173–181). Norwood, NJ: Ablex.

Hirsh, M. (Producer/director). (1988). *Inside Family Ties* [Videotape]. Chicago: WTTW (PBS).

Larson, M. S. (1989). Interaction between siblings in primetime television families. *Journal of Broadcasting & Electronic Media, 33*(3), 305–315.

Long, M., & Simon, R. (1974). The roles and statuses of women on children and family TV programs. *Journalism Quarterly, 51*, 107–110.

Manes, A. L., & Melnyk, P. (1974). Televised models of female achievement. *Journal of Applied Social Psychology, 4*, 365–374.

McLeod, J. M., Fitzpatrick, M. A., Glynn, C. J., & Fallis, S. (1982). Television and social relations: Family influences and consequences for interpersonal behavior. In D. Pearl, L. Bouthilet, & J. Lazar (Eds.), *Television and behavior: Ten years of scientific progress and implications for the eighties, Vol. II: Technical reviews* (DHHS Publication No. ADM 82-1196, pp. 272–290). Washington, DC: U.S. Government Printing Office.

McNeil, J. (1975). Feminism, femininity, and the television series: A content analysis. *Journal of Broadcasting, 19*(3), 259–269.

Raush, H. L., Barry, W. A., Hertel, R. K., & Swain, M. A. (1974). *Communication conflict and marriage*. San Francisco: Jossey-Bass.

Schramm, W., Lyle, J., & Parker, E. B. (1961). *Television in the lives of our children*. Palo Alto, CA: Stanford University Press.

Selnow, G. W. (1986) Solving problems on prime-time television. *Journal of Communication, 36*(2), 63–72.

Shaner, J. (1982). Parental empathy and family role interactions as portrayed on commercial television. *Dissertation Abstracts International, 42*, 3473A.

Signorielli, N. (1982). Marital status in television drama: A case of reduced options. *Journal of Broadcasting, 26*(2), 585–597.

Skill, T., Robinson, J., & Wallace, S. (1987). Family life on prime-time television: Structure, type and frequency. *Journalism Quarterly, 64*(2/3), 360–367, 398.

Skill, T., & Wallace, S. (1990). Family interactions on primetime television: A descriptive analysis of assertive power interactions. *Journal of Broadcasting & Electronic Media, 34*(3), 243–262.

Skill, T., Wallace, S., & Cassata, M. (1990). Families on prime-time television: Patterns of conflict escalation and resolution across intact, non-intact, and mixed family settings. In J. Bryant (Ed.), *Television and the American family* (pp. 129–163). Hillsdale, NJ: Lawrence Erlbaum Associates.

Sweeper, G. (1984). The image of the black family and the white family in American prime-time television programming 1970 to 1980. *Dissertation Abstracts International, 44*, 1964A.

Thomas, S., & Callahan, B. P. (1982). Allocating happiness: TV families and social class. *Journal of Communication, 33*(3), 184–190.

United States Commission on Civil Rights. (1977). *Window dressing on the set: Women and minorities in television*. Washington, DC: U.S. Government Printing Office.

4

THE EFFECT OF MEDIA ON FAMILY INTERACTION

Alison Alexander
The University of Georgia

The social changes that followed the shift from traditional to modern society have given the family a great deal of "leisure" time to be filled in the home (Laslett, 1973; Sennett, 1970). For several decades, the family's use of this time has been dominated by television, which is deeply interwoven into the fabric of daily family life (Leichter et al., 1985; Morley, 1986).

Directly and indirectly, television provides bases for family interaction (Bryce & Leichter, 1983; Lull, 1980a), and these interactions teach and reinforce conventional ways of comprehending both the medium and social reality in general (Alexander, Ryan, & Munoz, 1984; Messaris, 1986). A number of studies convincingly demonstrates the *potential* for family interaction to mediate the impact of exposure to media. In experimental settings, parental or adult comments have been found to aid children's understanding of program content (Collins, Sobol, & Westby, 1981; Prasad, Rao, & Sheikh, 1978), to foster critical viewing skills (Corder-Bolz & O'Bryant, 1978), and to increase recall of information from educational programs (Salomon, 1977; Singer & Singer, 1976). However, co-viewing in a context of limited interaction tends to be the norm, restricting the learning that interaction could promote (Anderson & Collins, 1988; Field, 1987).

Much of the family interaction about television focuses on its *use*. Numerous studies have focused on parental rules about viewing, how families select programs, and other control issues. Extensive reviews of these studies are available (McLeod, Fitzpatrick, Glynn, & Fallis, 1982). From this work we can arrive at several conclusions. Television viewing can create conflicts among family members as to how much and what children view, as well as conflicts over program choices (Alexander et al., 1984; Zahn & Baran, 1984). At the same time, Goodman (1983) noted that family members may find it easier to fight over television than over more "important" things.

Moreover, some parents use television to unite their families (Johnsson-Smaragdi, 1983; Messaris, 1986). Although talk declines during viewing, touching increases (Brody & Stoneman, 1983; Brody, Stoneman, & Sanders, 1980). Still, previous studies have produced quite divergent results: An early study by Maccoby (1954) found that amount of viewing and "frustration" were positively related, among those of higher social class. Also, Rosenblatt and Cunningham (1976) found that the amount of television viewing was related to the amount of tension in the family; the more viewing, the greater the family tension level.

Yet, the public fears associated with the influence of television on family interaction have not been clearly demonstrated by research. The ability of television to replace interpersonal communication, to promote conflict, and to reduce family unity remains unproven. Given the variety of roles television may play in the family, the most valid conclusion of several decades of research is that the domestic uses of media essentially extend pre-existing family communication patterns. Television use is predicted by family rules rather than television rules (Andreason, 1990).

Examining the Application of Family Systems Perspectives

By now it has become axiomatic to argue that family-based media uses and effects research should focus on the family system. Recently, I have argued that a communicative perspective on the role of television in family interaction must begin by examining the family as the context in which viewing is performed and made meaningful (Alexander, 1990).

Of the many contexts that influence meaning and behavior, none is more ubiquitous than the family. And it is through communication that the structures and processes that regulate a family are created. This *interactionist* perspective from family process research has been modified by communication researchers with a strong symbolic interactionist view, to become the predominant position in the field of communication (Meadowcroft & Fitzpatrick, 1988). Because communication is seen as fundamental to family process, researchers have attempted to identify dimensions of family interaction that illuminate the processes whereby communication operates within the family to create family systems (Reiss & Oliveri, 1983).

This perspective assumes that there are patterns and regularities in marriage and family communication. "Uncovering" these patterns, their characteristics, causes, and consequences, has been a primary focus of family research. Although interactionists agree that communication is the process whereby families create a social reality, such agreement has not led to common research strategies or perspectives. Research has conceptualized the family as a system, as a small group, as a type, as part of a network, in a life stage, in family therapy, or negotiating power (cf. Bochner, 1976). Similarly, the examined outcomes of communication are quite varied. Concepts such as conflict, dominance, intrusion, and influence are frequently studied. More rarely support or encouragement are examined.

With the emergence of interest in qualitative investigations of how media are used in everyday life, researchers began to observe the nature and consequences of television-related interaction in the home (Alexander, Ryan, & Munoz, 1984; Brody, Stoneman, & Sanders, 1980; Lemish, 1986; Lull, 1980a; Reid & Frazer, 1980a, 1980b; Wolf, Meyer, & White, 1982). One major conclusion from this line of research is that television may serve an almost limitless range of diverse uses and functions. Family members can watch television to be together, or to get away from each other; as a basis for talk or to avoid talk; television can be a source of conflict or an escape from conflict; and so on. Because much of the time that family members spend together is in the presence of television, television at least partially defines the context within which family interaction occurs and therefore helps determine the meaning of that interaction. From this perspective, family themes, roles, or issues are carried out in a variety of contexts, and the television viewing context becomes one in which it is useful to study patterns of family interaction in general. For example, if one assumes that there is stability in family interactions, then differences between the viewing and nonviewing context could be explored as to whether the task (television viewing) alters the interactional patterns in some unique way. As such, media are implicated in the accomplishment of numerous family functions, including defining role expectations, articulating the nature of relationships, and using economic and relational currencies in the negotiation of intimacy and power.

Such a perspective, however, cannot naively assume a communicatively generated family system. For although families do jointly create rules, roles, and systems, that creation occurs within a larger cultural context that provides frames and boundaries, just as media texts and technologies are associated with social values in everyday life that affect how, when, and where they are used in the domestic sphere (Lindlof, 1986, 1991). It is, I suspect, our failure to properly embed our examination of family interaction within just such a larger cultural context that has resulted in the depressing, limited-effects conclusion that media effects on the family are complex, are mediated by a variety of intervening variables, and are less powerful than we have thought. In part, our research has betrayed our impoverished image of the family system. By focusing on differences across families (such as family types), we have ignored the variabilty of tasks faced *within* families. Yet all families are engaged in behaviors with major consequences for the system of meanings within that family and for the individual members of that system: the creation of family and individual images, the creation and communication of intimacy, the creation and communication of family roles and types, the creation and communication of power, the management of decisions, and of conflict.

Labeling the activity through which family systems are created and maintained is a significant task. Differing implications are derived from the choices of "talk," "interaction," and "communication." I would propose that the question "How do media influence family interaction?" organizes one's attention differently from "What is the relationship of media and family communication?" If communication can be defined as a process of creating and sharing meanings, then mass communication scholars might profitably focus their attentions on the ways in which media affect the process of creating and sharing meanings within the family, as well as asking the ways in which the process of creating and sharing meanings within the family affects the place of media within the family. This chapter challenges us to rethink some of the limitations of our current perspectives on media and the family.

Rethinking our Research Site: Interaction Outside of the Viewing Context

Television can influence family interaction even when family members are not watching it and even when they are not at home (cf. Bryce & Leichter, 1983). Media influence is embedded in peoples' daily lives. I have talked to viewers of soap operas — perhaps the most heavily stigmatized viewing behavior that you can choose. When it emerges in conversation with others that these individuals are soap opera viewers, they find they have to accomplish a lot of what Goffman (1967) called "conversational repair" to restore their identity, and they accomplished that repair through conversational strategies that detached their "selves" from their viewing. They said, in essence, don't judge me by my viewing because, as was argued in several cases, they were really superior to the messages themselves; that is, they watched soaps in order to laugh at them, or they saw soap operas for what they truly are, mere entertainment, certainly nothing that would influence them, certainly nothing to which they could arguably be described as being addicted or even as being involved. They saw through them. Mark Crispin Miller (1988) called this the "jeering gaze" of contemporary audiences that fosters an illusion of "knowing" (about the medium) we wrongly assume protects us from the consequences of consumption. Even those who argued that viewing was not unproductive, that they were in fact doing other things as well—cooking dinner, doing their homework, watching the kids—still said don't judge me by my viewing. It's mere entertainment. It's not a problem. Central to these claims is the statement that soap opera viewing is a peripheral activity—nothing that should have any consequences for defining the self.

This is a clear demonstration that the effects of television on family interaction are not contained nor can they be fully accounted for if we study only the primary exposure context. The media has impact on family interaction not only within the primary media exposure context, but also in numerous ongoing and communicative contexts (Fry, Alexander, & Fry, 1990). These contexts are separated spatially and temporally from the primary exposure context but are, nonetheless, important for understanding media influence. A research focus on "extratextual" communicative contexts may be crucial in understanding the production and reproduction of meaning, because it acknowledges the range and complexity of the different ways in which texts and individuals can come together. Therefore, media effects on family interaction include discussions, direct or indirect, of the media or media content outside the viewing context.

Rethinking the Indirect Relation of Text and Interaction

Although most research reports seem to indicate scholars' awareness of the ability of certain media content to provide interaction, theory about the linkage of media content and interaction remains rare. From the perspective developed previously, it is explicitly assumed that as mediated content passes from the primary media consumption contexts into and through various communication contexts, it does not necessarily remain the same; it may be transformed and recreated within each context. This is not to suggest that the content is distorted, because that would imply that there was a "true" meaning. Instead it suggests that ordinary discourse about television is tied closely to the demands of the communicative situation, the identity of the speakers and listeners, and the cultural evaluation of the text. Indeed, an individual's experience with text is not limited to the consumption context and may be fundamentally different when that text is encountered as an object of talk.

Anderson (1986) made a similar point when he described meaning as promiscuous and prolific. Meaning does not end at the point of reception. It is promiscuous because meaning is aroused in each of us as we interpret content and prolific because new meaning arises with each content encounter. "Meaning construction, then is an ongoing process which reaches well beyond the moment of reception. It is continued in the circumstances of each situation demanding interpreted content" (p. 167).

However, research that attempts to locate the influence of communication about media outside of the exposure context is rare. Despite an interest in such a process that dates back to the work of Lazarsfeld in the 1940s, the interaction process that presumably creates these affects has been assumed rather than studied.

Rethinking the Integration of Story and Family System

One way to examine the creation of meaning in family contexts is to explore the relationship of media's storytelling function to self-narrative and family themes. The generative force of conversation and storytelling as audience members take up information and narratives from the media has tended to be overlooked by media scholars.

Gergen (1984) has argued that narrative is central to understanding the social world (also see MacIntyre, 1981; Milk, 1970). We tell stories as a means of organizing the social world, placing ourselves in that social world, and justifying, explaining, criticizing, and solidifying that social world. We, as individuals and as families, selectively take the raw material of life and put it into narratives (or stories) and, through that process, come to understand our life or some component of it. The ability of families and individuals to make their own narratives for and about themselves can be contrasted to a view of individuals as manipulated by the producers of narratives for their own ends.

In consuming the media we are, in effect, consuming narratives, narratives that are fundamentally controlled by the media. We may respond positively or negatively to the narrative, we may be interested and involved or uninterested and distracted, but we remain more responsive than creative. As Ang (1985) noted, we engage the media as a routinized form of cultural practice. In nonmediated communication contexts, though, we are engaged in a fundamentally more direct fashion in the creation of stories to accomplish relational and interactive goals. The communication context is far less reactive and more productive (in the sense of production of text) than is the primary media consumption context (Fry et al., 1990). This does not posit that the audience is totally reactive in mediated contexts and totally active and creative in nonmediated communication contexts. Nonetheless, it would seem reasonable to suggest that this distinction does in some form exist, and that it has some analytic significance.

The heuristic value of this distinction lies with the presumption that events, information, and experiences become meaningful to us as we build narratives about them or as we integrate them into our narratives to accomplish related goals. Thus, the force of the mediated experiences that audience members have may well not become manifest in the media consumption contexts per se; instead, those mediated experiences become significant only after audience members take up mediated narratives and integrate them wholly or in parts into self-narratives. Certainly, significant processes occur in the media consumption contexts. We engage cultural products, we learn plot lines, we memorize bits of information. But, that which we take in during media consumption contexts may remain peripheral to self until we integrate it into our self-narratives. Simply, we learn a great deal from the media in a number of forms, but the relative significance of this to the individual audience member is minimal until it is used, either in the way it was intended by the media or in particular idiosyncratic ways, in self-narratives or in the development of family themes. Thus, audience members are constrained by the mediated text in that there is a limited range of likely interpretations in media consumption contexts. The actual creative control by audience members occurs when audience members selectively *use* mediated content in communication contexts.

This integration of text within context leads the research to pursue a more systematic exploration of how we integrate, or for that matter do not integrate, the media and mediated texts into our self-and family narratives. Thus, the naturalistic stories that individuals and families construct should become a significant data base for mass communication research because it is at this point that mediated texts become integrated into other social processes. It is here that audience members draw from the narrative resources available to them (both mediated and nonmediated) and actually make use of those resources to accomplish social goals.

In conclusion, the research goals posed here are far from easy to accomplish. Most research has assumed that interaction is an intervention that modifies the influence of exposure, thus telling us little about how interaction within the family relates to larger cultural patterns and social structures. Such an orientation will require that mass communication researchers begin to think differently about mass communication and its boundaries. Nonetheless, this offers the potential of repositioning mass communication within a range of other social processes. It begins to move mass communication research away from the simple, and generally unproductive, causal models to one that treats mass communication as one component of a complex social environment.

REFERENCES

Alexander, A. (1990). Television and family interaction. In J. Bryant (Ed.), *Television and the American family* (pp. 3–55). Hillsdale, NJ: Lawrence Erlbaum Associates.

Alexander, A., Ryan, M. S., & Munoz, P. (1984). Creating a learning context: Investigations on the interaction of siblings during co-viewing. *Critical Studies in Mass Communication, 1,* 345–364.

Anderson, D. R., & Collins, P. (1988). *The impact on children's education: Television's influence on cognitive development.* Washington, DC: U.S. Department of Education.

Anderson, J. (1986). Commentary on qualitative research and mediated communication in the family. In T. Lindlof (Ed.), *Natural audiences: Qualitative research of media uses and effects* (pp. 161–171). Norwood, NJ: Ablex.

Andreason, M. S. (1990). Evolution in the family's use of television: Normative data from industry and academe. In J. Bryant (Ed.), *Television and the American family* (pp. 3–55). Hillsdale, NJ: Lawrence Erlbaum Associates.

Ang, I. (1985). *Watching Dallas: Soap opera and the melodramatic imagination.* London: Methuen.

Bochner, A. (1976). Conceptual frontiers in the study of communication in families: An introduction to the literature. *Human Communication Research, 2,* 381–397.

Brody, G. H., & Stoneman, Z. (1983). The influence of television viewing on family interaction: A contextualist approach. *Journal of Family Issues, 4,* 329–348.

Brody, G. H., Stoneman, Z., & Sanders, A. K. (1980). Effects of television viewing on family interactions: An observational study. *Family Relations, 28* 216–220.

Bryce, J., & Leichter, H. J. (1983). The family and television: Forms of mediation. *Journal of Family Issues, 4,* 309–328.

Collins, W. S., Sobol, B. L., & Westby, S. (1981). Effects of adult commentary on children's comprehension and inferences about a televised aggressive protrayal. *Child Development, 52,* 158–63.

Corder-Bolz, C. R., & O'Bryant, S. (1978). Can people affect television: Teacher vs. program. *Journal of Communication, 28*(1), 97–103.

Field, D. (1987). *Child and parent coviewing of television: Relationships to cognitive performance.* Unpublished doctoral dissertation, University of Massachusetts, Amherst.

Fry, V., Alexander, A., & Fry, D. (1990). Textual status, the stigmatized self, and media consumption. In J. Anderson (Ed.), *Communication Yearbook 13* (pp. 519–544). Newbury Park, CA: Sage.

Gergen, K. J. (1984). Theory of the self: Impasse & evolution. In L. Berkowitz (Ed.), *Advances in experimental social psychology* (Vol. 17, pp. 49–115). New York: Academic Press.

Goffman, E. (1967). *Interaction ritual: Essays on face-to-face behavior.* Garden City, NY: Anchor.

Goodman, I. F. (1983). Television's role in family interaction: A family systems perspective. *Journal of Family Issues, 4,* 405–424.

Johnsson-Smaragdi, U. (1983). *TV use and social interaction in adolescence: A longitudinal study.* Stockholm: Almqvist & Wiskell.

Laslett, B. (1973). The family as a public and private institution: An historical perspective. *Journal of Marriage and the Family, 35,* 480–492.

Leichter, H. J., Ahmed, D., Barrios, L., Bryce, J., Larsen, E., & Moe, L. (1985). Family contexts of television. *Educational Communication and Technology Journal, 33,* 26–40.

Lemish, D. (1986). Viewers in diapers. In T. Lindlof (Ed.), *Natural audiences: Qualitative research of media uses and effects* (pp. 33–57). Norwood, NJ: Ablex.

Lindlof, T. (1991). The qualitative study of media audiences. *Journal of Broadcasting & Electronic Media, 35,* 15–30.

Lull, J. (1980a). The social uses of television. *Human Communication Research*, *6*, 197–209.

Lull, J. (1980b). Family communication patterns and the social uses of television. *Communication Research*, *7*, 319–334.

Maccoby, E. E. (1954). Why do children watch television? *Public Opinion Quarterly*, *18*, 239–244.

MacIntyre, A. (1981). *After virtue*. South Bend, IN: University of Notre Dame Press.

McLeod, J. M., Fitzpatrick, M. A., Glynn, C. J., & Fallis, S. F. (1982). Television and social relations: Family influences and consequences for interpersonal behavior. In D. Pearl, L. Bouthilet, & J. Lazar (Eds.), *Television and behavior: Ten years of scientific progress and implications for the eighties* Vol. 2, (pp. 272–286). Washington, DC: U.S. Government Printing Office.

Meadowcroft, J. M., & Fitzpatrick, M. A. (1988). Theories of family communication: Toward a merger of intersubjectivity and mutual influence processes. In R. P. Hawkins, J. M. Wiemann, & S. Pingree (Eds.), *Advancing communication science: Merging mass and interpersonal processes* (pp. 253–275). Newbury Park, CA: Sage.

Messaris, P. (1986). Mothers' comments to their children about the relationship between television and reality. In T. Lindlof (Ed.), *Natural audiences: Qualitative research of media uses and effects* (pp. 95–107). Norwood, NJ: Ablex.

Milk, L. O. (1970). History and fiction as modes of comprehension. *New Literacy*, *1*, 541–558.

Miller, M. C. (1988). *Boxed in: The culture of TV*. Evanston, IL: Northwestern University Press.

Morley, D. (1986). *Family television: Cultural power and domestic leisure*. London: Comedia.

Prasad, V. K., Rao, T. R., & Sheikh, A. A. (1978). Mother vs. commercial. *Journal of Communication*, *28*, 91–96.

Reid, L. N., & Frazer, C. (1980a). Children's use of television commercials to initiate social interaction in family viewing situations. *Journal of Broadcasting*, *24*, 149–157.

Reid, L. N., & Frazer, C. (1980b). Television at play. *Journal of Communication*, *30*(4), 66–73.

Reiss, D., & Oliveri, M. E. (1983). The family's construction of social reality and its ties to its kin network: An exploration of causal direction. *Journal of Marriage and the Family*, *45*, 81–91.

Rosenblatt, P. C., & Cunningham, M. R. (1976). Television watching and family tensions. *Journal of Marriage and the Family*, *38*, 105–111.

Salomon, G. (1977). Effects of encouraging Israeli mothers to co-observe *Sesame Street* with their five-year-old child. *Child Development*, *48*, 1146–1151.

Sennett, R. (1970). *Families against the city*. Cambridge: Harvard University Press.

Singer, J. L., & Singer, D. G. (1976). Family television viewing habits and the spontaneous play of preschool children. *American Journal of Orthopsychiatry*, *46*, 496–502.

Wolf, M. A., Meyer, T. P., & White, C. (1982). A rules-based study of television's role in the construction of social reality. *Journal of Broadcasting*, *26*, 813–829.

Zahn, S. B., & Baran, S. J. (1984). It's all in the family: Siblings and program choice conflict. *Journalism Quarterly*, *61*, 847–852.

5

MEDIA IMPLICATIONS FOR THE QUALITY OF FAMILY LIFE

Robert Kubey
Rutgers University

T his chapter considers general tendencies in how the commercial media, particularly television, present information and what potential broad effects these media might have on the family. Some of what follows is necessarily speculative. The aim is to stimulate consideration of these ideas, particularly by researchers. Before launching into these ideas, a brief summary of some of my research findings on media use and family life is presented. Complete presentations can be found elsewhere (Kubey, 1990a, 1990b, 1991a; Kubey & Csikszentmihalyi, 1990).

Since the mid-1970s, I have used the Experience Sampling Method (ESM) to study media behavior. In the ESM research subjects are given paging devices — beepers — and small booklets of self-report forms. Each time we randomly signal the respondents — usually 6 to 8 times each day for a week — they fill out a report form telling us where they were, what they were doing, and how they were feeling on a set of standard psychological measures. In this way we obtain behavioral reports as people actually engage in media use. We are also able to compare these reports to all the other things that people do on a daily basis.

One of the things that people do when they watch television is talk — in one study, talk accounted for roughly 20% of the time adults viewed with their family members. When adults were with family members but not watching television, they talked 36% of the time. In other words, television viewing reduced talking but not by the amount suggested by those who have long held that family viewing experience is purely parallel (Maccoby, 1951).

Partly because of talking, and for other reasons as well, respondents report familial television viewing to be a significantly more challenging activity than when they view alone. Respondents also feel more cheerful when viewing with the family than when they view TV alone (Kubey, 1990b). However, much larger experiential differences are observed between family time without TV and family time with TV. Without TV, adult respondents reported time spent with the family as being more challenging and significantly more psychologically and physically activating, but significantly less relaxing than time spent with the family *with* TV.

Overall, there is somewhat more evidence in this research to suggest that television brings family members together than that it renders them apart. Generally, more time spent viewing is correlated with more time spent with the family.

This relationship is particularly telling among children and adolescents (Kubey, 1990a). Indeed, one marker of becoming adolescent in contemporary society may be a movement away from television and time spent with the family, and a movement *toward* more time spent outside the home with friends and listening to music (Larson, Kubey, & Colletti, 1989). We have also found that adolescents who watch more television report feeling better during time spent with the family and relatively worse with friends, whereas adolescents who listen to more music feel worse with the family and better with friends (Larson & Kubey, 1983). Heavier television use among teenagers was also correlated with better academic performance — controlling for IQ — whereas heavier music use was correlated with poorer academic performance.

We have also found evidence that the longer people view the worse they feel, yet they continue to view. This and other findings speak to the seductive nature of the television medium and the habitual nature of much viewing (Kubey & Csikszentmihalyi, 1990; McIlwraith, Jacobvitz, Kubey, & Alexander, 1991). Television habits are often quite difficult to break especially within the context of a family (Daley, 1978; Winn, 1977). But as noted, these ideas and findings are discussed elsewhere. Let us move to broader considerations.

DOES COMMERCIALISM CONFLICT WITH FAMILY VALUES?

The rise of the mass media has constituted an alteration in the frequency with which certain kinds of messages are communicated about what is to be valued in society. Prior to the rise of the mass media, there were three primary societal institutions charged with the responsibility of socializing the young and moving them toward particular ideals of what they should know about and value on reaching their majority. These three institutions were the church, the family, and the school. The mass media that rose up in the first three decades of this century constitute a fourth voice heard by the young. But this fourth institution is unlike the others in being only marginally responsible for *formal* socialization. Yet it does socialize.

Rather, the fourth socializing institution of the mass media is operated by individuals and corporations who stand to make money by attracting and holding the attention of audiences. Their prime responsibility is to themselves and to stock holders, and only secondly, at best, do they operate in the public interest and to the varying and often minimal requirements of the FCC or Congress.

Although it is the case that many of the messages promulgated on television are conservative and in the mainstream, and supportive of family values, it is also the case that other messages may either directly or indirectly controvert processes and orientations that are critical to sustaining families.

One of the primary messages of the commercial media is that, in order to be happy, one must own things and avail oneself of commercial services Ewen, 1976; Kubey & Csikszentmihalyi, 1990). Every few minutes television and radio programs are interrupted by advertising with the message being communicated either implicitly or explicitly that owning something will improve the quality of one's life. The question arises whether a culture obsessed with material goods may also be a society in which people are less likely to recognize that nonmaterialistic family life can be quite rewarding in its own right. The notion that the best things in life are free must compete with the more frequent message in the commercial media that the best things in life cost money.

That television's dominant message is a materialistic one is no coincidence. Those who own television networks and stations, and especially businesses that sponsor television programs, stand to profit from the dissemination and adoption of materialistic messages. Media outlets increase advertising revenue by attracting and holding attention. And a whole series of phenomena spill out from this bottom-line goal. For example, the mass media may be reluctant to present ideas that conflict with too many people's values too much of the time lest viewers turn away and advertising revenue dry up (Gitlin, 1972, 1983). For this reason, many mass media messages are thought to be conservative, tending to reinforce and maintain the economic status quo (Gerbner, 1972; Parenti, 1986; Schiller, 1973; Turow, 1985). But simultaneously, media outlets deliberately inject sex and violence into film and television content in order to attract audiences. This mix of conservative values with material that appeals to base instincts and hedonism is what Bell (1976) referred to as "cultural contradictions of capitalism."

Because holding attention is the sine qua non of the commercial media, other things happen as well. Sound bites in television and in radio must be short and scenes must change rapidly lest the audience grow bored or change the channel (Adatto, 1990; Hallin, 1992).

What might this mean for the family? With ads promising quick solutions and with the propensity to convey information quickly, the commercial electronic media may be contributing to an expectation that we should obtain gratification immediately and that solutions should come easily and quickly.

Immediate Gratification

This orientation toward immediate gratification and quick solutions is in conflict with many of the basic commitments and slow, gradual processes necessary to sustain the family, a social arrangement that one hopes will endure for at least the 18 odd years that a child lives with his or her parents.

If some people have been conditioned to expect quick and easy solutions, if they are impatient and not prepared to persist and to endure difficult times, complexity, and uncertainty from time to time, then being a husband or wife, and parent, may well be roles that they are not well suited to successfully enact.

The commercial media and the advertising that supports the media also suggest to us that one should never feel badly for too long. After all, there is one nostrum or another for almost anything that ails us. This message, and the emphasis in much advertising that a product can make one feel better almost immediately, may be related to some of our culture's problems with drug abuse. And given that drug abuse can seriously disturb a family's life, this may be another way that the form, style, and content of the commercial mass media indirectly contribute to familial problems.

In a review written for the U.S. Dept. of Education on the effects of television on scholastic performance, one of the few consistent findings cited across many studies was that children who used television heavily, especially violent programming, had more difficulties in impulse control, task perseverance, and delay of gratification (Anderson & Collins, 1988). That such children grow into adults is unquestionable. Whether these problems are sustained into adulthood is not clear.

There is also evidence to show that, at least among adults, heavier TV viewers are significantly more likely to report feeling badly emotionally in "unstructured situations" (i.e., when they have nothing to do; Kubey, 1986).

Put another way, heavy adult television viewers are more likely than light viewers to have difficulty tolerating open or unfilled time.

In other research, self-labeled television "addicts" scored significantly higher than "nonaddicted" viewers on measures of mind wandering, distractability, boredom, and unfocused daydreaming (McIlwraith, 1990; Smith, 1986). Whether television itself can be held directly responsible remains unclear. But it seems plausible that some of the people who spend 4 and 5 hours almost every day over decades watching television may be less practiced in directing their own attention, in entertaining themselves, and in maintaining psychological equilibrium when left to their own devices than infrequent viewers. And if self-control is a problem for a parent, there are almost certainly going to be repercussions for the family as a whole.

Commercial pressures in the mass media, along with the general speed of technological development, also result in an emphasis on "the new"— products, programs, fashions—things are better if they are *new*. Not only is the family not new, but this orientation may contribute to older people— important extended members of the family—such as grandparents, being more easily deemed obsolete, not "with it," and useless (Kubey, 1980). Grandparents may not know how to program a VCR, or about CD players or the latest rap group, but they may well be wise about life.

Competing for Attention

Another area worth examination concerns family members who feel that they must compete with the people on television for the attention of other family members. This is not an insignificant problem, yet there is very little, if any, research that bears on it directly.

Never before in the history of the human species has there been such a form of distraction in the home wherein the most beautiful and interesting and engaging people that a culture can find are presented incessantly in full living color. And it is undeniably the case that from time to time, and in some families frequently, people are neglected or ignored by other family members because of TV. The image of the father who comes home from work to find that his children can barely greet him with a hello because they are watching a rerun of "Bonanza" is legion in film, and although fictionalized, such images retain a basis in reality. Our society even has a term—*football widow*—to describe a woman who feels neglected by her husband because he watches so many football games on television over his 2 days at home with her each fall weekend.

Most problematic of all are cases where the emotional and physical needs of children are neglected because of a parent's extreme involvement with television. Although inconclusive, there is research suggesting that hyperactive and attention deficit disorder children do not watch more television than nonhyperactive children. Instead, this research found that the *parents* of ADHD children watch more television than parents of non-ADHD children (Shanahan & Morgan, 1989). One of the researchers' interpretations is that some children may be mimicing television's kinetic nature in an attempt to be as exciting as the tube in order to win parental attention. There may well be more sound interpretations, but this interpretation remains a disturbing one to consider.

Devaluation of Spouses

There is also constant pressure in our culture on women to compete with the thousands of attractive women who appear on television. (The same phenomenon goes on for men as well, but its effects are likely to be less pervasive if for no other reason than that women have been historically valued for their appearance more than have been men.)

The question arises whether this constant barrage of attractive opposite-sex celebrities on television brings any new pressures to a marriage, whether men in particular, and women to a somewhat lesser degree, are more likely to feel that they are somehow missing something if their spouse is not as young, as beautiful, or as svelt as the people on television.

We might also ask whether film and television over-romanticize the intensity of love between men and women thereby making it more likely for some people who have been married for a number of years to feel that the reduced intensity of their own romance and lovemaking pales by comparison. Put another way, does television leave some people thinking to themselves, "I'm missing something"? Although, a clear directional cause is not established, there already exists evidence to show that heavy viewers of pornography are more dissatisfied with their spouses (Zillmann & Weaver, 1989).

The possibility arises that some people may be more likely to look outside the marriage for romantic and/or sexual satisfaction to get for themselves that *something* that they already miss, but that they are more intensely aware that they are missing because of what they see routinely in the media. It is no accident that on average women on TV are roughly 10 years younger than men (Kubey, 1980; Signorielli & Gerbner, 1978). Television and film are thick with extremely attractive young adults as well as intense love scenes, in part, again, because of the commercial domination of these media and the goal of attracting and holding audiences.

Media Courtship Behavior as Preparation for Marriage and Family Life

Married couples and families can also be conceived of as audiences or members of an audience. Indeed, for many married couples and in many families, the majority of time spent together is as an audience. This is an important fact that is rarely dealt with in research. A question develops. How critical in courtship and the decision to marry have similar leisure orientations and film and television tastes become?

Contemporarily, an increasing number of people meet their future spouses through shared leisure and sporting activities. To focus on media, consider the period of courtship in which a couple spends a huge percentage of its time together on dates, at movies and concerts, or watching TV. Modern courtship could be increasingly thought of as a testing period for a lifetime of sharing entertainment and being members of an audience together. Presumably, some relationships break down in the early courtship stage, partly because the two people's tastes in leisure activities and in film and television vary severely.

Certainly in previous centuries, similar tastes for entertainment had to be of far less import if for no other reason than that so much less time was spent being entertained. Today, in contrast, millions of married couples spend 15-20 hours most every week, week in and week out, over decades receiving entertainment and information together as audience members. Viewed in this way, there may be effects of the media on family life that are much greater and pervasive than we typically think.

Avenues for Action

As for what might be done. First, parents need to be encouraged to exercise greater control and become more vigilant with regard to what their children are being exposed to. With the new modes of delivery, and the greater diversity of what is now available, especially via cable and the VCR, the challenge to parents is greater than it has ever been, but many parents exercise very little control over what their young children view or are unaware of potential problems that the media pose (Kubey, 1991a). For example, not a few parents permit—or even encourage—their young children to watch horrific and graphically violent material on TV. Other parents are unaware that their young adolescents are watching hardcore pornography.

There is also a role for the government, as well as for political action groups, and for citizens working with one another or alone. There will remain disagreements on the effects of different kinds of content and different media on both individuals and on families. Because in most cases we cannot predict precisely what the effects might be, many researchers are reluctant to prescribe solutions. But some solutions can involve common sense. Children should not be exposed to excessively graphic violence or pornography (Kubey, 1987). Nor do we need to wait for definitive social science research findings in order to set policy in these areas. My personal judgment is that we should be urging the media industries to more effectively regulate themselves and exercise greater restraint. And we should be urging the government to bring greater pressure on media industries to better serve the public interest. One avenue is for parents and educators to use the recent Children's Television Act to encourage local TV stations to provide more programs of value to children.

The Supreme Court decided years ago that commercial speech was different from other forms of speech and did not always deserve the same protections. In my view, with media such as videos, television, and radio that are widely available and that enter peoples' homes, the government retains a limited right to take steps to serve the greater good.

The other thing that we must do as a society is to encourage media literacy training and critical viewing skills to be taught formally in our school systems (Kubey, 1991b). Since 1987, the province of Ontario — Canada's largest — has required media literacy instruction for all students from Grades 7 to 12. Media literacy is also well developed in regions of England, Scotland, and Australia, as well as in many European countries.

Media education is important because parents cannot do the job entirely by themselves, and some parents will not do the job regardless. Nor are the commercial media industries likely to change the practices that they employ to attract and hold attention, nor is the FCC or the government likely to significantly alter the commercial dominance of the media in our society. What we can do is better prepare future citizens to analyze and think critically about what they view, read, and listen to.

REFERENCES

Adatto, K. (1990). *Sound bite democracy: Network evening news presidential campaign coverage, 1968 and 1988* (Research Paper R-2). Cambridge, MA: Harvard University, Joan Shorenstein Barone Center.

Anderson, D., & Collins, P. (1988). *The impact on children's education: Television's influence on cognitive development.* Washington, DC: U.S. Dept. of Education.

Bell, D. (1976). *The cultural contradictions of capitalism.* New York: Basic Books.

Daley, E. A. (1978). *Father feelings.* New York: William Morrow.

Ewen, S. (1976). *Captains of consciousness: Advertising and the social roots of the consumer culture.* New York: McGraw-Hill.

Gerbner, G. (1972). Communication and social environment. *Scientific American, 227,* 152-160.

Gitlin, T. (1972). Sixteen notes on television and the movement. In G. White & C. Newman (Eds.), *Literature in revolution* (pp. 335–366). New York: Holt, Rinehart & Winston.

Gitlin, T. (1983). *Inside prime time*. New York: Pantheon.

Hallin, D. C. (1992). Sound bite news: Television coverage of elections, 1968–1988. *Journal of Communication, 42*, 5–24.

Kubey, R. W. (1980). Television and aging: Past, present, and future. *Gerontologist, 20*, 16–35.

Kubey, R. W. (1986). Television use in everyday life: Coping with unstructured time. *Journal of Communication, 36*, 108–123.

Kubey, R. W. (1987, June 24). *Testimony on Senate Bill 844, 100th Congress, a Television violence antitrust exemption*. Hearing before the Subcommittee on Antitrust, Monopolies and Business Rights of the Committee on the Judiciary, U.S. Senate, Serial No. J–100-27. Washington, DC: U.S. Government Printing Office.

Kubey, R. (1990a). Television and family harmony among children, adolescents, and adults: Results from the experience sampling method. In J. Bryant (Ed.), *Television and the American family* (pp. 73–88). Hillsdale, NJ: Lawrence Erlbaum Associates.

Kubey, R. (1990b). Television and the quality of family life. *Communication Quarterly, 38*, 312–324.

Kubey, R. (1991a, Fall–Winter). Growing up in a media world. *Media and Values*, pp. 8–10.

Kubey, R. (1991b, March 6). The case for media education. *Education Week*, p. 27.

Kubey, R. W., & Csikszentmihalyi, M. (1990). *Television and the quality of life: How viewing shapes everyday experience*. Hillsdale, NJ: Lawrence Erlbaum Associates.

Larson, R., & Kubey, R. (1983). Television and music: Contrasting media in adolescent life. *Youth and Society, 15*, 13–31.

Larson, R., Kubey, R., & Colletti, J. (1989). Changing channels: Early adolescent media choices and shifting investments in family and friends. *Journal of Youth and Adolescence, 18*, 4.

Maccoby, E. (1951). Television: Its impact on school children. *Public Opinion Quarterly, 15*, 421–444.

McIlwraith, R. D. (1990, August). *Theories of television addiction*. Talk to the American Psychological Association, Boston.

McIlwraith, R. D., Jacobvitz, R. S., Kubey, R., & Alexander, A. (1991). Television addiction: Theories and data behind the ubiquitous metaphor. *American Behavioral Scientist, 35*, 104–121.

Parenti, M. (1986). *Inventing reality: The politics of the mass media*. New York: St. Martins.

Schiller, H. (1973). *The mind-managers*. Boston: Beacon Press.

Shanahan, J., & Morgan, M. (1989). Television as a diagnostic indicator in child therapy: An exploratory study. *Child and Adolescent Social Work, 6*, 175–191.

Signorielli, N., & Gerbner, G. (1978). The image of the elderly in prime-time television drama. *Generations, 3*, 10–11.

Smith, R. (1986). Television addiction. In J. Bryant & D. Zillmann (Eds.), *Perspectives on media effects* (pp. 109–128). Hillsdale, NJ: Lawrence Erlbaum Associates.

Turow, J. (1985). Learning to portray institutional power: The socialization of creators in mass media organizations. In R. D. McPhee & P. K. Tomkins (Eds.), *Organizational communication: Traditional themes and new directions* (pp. 211–223). Beverly Hills, CA: Sage.

Winn, M. (1977). *The plug-in drug*. New York: Viking.

Zillmann, D., & Weaver, J. (1989). Pornography and men's sexual callousness toward women. In D. Zillmann & J. Bryant (Eds.), *Pornography: Research advances and policy considerations* (pp. 95–125). Hillsdale, NJ: Lawrence Erlbaum Associates.

Part II

DEVELOPMENTAL AND EDUCATIONAL IMPLICATIONS

6

Educating Children With Television: The Forms of the Medium

Aletha C. Huston
John C. Wright
University of Kansas

Parents are often told that their children would be better off if they turned off the television set. Many critics argue that television as a medium is harmful to children and adults alike. This argument implies that it is not just the content of television, but something about the medium itself that may induce laziness, passivity, hyperactivity, or many other ills. What distinguishes television from radio, books, and other media are the forms in which information is presented, not the content messages. In this chapter, we describe a program of research investigating the forms or formal features of television for children. We argue that children attend to and learn from television actively, and, that used optimally, television is particularly well suited to educate and inform them about a wide range of content areas. Parents can use television as a positive force for their children as well as taking an active role in protecting their children from harmful content.

The Medium of Television

Formal features of television are relatively content-free attributes that are a result of production and editing. They include visual techniques (e.g.,

73

zooms and special effects), auditory features (e.g., sound effects and music), and more global dimensions of program pace, action, and variability of scenes.

We began to study television forms in the mid-1970s with two major goals. First, we were interested in identifying those forms that influence children's attention and comprehension of content, in part because such information seemed basic to optimal production of educational programming. Second, we were testing several hypotheses concerning the effects of the television medium on basic modes of cognitive processing. These hypotheses were derived from the initial ideas of McLuhan (1964) and later theoretical propositions by Salomon (1979) and others concerning the effects of television as a medium and specific production techniques on the fundamental modes of processing information.

One purpose of this chapter is to discuss the effects of formal features on children's intellectual activity with particular attention to forms used in educational television. We have chosen "Sesame Street" as a specific example of educational programming because it is the most widely viewed and most extensively studied children's educational program. It is also the most frequently attacked, perhaps in part because it is so successful in drawing child viewers. The most recent of these attacks is a highly emotional and poorly informed polemic by Jane Healy (1990), which is being published in popular book form. The themes of the critics have remained remarkably constant over the years; they center on the medium of television and the forms used to attract child audiences, not on the content. One of the most frequent assertions is that rapid pace and perceptually demanding forms lead to poor comprehension, little time for reflection, and reduced attention spans. A second major theme in these critiques is that television leads to intellectual passivity, either because it does not allow time for processing information or because it does not allow for repetition, imagination, or control by the viewer. A final common complaint is that television viewing occupies portions of children's time that would otherwise be devoted to leisure reading.

We present a different view in this chapter. Although each of these critiques probably has a germ of truth, they do not represent what really happens when children watch and learn from carefully designed educational programs like "Sesame Street." First, we show that educational programs for children, including "Sesame Street," use a combination of formal features that includes not only perceptually salient techniques but a judicious mix of forms and formats that are carefully designed to encourage learning and intellectual processing of content. The goal is not just to get and keep children's eyeballs on the screen, but to promote learning and comprehension. Their forms are quite different from advertisements, cartoons, and other commercial programs for children. Second, we summarize a large literature on children's cognitive processing of television that demonstrates persuasively that children are active, selective viewers. Their attention patterns are guided by what they find interesting and comprehensible, not by flashing lights, bells, and whistles. The image of the zombie child being sucked into viewing against his or her will does not fit the data. Children are smarter than that. Third, we cite evidence that viewing television, especially educational programs made for children, does not interfere with and may facilitate leisure-time reading. Finally, we discuss ways in which parents and families can use television as an ally, not an enemy. Quality television can be a contributing part of a family environment that provides intellectual stimulation, emotional security, and prosocial values.

Forms of Educational Programs

When we began our research on formal features of children's television, we were guided by a theory of children's information getting that proposed a gradual shift from the process of exploration to the process of search as a person has increasing exposure to a stimulus. Exploration is a mode in which attention is disjointed and responsive to perceptually salient events (i.e., to rapid movement, loud sounds, changes in events). Search is a mode in which attention is guided by the viewer's goals and interests; it occurs more readily once the individual has become familiar with a stimulus. Then a person typically ignores the sensory intensity of the stimuli and instead attends to things that are relevant to his or her goals and interests (Wright & Vlietstra, 1975). Therefore, we initially classified formal features of television as those that are primarily perceptually salient in contrast to those that might encode interesting or useful information and thus encourage comprehension and reflection.

Our first step was to amass two samples of available programming and code them for formal features and violent content. For 1 week in November 1977 and another week in February 1978, we recorded all programs designed for children broadcast on the three commercial networks and on public television. One hundred thirty-seven programs were coded for the three types of formal features shown in Table 6.1 (Huston et al., 1981). Perceptually salient features included rapid action (characters moving faster than a walk), variability of scenes, pace (rate of change of scenes), music, noise (e.g., sound effects, animal sounds), visual tricks (e.g., special effects), and visual change (e.g., cuts). The other two groups of features were considered likely to aid comprehension and reflection. Dialogue has fairly obvious value because verbal representation should promote comprehension. Singing, long zooms, and moderate action (moving at the pace of

TABLE 6.1

Frequencies of Formal Features in "Sesame Street" as Compared to Averages for All Educational Daytime and Saturday Morning Children's Programs

Formal Feature	"Sesame Street"	Educational Daytime	Saturday Morning
Perceptually Salient			
Rapid action	0.4	0.8	1.6
Variability	2.3	2.2	2.6
Pace	4.8	4.4	5.8
Music	2.8	3.1	4.3
Noise	3.9	3.0	4.9
Visual tricks	3.4	4.6	5.2
Visual change	6.6	6.9	7.4
Dialogue and Narration			
Nonhuman speech	3.1	1.0	1.6
Child speech	2.4	1.6	0.6
Adult speech	3.1	3.1	3.1
Reflective Features			
Singing	1.1	0.8	−.2
Long zooms	−.1	0.1	−.3
Moderate action	2.0	2.1	1.3

Note: Except for rapid action, moderate actions, and long zooms, numbers represent frequencies transformed into log (0.5) in order to normalize distributions.

a walk) were expected to promote rehearsal and reflection because they allow for repetition and time to process information. Because young children often represent information in images rather than abstract concepts, physical activity of moderate speed may provide them with visual images for encoding information.

In the overall analysis, Saturday morning commercial programs contained high levels of perceptually salient features and low levels of dialogue and reflective features. Educational programs were characterized by features involving reflection and by frequent child dialogue. A more detailed linguistic analysis of the dialogue was conducted by our colleague, Mabel Rice (1984). She found that "Sesame Street" and "Mr. Rogers' Neighborhood" both used language in ways that should enhance comprehension. For example, they often contained single words, repetitions, literal meanings, and pictures of the objects being referred to. By contrast, commercial TV cartoons contained complex language, nonliteral meanings, and few opportunities to match words with visual presentations.

Educational programs for children also contained some perceptually salient features, but the levels were generally lower than those in entertainment programming. The mean levels for three episodes of "Sesame Street" are shown in Table 6.1. Its features were similar to other educational programs except that it contained more child and nonhuman dialogue (muppets were coded as nonhuman). These data show clearly that educational programs like "Sesame Street" are not carbon copies of the forms used in popular entertainment programs. They use some perceptually salient forms, but they also incorporate techniques and forms that would be expected to encourage comprehension and learning.

Recurrent formats are used planfully to encourage active processing and learning on several educational productions. For example, the song beginning "One of these things is not like the others . . ." signals a segment involving sorting and classification. A frequent viewer knows immediately the type of problem-solving task about to be presented and can prepare to think about similarities and differences rather than, say, numbers or body parts. Some formats are designed to elicit activity by omitting some of the elements and letting the viewer fill them in. For instance, in a segment from "Electric Company," street signs were shown while they were named in a catchy song; then the visuals and music were replayed without the words in the song, providing an invitation for the viewer to supply the words (Palmer, 1978).

Children's Attention and Comprehension

Having confirmed through the formal feature analyses that educational programs, including "Sesame Street," use a different combination of forms than commercial programs, we next needed to ask how these forms influence children's patterns of attention and learning. Do children attend to the most immediately and perceptually demanding forms? How do pace, levels of action, animation, and other formal features affect learning and comprehension?

We mentioned earlier that our work on this topic was originally based on a theory that attention patterns shift from exploration to search modes as a result of cognitive development and exposure to television. On the basis of this theory, we initially predicted a developmental shift in children's attention patterns. We expected preschool children with little viewing experience to attend to perceptually salient formal features, and we expected children to attend to informative formal features as they moved into middle childhood and/or became more experienced with television. The results of our research and those of several other investigators indicate clearly that this shift probably happens much younger and faster than we originally expected.

Even 3- and 4-year-old children attend to television forms that provide them with information about the program content rather than to those that are merely perceptually salient.[1] Children do attend to programs with high levels of physical activity, or visual and auditory special effects. However, rapid pace (that is, frequent change of scene and character) alone does not hold attention (Wright et al., 1984). Moreover, children attend to children's and women's voices but lose interest when adult men talk. They attend to a simple story cartoon more when it contains narration than when it does not. By the time they reach kindergarten, a continuous story line holds their interest better than disconnected segments in a magazine format (Alwitt, Anderson, Lorch, & Levin, 1980; Huston & Wright, 1989).

These patterns led us to propose the "feature signal hypothesis" (Huston & Wright, 1983; Wright & Huston, 1983). Children appear to guide their attention actively to content that is interesting and comprehensible. They use formal features as signals to help them decide whether particular content is worth attending to. Such formal features as animation, children's voices, and visual special effects tell a child at a glance (or a listen) that the program content is intended for children and thus elicit greater interest. Adult men's voices, by contrast, signify a program intended for adults. A laugh track signals that a program is a comedy. As children gain experience with television, they learn the codes represented by different formal features, and they use that knowledge to make attentional choices.

Forms that signal child-appropriate content not only elicit visual attention; they induce children to learn the content. In one study performed in our laboratory, for instance, public service announcements about nutrition were produced in two parallel versions. The content of the two versions was identical, but the forms were different. One version was made with animation, lively music, and child voices—features designed to signal child-appropriate content. The other version was made with "adult" formal features—live photography, serious music, and adult male voices. Five-year-old children attended more to the version with child features than to the adult version and learned more of the nutritional messages presented (Campbell, Wright, & Huston, 1987).

Television forms can also be used to help children to process the information presented in a program. For instance, formal features can highlight particularly important aspects of a message. Just as a spotlight on a stage guides the gaze of an audience, judicious use of sound effects, character action, camera techniques, and visual special effects can guide the attention of the child viewer. This principle has been refined in some types of educational production. For example, "Electric Company" contains segments showing two profiles facing one another and mouthing phonemes

---

[1]Attention in the studies cited here is almost always defined as looking at the television screen, but comprehension of content is often measured after viewing as well to determine whether the televised material was understood.

that form words. The profiles rather than full faces were chosen because careful studies of eye movements demonstrated that, when full faces were used, children looked at the faces rather than the phonemes. Once the faces were deemphasized by making them black, featureless profiles, children looked at the letters that were the "central" content of the segments (Palmer, 1978).

Television forms can also help children to form mental representations. Young children encode visual concrete information more readily than verbal abstract content. When content is shown with a concrete visual referent, or when a theme is demonstrated in physical action as well as verbal, young children understand it better. For instance, in an episode of "Fat Albert and the Cosby Kids," some elements of the plot were portrayed in actions; others were primarily verbal. Preschool and kindergarten-age children understood the themes shown with action better than those that were presented primarily in dialogue (Calvert, Huston, Watkins, & Wright, 1982).

Moving from the laboratory to home viewing, there is ample evidence that "Sesame Street" and other educational programs are effective teachers. The combination of forms used in "Sesame Street" is especially successful, not only for drawing and holding a child audience but for transmitting information and knowledge. The early evaluations of the program demonstrated that viewing led to improvements in letter and number skills, understanding of concepts, and the like (Ball & Bogatz, 1970). In the early 1980s, we conducted a 2-year longitudinal study of media use by children ages 3 to 5 and 5 to 7. We collected information about all programs watched by the children and their families, and we tested the children at the beginning and end of the 2-year period (Huston, Wright, Rice, Kerkman, & St. Peters, 1990).

The findings indicated that the more time children spent watching "Sesame Street" between ages 3 and 5, the more their vocabulary scores improved over time. Even when other factors contributing to vocabulary (e.g., parent's education, preschool experience, birth order) were controlled, "Sesame Street" viewing made an independent contribution to improvement in vocabulary (Rice, Huston, Truglio, & Wright, 1990). Although "Sesame Street" is not specifically designed to teach vocabulary, language is presented in ways that should promote comprehension. There were not comparable benefits of viewing from age 5 to 7; that age group is beyond the target audience of the program.

Television can also transmit prosocial values and behavior to young children (Stein & Friedrich, 1975). In one of the early studies, Friedrich and I (ACH) showed children at preschool several episodes of "Mr. Rogers' Neighborhood." When compared to groups shown other types of programs, they were more cooperative, helpful, and verbally expressive with their peers, and they were more likely to persist at tasks and activities (Friedrich & Stein, 1973). Other investigations demonstrated that 3- and 4-year-old children who watched "Mr. Rogers" were more imaginative than control groups (Singer & Singer, 1981).

Educational Uses of Television in the Family

The evidence for positive effects of carefully designed television indicates that television can be an ally, not an enemy, for parents. Parents can use television programs for their children's benefit just as they use books and toys. In our longitudinal study, we asked parents about what they encouraged their children to view and what they prohibited. Many parents said they encouraged their children to watch educational programs and children's specials, particularly at times of day when the parents could not spend quality time with their children (e.g., during meal preparation). Critics often condemn parents for using television as a babysitter, but no parent can spend every waking moment in active interaction with a child. The real question seems to be whether it is a good or a bad babysitter. It can be either.

In a more recent investigation of 2- and 4-year-olds from low-income families, we have collected extensive information about the parents' backgrounds and about the kinds of intellectual stimulation and emotional support provided at home. Children who frequently watch informational programs designed for a child audience have parents who also provide them with stimulating toys and activities and who are attentive and affectionate to them. Children who frequently watch cartoons and other "pure" entertainment programs come from homes with lower levels of stimulation and affection (Murphy, Talley, Huston, & Wright, 1991).

Parents can use television actively in interactions with their children. One set of investigators in our lab at CRITC called television a talking picture book (Lemish & Rice, 1986). They observed children ranging from 6 months to 3 years in their homes as they watched "Sesame Street" and other programs. Children watched television while they played, had their diapers changed, and while they ate. From early in the second year of life, children talked to their mothers about the characters, objects, and content of the program much as they do when they look at picture books. They labeled objects on the program (e.g., "kitty," "balloon"). They asked questions such as "What's that?" "What happened to the monkey?" "Where Ernie go?" They also repeated slogans: "Diet Pepsi, one less calorie," "Sesame Street is brought to you today by the letter B." Mothers also talked to their children about the objects and events on the screen just as they talk about pictures and events in books when they read to children.

For children in the age range from 3 to 5, watching programs like "Sesame Street" with an adult can add to enjoyment and learning. Israeli children whose mothers were asked to watch "Sesame Street" with them learned even more than those who watched without maternal intervention (Salomon, 1977). Laboratory experiments have also demonstrated that an adult co-viewer who discusses and explains the content of a program helps children to understand central program themes and to make appropriate inferences about implied events in stories (Collins, Sobol, & Westby, 1981; Watkins, Calvert, Huston-Stein, & Wright, 1980).

Television can be a positive part of family life if it is carefully designed and selected. With home video players and tapes in the majority of households with children, parents have considerably more choice of programs than they did when broadcast television was the only option. However, many parents do not exercise much selectivity or control over their children's viewing (Wright, St. Peters, & Huston, 1990). Educating parents to use television to their children's advantage rather than admonishing them to turn it off might lead parents to be more active in guiding their children's television use.

Most of the examples demonstrating the positive influences of television are based on preschool children, largely because there are fewer quality programs for school-age children and adolescents. When such programs are available, they can lead to positive outcomes. One example is "De Grassi Junior High," a program discussed in detail in another chapter in this book (Singer & Singer).

Parents can be educated to become active in influencing the production and distribution of quality programs for children of all ages. The Children's Television Education Act, passed in 1990, requires television stations to meet the educational and informational needs of children. The act can provide an impetus for better programming, but parents and other citizen groups need to make clear to broadcasters their interest in such programming.

CONCLUSION

We began by addressing some common assertions about television in general and "Sesame Street" in particular. Critics persistently argue that rapid pace and perceptually demanding television forms gain children's attention but interfere with deep processing and comprehension. They sometimes make the more sweeping generalization that television as a medium inherently produces passive mental responses. We dispute these beliefs with three kinds of evidence. First, the formal features used by

"Sesame Street" and other educational programs for children are not all perceptually salient, and they are distinctly different from the features commonly used in advertising and commercial programs for children. Informative programs for children, including "Sesame Street," contain moderate levels of some perceptually salient features including animation, visual, and auditory special effects. They also contain a considerable amount of speech that is carefully tailored to the comprehension abilities of their target audience, as well as some nonverbal features that are apt to stimulate reflection and thought.

Second, a large body of evidence demonstrates clearly that children's attention to television is actively guided by their interests and their ability to understand the content. Mere bells and whistles do not hold them very long. Instead, they attend to formal features that signal content that is interesting, funny, or comprehensible, and they turn away from features that signal content that is incomprehensible or uninteresting. Formal features can stimulate active processing and learning from television as well as draw children's eyes to the set. The forms used in "Sesame Street" are successful, not only in attracting a child audience but in teaching the curriculum of language, concepts, and skills that the program presents.

Third, television can be a positive force in family life as well as a negative influence. Well-designed programs for children can be selected by parents for their children's benefit just as books and toys are selected. Parents can use programs like "Sesame Street" as occasions for conversation, teaching, and pleasant interaction with their children. Parents can offer explanations and answer questions during viewing in order to help children learn and understand the messages being conveyed. They can use television as an occasion to discuss values and opinions. Television as a medium is neither good nor bad for family life; its influence depends on what kind of television is viewed and how it is used during interactions among family members.

ACKNOWLEDGMENTS

Much of the research described was supported by grants from the National Institute of Mental Health and the Spencer Foundation to the Center for Research on the Influences of Television on Children (CRITC).

REFERENCES

Alwitt, L. F., Anderson, D. R., Lorch, E. P., & Levin, S. R. (1980).Preschool children's visual attention to attributes of television. *Human Communication Research*, 7, 52–67.

Ball, S., & Bogatz, G. (1970). *A summary of major findings* in *"The first year of Sesame Street": An evaluation.* New York: Educational Testing Service.

Calvert, S. L., Huston, A. C., Watkins, B. A., & Wright, J. C. (1982). The relation between selective attention to television forms and children's comprehension of content. *Child Development*, *53*, 601–610.

Campbell, T. A., Wright, J. C., & Huston, A. C. (1987). Form cues and content difficulty as determinants of children's cognitive processing of televised educational messages. *Journal of Experimental Child Psychology*, *43*, 311–321.

Collins, W. A., Sobol, B. L., & Westby, S. (1981). Effects of adult commentary on children's comprehension and inferences about a televised aggressive portrayal. *Child Development*, *52*, 158–163.

Friedrich, L. K., & Stein, A. H. (1973). Aggressive and prosocial television programs and the natural behavior of preschool children. *Monographs of the Society for Research in Child Development*, *38*, (No. 4, Whole No. 151).

Healy, J. M. (1990). *Endangered minds: Why our children don't think*. New York: Simon & Schuster.

Huston, A. C., & Wright, J. C. (1983). Children's processing of television: The informative functions of formal features. In J. Bryant & D. R. Anderson (Eds.), *Children's understanding of TV: Research on attention and comprehension* (pp. 37–68). New York: Academic Press.

Huston, A. C., & Wright, J. C. (1989). The forms of television and the child viewer. In G. A. Comstock (Ed.), *Public communication and behavior* (Vol. 2, pp. 103–158). New York: Academic Press.

Huston, A. C., Wright, J. C., Rice, M. L., Kerkman, D., & St. Peters, M. (1990). The development of television viewing patterns in early childhood: A longitudinal investigation. *Developmental Psychology*, *26*, 409–420.

Huston, A. C., Wright, J. C., Wartella, E., Rice, M. L., Watkins, B. A., Campbell, T., & Potts, R. (1981). Communicating more than content: Formal features of children's television programs. *Journal of Communication*, *31*, 32–48.

Lemish, D., & Rice, M. L. (1986). Television as a talking picture book: A prop for language acquisition. *Journal of Child Language*, *13*, 251–274.

McLuhan, H. M. (1964). *Understanding media: The extensions of man*. New York: McGraw-Hill.

Murphy, K. C., Talley, J. A., Huston, A. C., & Wright, J. C. (1991, April). *Family ecology and young children's viewing of television designed for children*. Paper presented at the Biennial Meeting of the Society for Research in Child Development, Seattle.

Palmer, E. L. (1978, June). *A pedagogical analysis of recurrent formats on Sesame Street and Electric Company*. Paper presented at the International Conference on Children's Educational Television, Amsterdam.

Rice, M. L. (1984). The words of children's television. *Journal of Broadcasting*, *28*, 445–461.

Rice, M. L., Huston, A. C., Truglio, R., & Wright, J. C. (1990). Words from Sesame Street: Learning vocabulary while viewing. *Developmental Psychology*, *26*, 421–428.

Salomon, G. (1977). Effects of encouraging Israeli mothers to co-observe "Sesame Street" with their five-year-olds. *Child Development*, *48*, 1146–1151.

Salomon, G. (1979). *Interaction of media, cognition, and learning*. San Francisco: Jossey-Bass.

Singer, J. L., & Singer, D. G. (1981). *Television, imagination and aggression: A study of preschoolers*. Hillsdale, NJ: Lawrence Erlbaum Association.

Stein, A. H., & Friedrich, L. K. (1975). The impact of television on children and youth. In E. M. Hetherington (Ed.), *Review of child development research* (Vol. 5, pp. 183–256). Chicago: University of Chicago Press.

Watkins, B. A., Calvert, S. L., Huston-Stein, A., & Wright, J. C. (1980). Children's recall of television material: Effects of presentation mode and adult labeling. *Developmental Psychology*, *16*, 672–674.

Wright, J. C., & Huston, A. C. (1983). A matter of form: Potentials of television for young viewers. *American Psychologist, 38,* 835–843.

Wright, J. C., Huston, A. C., Ross, R. P., Calvert, S. L., Rolandelli, D., Weeks, L. A., Raeissi, P., & Potts, R. (1984). Pace and continuity of television programs: Effects on children's attention and comprehension. *Developmental Psychology, 20,* 653–666.

Wright, J. C., St. Peters, M., & Huston, A. C. (1990). Family television use and its relation to children's cognitive skills and social behavior. In J. Bryant (Ed.), *Television and the American family* (pp. 227–252). Hillsdale, NJ: Lawrence Erlbaum Associates.

Wright, J. C., & Vlietstra, A. G. (1975). The development of selective attention: From perceptual exploration to logical search. In H. W. Reese (Ed.), *Advances in child development and behavior* (Vol. 10, pp. 196–236). New York: Academic Press.

7

STRATEGIES FOR THE 1990S: USING THE MEDIA FOR GOOD

Ernest E. Allen
National Center for Missing and Exploited Children

In 1984 President Ronald Reagan announced the opening of the National Center for Missing and Exploited Children (NCMEC), a private nonprofit corporation dedicated to child protection. In his message the President quoted from a Helen Kromer poem: "One man awake can waken another. The second can awaken his next door brother. The three awake can rouse the town by turning the whole place upside down. And the many awake make such a fuss they finally awaken the rest of us."

There is no more important factor in our crusade to "wake up America" than the media. We have seen and heard ample and growing evidence of the power and influence of media in shaping attitudes and affecting behavior, most of it focused on the negative impacts of media. Yet, there is an abundance of information to demonstrate its positive effects as well. Information on the positive effects of such social action can be found in *Strategies of Community Organization* (Cox, Erlich, Rothman, & Tropman, 1987) and *Rules for Radicals* (Alinsky, 1971).

The media can be the best friend the parents of a missing child may have. A dedicated community can rally around the family of a missing youth in the early days and months following an abduction, prepare bulletins about the child's disappearance, stuff and mail them nationwide, and volunteer to law enforcement to help comb the woods and surrounding areas in the hopes of locating the child. But the power of the media can be harnessed, and in a matter of hours that local effort can be taken to the entire nation, while capturing the emotion associated with the tragedy. A moving article or television newspiece can burn a child's smiling face into the consciousness of the country and move people thousands of miles away to join the search for a child they will never know.

Just as television brought the atrocities of Korea and Vietnam into our living rooms and changed the way Americans perceive war, it has brought the realities of world famine, crime, and illness into our lives as never before. Without being victimized personally, we can instantly be touched by the heartbreak others endure.

With regard to child abduction, perhaps Americans in the 20th century learned best the new power of the media when, in 1932, Charles and Ann Lindbergh's baby was kidnapped and later found dead. Certainly because of their celebrity, the Lindbergh's tragedy was reported internationally. This case has been recounted in numerous books and articles and was a major influence in the passage of the federal kidnapping law: 18 USC 1201. It was not until 50 years had passed, however, that other cases, like that of 6-year-old Etan Patz who was last seen walking to his school bus stop the morning of May 25, 1979, in New York City and is still missing, and Adam Walsh, the 6-year-old boy who was abducted from a Florida shopping mall in 1981 and found murdered 2 weeks later, touched families from coast to coast and prompted a massive public outcry for change.

Now, thanks to the media, when most Americans think about missing children, certain symbols come to mind immediately; the green ribbons worn by people from Washington State to Washington, DC, in 1981 — at the request of and as a symbol of solidarity with the frightened and frustrated families and community members from Atlanta, Georgia, who saw 29 of their youth abducted and murdered more than a decade ago; milk cartons, grocery bags, and the familiar "Have You Seen Me?" cards we all receive in our mail each week, each bearing a different child's face, each asking for our help.

Although missing children photographs have become a regular feature of American life, many people doubt their efficacy. Yet, these photographs work. Many children are located because someone took the time to look at the picture and then called NCMEC with information. One child in seven featured in the NCMEC photo distribution system is recovered.

The system for distribution of missing children photographs throughout the United States and Canada has involved NCMEC and 1,518 private-sector partners, plus 113 using mail inserts. Since the photo distribution system began in October 1985, photos–bios of 1,593 missing children have been distributed nationwide.

Today, there are 371 active private-sector companies using photos and 30 federal agencies placing pictures in all their mail. Two hundred thirteen children are known to have been recovered as a direct result of the use of photo distribution nationally—a rate of 1 in 7. The largest distribution program, ADVO's direct mail effort, reaches 50 million homes each week and has produced a recovery rate of approximately 1 in 6.

Missing children are recovered through photo distribution because, in virtually every case, someone knows the whereabouts of the child or what happened to him or her. But, people may not know that a child living in their community is a missing child until they see that child's picture through this program. The greater the number of people we can reach with these pictures, the greater the likelihood of recovering these children.

The media, in all its forms, have helped to raise the level of awareness about the tragedy of child abduction and molestation to a height no advertising budget alone could match. The influence of the media on the issue of missing children is fourfold and has resulted in a domino effect:

- It has helped to create a powerful grass-roots level campaign, educating millions of people nationwide, moving them to become involved, to volunteer at the local level, and to work to prevent crimes against children in their own community.
- In turn, it has helped to prompt the involvement of elected officials at the state and federal levels to pass meaningful legislation to better safeguard our children.
- It has interested and involved the powerful American private sector to support efforts to locate and reunite missing children with their loved ones.
- And, perhaps most importantly, the media themselves have become a vehicle for successfully locating missing children.

A journalist in the 1990s is no longer merely reporting the news when a child disappears; he or she is performing a public service. He or she is helping to spread the word about the child's abduction and is prompting millions of readers, listeners, and viewers to become involved in the search.

There are other important examples of the power of the media. The disappearance of Etan Patz, and abduction and murder of Adam Walsh, garnered national media attention, and each child's story was retold for millions of Americans in heart-wrenching, made-for-television films.

The movie depicting Etan's story, *Without a Trace*, and *Adam*, as well as *Adam: His Song Continues*, helped to bring home the senselessness of these

TABLE 7.1

Film	Air Date	Number of Children Featured	Number of Children Recovered
Adam	October 10, 1983	55	13
Adam	April 30, 1984	51	19
Adam	April 29, 1985	60	6
Adam: His Song Continues	September 29, 1986	50	7

crimes and the devastation they leave behind for victimized families and communities. *Adam* influenced so many people nationally that it has been rebroadcast three times since 1983, each closing with a "roll call" of photographs of 50 missing children. In each case, NBC allotted 2 minutes of network air time, barely 30 seconds of television exposure per child, and still Americans responded. Each time the films aired, many children were quickly located as a direct result. In fact, 21% of the children featured at the conclusion of *Adam* and *Adam: His Song Continues* were recovered as a direct result of the leads called in by citizens who viewed those films.

Above and beyond moving parents to better educate their own children about the need for increased child safety, coverage of the missing children issue has moved people to work to change "the system." Led by victimized families nationwide, a grass-roots level campaign began in the early 1980s that resulted in sensitizing elected officials in state legislatures and the U.S. Congress to pass laws to better protect our children.

Following highly publicized hearings held on Capitol Hill and field sites in 1981 and 1982, the Missing Children's Act was signed into law by President Ronald Reagan in 1982. What may have seemed an easy bet for passage, the Missing Children Act was actually quite controversial—its passage opening the Federal Bureau of Investigation's files at the National Crime Information center's computer to the intake of cases of missing children. Many questioned the appropriateness of entering missing children information into the national crime computer, arguing that there were too many cases. Media attention remained at a fevered pitch in the early 1980s, giving an open forum to parents of missing children and child advocates and keeping the heat on politicians. Soon came the passage of the Missing Children's Assistance Act of 1984, which carried a congressional mandate for the newly established national resource center and clearinghouse for victimized youth, the National Center for Missing and Exploited Children.

This organization, working hand in hand with the media, has continued to spearhead efforts to keep the spotlight on the continued need for better laws to protect children. And although hard fought, progress in the past decade has been remarkable. NCMEC serves as America's resource center for child protection. In cooperation with the U.S. Department of Justice,

NCMEC works to find missing children and to prevent child abduction, molestation, and sexual exploitation. Since its creation in 1984, NCMEC has seen the establishment of 42 state clearinghouses nationally and one in the District of Columbia. In 1982, there was only one. And systematically, NCMEC has pushed for a rehaul of state legislation for children, including the implementation of a "Children's Bill of Rights."

Thanks to the growing public awareness of crimes against children fostered by media attention, NCMEC has handled more than 615,000 telephone calls through its national Hotline, 1-800-THE-LOST, and is currently averaging nearly 586 calls per weekday. These calls come from parents, law enforcement officers, and justice system professionals, but they also come from citizens who have seen the photographs of missing children and want to help. Since NCMEC's opening in 1984, more than 89,000 calls have been received from citizens reporting the sighting of a missing child.

Further, because of media visibility and resultant public interest and concern, NCMEC has disseminated more than 6.7 million copies of its publications and brochures addressing a host of child protection and child safety issues. Citizens from around America call the Hotline to request information and recommendations regarding safety in daycare, selecting a babysitter, safety rules for children, and dozens of others.

NCMEC has received more than 380 leads and tips through its Hotline regarding the manufacture and distribution of child pornography. That information has led to more than 80 successful prosecutions of child pornographers to date.

The discovery of crimes against children has awakened the official system as well. Since 1984, NCMEC has trained more than 119,000 law enforcement, criminal–juvenile justice, and healthcare professionals nationwide and in Canada on investigative, interviewing, search, and other child protection techniques.

There is new awareness, new sophistication, new technology, and new sensitivity to the vulnerability of American children. And, perhaps most importantly, this growth in awareness has had an impact on real children and families. Since 1984 NCMEC has dealt with the cases of 34,000 missing or sexually exploited children and has played a role in the recovery of more than 21,000 of them.

The level of media attention given a worthy cause can also prompt the private sector to become involved in public service programs, and the effort to locate missing children is a classic example. Most companies, whether a top executive has been touched personally by the cause, or whether cause-related marketing is a part of the company's philanthropic philosophy, are looking for partnerships that will enhance their image as a caring corporation. As the tide of media attention rises on a given social concern, so too does the public interest and the private sector's involvement in helping to address it.

The images that come to mind when one thinks of missing children are in large part all successful examples of companies participating in programs to help these children and their families. The milk carton and shopping bag campaigns, for example, were public service programs designed to reach millions of Americans as they shopped for groceries. The "Have You Seen Me?" ADVO direct address label program has delivered 50 million pictures of missing children weekly to American homes over the course of the past 8 years as a public service.

And there are other corporations, who for more than 8 years have also participated in the effort to help reunite families, but who have done so without the spotlight of the media. For example, American and Continental Airlines reunite families of missing children, and Quality Inns International hosts the families while they are getting reacquainted — all as a public service. These long-term philanthropic programs are undoubtedly beneficial to the corporations involved, because they are programs that give something back to the communities where they are headquartered and give them an opportunity to make a real impact on people's lives. There is no question, however, that media attention of the problem of child abduction throughout the past decade made a tremendous impact on the corporate executive's decision to join the fight.

In NCMEC's ninth year of operation, the media continue to play a critical role in maintaining the height of public awareness about crimes against children. Individual cases of child abduction are often front-page news, and in-depth coverage of each aspect of the problem has been scrutinized in the press.

In fact, the media themselves have been proven a powerful tool in directly locating children. Articles on the issue, and on individual cases of missing children, have appeared in nearly every major daily newspaper, and in hundreds of weeklies. The power of the radio has brought word of the problem to millions of Americans. Whether profiled in the print or broadcast media or televised on such current national talk shows as "Donahue," "Geraldo," "Sally Jessy Raphaël," or "The Oprah Winfrey Show," national forums are now open to parents of missing children to tell their story to a national audience and solicit its help. And there are families who have been reunited due to such coverage in the media:

• In 1985, Mallory Elizabeth Sutton was abducted by a babysitter from her Texas home. Within days, her photograph was aired on ABC's "Good Morning America" and a viewer who recognized the child telephoned NCMEC's Hotline. Mallory's mother was reunited with her in a matter of days.

- In 1986, Jeremiah Thate was abducted in the metropolitan Washington, DC, area and remained missing for several months. One weekend, a local firefighter read an article in The *Washington Post Magazine* about the suffering the infant's parents were enduring. A few days later, he was working at the scene of a fire when he looked up to see the face of that missing child. Because this firefighter was so touched by the article he had read and paid such close attention to the child's picture, the infant was recovered and reunited with his family.
- In 1988, a 17-year-old runaway who happened to watch a special on "The Oprah Winfrey Show" focusing on missing children was moved to contact her mother after 12 years.
- In 1989, a mother of a child abducted by her noncustodial father appeared as a guest on the "Sally Jessy Raphaël Show." Private investigators watching the program later volunteered their services to help recover the child, and, once located, Fox Television's "A Current Affair" arranged to reunite the mother and child.
- In 1990, Nicole Ravisi was abducted by a family acquaintance. Fox's "America's Most Wanted" profiled her case repeatedly and helped to successfully locate the child due to a viewer's tip.

Other nationally televised programs such as NBC's "Unsolved Mysteries" and "Missing! Have You Seen This Person?" Fox's "The Reporters," and nationally syndicated "Missing/Reward" have featured cases of missing children and played significant roles in their recovery. Network television news magazines have also focused on the issue of missing children and what is being done to combat it. CBS's "60 Minutes" featured a segment entitled "Underground Railroad" that aired on October 16, 1988, discussing the problems faced by parents who illegally take and conceal their children from allegedly abusive spouses; "48 Hours" on June 6, 1990, aired the story of Matthew Roberts, a 6-year-old boy missing from New Mexico who was found deceased; and ABC's "20/20" aired a segment entitled "Where's My Baby" on November 7, 1988, that discussed the problem of infants who are abducted from hospital settings and ways to prevent that crime. The ABC, CBS, and NBC networks have also aired made-for-television movies about such crimes against children. In addition to NBC's *Adam* and *Adam: His Song Continues, I Know My First Name is Steven* has now been broadcast twice, detailing the long-term abduction and recovery of a missing boy from California, Steven Stayner.

In January 1990, ABC aired the made-for-television movie, *Unspeakable Acts*, based on the true story of sexual abuse at the Country Walk Babysitting Service located 30 miles from Miami, Florida, and adapted from a book of the same title by Jan Hollingsworth (1986). This case is significant because it is the first successfully prosecuted case in which a daycare operator was convicted of multiple child sexual abuse. Prior to airing the show, the producer of the film contacted NCMEC and asked the organization to prepare a brochure for families on selecting safe daycare. At the close of the film, the leading actor, Jill Clayburgh, appeared to tell the national audience that daycare in America is safe, but that we must all be cautious and use common sense in protecting our children. She added that free information was available to viewers by calling the displayed NCMEC toll-free Hotline number.

During the ensuing 3 days, NCMEC handled more than 10,000 calls from citizens requesting the information. Further, NCMEC received 893 calls from parents who felt that their children were being sexually abused in daycare. In each case NCMEC assigned a case manager, gathered information, and worked with law enforcement authorities in that community.

CBS aired the afterschool special, "Maggie's Secret," about a school girl's fight to survive in a dysfunctional family. As in the other cases cited previously, the Hotline became a vehicle for helping families, providing positive information, and identifying cases in need of assistance. NCMEC joined with the American Council on Alcoholism and the National Committee for Prevention of Child Abuse in handling the calls and disseminating information to families and children across America.

The problem of child abduction and how the United States has moved to combat it has not only been a source of interest to the American press but to international media as well. Over the past 8 years, NCMEC has provided information to or hosted representatives of the press from Belgium, Canada, China, France, Germany, Great Britain, Japan, Korea, the Netherlands, and the former USSR.

The importance of the media's involvement in the fight to reduce crimes against children cannot be overstated. Without their tremendous voice and ability to reach out to millions of Americans, efforts to curtail abduction and molestation would certainly be diminished. Above and beyond the individual cases of success, there would not currently be an American population mobilized to fight for the rights of children. A law enforcement officer once said, "The only way not to find this problem in your community is simply not to look." With the help of the media, Americans have found it hard to turn away from the problem of child victimization, and for that we are all in their debt.

But what about strategies for the future?

We Must Rethink and Redefine Media Public Service Requirements. The concept of public service too often is viewed as an obligation rather than an opportunity. In far too many media markets it is met by airing public service announcements at 3:00 a.m. on Sunday mornings.

I would urge creativity and imagination, to think about the media and public service in a broader context. Working together we can ensure that compelling issues and challenges facing American families are addressed in a positive informative manner by media, beneficial to both the media and community.

There are countless examples of conveying valuable information in an attractive, entertaining way. For example, NCMEC has worked directly with television networks to build valuable information into the story lines of entertainment programs, and to ensure that the message is proper and appropriate, based on available research and expert opinion. Television series including Fox's "21 Jump Street," ABC's "Who's the Boss," CBS's "The Equalizer," as well as daytime television programming such as "The Guiding Light" have worked with NCMEC on episodes addressing issues such as child abduction, parental kidnapping, child prostitution, child pornography, runaways, and so on.

Whereas deeply concerned about the Nielsen ratings, producers have begun to recognize the benefits to the public and to their ratings that flow from conveying useful, beneficial program content, which is also entertaining. In addition, through tie-ins with viable, credible, national organizations, the producers offer something more than just an hour's entertainment. They offer viewers the opportunity to receive free, useful, usable information.

The media become more interactive with their audience, attempt to address the problems and concerns of the audience, and by so doing become a more vital and irreplaceable part of the viewers' lives.

We Must Remove Some of the Traditional Barriers to More Direct Media Involvement in Matters of Great Public Importance. Traditionally, and appropriately, the media have avoided becoming a participant in a story or event. They have maintained distance to ensure objectivity and perspective. Yet, there are many cases in which there is a higher need or calling.

In a time of crisis the media are often the only meaningful purveyor of information, counsel, advice, and direction to a traumatized frightened community. It is not enough to merely report.

In communities that experience a highly publicized abduction or murder of a child or children, parents become paralyzed with fear and are reluctant to ever allow their children out of their sight. School systems often send the wrong messages, whereas media reporting may inflame, rather than inform.

Many media organizations today are more involved than ever before in efforts to provide calm practical information to families. Working with local and national experts, the media are the most pervasive and most effective source of help and support and must broaden their view of their mission.

We Must Work to Ensure that the Media Treat the Cases and Problems of Individual Families Fairly and Equitably. In missing child cases many parents become frustrated when they literally have to fight with media to create interest in their missing child's case, whereas the circumstances surrounding the disappearance of another missing child receive constant local and national exposure. For a variety of reasons the cases of children like 11-year-old Jacob Wetterling of St. Joseph, Minnesota, who was abducted at gunpoint on October 22, 1989, by an unknown assailant and has not yet been located, or 5-year-old Melissa Brannen of Lorton, Virginia, who was last seen on December 3, 1989, at a holiday party held at her apartment complex and believed to have been abducted by a nonfamily member, may receive enormous media coverage, whereas other cases, equally tragic and equally in need of visibility, may be largely ignored. What many editors and producers do not realize is that their decision not to cover a case of an abducted child following his or her disappearance may mean the difference between that child's life and death.

NCMEC works to give missing children from every race, age, and geographic location in the United States the equal opportunity for media attention. However, we must do more to sensitize the media to the fact that all missing children are at risk, regardless of their situations, and they all need and deserve our help.

Further, although recognizing the limitations of space, time, and interest, media must work to create a decision-making process that minimizes arbitrariness and eliminates coverage decisions based solely on perceptions or survey data on the interests of the viewing audience.

We Must also Work to Create an Evenhandedness in the Exposure of Causes or Issues. Just as some cases of missing children garner more media coverage than others, the media can also play favorites with their coverage of social issues and concerns. Certainly, extensive coverage of an issue of particular concern to the community translates to greater viewership or readership, and more advertising dollars to the station or periodical involved.

We must work to overcome this "cause of the month" syndrome that puts a valid issue like that of child victimization in the headlines one week and buries it in Section B the next. Media often help to create movements and then seek to debunk or destroy them.

We must work to educate the media and the public at large that every social concern requires our attention, but just because a problem moves from the front page periodically is no indication that the need has been removed. A study of the life cycles of a cause or movement often reflects the disproportionate impact of media attitudes and media coverage.

A decade ago an author titled his book on the victimization of America's children, *Hidden Victims*. Thanks to the attention of media and the resultant growth in public awareness and recognition, the problem is less hidden today. Let us hope that in the 1990s the media will recognize the positive proactive role they must play in addressing the many problems faced by families and truly help us "Wake Up America."

REFERENCES

Alinsky, S. D. (1971). *Rules for radicals*. New York: Random House.

Cox, F. M., Erlich, J. L., Rothman, J., & Tropman, J. E. (Eds.). (1987). *Strategies of Community Organization*. Itasca, IL: Peacock.

Hollingsworth, J. (1986). *Unspeakable acts*. New York: Congdon & Weed.

8

EVALUATING THE CLASSROOM VIEWING OF A TELEVISION SERIES: "DEGRASSI JUNIOR HIGH"

Dorothy G. Singer
Jerome L. Singer
Yale University

Researchers studying the behavioral correlates of television viewing for children in the 11- to 15-year-old age group have generally reported associations of gender stereotyping and potentially at-risk attitudinal orientations with heavy television viewing. One reason may be that entertainment television contains frequent examples of gender stereotyping, substance abuse (especially alcohol), maladaptive ways of coping with problems, and other high-risk behaviors (Greenfield et al., 1987; Harwood & Weissberg, 1987; Morgan, 1987; Signorielli, 1987). One effort to counteract this programing trend eventuated in the development of a joint United States–Canadian television series, "Degrassi Junior High," aimed at a late puberty to early adolescent target population. Increasing awareness of persisting substance abuse and poor social problem-solving skills in many children within this age bracket also has led to calls for more imaginative use of the natural interest of these children in television as a means of supplementing primary prevention efforts in the classroom (Harwood & Weissberg, 1987). In this chapter we examine a research intervention and process evaluation of the use of episodes of the "Degrassi" series with and without teacher-led discussion as part of a school system's substance abuse prevention and problem-solving skill promotion program.

Our goal is to indicate not only some concrete findings of the study but to suggest methods for further formative evaluations for producers of programing that might be part of school-based prevention curricula.

BACKGROUND

Far from being a so-called "latency period," the phase of puberty and early adolescence in children may be of great importance in the development of internalized socialization through fantasy and imagination about possible social and sex roles, career choices, adventure, and romance (D. Singer & J. Singer, 1990). The television medium now provides a major source of content and structure for children's knowledge, beliefs, and future world because children average more than 23 hours per week in viewing, an amount of time that in many cases exceeds all their time in school, reading, or doing homework. Signorielli (1987) stated: "For the first time in human history a centralized commercial institution rather than parents, church, or school tells most of the stories most of the time" (p. 255). The special properties of the world as filtered through television fiction content, the especially attractive medium of music video with its well-documented emphasis on male–female violence, sadomasochism, and materialism may well be reinforcing certain types of gender stereotypes, career expectancies, and role models that may put many children at risk for substance abuse and delinquency. This may be especially the case when parental mediation of the children's viewing is neglected or unavailable (Desmond, Singer, Singer, Calam, & Colimore, 1985; Greenfield et al. 1987; Morgan, 1987; Prinsky & Rosenbaum, 1987; Signorielli, 1987; Wroblewski & Huston, 1987).

Children at this early adolescent age level are also at a high risk for delinquency and substance abuse. There may be an added impact of unsupervised television viewing on at least attitudes and beliefs that may predispose toward conduct disorder, especially when children face stressful life events and grow up in fractionated households (Bruns & Geist, 1984; Dornbusch et al., 1985; NIDA, 1989; Wills 1985). To counteract the risks of substance abuse and conduct disorder development, schools are increasingly building in prevention programs as part of their social studies and health curricula. A possible role for television in school-based programs providing social competence skill training has been outlined by Harwood and Weissberg (1987). After summarizing the extensive evidence of modeled experience versus verbal instruction, these investigators cite the motivating advantages of video presentations with characters with whom children can identify and of teachers' guides and relevant instructional material following up on the video presentations. Whereas several programs have been developed for skill development (Beyth-Maron, Fischoff, Jacobs, & Furby, 1989), Harwood and Weissberg point to the need to incorporate video materials to capitalize on children's established attraction to television viewing.

In our own work with elementary school-aged children, we found it useful to employ a curriculum to teach children how to become effective, intelligent consumers of television (Singer, Zuckerman, & Singer, 1980). We also have assessed the use of afternoon specials geared to adolescents and found that TV programs accompanied by teachers' guides and discussion produced positive changes in these students' attitudes (Singer, 1979). Although there is ample evidence that well-designed programming geared to constructive values and to appropriate age levels can have a useful impact on children and adolescents, the paucity of such programming on a *regular* basis presents a special problem (Huston, Watkins, & Kunkel, 1989; Pearl, Bouthilet, & Lazar, 1982; Williams, LaRose, & Frost, 1981).

What is clearly needed is an increase in regular series or specials that afford teenagers opportunities to engage in critical thought or the development of problem-solving strategies. An early effort in this regard, Public Television's "Freestyle," represented an example of how research could be used in a formative fashion and in evaluation, the assessment of the effects of viewing this series, on early teenagers' awareness of career options and on their overcoming occupational stereotypes (Johnston & Ettema, 1982; Williams, LaRose, & Frost, 1981).

The research literature indicates that teenagers do rely on television to form attitudes and values, but their current uncritical viewing of available programming may put them more at risk for negative behavior rather than arm them for effective coping with the stressors of transition to early adulthood. For this reason, a program such as "Degrassi Junior High" seemed like an excellent vehicle to test whether or not thoughtful programming can have an effect on young people's attitudes and behaviors. The use of such a program in classrooms with and without discussion at the conclusion of each show presented an opportunity to assess the value of discussion plus program viewing compared to the effects of simply viewing an episode without follow-up. We have found in past research that discussion of programming helps children to comprehend television themes and to understand television's special effects and its formal conventions (Desmond et al., 1985).

"DEGRASSI JUNIOR HIGH": THE TELEVISION SERIES

The "Degrassi Junior High" series, targeted to an 11- to 15-year-old audience, is intended as an alternative to the situation comedies produced in Hollywood where precocious, "well-adjusted," witty young people are presented in designer clothing, living in beautiful surroundings, and parented by loving, understanding adults. Solutions to problems in these shows are simple and immediate. "Degrassi Junior High," in the words of its producer, Kate Taylor, "tries to portray the complex experiences of early adolescence with insight, humor, compassion, and respect." The programs have dealt with sexual awareness, alcoholism, smoking, drugs, pregnancy, shoplifting, illness, and death, and the more common adolescent issues of grades, friendship patterns, popularity, parent–child relationships, and social justice.

The programs maintain continuity of character and recurrence of themes in this same junior high school. There is no particular "star"; each week different characters from the core group of about 10 are highlighted, and they usually confront a particular dilemma. The varied use of characters affords the young people an opportunity to identify with youths like themselves or like someone they would like to be. Although humor and suspense are employed, there is no effort to present "quickie" solutions. Useful ways of confronting problems are presented, however.

Five programs were selected from the series to test their effect on the attitudes and behavior patterns of fifth- to eighth-grade students and to determine their preferences for themes, plots, characters, and their understanding of the issues raised. Teachers were also asked to evaluate the programs and to express their opinions regarding the usefulness of such programs in a health-oriented curriculum.

RESEARCH METHOD

The goal of this study was to examine how episodes of the series shown in the classroom would, first of all, be received by the students. Second, we sought to evaluate the extent to which the viewers' response to plots and characters and to the issues of problem solving would be enhanced by specific classroom discussion of the episodes. Whereas we also attempted to assess students' substance use and various problem-solving attitudes before and after their classroom exposure to the the "Degrassi" episodes, we had little reason to expect any gross attitudinal change after such a brief 3 weeks of exposure. Rather, we were interested in patterns of response to the programs with and without discussion by the children who showed different styles of substance use and coping or problem-solving styles.

PROCEDURE

Informed Consent

The superintendent and principals of two schools in a mixed rural and suburban district in Connecticut were contacted in the spring of 1988 by the principal investigators to seek permission to carry out the project. Sample tapes of the programs and copies of all instruments were presented to the administration and to the staff who would participate (principals and teachers in the two schools). Once the school personnel approved of the study, we presented the project to parents at an evening meeting. With the approval of all, we then prepared a consent form as required by Yale University's Committee on Research Involving Human Subjects. This form was distributed to all parents of children in both schools in order to obtain their written consent. In addition, parents filled out a questionnaire concerning demographic data. Only those children whose parents signed the forms were included in the study. All participants were code numbered to maintain anonymity. Because the school collected data on substance use attitudes for all children, these data were available even if the children did not participate in the "Degrassi" viewings.

Teacher Participation

Six teachers agreed to participate in the study, three from each school, covering Grades 5 to 8. Meetings were held in each school to familiarize the teachers with the "Degrassi Junior High" programs that we selected and to discuss the teachers' guides that would be used with the discussion group. Schedules were arranged for each participating class for collection of pre-experimental data, for showing of the particular videotapes, for postexperimental data collection, and for teacher feedback sessions. In addition, all children's instruments were provided for the teachers in advance of the study so that any clarifications regarding instructions could be made if needed. Teachers had the opportunity to screen the videotapes before the experiment began and to ask any questions about the instruments, teachers' guides, and the "Degrassi" series. Hypotheses of the study were not discussed with the teachers in order to prevent their influencing the participants' responses to the questionnaires.

PARTICIPANTS

Characteristics of the Sample

The children who participated in this study were drawn from Grades 5 to 8 (elementary and middle school) of a school district in central Connecticut. The sample of children on whom we have basic information concerning reading levels, television-viewing patterns, socioeconomic level, parental marital status, and so on made up the full population of the grades in the schools ($N=621$). Of this number 294 received parental consent to participate in the "Degrassi" classroom viewing phase of the experiment. Because of absences, there were 284 in the formal experiment of whom 146 were girls, 138 boys. The average grade level of the participants was 6.6; thus the average age was 11.5 years of age. Somewhat more than one third of the children were in Grades 5 and 6, whereas about 65% were in Grades 7 or 8. For those children on whom data could be gathered using the 5-point Hollingshead-Redlich scale, the average was 2.8, suggesting a clearly "middle–middle SES level" with almost no representation from either the lowest or highest economic strata of the society. There was, however, a sizable representation (24%) from blue-collar backgrounds, suggesting that the sampling reflected the more general Connecticut population outside of the inner areas of the state's largest cities. Marital status was categorized by parents currently married, divorced, widowed, or other. For this sample 83% of the children came from two-parent households with 15% from divorced families. Data on reading levels were also available. Sixty-five percent of the children were reading at grade level or above, whereas 35% were categorized as below grade level.

An analysis of the questionnaire scores of the children whose parents did not grant consent or who had neglected to respond showed no significant differences between them and the 284 children who participated on reading levels, television-viewing patterns, or parental marital status. When the children were divided for demographic characteristics on all the preceding variables after random assignment to the two experimental groups (Classroom "Degrassi"-viewing versus Classroom "Degrassi"-viewing plus Discussion), no significant differences emerged. Thus the random assignment to conditions was quite effective.

In summary, this sample of children came from essentially the socioeconomic center of the population with adequate representation for this state of the white- and blue-collar family backgrounds. They seemed solidly representative of the state norm and, more generally, of national norms. The sample of the school population from whom we received parental consent did not differ significantly in demographics from the nonparticipants.

MEASURES

Parents' Questionnaires

In addition to the Informed Consent, parents filled out a background information sheet yielding data concerning parents' education, employment, marital status, ethnicity, number of children, languages spoken at home, child's average grades in school.

Children's Measures

TV Information Form. This form was administered pre and postclass-room exposure to all school classes. It yielded information concerning the Viewing and Viewing with Discussion participants' television habits: the programs viewed on the previous day of testing; number of hours of TV viewing on weekdays; number of hours of TV viewing on Saturday: number of hours of TV viewing on Sunday; and three favorite television programs. In addition, participants were asked how many times they had watched specific popular programs. "Degrassi Junior High" was included among such titles as "Family Ties," "Star Trek," "Wonderworks," and "Kate and Allie". This was to ascertain whether or not our participants had seen "Degrassi Junior High" prior to the experiment. Programs viewed were coded into 15 distinct categories (e.g., news, sitcoms, soaps, action–adventure).

Opinions Questionnaire. This was administered pre and post classroom exposure to all school classes. Three short tests consisting of 31 questions dealt with students' attitudes toward smoking cigarettes, drinking alcohol, and using drugs. Answers were recorded from "Strongly Agree" to "Strongly Disagree" on a 5-point scale. The measures were adapted from tests used by Roger Weissberg in the New Haven Schools in the "decision-making" project (Harwood & Weissberg, 1987).

Coping Questionnaire. This measure was administered pre and post to *all* school classes. It contains 47 items dealing with how a person copes with stress either through focusing on *emotional coping*, such as "I like to go to some place calm and peaceful to settle down," or *problem solving*, such as "I talk to my parents to figure out how to solve a problem." Two separate scores were obtained — one for *emotional coping* and one for *problem-solving coping*. Answers were marked from "Never" to "Most of the Time." In addition, eight questions were asked concerning how one *handles problems* as a further check on the Coping Questionnaire. Answers on this measure were marked from "Strongly Agree" to "Strongly Disagree" on a 5-point scale.

Whereas there may be adaptive features to both emotional coping and more active problem solving, some studies suggest that more problem-focused coping may be characteristic of better functioning children. Emotional coping seems more often associated with attempted mood change without realistic efforts at dealing with the stressful situation (Beyth-Marom et al., 1989; Bruns & Geist, 1984; Wills, 1985).

Mood and State Questionnaire. This measure was administered pre and post to *all* school classes. It has 11 questions tapping a person's moods during the past month. For example, "I felt relaxed and free of tension," and "I woke up feeling fresh and rested." Answers were checked from "None of the Time" to "Most of the Time" on a 5-point scale.

Story Comprehension. This measured, Viewing-only and Viewing with Discussion Groups. Tailor made for the five "Degrassi Junior High" episodes, it asked children to state the main points of each episode they had watched and to provide 5-point ratings on Agreement with the Way the Story Ended, Arousal of Ideas or Problems you Might Think of in Future, Particular Feature that Stays in Mind or Made Strong Impression, Similarity of Story Kids to the Kids in Own School, Did Characters Act as they did because of Peer or Adult Pressure?

These questions were answered immediately after viewing in the Viewing-only Group but after the Viewing and Teacher-led discussion in the other group. We hoped in this way to assess the children's general grasp of the material, the characters' motives, identifiability, and the like. Whereas the producers hoped that a showing by itself (as in natural home viewing) would yield good comprehension and subsequent reflection, we believed from our previous research that the Discussion Group would show more understanding and impact of the individual and combined shows.

Emotions Questionnaire. This measure was for Viewing Groups only. Consisting of 11 items, it tapped the way the participants felt after viewing each show to determine such moods as sadness, disgust, interest–enjoyment, anger, and embarrassment or shame. The Discussion Group answered these items *after* the teacher-led discussion. In addition, two questions relating to the viewers' liking of the music, a special concern of the producers, were included.

Characters Questionnaire. This measure was for Viewing Groups only. It consists of 21 questions relating to participants' reactions to the various main characters on the five programs presented. Questions dealt with such items as "which character seemed most like you?", "Which character would you hate to be the most?" This measure was administered at the end of all five video presentations to both experimental and control groups.

Teachers' Measures. Two measures were administered to the six participating teachers: (a) an evaluation form to determine teachers' ratings of the programs; their own viewing of "Degrassi Junior High" prior to the study; their preferences for various characters in the shows; the relevance of the shows for their students; their future use of the programs; and (b) an evaluation form dealing with the value of the teachers' guides and their evaluation of how the programs were received by their students. The *Teacher Evaluation Report*, although of use for producers, is summarized only briefly in this chapter.

VIDEOTAPES USED IN THE STUDY

Five videotapes were selected for this study based on their appropriateness for this age group and relevance and interest of topics. The tapes selected were: (a) *Bottled Up*, dealing with alcoholism in the family, confronting problems, smoking; (b) *The Big Dance*, dealing with themes of parent–child relationships, cultural differences, lying, alcohol, and dating; (c) *Stage Fright*, dealing with handicaps, shyness, jealousy; (d) *What a Night*, dealing with shoplifting, judgment, decision making, peer pressure, media images; and (e) *A Helping Hand*, dealing with sexual harassment by a teacher, latchkey kids, self-image.

Each episode played for about 25 minutes. During each presentation, large photographs of the characters in the particular program viewed were on display in front of the classroom. Each photograph had the name of the character printed with it so that students would become familiar with the various members of the cast.

RESULTS

Television-Viewing Patterns

Of the school population ($N = 621$), 59.6% reported they had never seen "Degrassi Junior High" on TV. Of those who had seen it, 27.2% reported only one viewing; only 3.5% had seen it four or more times. For the total sample the average weekly hours of TV reported by the children was 31.78 ($S.D. = 11.68$, $N = 568$). The "Degrassi" home viewers, contrary to what we expected, came from the heavier viewing segment of the sample averaging 33.64 hours of weekly TV ($S.D. = 10.64$, $N = 109$). There were, however, no significant differences between the experimental groups or between them and the nonparticipants in overall TV viewing. With respect to the formation of the two experimental groups, neither differed in the extent of viewing of the "Degrassi" program prior to the formal study.

To establish the children's television-viewing favorite shows (by category, e.g., Action–Adventure, Cartoons, Sports, Music Video), we asked for a ranking of favorites. These responses were weighted from 1 to 3 by category. Scores were created for each category based on the percentage of the sample of 621 who listed a program in that category as their top favorite and its rank as 3 (top favorite) down to 1. The overall average for more violent programing among top three favorites was .231; Sitcoms by comparison rated at .873, Music Videos .113, Soaps .138, with all other programing (including, alas, PBS adult and children's shows) showing far lower scores. Clearly, for this sample family Sitcoms like "The Cosby Show" dominated as favorites followed next but well behind by Action–Adventure, Soap dramas, and Music Videos.

When we tested for favorite programming in a follow-up 4 weeks after the "Degrassi" classroom exposure, the pattern of overall favorites changed slightly. Pre-experimental to postexperimental changes in viewing categories were negligible except for a significant shift in Action–Adventure viewing. Following both experimental groups' exposure to "Degrassi" in the classroom, they were subsequently significantly less likely to list the violent Action–Adventure shows among their favorites. The children who had not seen "Degrassi" in class showed no appreciable change in this violent viewing category as a favorite.

In general, for our sample, the major thrust of children's viewing patterns pits the choice of Action–Adventure programming against other kinds of favorites. Thus, children who prefer Music Video, Sitcoms, or Soaps are less likely to be caught up in the more violent programming as their favorites. Of special interest is the finding that home "Degrassi" viewing *subsequent* to the experiment went up dramatically for the exposed groups, seven or eight times greater than for those not exposed. To the extent that the series may be considered "worthwhile" fare specifically produced for children, this shift is encouraging even on a temporary basis. In effect, then, the children who had participated in the school viewings of "Degrassi" subsequently became more interested in that show for home viewing and also seemed less likely to list violent programming among their favorite shows.

Substance Use Attitudes

The children from all grades involved in the study filled out questionnaires about their opinions concerning cigarette smoking prior to and following the experimental groups' exposure to the "Degrassi" films. In general, the children in this school were already somewhat sensitized to the risks of smoking, drinking, and the use of drugs. The overall average for Opinions about Cigarette Smoking was 15.58 ($S.D.$ = 4.63) for the full sample prior to the experimental procedures, a score suggesting a strongly unfavorable view because 50 was the maximum positive attitude toward smoking. Under those circumstances little change could be anticipated; the overall postviewing score for the experimental participants score was 15.4 (*S.D.*;eg4.8), with no indication that exposure to "Degrassi" in the classroom had any special effect. With respect to alcohol use, the overall group attitude, whereas still strongly negative, was slightly more accepting with an overall group average of 16.51 (*S.D.* = 5.66). Subsequent to the classroom showing there was no significant change, chiefly again we believe because scores were already so low (Post = 16.41, *S.D.* = 6.00). Finally, Attitudes toward Drugs were most negative with an overall group average of 14.81 (*S.D.* = 4.50) compared with a mean prior to the "Degrassi" of 15.01 (*S.D.* = 5.1), a trivial change. Thus, it appears as if the children's attitudes toward all substances were so negative at this age level and for this particular sociocultural group that a statistical reduction in positive attitudes could not be expected, a so-called "basement" effect.

Although we could not report an experimental influence on substance use attitudes, we did find a general patterning in our sample (e.g., Cigarette Smoking Attitudes correlate highly significantly with Alcohol and with Drug Use: $r = +.58, +.61$, respectively). The substance variables form a cluster negatively associated with the Problem-Oriented and General Problem-Solving variables but also correlated positively with the Emotionally Focused Coping. Factor analyses were conducted on the total original population and then separately on the two experimental groups (the children who viewed "Degrassi" episodes in class with or without teacher-led discussion). These analyses indicated that, despite the overall low scores on acceptance of substance use, there was still sufficient variability in our sample to demonstrate a single bipolar factor.

Those children who tend to show scores reflecting more positive attitudes about smoking, drinking, or drug use are also likely to score lower on the measures reflecting taking action to solve problems or experiencing efficacy in their efforts at using problem-focused skills. These children are also likely to seek emotional relief in the face of adversity rather than turn their attention to active solutions to the problems.

We had also obtained mood ratings for the total school population as well as before and after the classroom showings for the two experimental groups. The children who scored higher on substance use acceptance were also more likely to report negative affective states such as sadness, anger, and distress.

These findings indicating a linkage between negative affect, more emotionally focused and less problem-focused coping, with more acceptance (if not use) of substances are in keeping with some earlier results (Bruns & Geist, 1984; Wills, 1985). We also found, however, some new evidence that heavy television viewing, especially *weekend viewing*, loads positively on this same factor along with emotionally focused coping and positive substance use attitudes. Our data point to a clustering of heavy television viewing, substance use inclination, "self-medication" through emotional reaction rather than a directed effort at problem solving as characterizing a segment of our school population. These results call to mind important findings in studies by McIlwraith and Schallow (1982–1983) and Kubey and Csikszentmihalyi (1990) that also point to a cycle of heavy television viewing to counteract dysphoric moods, followed by further often heightened dysphoria following the viewing of more violent programming.

Attitudes Following "Degrassi" Classroom Viewing

As already suggested, the possibilities that we could demonstrate statistically reliable changes reflecting negative attitudes about substance use were severely limited by the children's initial scores on these measures. As a result, the likelihood of changes that were not simply regressions to the mean were difficult to demonstrate.

Examining the entire sample including those children who were not exposed to the "Degrassi" programming but who filled out substance use and TV-viewing questionnaires, we find only slight differences suggesting less acceptance of smoking and alcohol use for the "Degrassi"-viewing groups, *especially* the group who also participated in Discussion. More striking are the shifts in general TV viewing where the nonclassroom viewers showed increased TV viewing, whereas the classroom "Degrassi" viewers, especially those with teacher discussion, reflected a reduction in their general home TV-viewing. These findings are generally supported by a Multivariate Analysis of Covariance with univariate results significant or tending so primarily for Experimental versus Control Group differences on subsequent TV viewing. Keep in mind that our controls were not randomly assigned but were those whose parents failed to give permission to participate in classroom viewings. As indicated, these nonparticipating children's scores did not differ on the various pre-experimental measures from the two classroom-viewing groups.

We also sought to examine effects when we subdivided our sample into comparisons of children at risk with those least at risk. Here again, Multiple Analyses of Covariance and univariate analyses failed to yield consistent statistically reliable differences between those children who watched "Degrassi" in class versus those who did not. Nor could we demonstrate any reliable evidence that classroom discussion led to better coping skills or problem solving than mere classroom exposure. The trends generally suggested the advantages of teacher-led discussion, but the effects were too small for us to assert that such discussion made a really appreciable difference. We do have indications both from the subsequent very sizable increases in postexperimental viewing of the "Degrassi" series at home and by the general reduction in TV-viewing hours for the experimental subjects that one influence of the experiment may have been to stimulate a more *discriminating* home-viewing orientation.

Qualitative discussions with students, teachers, and some parents subsequent to the study support the previous conclusion about more selective viewing. Our follow-ups also indicated a general attitude of curiosity about the issues raised in the provocative series of films we showed. Only the programs that dealt with sexual misconduct by a teacher led to some confusion among the children who seemed less able to comprehend the plot and its implications.

Although we felt confident that our sample was representative in its socioeconomic and sociocultural aspects, the well-established and consistent policies of the school system concerning substance abuse may have operated to minimize the likelihood that this experimental design could show any appreciable substance use or coping skill effects of "Degrassi" viewing for these children. Qualitative response was excellent, but we must assert clearly that our "objective" testing measures yielded minimal evidence of the benefits of the experiment.

Response to Specific "Degrassi" Episodes

The children were exposed to five "Degrassi" episodes: *Bottled Up*, *The Big Dance*, *Stage Fright*, *What a Night*, and *Helping Hand*. Following each episode viewing (and the Discussion, for those in that condition), they answered questions on (a) grasp of the main points of each story, (b) Degree of Agreement with the way the story ended, (c) Degree to which the episode evoked Thought-provoking Ideas, (d) Degree of Impressive Effect, (e) Degree of Identification with story characters as typical school students, (f) Degree of Adult Pressure seen as motivating. They also filled out scales for liking of the episode generally and then reported the degrees of emotional response while watching or immediately afterward. The emotions rated on a 5-point scale (1 = hardly at all, 5 = very, very much) were Sadness, Disgust, Interest, Anger, Embarrassment, and Joy. They also rated degree of shifts of mood Upward and Downward. Finally they reported on Awareness of the Music and Degree of Liking of Music. For all these ratings, then, scores vary along a 1 to 5 scale.

Comparison of Main Points of Episode

As evaluated by comparison with scores produced by adult raters, the children showed a slightly below-midpoint comprehension score for identifying the main points of the episodes. There was an overall statistical difference across episodes; the comprehension scores ranged from 2.85 and 2.59 for *Big Dance* (With and Without Discussion, respectively) to a low of 1.95 and 1.93 for *Helping Hand* (the sexual harassment, self-image episode). The Discussion group's scores are consistently but not significantly higher for 4 of 5 episodes. Thus, for our sample the Teacher Discussion did not yield a really major improvement in the children's grasp of the main points of each episode. Overall, for these children, they showed a very modest ability to identify the conceptual "lessons" of the episodes but were consistent in their differential grasp of the themes of the shows. The *Big Dance* theme of Voula's conflict with her puritanical father produced a much clearer understanding among the viewers than the theme of teacher sexual provocation in *Helping Hand*.

Agreement with Ending

In general, agreement with the ending of the shows averaged well above 3 for the five episodes. Once again, Teacher Discussion was not a clear influence, although the general trend in this instance (nearly statistically significant) was for the children who participated in Discussions to be *less* satisfied with the endings. The ratings across shows indicated highest agreement with the conclusions of *Helping Hands* and *Stage Fright*, the least agreement with how *Big Dance* concluded. The differential response across shows was once again highly significant statistically, indicating that children do react differentially to particular episodes.

Ideas for Future Thought

Whereas overall the average rating for provocative ideas from the shows was slightly below the midpoint of 3, the range across episodes (from 2.75 for *Big Dance* to 2.57 for *Helping Hand*) was less impressive than the very striking difference for the Discussion versus No Discussion groups. Here Teacher-led review was consistent in generating higher scores for this measure, yielding a statistically significant advantage for Discussion. Lowest scores for idea provocation emerged from *Helping Hand* when there was no teacher assistance.

Impressive Events

The overall average for degree to which children rated the shows as having made a strong impression was just slightly below the scale midpoint (2.8).

There were no really clear-cut differences across episodes—*Stage Fright* rated 3.01 with Teacher Discussion and *What a Night* 2.44 with Discussion. Teacher Discussion yielded higher ratings for all five shows but at only a marginally statistically significant level.

Perceived Similarity or Identification

By and large, this sample rated each episode below the midpoint for perceived similarity to "the kids in school" (an average of 2.52). Teacher Discussion had very modest influence yielding higher similarity scores for 4 out of 5 episodes but with slight differences. No episode stood out as yielding either greater identification or very little perceived similarity.

Influence by Peer Pressure

Results here indicate a marked episode difference with almost no variation as a function of Discussion–No Discussion. The children reported that *Bottled Up* and *Big Dance* both reflected the most peer pressure. Teacher Discussion was not a significant factor overall.

Adult Pressure

For this variable the children clearly reflected an awareness of plot differences. *Helping Hand* and *Bottled Up* yielded the highest scores (2.9 and 2.73, respectively), with *Stage Fright* showing the least influence of adults. Teacher Discussion had no consistent effect here.

Liking for the Music

The children generally rated their liking for the music of all shows at well above the midpoint of the scales. The average score was 3.6, with perhaps a slight edge overall for the music in *Stage Fright* and *Helping Hand*. Overall, there was little variation between episodes or experimental groups here. Because the children generally rated conservatively, rarely according "5"s, the general impression seems quite favorable to the musical background. *Noticing* the music yielded generally low ratings, suggesting that the music was not intrusive even though generally enjoyed.

Specific Emotional Reactions

As might be expected specific emotions evoked by the shows varied considerably from episode to episode. *Big Dance* and *What a Night* evoked highest scores for Joy, with *Bottled Up* and *Helping Hand* showing lowest scores. In general, more positive ratings emerged after Teacher-led discussions. Highest ratings for experiencing Sadness were obtained for *Stage Fright* and *Bottled Up*, but overall this emotion was not a prominent mood evoked by the episodes. No experimental group effect emerged. For the feeling of Disgust there is little variation or Teacher Discussion effect, but one show, *Helping Hand* with scores of 2.94 (Discussion) and 3.08 (No Discussion), was well above the others in evoking this emotion. One senses the queasiness these 11-year-olds or younger children experience at the sexuality and adult–child intimacy of that film. Here, Teacher Discussion may have slightly moderated the effect. For the positive emotion of Interest, scores were high overall for this sample (close to the midpoint), with *Big Dance* and *What a Night* yielding the highest scores and *Helping Hand* the lowest, but with relatively little variation. Whereas Anger was generally not provoked much, it was most often listed by the children for episodes that involved adults who step out of their appropriate roles. In general, Embarrassment was relatively rarely rated except for the *Helping Hand* episode about the sexually provocative teacher, which stood out as evoking this emotion much more than the other episodes. In producing a downward shift in mood, *Bottled Up* stood out from other episodes followed closely by *Helping Hand*. *What a Night* and *Bottled Up* also evoked the highest scores for mood enhancement, chiefly following Teacher Discussion.

In summary, the analysis suggests fairly clear differences in the children's grasp of the shows, their reaction to particular points. The theme of adults behaving "badly" or stepping out of their quasi-parental roles as in *Bottled Up* and *Helping Hand* evoked the greatest ranges of emotion and the most negative ones.

Evaluating Identifications and Character Appeal.   We also carried out extensive analyses of the children's reactions to specific child and adult characters. Because these were chiefly designed to be informative to the producers in developing future episodes, we summarize here only the more general implications of our study. A major result was that, of the female characters, certain girls stood out as appealing and identifiable. One, Stephanie, was memorable as the repository for fantasies about hairstyles, dating, and clothing, but she was also viewed as too risk taking and outrageous for identification purposes. There were interesting differences in "Degrassi" character popularity or identifiability as a function of the students' reading scores and socioeconomic status. Thus the character of Joey, a kind of "Dead End Kid," was most appealing to children with lower reading level scores, whereas other characters especially appealed to better readers, school achievers, or children from higher socioeconomic backgrounds. This differential reaction to characters was also evident for the few adults in the story. Thus, Kathleen's Mom, an alcoholic, was favored only by children who scored at average or below-average reading levels. Our data also allowed us to make a strong recommendation to the producers to increase the variety and differentiation in male characters, as the female characters emerged from the episodes much more vividly for viewers from both genders.

Teachers' Evaluations

Although the extensive ratings and qualitative reports we obtained from teachers were chiefly of specific use to the producers, a few general comments can be made. The overall response to the showings in classroom, especially as a basis for discussions about problem-solving and coping skills, was very positive. Teachers reported that children were more able to talk openly about significant general as well as personal problems stimulated by program content than they had been in previous classes on substance use or problem solving. They reported "positive, open attitudes," "receptivity to ideas," and "insightful" discussions. They seemed to feel that, were such television materials readily available, they could be used very effectively in social studies classes.

SOME CONCLUDING REMARKS

This project involved two general objectives: The first called for relatively rapid feedback to the producers of "Degrassi Junior High" concerning response of children and teachers to the shows and their characters and to the discussion guides; the second called for a more extensive evaluation of children's comprehension, emotional reactions to the episodes and specific characters, and an assessment of whether school showings with or without teacher-led discussion modified substance use attitudes or coping skills.

The first objective was met in part by providing the producers with information that indicated an extremely positive response to the episodes shown by both teachers and students. The research data also indicated that junior high schoolers, as a target audience, comprehended the program content moderately well, were attracted to a variety of characters (with interesting differences for middle and lower socioeconomic status groups), and, following exposure to the five episodes in school, markedly increased their home viewing of the series. It was also possible to say that the lack of one or two central heroic characters did not seem to mar the children's responses. Rather they showed a range of identifications. What did emerge clearly was that children in this sample were less attracted to the male than to the female characters in the episodes shown. It was recommended to the producers that attention be paid to developing livelier male characters to appeal to both boys and girls.

A second objective involved assessment of the usefulness of "Degrassi" showings in the schools with and without teacher-led discussions based on available Discussion Guides. There was special concern about whether the children's opinions about drugs, alcohol, and cigarettes, and their television-viewing patterns might be influenced by the content of the episodes. In addition, the emphasis in the programming on children's coping skills and problem solving might affect the viewers, especially if amplified by teacher discussion. Despite the fact that the statistical data evaluating attitude changes for children viewing the episodes were not conclusive, there were strong qualitative indications from subsequent parent, teacher, and child interviews, suggesting the benefits of the series as a method of stimulating children to think seriously about substance use and about practical approaches to their common problems. The discussions seemed especially helpful, but showings without discussion were also useful. Children who participated in the classroom discussions subsequently showed more evidence of selective TV viewing. Although we cannot state that showings of five episodes can produce any major attitudinal changes, the receptiveness of the children and teachers to the episodes and to the possibilities for using such material to examine their own beliefs was exhilarating.

Acknowledgments

The research described in this chapter was carried out with support from WGBH–TV Boston and the "Degrassi Junior High" series, Kate Taylor, Producer, as well as from the W. T. Grant Foundation. The cooperation of the Berlin Connecticut School District is gratefully acknowledged.

References

Beyth-Marom, R., Fischoff, B., Jacobs, M., & Furby, L. (1989). *Teaching decision making to adolescents: A critical review* (Carnegie Council on adolescent development, working paper) Washington DC: Carnegie Corporation of America.
Bruns, C., & Geist, C. S. (1984). Stressful life events and drug use among adolescents. *Journal of Human Stress, 10*, 135–139.

Desmond, R., Singer, J. L., Singer, D. G., Calam, R., & Colimore, K. (1985). Family mediation patterns and television-viewing. Young children's use and grasp of the medium. *Human Communications Research*, *2*, 461–480.

Dornbusch, S. M., Carlsmith, J. M., Bushwall, S. J., Ritter, P. L., Leiderman, H., Hastorf, A. H., & Gross, R. T. (1985). Single parents, extended households, and the control of adolescents. *Child Development*, *56*, 326–341.

Greenfield, P. M., Burzone, L., Koyamatsu, K., Satuloff, W., Nixon, K., Brodie, M., & Kingsdale, D. (1987). What is rock music doing to our youth? A first experimental look at the effects of rock music lyrics and music videos. *Journal of Early Adolescence*, *7*, 345–364

Harwood, R. L., & Weissberg, R. P. (1987). The potential of video in the promotion of social competence in children and adolescents. *Journal of Early Adolescence*, *7*, 345–364.

Huston, A. C., Watkins, B. A., & Kunkel, D. (1989). Public policy and children's television. *American Psychologist*, *44*(2), 424–433.

Johnston, J., & Ettema, J. S. (1982). *Positive images: Breaking stereotypes with children's television*. Beverly Hills, CA: Sage.

Kubey, R., & Csikszentmihalyi, M. (1990). *Television and the quality of life*. Hillsdale, NJ: Lawrence Erlbaum Associates.

McIlwraith, R. D., & Schallow, J. R. (1982–1983). Television-viewing and styles of children's fantasy. *Imagination, Cognition, and Personality*, *2*, 323–331.

Morgan, M. (1987). Television, sex role attitudes and sex role behavior. *Journal of Early Adolescence*, *7* 269–282.

NIDA. (1989). *National household survey on drug abuse:Population estimates 1988*. Rockville, MD: Author.

Pearl, D., Bouthilet, L., & Lazar, S. J. (Eds.). (1982). *Television and behavior: Ten years of scientific progress and implications for the eighties* (DHHS Publication Nos. ADM 82-1195, Vol. 1 and ADM 82-1196, Vol. 2). Washington, DC: U.S. Government Printing Office.

Prinsky, L. E., & Rosenbaum, J. L. (1987). Lear-ics or lyrics? *Youth and Society*, *18*, 384–394.

Rosenbaum, J., & Prinsky, L. (1987). Sex, violence, and rock and roll: Youth's perceptions of popular music. *Popular Music and Society*, *11*, 79–90.

Signorielli, N. (1987). Children and adolescents on television: A consistent pattern of devaluation. *Journal of Early Adolescence*, *7*, 255–268.

Singer, D. G. (1979). The constructive uses of television in the classroom. In S. L. Lustman (Ed.), *Proceedings, international year of the child: Child advocacy* (pp. 255–266). New Haven, CT: Child Study Center, Yale University.

Singer, D. G., Zuckerman, D. M., & Singer, J. L. (1980). Teaching elementary school children critical television viewing skills: An evaluation. *Journal of Communication*, *30*(3), 84–93.

Singer, D. G. & Singer, J. L. (1990) *The house of make-believe: Children's play and the developing imagination*. Cambridge, MA: Harvard University Press.

Williams, T. M., LaRose, R., & Frost, F. (1981). *Children television and sex role typing*. New York: Praeger.

Wills, T. A. (1985). Stress, coping, and tobacco and alcohol use in early adolescence. In S. Shiffman & T. A. Wills (Eds.), *Coping and substance use* (pp. 67–94). New York: Academic Press.

Wroblewski, R., & Huston, A. C. (1987). Televised occupational stereotypes and their effects on early adolescents: Are they changing? *Journal of Early Adolescence*, *7*, 283–298.

9

Media Influences and Personality Development: The Inner Image and the Outer World

Charles Ashbach
Clinical Psychologist, Philadelphia

Statement of the Problem

Why are television and movies so powerful? What is it about TV that motivates people to watch it 3, 4, 5 even 6 hours each day? What makes it so compelling? Why is it referred to as the "plug-in drug" (Winn, 1985)? Why are so many negative effects associated with it? Can it "cause" violence? Can it affect the personality in a profound way so as to cause ill? Why are we so enthralled when watching movies? What causes us to be transported and transfixed into stuperous and trancelike states by the images and sounds experienced within the movie theater?

The argument advanced here is that visual media (TV and movies), in and of themselves, are not powerful. They are simply technologies for the delivery of images on flat screens. What is powerful are those aspects of mind and emotion that respond with such total attention and surrender to the experience of watching and, as importantly, feeling those images projected onto to those screens.

This chapter utilizes psychoanalytic developmental psychology to study some aspects of mind and imagination that may shed light on some of the more pressing questions confronting us regarding the impact of visual media. Further, I examine certain developmental periods that individuals go through and relate them to the use or abuse of media images.

A Developmental Overview

From a psychoanalytic developmental perspective, the growth and emergence of personality can be conceived as the slow unfolding of biologically based bodily needs as they interact with the mental and psychological dimensions of the individual. The fundamental needs of the human animal (e.g., sex, aggression, attachment, learning) become powerful sources of motivation. Freud (1933/1964) called these the drives. They are like instincts in the animal world but they lack the specific behaviors and relationships that animal instincts cause.

The child's drives produce both the desire and the readiness to learn and behave. The final form of these motivations, desires, and activities are shaped through interactions with significant others: at first the mother, then the father, then the family, and then outward to the group and social collective. What start out as bodily needs evolve into the complex phenomenon of mind and mental life.

Due to the conflict, pain, and anxiety caused by our wishes clashing with the demands and limitations of external reality, mind becomes differentiated into conscious and unconscious aspects. Within consciousness reside those aspects of mental life dealing with rationality, memory, decision making, acceptable desires and wishes, communication, and social relations.

The unconscious is the vast storehouse for the repressed: those wishes, needs, desires, fears, anxieties, dreams, and fantasies that are unacceptable to the conscious mind. Also located in the unconscious are those mechanisms of defense used to ward off fear and to realize dreams and pleasure. Fantasy is the aspect of the unconscious that helps to explain media's impact on the personality.

Unconscious fantasy is the form that drives take as they express themselves. Thus, a wish for food or love expresses itself in an image or narrative (visual and verbal) that has as the outcome the gratification of that wish. A hungry child's wish for food might be transformed into an unconscious image of a satisfying, available breast. The child may make that image conscious by having a daydream of an ice cream cone, or a night dream of drinking from a cool and refreshing stream. Freud (1916/1963) said that "Every desire takes . . . the form of picturing its own fulfillment" (p. 372).

The very bedrock of mind is built on this vast unconscious reserve of images and narratives. Expression in consciousness of these unconscious images occurs through play, dreams, symbolism, artistic creations, metaphor, and daydreams. Pathological forms of expression are seen in neurotic symptoms, antisocial behavior, or the delusions and hallucinations of the mentally ill. At the group and society levels, these images become the common language of fairy tale and myth that allows for the social sharing of deep inner experience and provides the basis for empathy, understanding, and community.

The relationship between media images and unconscious fantasy can be seen in a child's wish to be secure and invulnerable. That wish may exist as an unconscious fantasy of a turtle, secure in its shell. The external, media image of "Teenage Mutant Ninja Turtles" would then be seen as an artistic creation that resonates with the child's deeply felt desire, and the child's pictorial form of the turtle, to be able to protect him or herself from all forms of threat and harm. The child's delight in the characters of the Turtles and their exploits (fairy tales) is obtained from the gratification of deeply held primitive wishes. The whimsy of the Ninja Turtles piggybacks on the timeless hope for complete safety, power, and invulnerability. The image of the turtle in its shell is the core of the unconscious fantasy and is a prime example of the "inner image" referred to in the title of this chapter.

This example shows that the unconscious fantasy may simply be a single image (turtle) or it may be a story about turtles struggling for good and against evil. In this way, the narrative structure of the fantasy provides the basis for explaining problems, resolving them, and generating morals concerning the proper conduct of future behavior. Thus, unconscious fantasy, as it links up with conscience, contains powerful moral messages and meanings.

The process of development is complex and multifaceted. The child must negotiate a series of vital tasks as he or she grows. The child must secure a sense of attachment to mother, father, and family (Bowlby, 1988). Then the child must move through the phases of separation and individuation (Mahler, Pine, & Bergman, 1975). Here, the baby begins to move toward being a person (i.e., toward developing an internalized world of thought, emotion, and judgment that will enable the baby to be autonomous and self-regulating). From there, the child must begin to deal with his or her issues of sexual identity, competition, power, and inclusion in the group, elements that Freud (1933/1964) termed the *Oedipal phase*.

The relationship between unconscious fantasy and the growth of the personality can be understood from the following:

> The growth of the personality occurs with the maturation of the perceptual apparatus, of memory as well as from the accumulated experience and learning from reality. This process of learning from reality is connected with

the evolution and changes in unconscious fantasy. There is a constant struggle with the child's omnipotent fantasies and the encounter of realities, good and bad. (Segal, 1991, p. 26)

This "constant struggle" between fantasy and reality can be seen in the child's deep ambivalence about accepting the difference between "what's real" and "what's made up." The child continually attempts to obliterate differences, especially those existing between the sexes and the generations (Chasseguet-Smirgel, 1986). The child wants to be everything; he or she wants to be his or her own cause, he or she wants to be unlimited. The child wants to be a boy *and* a girl; to be his or her own father and mother; to know everything without learning and so forth. One can readily see that TV (as well as movies and video games) can be experienced as a means to gain the illusion of gratifying those wishes.

However, parents know that fantasy and daydreams continue to play an active, sometimes predominant, aspect of the child's development throughout his or her formative years. In many cases, it is not until early adolesence (12 to 14 years of age) that we see children able to integrate their fantasies with rational thought in a way that ensures that external reality takes an increasing hold over perception, reasoning, and behavior. But many more years are required before the child matures into a person who competently and consistently discriminates the internal from the external in a generally integrated fashion. It is this slow and accumulating process of thought and fantasy being integrated with the resulting increase in the growth of the personality that seems to suffer the most inhibition when the consumption of media images becomes excessive or defensive.

Children's animated cartoons show how external, media-based images "mimic" the form of unconscious fantasy. The cartoon is an emotionally charged, exciting portrayal of fantastic (animated) characters. Its form is simple: An underdog (disguised child) comes into conflict with others (the top dog = parents or older children). There is danger, threat of destruction or death that are overcome in a magical and effortless fashion where pleasure and laughter are the outcome. The Coyote wants to eat the Roadrunner, Elmer Fudd wants to shoot Daffy Duck. Through complex and irrational activities, the "victim" triumphs over the "villain." Furthermore, there are no real consequences attendant to the use of massive aggression and force. Magically, all characters reappear in the next cartoon and the cycle of conflict and resolution, gratifying the child's wish to overcome limitation and smallness, is repeated once more.

The responsible parent knows that children need to have a safe and secure context within which to check out the magical and omnipotent world of the wish and cartoon. This is the world of the child–parent dyad and the family. Within the reality of the family, the omnipotent and grandiose desires of the child may be modulated and transformed. The love and availability of the parents are internalized and the wish to be singular, heroic, and possessing magic (Superman, Batman, Wonderwoman) begins to exist along side of the awareness of the importance of dependency, relationships, and cooperation. Relationship begins to neutralize omnipotence. Gradually, the child is able to give up his or her wish to overcome all obstacles and challenges, or to be able to defeat all opponents and begin to accept defeat, hurt, and ultimately limitation. This process of increased reality testing and frustration tolerance leads to the painful experiences of guilt and shame.

Because unconscious fantasy is the foundation that dreams are built on, we can now understand the reason that excessive TV viewing becomes problematic for children. In essence, the TV viewing experience itself, regardless of the content viewed, lends itself to be experienced as a form of unconscious fantasy. That is, the more a person (regardless of age) watches TV, the more he or she begins to feel as if he or she is dreaming even though awake. Like the hypnotic subject, who gives over his or her power of conscious thought and critical judgment to the hypnotist, the child (or adult) surrenders those reflective, active, and rational aspects of mind as he or she is entranced and mesmerized through the magic of the dancing images on the screen.

The use of the remote control channel changer (the "zapper") adds even further to the sense of magic and omnipotent force. With just a flick of the finger the child is able to gratify his or her every desire, or at least this is the impression. The child can move from cartoons, to sport, to horror movies or science fiction, to drama or sexual soap operas without having to think or engage the mind. Like Adam in the Garden of Eden, the child is king of all he or she surveys and is able to control and change everything based on his or her whim. The frequent outcome of this process is paradoxically an inflated sense of omnipotence and grandiosity as well as a heightened sense of passivity. Unfortunately, the true situation for the child is closer to that of Mickey Mouse in the *Sorcerer's Apprentice*. The child has acquired the use of Merlin's "magic wand" but is unable to anticipate or control the consequences.

Accordingly, arguments about the content of children's programming miss this vital aspect. The child's very experience of reality (i.e., the relationship between inner world and outer realm) is compromised to the extent that TV viewing begins to interfere with the process of reality testing and active relating with others.

Further, the child's ability to be creative, to construct a "transitional space" (Winnicott, 1978) within which to form new combinations of inner and outer, is inhibited to the extent that the child's mind is saturated with media-based images, characters, stories, and stimulation. The child must transform the "raw material" of both his or her inner and outer world in a pleasing synthesis in order to feel truly competent and in charge of his or her existence. The passivity by-product of TV viewing leads to a restriction of autonomous creativity and produces what teachers are seeing more and more: anxious, irritable, resentful, and demanding children who are unable to "play" and who demand to be "entertained" in a mode that approximates their experience of TV viewing.

TV commercials are like cartoons in that they too "mimic" the form of unconscious fantasy. They are powerfully seductive little "daydreams" that bring the dreamer (the viewer) the image of fulfillment and gratification of their wishes, and most importantly, without effort or delay. When it comes to commercials for adults the addition of the sexual factor brings about an incredibly charged "commercial cartoon." Here, the wish to be fulfilled is saturated with sexual longing and aggression. Beer commercials are perhaps the best example of adult cartoons. What is promised is a magical transformation of an "average guy" into a sexually attractive and powerful idol over whom women swoon. This false transformation, through the agency of the product (the beer), leads to a dimunition in reality testing and an increased tendency toward the use of things (substances) to control anxiety and personal insecurity.

The use of drugs and alcohol employ the same mechanisms as TV to achieve their psychological effects. As the substance user's body and mind are chemically altered, deep unconscious fantasies of security, attractiveness, power, or limitlessness are activated. Hence, Winn (1985) was accurate in describing TV as the "plug-in drug" because the "use" of TV to fend off depression, anxiety, and conflict is identical in its function to that of drugs and alcohol.

The cult of "instant gratification" can be seen to appeal to the universal wish to be the satisfied infant sucking at the breast: a mere cry, the feed and the bliss of satisfied sleep. The reality is unfortunately much more complex, for what we see are increasing numbers of frustrated, angry, and uncooperative children, experiencing their wishes as demands, and their hopes as entitlements.

Postman (1992) estimated that by the age of 65 the average American will have seen approximately 2 million TV commercials! He characterized this as a devouring assault on the psyches of consumers, leading to a "symbol drain" where all possible meaningful images, sacred and profane, have been employed to sell products. From the standpoint of unconscious fantasy, millions of moments of commercial stimulation involving the deepest forces in the human personality will have to be endured due to the impact of television.

When the TV commercial cries out its ominous message, "ring around the collar," the worried housewife's sense of shame is appealed to as a motivator for the purchase of laundry detergent. This seemingly "innocent" use of shame (Wurmser, 1981) draws on a much more regressive and profound experience when we once soiled more than our collars, and this soiling was a powerful occasion for the threat of exclusion from the love and respect of the family. It is a hallmark of commercial advertising that unusually primitive and powerful emotion is mobilized for the sale of products.

An important point remains to be made. Obviously, the quality of mind and personality of the TV or movie viewer plays the decisive role in the "meaning," "impact," or "effects" that the media message will eventually achieve. A competent child or adult has a rich and integrated inner world as well as a related and active interpersonal life. These realities act as strong countervailing forces against any tendency that might emerge in the person to allow for a regressive blurring of the boundaries between the real and the imaginary. Therefore, TV and movies can be genuine means of gathering information or of being entertained in a growth-enhancing (nonaddictive) experience. The personal, familial, and relationship contexts are primary in anchoring a person to the realities of life as he or she deals with dreams and fantasies from whatever source. If relationships within the family are impoverished or absent, a child is much more likely to flee into the world of the media daydream and unconscious wish fulfillment as a defensive maneuver designed to fend off the painful and depressive emotions assicated with his or her life.

In considering pornography, a similar perspective is advanced. The use of pornographic images, actually bizarre and aggressively degraded pictures of women based on the pathological fear of them, become a means to temporarily regulate an empty and chaotic inner experience of the individual who uses such media images (Rosen, 1979).

MEDIA INFLUENCES AND PHASES OF PERSONALITY DEVELOPMENT

Having established the connecting linkage between the power of unconscious fantasy and media image, it is helpful to characterize the dynamics associated with children's use of media at three different points of psychological development: childhood (18 months to about 4 years), latency (7 to 10 years), and adolescence (12 to 18 years). We follow Parens' (1988) outline of these developmental periods.

The Childhood Period

The child during this period experiences the coalesence of basic personality structures. At the end of this phase, we may truly say the child possesses a full inner, which is to say symbolic, life.

Due to the vast array of changes and transformations of this phase, children need their parents to validate, explain, support, mirror, and limit their emerging realities. Their skills, although amazing and exciting, are not fully acquired and are still reversible. Parents act as auxilliary egos to protect against regression, and the fragmenting effects of anxiety. With the rise of the aggressive and sexual tensions of the Oedipal phase (ages 3 to 6), children frequently demand rigid, even harsh, boundaries.

Accordingly, we may point out that young children experience media images through the context and agency of the family. Vulnerability seems to be not so much in the content of specific messages but in the amount of time spent viewing both videos and television. In this phase, excessive consumption of media for a child points to a "gap" in the child's relationship to the parents. Media, in many cases, can be used by the child as a "fix" to compensate for the gap (lack of emotional closeness with the parents) and can therefore become a compulsive, defensive process employed to ward off dysphoria, rage, disorientation, and loneliness.

Excessive television or video viewing in this early developmental period can act as a powerful inhibitor against the child's emerging creative capacity. The stifling of spontaneous imagination due to the "consumption" of external images threatens to flatten the inner world, possibly depersonalize it, and flood it with a set of conventional (externally supplied) images and connotations.

A preponderance of mass-produced imagery likewise flattens the emotional world and decreases the capacity for empathy, concern, and morality itself. This last point is so because true morality emerges out of a context of being able to "feel for" the other, and to adjust the self so as not to hurt or harm the other.

As the child brings "home" the imagery he or she has learned in the beyond-family social-media world, it is the task of the good-enough (not ideal) parents to filter out, explain, or exclude those elements that are damaging or overstimulating. Even the most violent and brutal media images can be neutralized if adequate and reciprocal emotional communicating occurs. Also, violent and sexual imagery becomes compelling to the child to the extent that such themes are powerfully at work within the family system.

Said differently, the "daydreams" and "nightmares" of collective-culture experience can be rendered manageable and nontraumatic if processed through the care and standards of the parents in an emotionally real and compelling way. This naturally assumes that the parents themselves are not fleeing into the dream world of TV to avoid confronting their own limitations, conflicts, and vulnerabilities.

Latency-Aged Children

The tasks of this developmental period include the institution of massive repression against residual sexual and aggressive feelings of the Oedipal period. With marked improvement in ego function and reality testing, the latency-aged child begins to turn to peer relations and experiences in the beyond-family world in a fundamentally new and important way.

For latency-aged boys, conflicts emerge in the form of fantasies, games, war games, robberies, attacks, car crashes, karate, knives, and other forms of defense. The child's consumption of media images will naturally reflect these themes as they seek out opportunities to externalize and dimensionalize their inner worlds as a means of mastery and management.

The mastery of skills, different for each gender, and the acquiring of new capacities looms very large. These children want to watch how older youths and adults handle life. There is a strong voyeuristic component, with a decided, but repressed, awakening of early sexual interests. The repression of sexual impulses and their transformation into all forms of activity and growth make latency-aged children especially vulnerable to media messages that portray them as "little adults."

Their need for mastery produces a love of repetitiveness. This accordingly makes latency-aged children prone to slogans and ideal targets for advertising. The hunger for brightness and activity exposes such children to the danger of advertising images penetrating deeply into the self-concept. This means that instant gratification, the expectation of action and excitement, and a perceptual apparatus accustomed to short, choppy imagery and information becomes internalized in the core of the self.

The Adolescent Period

The adolescent's world is more complex. This phase brings with it a lessening of the primary child–parent bond, and an increasing incorporation of the external world. A central conflict of this phase is battle between giving up the childhood (and childish) relatedness to parents, and the wish to develop the personal and social skills necessary for adult living.

With the decrease in the child–parent bond comes a greater dependence on the peer group, and hence more vulnerability to group influences. What the group wears, watches, smokes, drinks, and thinks impinges forcefully on the not-yet coalesced self. Advertising images are accordingly more persuasive, compelling, and seductively reassuring.

The teen's awareness of his or her vulnerability and realization of the manifold threats and challenges that one must face in dealing with an increasing complex world generates massive anxiety in the adolescent and this must be defended against.

The "loudness" and "shocking" quality of the adolescent's world is a function of using "controlled chaos" to defend against "uncontrollable chaos." Naturally, music is an obvious means of both suppressing inner conflict with outer stimuli and an attempt to master the themes contained in the music.

Further, the need to counteract the rampant internal biological forces of sex and aggression as well as the psychological pressures of separation anxiety lead adolescents to be ideal consumers of "slasher" or gore movies. The fundamental appeal of movies such as *Friday the 13th*, *Halloween*, and *Prom Night* lies in their ability to help the adolescent both control deep-seated anxieties and simultaneously obtain relatively guilt-free pleasure and gratification from the process. Ironically, the internal artistic and psychological mechanisms of these films are fundamentally no different from those of the classic fairytales recorded by the Brothers Grimm. The woodsman in "Little Red Riding Hood," who kills the wolf with his ax, is only slightly different from the hero or heroine who dispatches the slasher maniac in gore movies of today.

The fundamental difference between the two lies in the fact that the "slasher" movie is a degraded fairy tale, and in this "story" the moral lesson is lost. Specifically,the gore and hyperrealism of such films act to overstimulate and destabilize the ego of the viewer. In such an aroused and charged emotional context, the teenage (or preteen) viewer is hard pressed to "learn" from this "story." The creative (learning) space afforded by the fairy tale ("long ago and far away") has been lost. Intense experience without symbolic meaning can lead to an inner world of chaos, impulse, and anxiety.

Finally, adolescence is the developmental period when disorders of regulation—alcoholism, drug abuse, eating disorders, gambling, compulsive work, and sexuality patterns—are all given final form. As Wurmser (1978) pointed out: "the grossest deficiencies in our culture can be found. . . in the emphasis on manipulation, on giving in to demands and not only on gratifying all needs but incessantly creating new ones" (p. 504). Adolescents are naturally more vulnerable to any message that promises both "freedom" from restraint and a sense of narcissistic entitlement to pleasure and reward. For the developing adolescent self, the pernicious impact of advertising's "false promise" exacts its greatest toll.

FINAL THOUGHTS

What, if anything, can be done? Because we know that it is the quality of the parent–child relationship, the quantity of time spent together, and the integrity and health of the family system that is fundamental to the buildup of a healthy inner image world of self (identity sense), it does not seem that merely changing the content of media programs can, in and of itself, lead to significant and lasting results.

Hope seems to lie in the education of parents and children in the underlying dynamics and long-term consequences of excessive TV viewing and media consumption. Whereas benefits are to be derived from increased knowledge and the experience of quality entertainment, the overwhelming emphasis must be placed on counteracting the most negative effects of television (i.e., the erosion of the reality sense, hyperstimulation of emotion, the isolation of the child from the family and peer group, and the installation of the belief that the possession of commodities and products will lead to security and happiness). Winn's notable attempts at helping parents (and schools) reduce children's exposure to TV viewing seems to be a step in the right direction.

From a psychological and developmental perspective, we must work to not allow our dreams and those of our children to become manipulated by commercial interests whose primary goal is the sale of products through the "capture" of the dream.

In an attempt to deal with the problem of the media, we must be careful not to reify it as if it exists outside of the individuals who create it, sponsor it, and consume it. Thus, there is no medium, per se, that acts with a will of its own to enslave and control our children and our families. The true nature of the threat exists in the erosion of the cohesion of families, relationships, and the psychic structure that is the internal map and compass guiding human activity.

I close with a quotation from Wurmser (1978). In his monumental study of the causes of drug addiction— *The Hidden Dimension*—he observed:

> Just as the pollution of air and water has been recognized as a self-suffocating factor only in our culture because of the tremendous expansion of technology, we have to learn how our culture and society far more potently than earlier cultures can attain or destroy those values which hold individual, family and society together: inner integration and self-discipline, integrity and honesty, beauty and a mature form of love, hierarchies and boundaries. (p. 505)

REFERENCES

Bowlby, J. (1988). *A secure base: Clinical applications of attachment theory*. London: Routledge.

Chasseguet-Smirgel, J. (1986). *Sexuality and mind: The role of the father and the mother in the psyche*. New York: New York University Press.

Freud, S. (1963). *Introductory lectures on psychoanalysis* (standard edition, 16). London: Hogarth Press. (Original work published in 1916)

Freud, S. (1964). *New introductory lectures on psychoanalysis* (standard edition, 22). London: Hogarth Press. (Original work published in 1933)

Mahler, M., Pine, F., & Bergman, A. (1975). *The psychological birth of the human infant.* New York: Basic Books.

Parens, H. (1988). Psychoanalytic explorations on the impact of the threat of nuclear disaster on the young. In H. B. Levine, D. Jacobs, & L. Rubin (Eds.), *Psychoanalytic explorations of the nuclear threat: Aggression,projection and identification* (pp. 123–132). Hillsdale, NJ: The Analytic Press.

Postman, N. (1992). *Technopoly: The surrender of culture to technology.* New York: Knopf.

Rosen, I. (1979). *Sexual deviation.* Oxford: Oxford University Press.

Segal, H. (1991). *Dream, phantasy and art.* London: Tavistock/Routledge.

Winn, M. (1985). *The plug-in drug: Television, children and the family.* New York: Penguin Books.

Winnicott, D. W. (1978). *Through paediatrics to psychoanalysis.* London: Hogarth Press.

Wurmser, L. (1978). *The hidden dimension: Psychodynamics in compulsive drug use.* New York: Aronson.

Wurmser, L. (1981). *The mask of shame.* Baltimore: Johns Hopkins University Press.

Part III

EFFECTS OF VIOLENCE AND HORROR

10

TELEVISION, FILMS, AND THE EMOTIONAL LIFE OF CHILDREN

Andre P. Derdeyn, M.D.
University of Virginia Health Sciences Center

Jeffrey M. Turley, M.D.
CSW Medical Center, Wiesbaden Air Force Base Germany

Selma Fraiberg (1987) introduced her classic article, "The Mass Media: New Schoolhouse for Children," with a look back at her childhood. She began:

> Many, many years ago when I was a child, a home was a shelter against the dangers outside. I had heard, as a child, that there was savagery in the world, that men committed murder, that homes were burglarized, that a child had been kidnapped and ravished, and that in far off lands there were revolutions and wars. But all these things happened in another world. Murders, kidnappers, and burglars lived on another planet—not so far away as dragons, witches, and monsters, but almost as far—and in any case that had not much more reality for me than the creatures of the fairy tales. (p. 573)

Fraiberg pointed out later in her article: "For today's child, a home is no longer a shelter against the dangers outside. The child is a fascinated spectator of the whole of our world" (p. 574). She continued:

> When the worst fears of a child can be confirmed in reality, the child loses his own best means of dealing with external danger. . . . None of us can imagine

131

what it is like to be a child today, to be helpless against the most extreme dangers and to be confronted in his own living room, in his classroom, with the full knowledge of the real dangers that exist in our world. (p. 578)

My first impulse is to vehemently agree, yes, children are surely exposed today by way of the media to more worrisome information, tacky domestic drama, and outright violence than any time in the past. Other responses also occur to me. Perhaps Fraiberg's home was uniformly serene and protective and is an unfair basis on which to measure the differences in how children are growing up today. Parents in the best of homes do and say things that make their children very anxious. Parental arguments have always been extremely concerning for children, although fear of divorce itself has surely become more common since the 1970s. Parental discussions about, if not arguments regarding, financial problems are regularly absorbed, distorted, and amplified by children. Unless they have parental concerns about money presented to them routinely, children tend to conjure up a desperate crisis and come up with solutions such as selling their bicycles or other prized possessions. Children have always fed upon the crumbs of parental anxiety or dissention, producing great anxiety within themselves that they tend to deal with in isolation. Generally, they do not share such worries with their parents because their perception is, and what makes them the most anxious is, that they see their parents as helpless to manage the problem or to agree with each other. The point is that unpalatable, difficult-to-manage information has always been provided to children and did not await the development of varied media modes. In fact, children are much more likely to be propelled to overwhelming anxiety by parental disturbances than by what they see or hear via media presentations.

A problem with media material that is widely recognized is that often viewing is done by children who are not in the presence of their parents. Theoretically, this prevents the child from being able to discuss confusion or concerns with the parent or to have it more fully explained by the parent. I am not sure how much difference this makes, however, for parents are not particularly talkative during television shows or films, and if a child is really anxious about something, he or she is just as likely to not talk about it at all as to share his or her concerns.

The lack of supervision, however, can allow a child to see things that most parents would not intend for their children to see, if they took the time to consider it. The concerns here are the recognized ones of explicit sexual matters and physical violence, in addition, of course, to the issue of the child spending excessive time being passively entertained.

I now move on to a clinical case involving a 13-year-old boy who was preoccupied with horror films. Working with one of these films, instead of categorically rejecting it as an unhealthy influence on this boy, allowed for a helpful therapy for the boy and an eye-opening experience for the boy's therapist and the therapist's supervisor.

CASE REPORT

Carl is a 13-year-old boy committed to a psychiatric facility after he became intoxicated on alcohol and destroyed the inside of his guardians' home with an axe. In the year prior to this hospitalization, his social and school functioning had deteriorated badly. Previously, a high-achieving and well-mannered student, he had become disruptive in class and refused to complete assignments. He became passively defiant of adult authority in his home and became involved in petty theft, truancy, and episodic alcohol abuse. His choice of friends changed gradually from teenagers who met with his guardians' approval to those who did not. He was popular with, and extremely loyal to, his many friends. There was no prior history of property destruction, assault, or cruelty to animals.

Development and Family History

The patient's mother had several brief psychiatric hospitalizations for bipolar illness during his infancy and early childhood. During this time, Carl was cared for by various relatives in succession. His early childhood behavior was marked by apathy, passivity, oppositionalism, and defiance of adult authority. At the age of 9, his mother abandoned him abruptly and absolutely. The next year, Carl was placed in the legal custody of his maternal uncle and aunt, who remain his current guardians. Married only a few years at that time, they had made the decision not to have children; they reluctantly took responsibility for this 10-year-old out of a sense of family duty. The uncle, an army lieutenant colonel now retired and working in an accounting firm, provided strict limits and clear standards of behavior for the boy. Carl quickly responded to this, spending fewer hours in front of the television and more time engaged in sports. He became popular among a group of friends and began to perform well in school. A period of 2 to 3 years of high functioning followed. Coincident with the onset of puberty came a return of defiant behaviors and Carl's concern about his place in the family.

Treatment

Medical and neurologic evaluations and a period of inpatient behavioral observation were carried out. Carl was passively noncompliant with staff authority. No disturbance of mood, impulse control, or social behavior was observed. Carl slept and ate well.

Individual psychotherapy and periodic family therapy were begun. Carl spent the initial individual meetings complaining about his uncle, school teachers, and other authority figures. He complained of being misunderstood and of being unable or unwilling to meet the expectations that these people had of him. He mentioned several times his resentment regarding his uncle and aunt's prohibiting his viewing of horror movies. He complained bitterly that they were prohibiting him from watching the films despite the fact that they had never seen one themselves and did not understand his interest in them. He expressed worry about his own preoccupation with death and killing. "It's as if I'm addicted to horror movies. Once you get started, it's very hard to stop." Initial family sessions were punctuated by frequent angry diatribes by the uncle and long periods of sullen silence on the part of the patient.

In individual work, the patient's frequent silences were often broken by his mention of horror movies. The therapist's inquiries about Carl's thoughts and feelings about them were followed by silent resistance. This pattern, which lasted several sessions, was resolved by the therapist's suggesting that the questions about the movies perhaps betrayed the same ignorance that his uncle demonstrated, and that perhaps the patient was experiencing the therapist as disapproving or critical. Although this interpretation was not accepted in any visible way, Carl responded by continuing on with a discussion of the films, his interest in them, and his anger that "adults don't understand." His favorite movies were the *Friday the 13th* and *A Nightmare on Elm Street* series. Although the films are artistically distinct, they have many characteristics in common. The bogeymen have been described as supernatural hybrids of the earlier monsters (Frankenstein, Werewolf, Mr. Hyde, Mummy) with the psychopathic murderer common to more recent genres of horror film. The bogeymen prey upon teenagers or young adults, many of whom are murdered during moral lapses such as making love or using drugs and alcohol. Typically, one teenager, who is depicted early in the film as timid and vulnerable, emerges as the most virtuous and resourceful. This person survives to vanquish the monster.

Viewing the Film

The therapist and patient agreed to a contract to spend 15 minutes of subsequent sessions watching videotape of a horror movie and 30 minutes to discuss the thoughts and feelings this experience provoked. Carl chose *A Nightmare On Elm Street Part IV*, *The Dream Master*, featuring the villain

Freddy Kruegger, a scarred supernatural killer with a glove consisting of five stilettos. Carl explained that Freddy was "conceived of the sperm of a thousand psychopaths." His mother, a nun, served God by working at a prison for the criminally insane. Accidentally locked up with the inmates one night, she was raped by them all and subsequently conceived her son. She died in childbirth, producing the ultimate "bad seed."

While explaining the details of the movie to the therapist, it occurred to Carl for the first time that loss of his mother was the motive behind Freddy's otherwise unexplainable violence. When the therapist suggested that perhaps the patient knew how angry such a loss could make a person, Carl spent the balance of the session angrily describing the deprivation he had suffered. Although the patient appeared physically normal, he felt his mother caused what he thought were dysmorphic body features and short stature by giving him soft drinks rather than milk. Carl seemed to identify himself with Freddy's ugliness and anger. There was also some envy of Freddy. Freddy has "ultimate power." He cannot be controlled by human means, and he knows no remorse for the destruction that results from his limitless rage. He is invulnerable. As Carl put it, "He can't die, he is already dead." Identification with Freddy's victims was strong as well.

The story is set among a group of high school students who conform to easily recognizable personal qualities and vulnerabilities. Thus, the victims have many qualities similar to those of the principal audience. The protagonist is a timid, underconfident 16-year-old girl with secret romantic longings for the football star. Like the patient, all the teenagers in the film appear to come from broken families. The few adults depicted exhibit inadequacies as parents, with problems ranging from excessive alcohol use to being preoccupied with their own lives. They are overtly hostile to their children.

During his natural life, Freddy Kruegger was a child-molesting murderer. Eventually, he had been cornered by the parents on Elm Street and burned alive by them. His revenge is to kill these parents' adolescent children, stalking them in their dreams. In *Nightmare on Elm Street, Part IV, The Dream Master*, the adolescents are seized abruptly during dreams in which they have placed themselves in compromising circumstances. One boy is stabbed during a masturbatory fantasy, another while sleeping in his history examination. The vain, body-centered beauty is transformed into a giant roach as she becomes drowsy while lifting weights. Her face is pulled off after being stuck to the adhesive in a huge roach trap, exposing the ugly insect inside, which is crushed by Freddy. The adolescents are very much on their own against Freddy. As Carl put it, "These parents are worse than useless. They can't protect their kids from Freddy. They don't even believe their kids." One mother treats her daughter's "adolescent anxiety" by drugging her with tranquilizers slipped into her drink. Discovering this, the daughter screams, "You've just killed me," which indeed turns out to be the case. The virtuous, timid protagonist is surprised to find that she becomes armed with the best features of her fallen classmates as they die one by one. Taking this terrific strength from her peer group, she forces herself to confront the monster and destroys him.

After Carl expressed his admiration of the "guys who make these stories up," the therapist suggested Carl imagine a film that he might make. First he imagined himself as Freddy, then constructed a scene wherein his uncle, dressed in full military uniform, was Freddy. Carl imagined himself as the lone surviving teenager. When Freddy–uncle raises his lethal hand to strike, the boy chops it off. "Then I'd joke: 'Somebody give that man a hand.' " The sadistic humor was followed by complaints about the uncle's humiliating criticisms and stern emotional distance. Carl commented, "He knows just how to hurt me." Empathic exploration of Carl's pain exposed his previously unrealized intense wish for approval by and closeness with his uncle and aunt. Carl made use of this new emotional experience in family therapy by approaching his guardians more with his pain than with his anger. This allowed them to recognize and express their own more tender feelings for him.

Following a series of successful family sessions and home passes, the patient was discharged to the care of his guardians. He was free of symptoms and functioning well at 6-month follow-up. Although he still watched horror movies, he no longer felt compelled to do so.

DISCUSSION

Bettelheim (1975) pointed out that fairy tales provide children meaning for their developmental tasks and help them to manage the fears and anxieties they experience. Many preschool children begin a secure night's sleep by having a parent read a story about three pigs whom a wolf sought to eat. The two pigs who quickly built shelters of straw and of wood so that they could play the rest of the day were devoured by the wolf. The third built his house of brick and would go out early in the mornings to obtain food while the wolf was still asleep. He eventually scalded to death and ate the big bad wolf. According to Bettelheim (1975), this story "teaches the nursery age child in a most enjoyable and dramatic form that we must not be lazy and take things easy, for if we do we may perish. Intelligence, planning, and foresight, combined with hard labor, will make us victorious over even our most ferocious enemy — the wolf!" (pp. 41–42). It may at first seem odd that a child would choose to be frightened at bedtime, a time often already characterized by anxiety brought on by darkness and by the prospect of being alone. The fairy tale initially increases that anxiety, then provides a mechanism for relief. The child's serial identifications with the helpless and terrified, then resourceful, then victorious pig lends strength to the child's struggle with his or her anxieties and facilitates sleep.

Young children require little in the way of graphic or literal images to produce the anxiety necessary to motivate mastery. Their capacity for imagination and magical thinking are sufficient to have the desired effect. In fact, a more graphic or realistic presentation (e.g., a film of a wolf thrashing in a caldron of boiling water or of pigs devouring flesh from his carcass) would likely flood the young child with fear and make a mastery experience impossible.

Fears of bodily damage, object loss, and the destructiveness of thoughts are shared with the preschooler by people of all ages. The adolescent, however is not likely to enjoy a fairy tale read at bedtime. The teenager's imagination is no longer quite so keen and literal as it was earlier in life. A consideration of both the uniqueness and universality of the themes of adolescent development helps to show the parallel between fairy tales for preschool-age children and horror films for adolescents.

Central developmental tasks of adolescence revolve about leaving the protection and control of parents, achieving relative emotional autonomy, and thus forming an adult identity. Developing an independent identity both in intimate relationships and in occupational situations is a challenge attended by considerable anxiety. As the fantasied protection of parents dissipates, there is a growing awareness of the possibility of injury and disease and the certainty of death and of the vagaries of love relationships and occupational success, adding further to an awareness of vulnerability.

Carl had many concerns about himself that were responsible for considerable suffering on his part and consternation on the part of his guardians. He worried about his worth to others, peers and adults alike. He worried about his bodily integrity and form. He felt himself to be unloved, unrespected, unheeded, and powerless. He worried about his sexual and aggressive impulses. These were concerns shared by the characters in the films he watched and by the audience of his peers at the shopping mall cinema where he spent so much of his time. Although he envied the monster's power and lack of remorse, he identified with the helpless victims of terrible danger, and, especially with the one among them who refused to accept the position of impotence. This one teenager survived to fight and win. He shared in her victory over and over in a vain attempt to master his own miseries. His longing to be accepted and cared for by his guardians was uncommunicated to them and complicated by the normal adolescent impulse to renounce dependency. His guardians made clear the emotional distance they wished to maintain and openly refused to allow him to consider them his parents. Without a secure attachment, his first attempts at separation were superficial and unsuccessful. He adopted a style of dress and a preference for music belonging to a peer group unacceptable to his guardians. These changes were unwelcomed by his uncle and resisted with some cruelty. Carl's subsequent rebellion took the form of antisocial behavior and the drunken cataclysm of anger that led to his hospitalization.

The therapist's use of the horror film as a means of grasping and working through unconscious conflict employed a technique common to the play therapy of younger children. Observation of play alerts the therapist to the repetitive but unsuccessful patterns of behavior that the child uses in attempting to master loss, trauma, or unconscious conflict. Because these patterns are unsuccessful, they often perpetuate anxiety rather than relieve it. The task of the therapist is to gain access to this material through play, and to interpret it appropriately to the child. The child is thus guided toward a process of repetition leading to mastery (Walder, 1933). If Carl's "addiction" to horror movies can be considered as an unsuccessful attempt to master anxiety, then it follows that the therapist's task is to join the "play." Of course, any therapist's willingness to accept the legitimacy of, and take interest in, the preoccupations of his adolescent patient is essential for a therapeutic alliance. Discussion with the therapist about the thoughts, concerns, and motives of the characters in the horror films allowed Carl access to his preconscious conflicts. Insight and the experience of being accepted by a trusted adult helped this adolescent to realize his affection for his guardians and to muster the courage to express his need for their love and acceptance.

Although there may be a population of children at risk to become violent in response to violent media images, the authors suggest that the modern horror movie may satisfy for the adolescent the same function that the bedtime fairy tale does for a younger child. Seen in this way, the popularity of this art form can be understood rather than feared. A reflex condemnation by parents and mental health professionals of any entertainment so widely enjoyed by adolescents as modern horror movies is not only irrational but also disrespectful of our young people.

REFERENCES

Fraiberg, S. (1987). The mass media: New schoolhouse for children. In L. Fraiberg, (Ed.), *Selected writings of Selma Fraiberg* (pp. 573–587). Columbus: Ohio State University Press.

Bettelheim, B. (1975). *The uses of enchantment: The meaning and importance of fairy tales* (pp. 41–42). New York: Vintage Books, Random House.

Walder, R. (1933, October 29). The psychoanalytic theory of play. *Psychoanalitic Quarterly, 2*, 208–224.

11

CONFRONTING CHILDREN'S FRIGHT RESPONSES TO MASS MEDIA

Joanne Cantor
University of Wisconsin—Madison

Anyone who has grown up in our culture knows that exposure to television shows, films, and other mass media presentations depicting danger, injury, bizarre images, and terror-stricken victims can scare an audience. Most of us seem to be able to remember at least one specific program or movie that terrified us when we were a child and that made us nervous, remained in our thoughts, and affected other aspects of our behavior for some time afterwards. Anecdotal evidence abounds, and, although research interest in this topic has been sporadic over the years, studies published in every decade starting with the 1930s have indicated that transitory fright responses to mass media stimuli are quite typical, and that enduring, and sometimes severe, emotional disturbances occur in a substantial proportion of children (Cantor, 1991).

The research literature also shows that parents are frequently unaware of their children's fright reactions (Cantor & Reilly, 1982; Preston, 1941), and that children are widely exposed to televised stimuli that were originally intended for adults and that are typically considered inappropriate for young children (Meyrowitz, 1985). A study by Sparks (1986), for example, reported that almost half of a sample of 4- to 10- year-olds had seen *Poltergeist* and *Jaws*, and substantial proportions of the sample had seen

Halloween and *Friday the Thirteenth*. Most of this viewing occurred in the home; most often it was on cable TV. Recent research shows that a substantial portion of children say they are sorry they have seen certain programs because of the intensity of the fright reactions they have experienced (Cantor & Reilly, 1982; Palmer, Hockett, & Dean, 1983). However, research also shows that children often say they enjoy being frightened, and that they do not want to be restricted from viewing scary media (Blumer, 1933; Cantor & Reilly, 1982; Sparks, 1986; Wilson, Hoffner, & Cantor, 1987).

DEVELOPMENTAL DIFFERENCES IN FRIGHT RESPONSES

Since the early 1980s, in collaboration mainly with Cindy Hoffner, Glenn Sparks, and Barb Wilson, I have been conducting research to find answers to two major questions: What types of mass media stimuli and events frighten children the most, and what are the best methods of preventing or reducing children's media-induced fears? Very early in our study of these issues, it became clear that a developmental perspective was appropriate. In other words, we have found that a child's age is a major determinant of the things that will be frightening and the techniques that will be most effective in counteracting emotional disturbances. It is simply not true that as children get older they become less and less susceptible to media-produced emotional disturbances. As children mature cognitively, some things become less likely to disturb them, whereas other things become potentially more upsetting.

Using observations and theories from developmental psychology as guidelines, particularly theories of cognitive development, we have conducted a series of experiments and surveys. The experiments have had the advantage of testing rigorously controlled variations in program content and viewing conditions, using a combination of self-reports, physiological responses, the coding of facial expressions of emotion, and behavioral measures. In some of our experiments, we have taken mass media stimuli and manipulated them in theoretically relevant ways, or, in rare instances, we have created our own stimuli. In other experiments, we have presented different treatments prior to exposing subjects to the same program. Usually, we have compared the responses of different age groups, while randomly assigning subjects to conditions within age groups.

Although our interest in strict control in experiments has meant testing children under somewhat artificial circumstances, our surveys have provided information about developmental differences in the responses of children who had voluntarily exposed themselves to a particular mass media offering in their natural environment, without any researcher intervention (see Cantor, 1989). Broad generalizations from our research are summarized here.

Perceptual Attributes of Threats

The first generalization is that the relative importance of the immediately perceptible components of a fear-inducing media stimulus decreases as a child's age increases. Research on cognitive development indicates that, in general, very young children react to stimuli predominantly in terms of their perceptible characteristics, and that, with increasing maturity, children respond more and more to the conceptual aspects of stimuli. Piaget referred to young children's tendency to react to things as they appear in immediate, egocentric perception as *concreteness* of thought (see Flavell, 1963); Bruner (1966) characterized the thought of preschool children as *perceptually dominated*. A variety of studies have shown that young children tend to sort, match, and remember items on the basis of their perceptible attributes, and that around the age of 7 this tendency is increasingly replaced by the tendency to use functional or conceptual groupings (e.g., Melkman, Tversky, & Baratz, 1981).

More specifically, preschool children (approximately 3 to 5 years old) are much more likely to be frightened by something that *looks* scary but is actually harmless than by something that looks attractive but is actually harmful; for older elementary schoolchildren (approximately 9 to 11 years), appearance carries much less weight, relative to the behavior or destructive potential of a character, animal, or object.

One set of data that supports this generalization comes from a survey we conducted (Cantor & Sparks, 1984), asking parents to name the programs and films that had frightened their children the most. In this survey, parents of preschool children most often mentioned shows with grotesque-looking, unreal characters, such as the television series, "The Incredible Hulk," and the feature film, *The Wizard of Oz*; parents of older elementary schoolchildren more often mentioned shows (like *The Amityville Horror*) that involved threats without a strong visual component, and that required a good deal of imagination to comprehend. Sparks (1986) replicated these findings when children responded themselves.

A second study that supports this generalization was a laboratory study involving an episode of the "Incredible Hulk" series (Sparks & Cantor, 1986). In this study, we concluded that preschool children's intense reactions to this program were partially due to their overresponse to the visual image of the Hulk character. When we tracked subjects' levels of fear during different parts of the program, we found that preschool children experienced the most fear after the attractive, mild-mannered hero was transformed into the monstrous-looking Hulk. Older elementary school-children, in contrast, reported the least fear at this time, because they understood that the Hulk was really the benevolent hero in another physical form, and that he always used his superhuman powers on the side of the "good guys," and against the "bad guys."

In another study (Hoffner & Cantor, 1985), we tested the effect of appearance more directly, by creating a story in four versions, so that a major character was either attractive and grandmotherly looking or ugly and grotesque. The character's appearance was factorially varied with her behavior—she was depicted as behaving either kindly or cruelly in an early scene. In judging how nice or mean the character was and in predicting what she would do in the subsequent scene, preschool children were more influenced than older children (6–7 and 9–10 years) by the character's looks and less influenced than older children by her kind or cruel behavior. As the age of the child increased, the character's looks became less important and her behavior carried increasing weight. A follow-up study revealed that all age groups engaged in physical appearance stereotyping in the absence of information about the character's behavior.

Fantastic Versus Realistic Threats

A second generalization that comes out of our studies is that as children mature, they become more responsive to realistic than to fantastic dangers depicted in the media. Data on trends in children's fears in general (e.g., Angelino, Dollins, & Mech, 1956) suggest that very young children are more likely than older children and adolescents to fear things that are not real, in the sense that their occurrence in the real world is impossible (e.g., monsters). The development of more "mature" fears seems to presuppose the acquisition of knowledge regarding the objective dangers posed by different situations. One important component of this knowledge includes an understanding of the distinction between reality and fantasy. Much research has been conducted on the child's gradual acquisition of the various components of the fantasy–reality distinction (see Flavell, 1963; Morison & Gardner, 1978). Until a child understands the distinction, he or she will be unable to understand that something that is not real cannot pose a threat, and thus the reality or fantasy status of a media depiction should have little effect on the fear it evokes. As the child comes increasingly to understand this distinction and increasingly appreciates the implications of real-world threats, depictions of real dangers should gain in fear-evoking potential relative to depictions of fantasy dangers.

This generalization is supported by our survey of parents, mentioned earlier (Cantor & Sparks, 1984). In general, the tendency to mention fantasy offerings, depicting events that could not possibly occur in the real world, as sources of fear, decreased as the child's age increased, and the tendency to mention fictional offerings, depicting events that might possibly occur, increased with age. Again, Sparks (1986) replicated these findings using children's self-reports.

Abstractness of Threats

Our third generalization is that as children mature, they become frightened by media depictions involving increasingly abstract concepts. This generalization is clearly consistent with the general sources of children's fears (Angelino et al., 1956). It is also consistent with theories and findings in cognitive development (e.g., Flavell, 1963), which indicate that the ability to think abstractly emerges relatively late in development.

Data supporting this generalization come from a survey we conducted on children's responses to the television movie, *The Day After* (Cantor, Wilson, & Hoffner, 1986). Many people were concerned about young children's reactions to this movie, which depicted the devastation of a Kansas community by a nuclear attack, but our research led us to predict that the youngest children would be the least affected by it. We conducted a telephone survey (using random sampling) the night after the broadcast of this movie. As we predicted, children under 12 were much less disturbed by the film than were teenagers, and parents were the most disturbed. The very youngest children were not upset or frightened at all. Most of the parents of the younger children who had seen the film could think of other shows that had frightened their child more during the preceding year. Most of the parents of the teenagers could not. We conclude that the findings are due to the fact that the emotional impact of the film comes from the contemplation of the potential annihilation of the earth as we know it — a concept that is beyond the grasp of the young child. The visual depictions of injury in this movie were quite mild compared to what most children have become used to seeing on television.

Effectiveness of Coping Strategies

The fourth generalization coming out of this research is that different strategies are appropriate for different ages when attempting to help children cope with their media-induced fears (Cantor & Wilson, 1988). In general, preschool children benefit more from "noncognitive" than from "cognitive strategies"; both cognitive and noncognitive strategies can be effective for older elementary schoolchildren, although this age group tends to prefer cognitive strategies. For example, "telling your child it's not real" is a very popular strategy among parents. When we questioned the parents of the children who had participated in one of our studies (Wilson & Cantor, 1987), 80% of them said they used this strategy, regardless of their child's age. Yet, our research also shows that this technique is largely ineffective for young children. In an experiment by Cantor and Wilson (1984), instructions to remember that what was being seen was not real caused a scene from *The Wizard of Oz* to be less frightening for 9 and 10-year-olds but did not reduce the fear of 3- to 5-years-olds.

In another experiment (Wilson & Cantor, 1987), we concluded that another cognitive strategy, verbally explaining the nonthreatening nature of a scary stimulus, may help older elementary schoolchildren, but it may actually "boomerang" with younger children. In this study, second and third graders who heard reassuring information about snakes (for example, that most snakes are not poisonous) were somewhat less likely to be frightened by the "snake pit" scene from the movie *Raiders of the Lost Ark*. However, kindergarten and first-grade children seem to have only partially understood this information, and for them negative reactions were more likely if they had heard the supposedly reassuring information than if they had not.

In contrast, less cognitively demanding approaches, such as visual desensitization (i.e., gradual visual exposure to a threatening stimulus), can reduce that object's fear-evoking potential for children in kindergarten through elementary school. This effect was demonstrated in the same experiment, involving *Raiders of the Lost Ark* (Wilson & Cantor, 1987). In this study, children were shown filmed footage of snakes gradually increasing in their closeness to the camera and in their size and amount of movement. Children who saw this footage tended to be less scared when they subsequently saw the "snake pit" scene than were those who had not previously seen the snake footage.

We have tested other techniques as well (e.g., Cantor, Sparks, & Hoffner, 1988; Hoffner & Cantor, 1990), and it is interesting to note that children's self-reports of the effectiveness of techniques have been shown to be consistent with our overall generalizations. In a self-report study (Wilson et al., 1987), we found that preschool children favored physical coping strategies, such as holding a cuddly toy or having something to eat or drink; older elementary schoolchildren favored cognitive strategies, such as telling themselves that what they were seeing was not real.

IMPLICATIONS FOR PARENTAL GUIDANCE

A general implication that emerges from the findings presented here is that how a child will respond to a particular mass media depiction is not always intuitively obvious from a parent's perspective. When we give advice to parents on how to guide their children's viewing, they must be made aware that it is not easy to categorize television shows and films as either "scary" or "not scary." Whether or not a program will be problematic for a particular child depends on many things, one of which is the child's age. Other things that might contribute to the impact of a program have to do with a child's own experiences and situation. In a recent study (Hoffner & Cantor, 1990), we found that children who believed that a depicted threat existed in their local environment were more frightened than were those who thought that it did not. Thus, a child on a first seaside vacation is apt to be more frightened by a film like *Jaws* than a child who has never been to the beach. Furthermore, a child left alone in the house for the first time is likely to be more upset by a film about someone terrorizing a babysitter than a youngster watching in the company of parents would be. Such generalizations may seem to amount to "common sense" in many cases, but it is important for parents to look at programs not from their adult perspective but from the perspective of the child. Many plots that seem whimsical or absurd to an adult can seem extremely real to a child. Most parents would be astonished to know that in our survey of responses to *The Day After* (Cantor et al., 1986), both "Captain Kangaroo" and *Charlotte's Web* were mentioned as programs that were more upsetting to preschool children than was this movie about nuclear holocaust.

In addition, many series that seem inherently benign can contain threatening issues and messages. In our survey of parents, we were more than a little surprised to see "Little House on the Prairie" mentioned as a source of fright for many children (Cantor & Sparks, 1984). What we discovered is that this program and others routinely shown in an after-school time slot often deal with extremely upsetting themes such as child molestation, kidnapping, and accidental death.

Exposure to Realistic Drama

Recently we conducted a study of the implications of children's exposure to dramatic depictions of realistic life-threatening events such as these (Cantor & Omdahl, 1991). We exposed children to dramatized events involving a fatal house fire or a drowning, taken from widely viewed television shows and movies, or to control programs depicting benign scenes involving fire or water. As expected, the threatening scenes induced more fear while viewing than did their neutral counterparts. In addition, children exposed to a particular threat subsequently rated similar events as more likely and the consequences as more severe; and reported more worry about such happenings than subjects exposed to neutral depictions. Moreover, in these children, liking for activities closely related to the observed threats was reduced. Specifically, children who had just seen a movie about a drowning reported a lower level of interest in the sport of canoeing than did children who had not seen the drowning; children who had just seen a television drama about a fatal house fire were averse to building a fire in a fireplace and much less interested than were those children who had not seen that drama. These findings suggest that the effects of exposure to scary media presentations may have broad and enduring implications in the life of a child.

Exposure to News

This brings us to the question of even more realistic presentations: news and current events programming. In our parent survey (Sparks & Cantor, 1984), news programs were among the top 10 offenders in terms of the frequency with which they were cited as distressing to children. At the time the survey was conducted, the most frequently mentioned news item was the Atlanta child murders case. Although studies of children's reactions to upsetting media events have been conducted from time to time (e.g., Wright, Kunkel, Pinon, & Huston, 1989), little attention was devoted to this concern until the outbreak of the War in the Persian Gulf in early 1991. At the time this chapter was written and first presented (November of 1990), I argued for the need to study children's emotional responses to upsetting news stories. The United States' entrance into the Gulf War and the media coverage thereof presented a unique opportunity to study such reactions.

We conducted a survey during the Persian Gulf War, in which we questioned a random sample of parents of children in Grades 1, 4, 7, and 11 (Cantor, Mares, & Oliver, 1993). The survey produced several findings of relevance here. First, a sizable number of parents reported that their child had been upset by television coverage of the war: Approximately one fourth mentioned the coverage spontaneously when asked to name something on television that had upset their child recently, and when asked directly about the impact of the coverage 45% said their child had been upset. Not surprisingly, the intensity of parents' responses was significantly correlated with the responses they observed in their children. An even stronger relationship was observed, however, between parents' attitudes toward the war and their child's perceived reaction. Moreover, we found that parents' reports of their own exposure to televised war news was more strongly related to their child's emotional response to the war coverage than to their own response to the war.

Of theoretical relevance was the finding that although there were no significant differences between age groups in the prevalence of negative emotional reactions to the coverage, children in different grades reportedly were upset by different aspects of the coverage. These differences were consistent with the developmental differences observed in our other studies. Parents of younger children, but not of older children, stressed the visual aspect of the coverage and the direct, concrete consequences of combat in their descriptions of the elements that had disturbed their child; as the child's age increased, the more abstract, conceptual aspects of the coverage and of the war in general were cited by parents as upsetting their child.

Challenges for Parents

The findings on the prevalence of emotional disturbances due to war coverage make it reasonable to speculate that the news media's current obsession with sensationalized violence, terror, and human misery (Kneale, 1988) can create an extraordinarily upsetting environment for children and an enormous two-fold challenge for parents who want to behave responsibly.

The first part of the challenge for parents is to decide how much of the news their children should be exposed to. At first, it might seem that this question is inappropriate. Indeed, most parents might consider restrictions on entertainment programming a matter worthy of debate, but they are apt to consider the news "educational" and therefore to assume that free access is the only defensible policy. But some people rightly question the age at which it is appropriate to burden children with graphic and gory images of traffic accident victims, terminally ill AIDS patients, sobbing parents witnessing the loss of their children in fires, and the like. The current prevalence of "tabloid" programs, such as "A Current Affair" and "Hard Copy," and the general tendency of news programs to present vivid visual images of brutal violence seem to make the lurid details of mayhem more available than ever before to anyone with access to a television set. Joshua Meyrowitz (1985) expressed the general problem well in *No Sense of Place* when he said:

> The widespread use of television is equivalent to a broad social decision to allow young children to be present at wars and funerals, courtships and seductions, criminal plots and cocktail parties . . . Young children may not fully understand the issues of sex, death, crime, and money that are presented to them on television . . . Yet television nevertheless exposes them to many topics and behaviors that adults have spent several centuries trying to keep hidden from children. Television thrusts children into a complex adult world, and it *provides the impetus for children to ask the meanings of actions and words they would not yet have heard or read about without television.* (p. 242, italics added)

The last sentence of this quotation brings us to the second facet of the challenge that exposure to current events in the mass media presents to parents. Our research shows that it is extremely hard to reassure children about real threats, no matter how unlikely the dangers are to be directly experienced by the child. And the process is further complicated by the need in some cases to warn children about the existence of a threat that they must avoid, without inducing an overly intense emotional reaction.

An article that appeared in *Parenting* magazine (Jacobson, 1989) captures the situation well. The author recounts his own experience:

> A few nights ago our six-year-old daughter crawled into bed with us, wanting to cuddle. She was upset. She said she'd had a bad dream. "What about?" I inquired. "Eagles? Elephants?" She shook her head and asked me if the police had caught "that man" yet.
>
> "What man?"
>
> "The one on the fire escape with the gun who shot through the window. The one on TV." . . .
>
> I could see this was a problem. How many other stocking-faced slashers and pump-gun snipers lurked inside my kid's tender little sponge of a brain? How many snapshots of AIDS sufferers, starving children, chemical-war victims? Attempting to swing into a purposeful parent mode, I had immediately pulled up a chair and told my daughter, yes, it is true, these terrible things happen. I'd tried to assure her, however, that they don't happen that often—that's why it's called "news." But, as is frequently the case when I try to impart my reassurances about the state of the world, those words left my lips and sank like stones. (p. 28)

The difficulty that the father was facing in this situation can be understood in the context of two of the studies discussed here. In our study of responses to *Raiders of the Lost Ark* (Wilson & Cantor, 1987), we found that telling young children that most snakes are not poisonous had the opposite effect of reassuring them. And in our study in which we manipulated the apparent proximity of a depicted threat (Cantor & Hoffner, 1990), we found it extremely difficult to communicate information about the likelihood of encountering a threat, and especially difficult to get children to differentiate between threats that were highly likely and those that were unlikely to occur. Our studies of children's understanding of common language terms may help us understand part of the problem. Studies we have conducted show that many young children have not fully grasped the differences between important relative quantifies such as "some" and "most," and probabilistic terms such as "possibly," "probably," and "definitely" (Badzinski, Cantor, & Hoffner, 1989; Hoffner, Cantor, & Badzinski, 1990).

In addition to these problems, our study in which we manipulated the appearance and behavior of the protagonist in a drama (Hoffner & Cantor, 1985) revealed how difficult it is to communicate to children in situations in which the outward appearance of something belies a contrary internal disposition. In other words, it is extremely difficult to communicate to young children that something that looks scary is in fact benign and something that is attractive is really dangerous.

These practical problems bring to light the importance of learning more about how to communicate effectively with children on the subject of coping with the threatening aspects of their environment. It is important to recognize that some level of fear is appropriate and indeed may be essential to survival in certain situations. On the other hand, overburdening children with fears of horrendous disasters that are either unpreventable or highly unlikely to threaten them personally may add undue stress to the process of growing up.

Because television is one of children's major sources of information about the world, we need to be able to make reasoned decisions about what to expose our children to and when. We also need to be able to explain crucial aspects of life to them in an age-appropriate way, that preserves their youthful optimism while promoting necessary and appropriate precautions.

REFERENCES

Angelino, H., Dollins, J., & Mech, E. V. (1956). Trends in the "fears and worries" of school children as related to socio-economic status and age. *Journal of Genetic Psychology 89*, 263-276.

Badzinski, D. M., Cantor, J., & Hoffner, C. (1989). Children's understanding of quantifies. *Child Study Journal, 19*, 241-258.

Blumer, H. (1933). *Movies and conduct*. New York: Macmillan.

Bruner, J. S. (1966). On cognitive growth I & II. In J. S. Bruner, R. R. Oliver, & P. M. Greenfield (Eds.), *Studies in cognitive growth* (pp. 1-67). New York: Wiley.

Cantor, J. (1989). Studying children's emotional reactions to mass media. In B. Dervin, L. Grossberg, B. O'Keefe, & E. Wartella (Eds.), *Rethinking communication. Vol. 2. Paradigm exemplars* (pp. 47-59). Newbury Park, CA: Sage.

Cantor, J. (1991). Fright responses to mass media productions. In J. Bryant & D. Zillmann (Eds.), *Responding to the screen: Reception and reaction processes* (pp. 169-197). Hillsdale, NJ: Lawrence Erlbaum Associates.

Cantor, J., & Hoffner, C. (1990). Children's fear reactions to a televised film as a function of perceived immediacy of depicted threat. *Journal of Broadcasting & Electronic Media, 34.* 421-442.

Cantor, J., Mares, M. L., & Oliver, M. B. (1993). Parents' and children's emotional reactions to televised coverage of the Gulf War. In B. Greenberg & W. Gantz (Eds.), *Desert Storm and the mass media* (pp. 325–340). Cresskill, NJ: Hampton Press.

Cantor, J., & Omdahl, B. L. (1991). Effects of fictional media depictions of realistic threats on children's emotional responses, expectations, worries, and liking for related activities. *Communication Monographs, 58*, 384–401.

Cantor, J., & Reilly, S. (1982). Adolescents' fright reactions to television and films. *Journal of Communication, 32*, 87–99.

Cantor, J., & Sparks, G. G. (1984). Children's fear responses to mass media: Testing some Piagetian predictions. *Journal of Communication, 34*, 90–103.

Cantor, J., Sparks, G. G., & Hoffner, C. (1988). Calming children's television fears: Mr. Rogers vs. The Incredible Hulk. *Journal of Broadcasting & Electronic Media, 32*, 271–288.

Cantor, J., & Wilson, B. J. (1984). Modifying fear responses to mass media in preschool and elementary school children. *Journal of Broadcasting, 28*, 431–443.

Cantor, J., & Wilson, B. J. (1988). Helping children cope with frightening media presentations. *Current Psychology: Research & Reviews, 7*, 58–75.

Cantor, J., Wilson, B. J., & Hoffner, C. (1986). Emotional responses to a televised nuclear holocaust film. *Communication Research, 13*, 257–277.

Flavell, J. (1963). *The developmental psychology of Jean Piaget.* New York: Van Nostrand.

Hoffner, C., & Cantor, J. (1985). Developmental differences in responses to a television character's appearance and behavior. *Developmental Psychology, 21*, 1065–1074.

Hoffner, C., & Cantor, J. (1990). Forewarning of threat and prior knowledge of outcome: Effects on children's emotional responses to a film sequence. *Human Communication Research, 16*, 323–354.

Hoffner, C., Cantor, J., & Badzinski, D. M. (1990). Children's understanding of adverbs denoting degree of likelihood. *Journal of Child Language, 17*, 217–231.

Jacobson, M. (1989, September). When evil lurks. *Parenting*, pp. 28, 31.

Kneale, D. (1988, May 18). Titillating channels: TV is going tabloid as shows seek sleaze and find profits, too. *Wall Street Journal*, pp. 1, 20.

Melkman, R., Tversky, B., & Baratz, D. (1981). Developmental trends in the use of perceptual and conceptual attributes in grouping, clustering and retrieval. *Journal of Experimental Child Psychology, 31*, 470–486.

Meyrowitz, J. (1985). *No sense of place: The impact of electronic media on social behavior.* New York: Oxford University Press.

Morison, P., & Gardner, H. (1978). Dragons and dinosaurs: The child's capacity to differentiate fantasy from reality. *Child Development, 49*, 642–648.

Palmer, E. L., Hockett, A. B., & Dean, W. W. (1983). The television family and children's fright reactions. *Journal of Family Issues, 4*, 279–292.

Preston, M. I. (1941). Children's reactions to movie horrors and radio crime. *Journal of Pediatrics, 19.* 147–168.

Sparks, G. G. (1986). Developmental differences in children's reports of fear induced by the mass media. *Child Study Journal, 16*, 55–66.

Sparks, G. G., & Cantor, J. (1986). Developmental differences in fright responses to a television program depicting a character transformation. *Journal of Broadcasting and Electronic Media, 30*, 309–323.

Wilson, B. J., & Cantor, J. (1987). Reducing children's fear reactions to mass media: Effects of visual exposure and verbal explanation. *Communication Yearbook 10* (pp. 553–573). Beverly Hills, CA: Sage.

Wilson, B. J., Hoffner C., & Cantor, J. (1987). Children's perceptions of the effectiveness of techniques to reduce fear from mass media. *Journal of Applied Developmental Psychology, 8*, 39–52.

Wright, J. C., Kunkel, D., Pinon, M., & Huston, A. C. (1989). How children reacted to televised coverage of the space shuttle disaster. *Journal of Communication, 39* (2), 27–45.

12

Television and Aggression: Recent Developments in Research and Theory

Russell G. Geen
University of Missouri

A brief presentation such as this is not an occasion for a review of the literature on the effects of observing televised violence, and I do not attempt one. Instead, I organize my discussion around two questions. The first is the more easily answered: Is watching violence presented on television associated with increased aggression in the viewer? The best answer that we can give on the basis of more than 30 years of research is that it is. The second question, one of greater interest to psychologists, is: When observation of violence is followed by aggression, what intervening processes connect the two? I take up the question of evidence for the connection first, after which I discuss some recent research on intervening variables.

EVIDENCE FOR THE RELATIONSHIP OF TELEVISED VIOLENCE TO AGGRESSION

Experimental Studies

The literature from laboratory experiments on the effects of televised violence on aggression has been reviewed many times (e.g., Geen &

151

Thomas, 1986; Hearold, 1986; Roberts & Maccoby, 1985) and I mention it here only to reiterate the general conclusion of most reviewers that observation of violence is often followed by increases in both physical and verbal aggression. This effect is most likely to occur when the viewer has been provoked in some way and is therefore relatively likely to aggress. This is not to say that all reviewers have drawn this conclusion; some (e.g., Freedman, 1984, 1988; McGuire, 1986) have been especially outspoken in their criticisms of the conclusions of laboratory experiments on aggression.

Critics of laboratory research base their arguments on allegations that such studies represent only analogs of aggressive behavior and not cross-sections of it (e.g., Freedman, 1984). Partly because of such arguments, interest in laboratory experiments began to wane in the 1970s as research on the effects of televised violence became based more and more on studies in natural settings. Some of these studies, usually called field experiments, involved the use of experimental methodology in natural settings. A number of such investigations were reported during the 1970s and, although they have been criticized as lacking internal validity (Freedman, 1984), these studies yielded consistent findings of a positive relationship between observation of televised violence and aggression.

A detailed discussion of the strengths and weaknesses of these studies has been provided by Friedrich-Cofer and Huston (1986). In addition, a meta-analysis of 28 field experiments conducted between 1956 and 1988 has recently been reported (Wood, Wong, & Chachere, 1991). The studies included in this analysis were chosen because they investigated the effects of media violence on aggression among children and adolescents during unconstrained social interaction with strangers, classmates, and friends. Wood and her colleagues concluded that media violence does enhance aggression in such settings and that, because all the experiments involved short-term immediate reactions to observed violence, the effects may be due to temporary changes in affect and arousal as well as to long-term processes like modeling.

Longitudinal Studies

The major emphasis of this chapter is on developments in the study of television and aggression that occurred during the 1980s. One such investigation was the final phase of a longitudinal project begun in the late 1950s by Eron and his associates (Eron, Walder, & Lefkowitz, 1971). The research began with the study of third-grade students in a rural county in upstate New York. Each child's level of aggressiveness was assessed through ratings made by parents, peers, and the children themselves; each child's preference for violent television programs was also measured. Measures of the same variables were obtained 10 and 22 years later from many of the same children. The method of cross-lagged panel correlation was used for analysis of the data[1].

The results of the 10-year follow-up (Lefkowitz, Eron, Walder, & Huesmann, 1977) revealed that among boys the amount of televised violence watched during third grade was positively correlated with aggressiveness 10 years later, whereas the correlation between aggressiveness during Grade 3 and the amount of violent television watched a decade later was essentially zero. Following the assumptions of cross-lagged correlation analysis, Eron and his associates inferred a causal relation between observing violence and aggressiveness from these data. For girls, both correlations were not significantly greater than zero. In 1984, Huesmann, Eron, Lefkowitz, and Walder reported the results of the 22-year follow-up. A positive relationship between childhood television viewing and subsequent aggressiveness was again suggested: The seriousness of crimes for which males were convicted by age 30 was significantly correlated with the amount of television that they had watched and their liking for violent programs as 8-year-olds. Again, aggressiveness at age 8 was not related to either overall viewing practices or preference for violent programs at age 30.

A connection between observing television violence and aggression has also been shown by Singer and Singer (1981) on the basis of a 1-year study involving children of nursery school age. At four times during the year, 2-week periods were designated as probes during which parents kept logs of their children's television viewing. Meanwhile, observers recorded instances of aggressive behavior by the children during school hours. When data were combined across all four probes, aggressive behavior was found to be significantly correlated with the total amount of time spent in watching "action–adventure" programs, all of which manifested high levels of violence. This effect was found for both boys and girls.

The pattern of cross-lagged correlations over the four probe periods led the Singers to conclude that the television viewing was leading to the aggressive behavior over the first two comparisons (i.e., from probe 1 to probe 2 and from probe 2 to probe 3). Over the final comparison (from probe 3 to probe 4), however, the cross-lagged pattern showed that not only was earlier viewing correlated with subsequent aggression, but also that earlier aggression was correlated with subsequent viewing. In other words, by the latter phase of the study a reciprocal effect was being shown. As in

---

[1]This method involves determining the degree of correlation between two events separated in time (e.g., television viewing at one time and aggression at some later time, and vice versa). A correlation between viewing during the earlier period and aggression during the later period that is greater than the correlation between early aggression and later viewing is usually interpreted as suggesting that viewing probably elicits aggression.

earlier periods, observation of violence was presumably eliciting aggressive behavior. In addition, aggressive children were also watching more of the violent "action–adventure" shows.

The latter finding—that aggressiveness may lead to a liking for violent television—is consistent with the results of a laboratory investigation by Fenigstein (1979). In that experiment, men who had aggressed physically against another person later selected material for viewing that was more violent than the material chosen by nonaggressing males. In a related correlational study, Diener and DuFour (1978) reported a positive correlation among males between scores on the aggressiveness subscale of the California Psychological Inventory and preferences for violent television programs. However, few studies of television and aggression have been designed to test the possibility of such a reciprocal relationship between the two variables. Friedrich-Cofer and Huston (1986) observed that the traditional emphasis on a unidirectional relationship was largely the result of the social learning and arousal theories that were once predominant. However, a bidirectional approach is consistent with more recent social learning theories that stress person–environment interactions.

Of the longitudinal studies reported during the 1980s, the authors of one drew the conclusion that no relationship had been found between viewing televised violence and subsequent aggression. Milavsky, Stipp, Kessler, and Rubens (1982) carried out two studies, each of which spanned a period of 3 years. One involved elementary schoolchildren between the ages of 7 and 12 and the other was done with boys aged 12 to 16. Over the 3 years, six probe periods were used with the elementary children and five with the adolescents. In each probe, children made self-reports of television viewing for a 4-week period; each program was judged for the violence of its content by adult ratings. Aggression in the younger children was assessed through peer ratings made by each child, and in the older boys through self-reports.

Milavsky and his colleagues devised a regression equation to assess the influence of both prior aggression and television viewing on aggression at each period and analyzed their data by LISREL. This method is more powerful than the cross-lagged correlation technique used in earlier studies. Regression coefficients were determined for all possible comparisons among the probes, so that any given comparison could cover a period from a few months to the full 3 years of the study. Milavsky et al. (1982) found that most of the coefficients were positive, but of little magnitude, and that the number that differed significantly from zero was not greater than would have been expected by chance. They also reported that when socioeconomic status was added to the structural model, even this small effect was attenuated. This finding raised the possibility that social and economic class status may have been correlated with both television viewing and postviewing aggression, a clear case of third-variable contamination.

From their findings, Milavsky and his associates concluded that observation of televised violence has no effect on aggression in children. However, after reanalyzing these data, Cook, Kendzierski, and Thomas (1983) drew a different conclusion. In addition to noting that most of the analyses yielded positive relations between viewing of violence and aggression, Cook et al. also discovered that the magnitude of this positive relationship increased as the amount of time between probes increased, and they argued that Milavsky and his associated did not examine this finding sufficiently. Furthermore, the subsequent analyses showed that, although some of the positive coefficients were an artifact of social class differences, others were not, so that the problem of possible contamination could be ruled out for at least that variable. Cook and his colleagues also criticized Milavsky et al. for failing to use better models in assessing the cumulative impact of television, for not considering possible interactions among television viewing, gender, and social class, and for not using statistical analyses of sufficient power.

Perhaps the most comprehensive set of studies on televised violence reported during the 1980s was carried out by a team of investigators working in five countries under the general direction of Huesmann and Eron (1986b). This research, like that of Milavsky et al. (1982), also benefited from the use of sophisticated regression analyses. In one of the studies from this program, involving two cohorts of American children spanning Grades 1 to 5, Huesmann and Eron (1986a) found that frequency of viewing televised violence was positively correlated with contemporary peer ratings of aggression. The effect was found in both boys and girls. In addition, aggression by boys was related to the degree to which the boys identified with aggressive characters seen on television. In general, findings similar to those obtained with the American sample characterized the investigations in the other countries: Finland (Lagerspetz & Viemero, 1986), Poland (Fraczek, 1986), Australia (Sheehan, 1986), and Israel (Bachrach, 1986). In each of these countries, a positive relationship was found between frequency of watching televised violence and peer-rated aggression. The only exception was that in Israel the effect was found among children living in cities but not among those living in a kibbutz. Aggression was also found to be linked to identification with violent characters in these countries, as in the United States.[2]

---

[2]Cook and his associates (1983) concluded, after reanalyzing some of the data from this study, that the mediation of aggression by identification with televised characters had not been proven.

Analysis of Archival Data

An ambitious and systematic attempt to account for real-world aggression with a hypothesis derived from laboratory research has been made in a series of investigations by Phillips (1986). Dealing entirely with material from public records, Phillips sought to show a causal connection between violence-related events shown on television or reported in other news media and increments in aggression, such as suicide and murder, in the immediate aftermath. The connection is attributed by Phillips to processes of suggestion and imitation similar to those described by Bandura (1973) and some other experimentalists. Despite criticism of his work on both methodological and theoretical grounds (e.g., Baron & Reiss, 1985), which Phillips has answered in later writings (Phillips & Bollen, 1985), the work appears to show some positive relationship between violence reported in the media and certain kinds of aggressive behavior.

Conclusion

What may we conclude from all this? Most laboratory evidence supports the notion of a causal connection between television viewing and aggression. Of the longitudinal studies reported during the 1980s, all but one lead to the same general conclusion, and that one may not be as negative as its authors have argued. The issue may never be settled to everyone's satisfaction, and certainly more research, using state-of-the-art methodology, is needed to settle the many remaining problems before conclusive evidence may be forthcoming. Even so, at the present time we do appear to have a fairly large amount of what Cook and his colleagues (1983) have called "circumstantial evidence" for a hypothesis that observation of violence on television produces some increase in aggressiveness of the viewers.

INTERVENING PROCESSES IN AGGRESSION FOLLOWING OBSERVATION OF TELEVISED VIOLENCE

Several explanations have been given for the relationship between television violence and aggression. Until recently, such explanations were based on theoretical concepts that were popular during the 1960s, such as disinhibition, arousal, and activation of conditioned responses. During the 1980s, two new theoretical explanations emerged, both of which are based on more recent cognitive models of behavior. These theoretical models are discussed in this section.

Cognitive Scripts

The first is the theory of cognitive scripting. Huesmann (1986) proposed that observation of violence on television provides material for the learning of complex behavioral scripts. The fundamental element in a script is a vignette, defined as "an encoding of an event of short duration" (Abelson, 1976), and which consists of a perceptual image and a "conceptual representation" of an event. A simple vignette might consist, for example, of an image of one person shooting another in anger over something the other person has done. The act of shooting provides the image, and the judgment regarding the "reason" for the shooting provides the cognitive representation. A script consists of a series of such vignettes. It may, for example, include several scenes of violence, and their conceptual representations, from television shows. The significance of scripts is that they serve as guides for behavior. Once a script has been learned, it may be retrieved on future occasions, at which time it may lead to specific actions.

The retrieval of any script depends in part on the amount of similarity between the situation at the time of retrieval and the situation at the time the script was encoded in memory. This is referred to as the principle of encoding specificity. As a child develops, he or she may observe instances in which aggression has been used to resolve interpersonal conflicts. Such events are common in television programming. The information may then be stored in a script, perhaps to be called up from memory at some later time when the child is personally involved in a situation of conflict. The retrievability of the script will depend partly on how closely the present conflict situation resembles those seen on television.

Certain stimulus conditions may, by directing attention, determine what happens in the encoding process. Any characteristic of the program that makes a scene stand out may enhance the extent to which that scene is encoded and stored in memory. Intensity of violence may be one such characteristic. Reality may be another. Acts of aggression that are perceived as real may be regarded as more instrumental to the solving of conflicts than less realistic ones. Studies have shown that when portrayals of violence are said to be real events they elicit more aggression than when they are described in less realistic terms (Geen, 1983).

When a cognitive script is retrieved as a guide for behavior, its enactment serves as a rehearsal that further establishes the script in memory. In addition, the script becomes elaborated and enhanced by the addition of of new scenarios peculiar to the situation in which it is called up. According to the principle of encoding specificity, this should make the script pertinent to an ever-widening range of situations the more often it is retrieved. One result of all this is that responding to television violence by enacting aggressive scripts can become a self-perpetuating process.

Cognitive Priming

A line of reasoning similar to Huesmann's, in that it also is based heavily on cognitive constructs, has been followed by Berkowitz (1984), for whom aggressive thoughts elicited by violent television programs "can prime other semantically related thoughts, heightening the chances that viewers will have other aggressive ideas in this period" (p. 411). Berkowitz bases this priming hypothesis on the notion of spreading activation proposed by Collins and Loftus in 1975: Thoughts send out radiating activation along associative pathways, thereby animating other related thoughts. In this way, ideas about aggression need not be identical to those observed on television to be activated by the latter. Thoughts are also linked along the same kind of associative pathways to related affective and emotional states and to expressive motor patterns (Bower, 1981; Lang, 1979). Observation of televised violence can therefore engender a complex of associations consisting of aggressive ideas, emotions related to violence, and the impetus for aggressive acts.

When an associative network has been primed, its likelihood of being activated by subsequent stimuli is increased. Berkowitz (1989) proposed that in the case of aggression this stimulus input is a state of negative affect that may be evoked by many situational conditions, among them frustration, attack, physical pain, or environmental stressors. Any condition that creates a sufficiently intense level of negative affect can cause aggression. Negative affect, however caused, initiates thoughts, emotions, and motor patterns for either aggression or escape ("fight or flight"). If aggressive associations have been primed by observation of violence, the "fight" option will be the more likely of the two to occur.

The priming hypothesis was first shown in aggression research in studies involving the judgments of hostility that people make of each other. For example, Srull and Wyer (1979) found that, when subjects had to rate the hostility of another person's ambiguous behavior, the ratings were higher if the subject had just performed a sentence completion task in which hostile material had been made salient. This material had primed related thoughts, making it more readily accessible for retrieval during the judgment phase of the study. An even more subtle illustration of this effect has been reported by Wann and Branscombe (1990), who showed that judgments of a target person's hostility were higher following a task in which the names of violent sporting activities, such as boxing and hockey, were prominent than after a task containing the names of nonviolent sports like billiards and golf.

To date, only one study has been reported in which the priming hypothesis was explicitly applied to the effects of television violence. In that study, Bushman and Geen (1990) found that subjects who had been shown brief videotapes of violent activity subsequently listed a larger number of aggressive thoughts than subjects who had seen a nonviolent control scene. This effect was moderated by individual differences in irritability, assessed by means of Caprara's (Caprara et al., 1985) Irritability scale: Subjects scoring high in irritability listed a greater number of aggressive thoughts than less irritable subjects when videotapes showing *moderate* levels of violence were shown. When an extremely violent videotape was shown, individual differences in irritability had no effect on the number of aggressive thoughts listed; in that condition all subjects had more aggressive thoughts than subjects who had seen less violent tapes. This finding is of interest because it tends to disconfirm an argument, long advanced by spokespersons for the television industry, that violent programs affect only viewers who are characteristically high in aggressiveness.

Questions Concerning Development

One final matter remains to be noted. The conclusions that have been drawn on the effects of televised violence have been based in part on studies involving children and in part on others involving young adults. Whether we can confidently generalize across age groups is a question that has not yet been answered. We should note, however, that certain developmental differences may have an effect on reactions to television. Young children have obviously not developed behavioral scripts of the same complexity as those of adults, nor have they had the same opportunities for rehearsal and elaboration. From another viewpoint, it is also obvious that, relative to adults, children probably have restricted and underdeveloped networks of thoughts and related affective states pertaining to aggression. To the extent that such variables mediate the responses that people have to televised violence, we might expect children to be less affected than adults.

On the other hand, there is evidence that children's perceptions and interpretations of violence may be simpler and less responsive to subtle variations than those of adults. For example, Collins, Berndt, and Hess (1974) found that, whereas teenagers were able to differentiate among violent acts seen on television in terms of the motives of the aggressors, children of kindergarten age and second graders tended to comprehend what they had seen only in terms of the level of violence and its ultimate consequences. Collins (1975) has also shown that older children are better able to construct meaningful sequences out of discrete violent scenes than are younger children. Studies have shown that adults modulate their aggression in response to television in terms of circumstances within which the violence occurs, such as the overall context of "justification" (e.g., Geen, 1981). If children are relatively insensitive to such differences in circumstances, they may, as a result, be more likely simply to react to violence with undifferentiated arousal and affect. Developmental factors in reaction of televised violence over the age span from childhood to adulthood remains an important problem for future research.

GENERAL DISCUSSION

Evidence from four types of study—laboratory experiments, field experiments, longitudinal studies, and archival studies—supports the conclusion that observation of television violence has a generally facilitating effect on subsequent aggression. These studies have involved children, adolescents and young adults, and a wide range of constrained and unconstrained behaviors. Admittedly, effect sizes are sometimes small, as critics have pointed out. Nevertheless, the large number of studies reporting the effect and the convergence of data from so many types of investigation indicates that the effect is a real one. Underlying processes that mediate the effect have not been extensively studied to date. However, some promising developments in theory are taking place, involving the development of models derived from affective, cognitive, and motivational psychology. The debate over the consequences of television violence for aggression is by no means over, and future studies of the problem will benefit from both the large literature on the subject and the emergence of the new theoretical approaches.

REFERENCES

Abelson, R. P. (1976). Script processing in attitude formation and decision making. In J. S. Carroll & J. W. Payne (Eds.), *Cognition and social behavior* (pp. 33–45). Hillsdale, NJ: Lawrence Erlbaum Associates.

Bachrach, R. S. (1986). The differential effects of observation of violence on kibbutz and city children in Israel. In L. R. Huesmann & L. D. Eron (Eds.), *Television and the aggressive child: A cross-national comparison* (pp. 201–238). Hillsdale, NJ: Lawrence Erlbaum Associates.

Bandura, A. (1973). *Aggression: A social learning analysis.* Englewood Cliffs, NJ: Prentice-Hall.

Baron, J. N., & Reiss, P. C. (1985). Same time, next year: Aggregate analyses of the mass media on violent behavior. *American Sociological Review, 50,* 347–363.

Berkowitz, L. (1984). Some effects of thoughts on anti- and prosocial influences of media events: A cognitive neoassociationist analysis. *Psychological Bulletin, 95,* 410–427.

Berkowitz, L. (1989). The frustration–aggression hypothesis: An examination and reformulation. *Psychological Bulletin, 106,* 59–73.

Bower, G. (1981). Mood and memory. *American Psychologist, 36,* 129–148.

Bushman, B. J., & Geen, R. G. (1990). Role of cognitive–emotional mediators and individual differences in the effects of media violence on aggression. *Journal of Personality and Social Psychology, 40*, 687–700.

Caprara, G. V., Cinanni, V., D'Imperio, G., Passerini, S., Renzi, P., & Travaglia, G. (1985). Indicators of impulsive aggression: Present status of research on Irritability and Emotional Susceptibility. *Personality and Individual Differences, 6*, 665–674.

Collins, A., & Loftus, E. (1975). A spreading-activation theory of semantic memory. *Psychological Review, 82*, 407–428.

Collins, W. A. (1975). The developing child as a viewer. *Journal of Communication, 25*, 35–44.

Collins, W. A., Berndt, T. J., & Hess, V. L. (1974). Observational learning of motives and consequences for television aggression: A developmental study. *Child Development, 45*, 799–802.

Cook, T. D., Kendzierski, D. A., & Thomas, S. V. (1983). The implicit assumptions of television research: An analysis of the 1982 NIMH Report on Television and Behavior. *Public Opinion Quarterly, 47*, 161–201.

Diener, E., & DuFour, D. (1978). Does television violence enhance program popularity? *Journal of Personality and Social Psychology, 36*, 333–341.

Eron, L. D., Walder, L. O., & Lefkowitz, M. M. (1971). *Learning of aggression in children.* Boston: Little, Brown.

Fenigstein, A. (1979). Does aggression cause a preference for viewing media violence? *Journal of Personality and Social Psychology, 37*, 2307–2317.

Fraczek, A. (1986). Socio-cultural environment, television viewing, and the development of aggression among children in Poland. In L. R. Huesmann & L. D. Eron (Eds.), *Television and the aggressive child: A cross-national comparison* (pp. 119–159). Hillsdale, NJ: Lawrence Erlbaum Associates.

Freedman, J. L. (1984). Effect of television violence on aggressiveness. *Psychological Bulletin, 96*, 227–246.

Freedman, J. L. (1988). Television violence and aggression: What the evidence shows. In S. Oskamp (Ed.), *Applied social psychology annual: Television as a social issue* (Vol. 8, pp. 144–162). Newbury Park, CA: Sage.

Friedrich-Cofer, L., & Huston, A. C. (1986). Television violence and aggression: The debate continues. *Psychological Bulletin, 100*, 364–371.

Geen, R. G. (1981). Behavioral and physiological reactions to observed violence: Effects of prior exposure to aggressive stimuli. *Journal of Personality and Social Psychology, 40*, 868–875.

Geen, R. G. (1983). Aggression and television violence. In R. G. Geen & E. I. Donnerstein (Eds.), *Aggression: Theoretical and empirical reviews* (Vol. 2, pp. 103–125). New York: Academic Press.

Geen, R. G., & Thomas, S. L. (1986). The immediate effects of media violence on behavior. *Journal of Social Issues, 42*, 7–27.

Hearold, S. (1986). A synthesis of 1043 effects of television on social behavior. In G. Comstock (Ed.), *Public communication and behavior* (Vol. 1, pp. 65–133). New York: Academic Press.

Huesmann, L. R. (1986). Psychological processes promoting the relation between exposure to media violence and aggressive behavior by the viewer. *Journal of Social Issues, 42*, 125–139.

Huesmann, L. R., & Eron, L. D. (1986a). The development of aggression in American children as a consequence of television violence viewing. In L. R. Huesmann & L. D. Eron (Eds.), *Television and the aggressive child: A cross-national comparison* (pp. 45–80). Hillsdale, NJ: Lawrence Erlbaum Associates.

Huesmann, L. R., & Eron, L. D. (Eds.) (1986b). *Television and the aggressive child: A cross-national comparison* (pp. 201-238). Hillsdale, NJ: Lawrence Erlbaum Associates.

Huesmann, L. R., Eron, L. D., Lefkowitz, M. M., & Walder, L. O. (1984). Stability of aggression over time and generations. *Developmental Psychology, 20,* 1120-1134.

Lagerspetz, K., & Viemero, V. (1986). Television and aggressive behavior among Finnish children. In L. R. Huesmann & L. D. Eron (Eds.), *Television and the aggressive child: A cross-national comparison* (pp. 81-117). Hillsdale, NJ: Lawrence Erlbaum Associates.

Lang, P. J. (1979). A bio-informational theory of emotional imagery. *Psychophysiology, 16,* 495-512.

Lefkowitz, M. M., Eron, L. D., Walder, L. O., & Huesmann, L. R. (1977). *Growing up to be violent.* New York: Pergamon.

McGuire, W. J. (1986). The myth of massive media impact: Savagings and salvagings. In G. Comstock (Ed.), *Public communication and behavior* (Vol. 1, pp. 173-257). New York: Academic Press.

Milavsky, J. R., Stipp, H. H., Kessler, R. C., & Rubens, W. S. (1982). *Television and aggression: A panel study.* New York: Academic Press.

Phillips, D. P. (1986). Natural experiments on the effects of mass media violence on fatal aggression: Strengths and weaknesses of a new approach. In L. Berkowitz (Ed.), *Advances in experimental social psychology* (Vol. 19, pp. 207-250). New York: Academic Press.

Phillips, D. P., & Bollen, K. (1985). Same time, last year: Selective data dredging for negative findings. *American Sociological Review, 50,* 364-371.

Roberts, D. F., & Maccoby, N. (1985). Effects of mass communication. In G. Lindzey & E. Aronson (Eds.), *Handbook of social psychology* (Vol. 2, pp. 539-598). New York: Random House.

Sheehan, P. W. (1986). Television viewing and its relation to aggression among children in Australia. In L. R. Huesmann & L. D. Eron (Eds.), *Television and the aggressive child: A cross-national comparison* (pp. 161-199). Hillsdale, NJ: Lawrence Erlbaum Associates.

Singer, J. L., & Singer, D. G. (1981). *Television, imagination, and aggression: A study of preschoolers.* Hillsdale, NJ: Lawrence Erlbaum Associates.

Srull, T. K., & Wyer, R. S. (1979). The role of category accessibility in the interpretation of information about persons: Some determinants and implications. *Journal of Personality and Social Psychology, 37,* 1660-1672.

Wann, D. L., & Branscombe, N. R. (1990). Person perception when aggressive or nonagressive sports are primed. *Aggressive Behavior, 16,* 27-32.

Wood, W., Wong, F., & Chachere, J. (1991). Effects of media violence on viewers' aggression in unconstrained social interaction. *Psychological Bulletin, 109,* 371-383.

Part IV

SEXUAL CONTENT AND FAMILY CONTEXT

13

CONTENT TRENDS IN MEDIA SEX

Bradley S. Greenberg
Michigan State University

It is a common gambit in popular discussions of media to begin by proclaiming that children will watch so many thousands of hours of television before they begin school, that teenagers will spend literally years in front of the TV set before they complete high school, and then to indicate that these same young people will have watched hundreds of acts of violence on TV and film each year that they have lived. After scrutinizing the literature on sex content in the most popular mass media, in this chapter I proclaim just how much sex our young people will see, and what kinds. To end with that pronouncement (so that you have something to look forward to), I first share information about what sex content prevails in today's mass media. I assure you, however, that it is far more difficult to write (and talk) about sex than to examine it (in content form). A videotape, a film, a TV show, and a music video would do much to clarify my conclusions and to keep your attention; instead, much as verbal sex content in the media does, I must trust your imagination and your experiences with the kinds of content described. Frankly, having what in locker room parlance is called a "dirty mind" would help.

Here, we describe current trends in the portrayal of sex in six forms of media content: music videos, X-rated videos, daytime soaps, primetime commercial network television, magazines, and movies.

Sex Content in Music Videos

Two comprehensive studies of the content of music videos, a much favored media experience for adolescents and preadolescents, were based on 1984 offerings from MTV and other television music programs. One study (Baxter, DeRiemer, Landini, Leslie, & Singletary, 1985) looked for many kinds of content, one of which was sex content; they found it in 60% of their sample of 62 videos. The content of the sex references was relatively mild, but the study is flawed by the fact that what was coded was whether or not a particular content element occurred in the video—and not how often anything occurred. Nevertheless, the sex content was such that 31% of the videos with sex content featured provocative clothing, 31% had embraces, 27% with dance movements that were sexually suggestive, 21% with nondance movements that were sexually suggestive, 15% with dating or courting, 11% with kissing, 11% with a male chasing a female or the opposite, and 8% in which someone used a musical instrument, typically a guitar, in a sexually suggestive manner. The authors (Baxter et al., 1985) concluded that:

> like other studies of televised sexual content, music video sexual content was understated, relying on innuendo through clothing, suggestiveness, and light physical contact rather than more overt behaviors.

> Thus, music video sexual content may have a decidedly adolescent orientation, suited to its audience; fantasy exceeds experience and sexual expression centers primarily on attracting the opposite sex. Sexual behavior, as portrayed in music videos may reflect actual or desired adolescent courtship behavior, or the expression of attraction impulses . . . The study's results indicate, however, that sexually oriented suggestive behavior is portrayed frequently in music videos. (p. 336)

Sherman and Dominick (1986) focused on the presence of sex and violence in 166 "concept" videos, videos in which more than half the screen time is given to story, drama, or narrative rather than to studio performance, and they drew their videos from the shows "Night Tracks" and "Friday Night Videos" as well as from MTV.

Analyzing only the visual dimension of the videos (and not the lyrics), they found sexual intimacy presented in more than three fourths of them, and an average of just under five sexual activities per video. MTV, however, was the sexiest, averaging more than six per video. The visible sexual activity consisted largely of nonintimate touching (45%), intimate touching (21%), kissing (13%), hugging (11%), and flirting (10%), leading the researchers to conclude that "kissing, hugging and suggestive behavior occurred at twice the rate that they occurred on conventional TV." The context of this activity was primarily heterosexual (71%), but there was substantial homosexual exchange (26%). However, all but one of the homosexual acts involved flirtation or nonintimate touching.

It is worth relating some of the findings from their examination of the violence content in these same videos. Foremost is the fact that four of every five videos containing violence also contained sexual imagery. The aggressors were male (73%), White (88%), and in the audience target age group of 18 to 34 (71%); the primary victims had these same characteristics, and the proportions did not differ by as much as 5% from the figures aforementioned. Also, two thirds of the characters were lower class. From this combination of sex and violence, Sherman and Dominick (1986) concluded: "In many cases, then, women were presented as upper-class sex objects for lower class males with visions of sexual conquest (p. 89) . . . adolescent sex in music television (is) long on titillation and physical activity, but devoid of emotional involvement (p. 91) . . . older women, who might resemble 'mother' figures, possess symbolic power through their exercise of aggression" (p. 92).

Sex Content in X-Rated Videos

Videos provide the newest medium of exchange for that content that borders on or crosses over into the realm of pornography. Before describing these videos, let us place video porn in at least one other context. In 1976, Smith described the content of 428 "adults only" paperbacks published from 1967 through 1974 that could be bought off the shelf; he bought every fifth paperback off the shelf of one store in each of eight communities in five states. Using as his key measure the proportion of the number of pages devoted to sex episodes (the detailing of physical sex acts with plot and story line doing little more than setting the stage for the sexual encounter), he found that in 1967 sex episodes consumed 29 of every 100 pages, by 1970, it was 64 of every 100 pages, and it remained at that level 4 years later. The typical character was 20 to 29 years old, 99 of every 100 were White, 94% of the men and 77% of the women were heterosexual, with 16% of the women as bisexual. As for the sex acts, in 9% there was some form of expressed love, in 60% it was sex for sex sake, with no involvement or commitment, and in one third there was physical or mental coercion. Smith (1976) reported: "these are the acts of virile, red-blooded males . . . there are no weird ones, kooks or sex freaks here." He also suggested the following as a prototype theme in these paperbacks: "the young, probably rich, sleek, cool, restrained, and posed beauty, the depths of her sexual desires unstirred as yet (particularly, if married, by her husband), until

Superstud arrives, who, despite her initial resistance and piteous pleas for mercy, rather quickly and relentlessly unlocks her real sexual passion to take her to hitherto unimagined heights, leaving her begging for his continued ministrations" (p. 23).

The reader is asked to retain this imagery as we move to describing contemporary X-rated video fare (not to include NC–17/18 ratings that postdate the research examined for this chapter). Cowan and her colleagues (Cowan, Lee, Levy, & Snyder, 1988) analyzed 443 explicitly sexual scenes in 45 X-rated videocassettes and found that over half those scenes were concerned primarily with domination or exploitation, mostly by men toward women. The four predominant themes were *domination* (28% of the scenes), in which one person controlled the sex act, *reciprocity* (37%), where there was mutual consent and satisfaction, *exploitation* (26%), where one participant used coercion and status inequality to get his or her way, and *autoeroticism* by masturbation or self-stimulation (9%). Primary indicators of dominance and inequality were status inequality (in 39% of the scenes), voyeurism (in 29%), verbal dominance (28%), physical aggression (23%), verbal aggression (20%), submission (14%), and rape (6%). In these videos, 60% of the minutes were explicit graphic depictions of sex acts, averaging 10 such scenes per video; 78% of the scenes were heterosexual acts, 11% (all female) were homosexual, 2% bisexual, and 9% autosexual. Of the females, 57% were heterosexual, 35% bisexual, and 8% homosexual, and none of the men were either bisexual or homosexual. The authors concluded: "The fusion of sex and aggression present in these videotapes, including the portrayal of rape, bondage, female submission and verbal abuse, supports the ideology that sexuality includes domination and abusive treatment of women . . . a significant level of hatred of women is now available for viewing in our living rooms and bedrooms" (p. 308).

Palys (1986) differentiated "adult" videos (*n* = 58) from what he termed *triple-X* titles (*n* = 92), with the latter corresponding to the Cowan et al. (1988) videos. Half the individual scenes were coded because they contained sexual acts (77% of the coded scenes), aggression (19%), and/or sexual aggression (13%), which were then rated (on a 1 to 7 scale) for explicitness. Adult and XXX titles averaged 11 sex scenes each, but this constituted 37% of all scenes in the former (averaging 1.8 on explicitness) and 56% in the latter (4.2 on explicitness).

The XXX videos had more frequent presentations of virtually all categories of sex measured, except for nudity that was in two thirds of the sex scenes in the adult and XXX titles: XXX videos had more oral–genital contact (72% of all scenes vs. 17%), the fondling of breasts or genitals (63% vs. 41%), genital–genital intercourse (52% vs. 27%), masturbation (27% vs. 10%), and anal intercourse (10% vs. 1%). By contrast, it was the adult videos that contained more aggression (e.g., more hitting, kicking, using weapons, attempted and actual murders, kidnapping, severe beatings, and torture) and indicators of more sexual aggression (e.g., more verbal humiliation and bondage). Palys (1986) noted: "the triple-X videos were less violent and less sexually violent than the adult movies, and the temporal analyses revealed significant decreases in the prevalence of this content in triple-X videos over time" (p. 34).

So, what does watching X-rated (or XXX) videotapes do? Peterson and Pfost (1989) showed different groups of undergraduate men one video that was an erotic–violent video, erotic–nonviolent, nonerotic–violent, or nonerotic–nonviolent. Both videos that contained eroticism (scantily clad women, breasts shown) produced more sexual arousal. The violent but nonerotic video had the strongest impact on "adversarial sexual beliefs," items that depicted a calloused and antagonistic orientation toward women, and on increasing anger, anxiety, and frustration among the viewers. Peterson and Pfost (1989) concluded: "High levels of anger, anxiety, frustration . . . can motivate aggressive behavior; such motivation might prompt men to think of women as adversaries as they seek an outlet for negative affect"(p. 321).

Zillmann and Bryant (1988) sampled male and female students and nonstudents and exposed them for 6 weeks to hour-long videos that were either "common, nonviolent pornography" or television situation comedies and, in the seventh week asked them to rate their personal happiness in several experience domains, and the relative importance of gratifying experiences. They found that exposure to these pornographic videos did not influence them outside the sexual realm but strongly impacted self-assessment of their sexual experiences in that they were less satisfied with their intimate partners — less satisfied with their affection, physical appearance, sexual performance, and sexual curiosity — and they gave more importance to sex without emotional involvement and less importance to faithfulness and family relations. Surprisingly, these effects occurred equivalently among men and women who watched the pornographic videos. They found that the principal message of such videos is, according to Zillmann and Bryant (1988): "great sexual joy and ecstasy are accessible to parties who just met, who are in no way committed to one another, and who will part shortly, never to meet again" (p. 450).

The somewhat romantic and clearly sanitized description of the adult paperbacks offered by Smith in 1976 is updated by the Zillmann and Bryant (1988) typology of video pornography:

> Only pornography details . . . men and, especially, women who are hysterically euphoric upon entirely common coital stimulation. Only pornography shows men and women to experience the greatest sexual pleasures from coition with many partners, one after the other, or from sexual activities with

several partners at the same time. . . . And only this genre provides specifics such as fellatio in which women make entire male organs vanish or coition in which penises of extreme proportion cause women to scream in apparent painful ecstasy. The sexual experience of normals must pale by comparison. Partners must seem prudish, insensitive, inhibited, frigid, . . . and deficient in endowment and skill. And who, confronted with the bounty of readily attainable sexual joys that are continually presented in pornography and nowhere else, could consider his or her sexual life fulfilled? (p. 452)

SEX IN SOAPS

Here we highlight results from our recent study of the most popular daytime soap operas among junior and senior high school students (Greenberg et al., 1993b). Ten episodes of each of the soaps were videotaped and analyzed. Finding 110 coded acts altogether, 3.67 sex acts were found per hour of soap opera. Individually, the averages in the 10 episodes coded for each soap were 5.2 per hour in "All My Children," 3.1 per hour in "General Hospital," and 2.7 per hour in "One Life To Live."

The most prominent sexual act referred to in each of the three soaps was *intercourse*. It accounted for 62% of all the coded sexual activity and occurred 2.29 times per hour; unmarried intercourse was twice as frequent as married intercourse. Only one other sexual activity, *long, passionate kisses*, occurred frequently, averaging just under one act per episode. Together these two activities accounted for 88% of all codings. Thus, prostitution, rape, and petting were very infrequent, and homosexuality was nil.

Among the 110 coded acts, 30% were visual and nearly all of those were long kisses. Thus, the nature of presenting all other sex acts on the soaps was primarily through verbal exchanges (e.g., people talked about having intercourse, or about other people having intercourse, but were rarely viewed doing so).

Next, we examined the marital status of participants in soap sex. Across all acts, about one fourth of the participants were married to each other, one fourth were married to someone other than their sex partner, one fourth were divorced–widowed, and one fourth were never-married pairings. In unmarried intercourse acts, more than one third were married to someone other than their sex partner and more than one fourth were divorced; thus, extramarital intercourse was nearly as prevalent as all the identifiable pairings in premarital intercourse.

For acts of intercourse in particular, only 16% were both present for the act that was coded, one was present for 50%, and a third of the time none of the participants being discussed were evident. In other words, someone was typically talking about someone else's sexual intercourse, or about one's activity to a third party.

The attitudes of participants and nonparticipants toward the coded activity were rated as positive, negative, or neither. Nonparticipants expressed significantly more negative attitudes toward the sexual activity than the participants, and in each comparison, the negative attitudes reflected a majority of the nonparticipants. Across all acts, 74% of the nonparticipants' attitudes were negative; for married intercourse it was 91% and for unmarried intercourse it was 69%. A majority of the participants are positive toward their sexual activity, but it is a slim majority for both married and unmarried intercourse; negative attitudes are more characteristic across the entire range of participants' sexual activity.

What is the context in which sex acts occur on the soaps? The most consistent feature was that there was a musical accompaniment to 87% of the visual sex activity. Consumption of alcohol was found 13% of the time, and physical aggression 13% of the time. None of the sex acts in the soaps were set in a humorous context. The most favored location was the living room (31%), outdoors (19%), the bedroom (13%), at work (9%), and a wide variety of unique locales (28%; e.g. cars, restaurants).

When did the sex activity occur? The predominant time frames were the past and the present. Fully 39% of the sexual activity identified happened earlier, 35% was occurring at the time, 16% was anticipated in the future, and 10% consisted of fantasies.

SEX IN PRIME-TIME COMMERCIAL TELEVISON SERIES

These results emerge from content analyses of the 19 prime-time commercial network fictional television series viewed most often by 9th and 10th graders (Greenberg et al., 1993b). On average, for each hour of programming, the average was just under three sexual activities. Two acts— *intercourse and long kisses*—predominated. The combination of married and unmarried intercourse occurred 1.14 times per hour, or 39% of the coded sexual activity. Long kisses were found nearly once per hour. Homosexuality and prostitution acts were identified once every 2 hours, with rape and petting extremely rare acts. Married intercourse itself was quite infrequent, accounting for only one sixth of the intercourse activity.

Among the sex acts, 37% were visual; 70% of these were long kisses and 21% were intercourse acts. The majority of sexual activity in prime time was verbal.

Prime-time series, however, are not all of one genre. The favored shows included five action–adventure series, 13 situation comedies, and one evening soap, "Dynasty." The show types are very different in both the magnitude of their sexual content and their categorical distributions.

"Dynasty" was the runaway leader in sexual activity. It provided an average of 10 sex acts per episode; these emphasized unmarried intercourse, long kisses, and homosexuality, with a smattering of rape, married intercourse, and petting. In all, "Dynasty" provided 26% of all the sex acts coded in the 19 series.

The overall rate of sex acts found in action–adventure series and situation comedies was equivalent, 2.61 acts per hour in the former, and 2.52 in the latter. However, there were substantial differences in emphasis. The action–adventure series featured unmarried intercourse (nearly 50% of its total acts) and prostitution (41%); kisses, homosexuality, married intercourse, rape, and petting were nil or nearly so. The situation comedies featured kisses (42%), intercourse (30%), and homosexuality (21%), with little if any of the other coded activities. Of nine visual acts involving intercourse, seven were in the action–adventure series and none were in the situation comedies.

Differences among the individual series, within program types, are also meaningful to describe. Among the five action–adventure series, the primary contributors, then, were "Hill Street Blues" (19 acts), "Riptide" (16), and "Miami Vice" (4). The primary providers of identified sex acts among the situation comedies were "Night Court" (12 acts), "Cheers," "Family Ties," and "Who's The Boss" (7 acts each), and "Three's A Crowd" (6). All others contained 0 to 3 acts across the three coded episodes. Thus, for both program types, the sexual activity was contained in relatively few series.

In terms of marital status for the 234 participants across all sex acts, the largest pairing was between those who were not ever married (28%), followed by those whose marital status was indeterminate (23%). If one combines those never married with those not now married (but whose history is unknown), nearly half the sex participants are accounted for. One in six participants was married to their sex partner. When the activity examined is unmarried intercourse, there is greater ambiguity as to marital status and greater variance; 32% of the intercourse partners provided no marital status information, and 20% were themselves known to be unmarried now. However, fully one fifth were engaging in extramarital intercourse and one fifth in premarital intercourse. Marital status for unmarried intercourse was also examined by program type. On "Dynasty," 50% of the acts were extramarital and 44% were among those whose marital status could not be determined. In action–adventure series, one fifth was extramarital, one fifth was premarital, and one third were not currently married, but their backgrounds were unclear. In situation comedies, there was no extramarital activity, one fourth of the participants were involved in premarital activities, and the largest groupings were among those whose marital status, present and prior, was not able to be identified.

Typically, both participants in prime-time sex were present for whatever activity was going on. Both were present 65% of the time, and one was present an additional 26% of the time. In the analysis of intercourse acts, 36% were both present and at least one was present half the time, reemphasizing the earlier finding that most of the activity is talking rather than doing, but in a large majority of the instances, one or both of the participants was involved in the conversation.

Consistently, across all acts and for each program type, the proportion of participants holding positive attitudes was significantly greater than the proportion of nonparticipants. Positive attitudes were expressed by 71% to 83% of the participants, with the highest proportion found in situation comedies; positive attitudes among the nonparticipants ranged from 15% to 27%, with the highest figure again found in the situation comedies. When this analysis is done for participants and nonparticipants in acts of unmarried intercourse alone, positive attitudes existed among 52% of the participants and 15% of the nonparticipants. Thus, in all cases, the onlookers are far more likely to frown at the goings-on, but for unmarried intercourse, those who participate express evenly divided feelings.

The most regular occurring feature in the context of visual sex acts on these prime-time series was musical accompaniment, 48% of the time. Eating (19%) and drinking (14%) also occurred with some regularity, whereas physical aggression was minimal (5%).

Sex acts were cast in a humorous context only in situation comedies — in 47% of the acts in that genre. The location of sex activity featured bedrooms (45%), work (23%), and restaurants (19%). Bedrooms dominated action–adventure series (90%) and "Dynasty" (83%), whereas situation comedy sex was located in restaurants (40%) and more unique locales (40%). For prime-time series, 43% of the sex acts were ongoing or current, 41% had already occurred, and 17% were future plans; there were no fantasy sequences.

Soaps Sex Versus Prime-Time Sex

The individual presentations of sexual content in soaps and prime-time series most watched by adolescent viewers may mask direct comparisons between them. Here those comparisons are made manifest:

Sex acts in preferred daytime soaps are more frequent per program hour than during preferred prime-time series.

Prime-time series have more varied sexual activity than the soaps; within prime time, in order of magnitude, "Dynasty" featured unmarried intercourse, long kisses, and homosexuality, action–adventure series featured unmarried intercourse and prostitution, and situation comedies featured long kisses, intercourse, and homosexuality. Soaps maximized intercourse and long kisses.

All favored soaps have sexual activity; among the most viewed prime-time series, three of five action–adventure series contained all the identified acts, and 5 of 13 situation comedies contained 81% of the identified acts. The vast majority of the prime-time sexual acts identified appeared in a minority of a series.

Sexual activity occurring among persons not married to each other nor to anyone is greater in the prime-time series; extramarital intercourse has more participants in the soaps; premarital intercourse has more participants in the prime-time series; marital status is less likely to be known–identified in prime time.

At night, it is more likely that both participants in intercourse activity will be present in the scene; in the soaps, it is more likely that someone is talking about sex to a third party.

Soaps' nonparticipants have more positive attitudes toward acts of sexual intercourse than prime-time nonparticipants, although the majority of each are negative. Participants are generally positive by a three-to-one margin.

There is no humor in sexual activity in the daytime; there is considerable humor as the context for sex in situation comedies in the evening.

Fantasizing or dreaming about sexual activities is unique to the soaps.

SEX CONTENT IN MAGAZINES

Let us begin with *Playboy* magazine, that bastion of male fantasies, and begin specifically with its cartoons. Matacin and Burger (1987) looked for sexual content in about 260 cartoons for the 1985 issues and found it in 61% of the cartoons. Then, they looked for four specific themes of sexual content; they found *seduction* as the core of the humor in 17% of the sexual cartoons, and both men and women were seducers to the same extent; they found *sexual coerciveness* (forcing sexual attention on someone) in 4%, and it was always the male who was the coercer; they found *sexual naivete* (innocence and vulnerability) in 6% of the cartoons, and in 90% of them, it was the woman who was naive; and they found an emphasis on *body shapes* in 11% of the cartoons, and the men had less attractive shapes 77% of the time.

Earlier, Malamuth and Spinner (1980) had compared *Playboy* with *Penthouse*, the two best-selling erotic magazines, for 5 years, and they examined pictures as well as cartoons specifically for the presence of sexually violent content (i.e., stimuli that depicted rape, sadomasochism, or exploitative, coercive, sexual relations). They found an increase in sexually violent pictorials in both magazines in both absolute numbers and as a percentage of all pictures. Sexually violent cartoons increased in *Penthouse*, but not *Playboy*; over the 5 years, 13% of the *Penthouse* cartoons were sexually violent, compared to half that percentage in *Playboy*. They added (Malamuth & Spinner, 1980): "While this constitutes a relatively small percentage, there exists the possibility that such materials contribute to a "cultural climate" which sanctions acts of violence against women . . . A message of female subordination communicated in varied forms may have summative effects in promoting a sexist ideology" (p. 235).

Winick (1985) expanded the scope of inquiry further by reading all 430 different sexually explicit magazine titles sold in an adult bookstore in New York City, and categorizing each one on the basis of its predominant content. In broad categories, his distribution of these magazines identified *content related to women* (35% of all pages) (e.g., with various degrees of undress, including genital details comprising 28%); *heterosexual activity* (25% of pages), comprised primarily of male–female sexual activity without showing actual body part interaction (18%), and male–female sexual activity including genital interaction (6%); *special sexual preferences* (23%) with no specific preference dominating, from among bondage (5%), oral–genital sexual interaction (3%), use of dildoes (3%), and the remainder — lesbians, swingers, sadomasochism, fetishes, group set, and so on at 1% to 2%; and *mixed content* (14%), which included one or more of the preceding categories, with none dominating.

If these magazines are not on your normal subscription or gift list, Scott (1986) analyzed *Reader's Digest, McCall's, Life, Time, Newsweek*, and the *Saturday Evening Post* for four decades, 1950 through 1980. He analyzed all articles in the first four issues at the beginning of each decade. The sheer number of sex references increased 84% from 1950 to 1960, 16% from 1960 to 1970, and another 68% from 1970 to 1980. One of his measures was the ratio of sex references per editorial page; if you read these magazines in 1950, you would have found 17 references in 100 pages of text, and if you read them in 1980, you would have found 88 references in 100 pages, or nearly one sex reference per page.

What did he mean by sex references? Between 1950 and 1980, the annual percentage of sex references that suggested *extramarital intercourse* increased from 18% to 26%; *sex relations leading to pregnancy* increased from 8% to 16%; *sex perversions* increased from 8% to 15%, whereas references to *noncoital sex* (e.g., kissing and hugging) fell from 20% of all references in 1950 to 5% in 1980; references to *censorship and sex education* fell from 20% to 12%; the only constant was references to *sex desires and sex organs*, which was 25% of the references in each decade. Scott also examined whether the text reflected these references in a conservative or liberal fashion; liberal references predominated in each decade, ranging from 41% to 46%, whereas conservative references decreased from 33% to 19% in the same time period.

SEX IN R-RATED MOVIES

Sixteen films were selected from the strongest box office R-rated films available over 3 years. They were selected because of their special appeal to young viewers and because their R-rating was based on sexual content rather than on violent content. Nine of the 16 films had been seen by 53% to 77% of the ninth and tenth graders surveyed; six of the remainder had been seen by 35% to 46% of the sample (Greenberg et al., 1993a).

There were 280 coded sex acts in the 16 films, or 17.5 per film. On a per-hour basis, the viewer had 10.8 acts available per film hour. The runaway winner was the category of *sexual intercourse between unmarried partners*. There were eight such coded acts per film, or 46% of all the sexual activity found. All films contained at least one incident-reference to sexual intercourse and the majority had at least half a dozen. Sexual intercourse between marriage partners occurred once every four films, or four times altogether. The ratio then of unmarried to married intercourse was 32:1.

Three other activities were identified two to three times per film. *Prostitution* was found an average of three times per film, but this average masks the concentration of this category in only two films—*Bachelor Party* and *Risky Business*—for 47 of the 48 prostitution acts. *Long kisses* and *"other"* acts averaged 2.38 and 2.19 acts per film and were located in all but one or two films. The other category included a variety of references to masturbation, virginity, sex with animals, and so forth. *Heavy petting* was found a little more than once per film, and in a majority of the movies. Little seen or discussed was *homosexuality* (in six films, and never more than twice in any one film). Intercourse between marriage partners has been discussed, and *rape* was not in any of the films.

Although a majority of the filmed references to sexual activities was verbal, 36% of all acts had some visual component. One sixth (17%) of the intercourse acts had some visual component, as well.

The attitudes of the participants in sexual activity toward what they are doing was also analyzed. Most simply, those participating were portrayed as either overtly positive toward what they are doing, or no codable attitude was indicated. Acts of intercourse were even more favorably received than the total group of acts.

The initiator of the sex act was identified. In 16% of the acts, there was clearly a single initiator; in these instances, that initiator was a male 55% of the time and a female 45% of the time. In 26% of the acts, initiation mutually involved both participants, and in the majority of the incidents (58%), it was not clear that there was any particular initiator.

The vast majority of the time, the sexual activity was presented in a serious context; 13% of the visual acts were humorous, as were 28% of the verbal acts. Half the time, the scene presented involved both sex act participants, one third of the time, only one was present, and the remainder were scenes involving discussions of the sexual activities of persons not present.

The sexual activities were typically presented as happening now; 54% were current, 29% were reports of past activities, 14% were future plans, and 2% were fantasy-dream situations. Behaviors concurrent with sexual activity featured the accompaniment of background music in 70% of the visual incidents; other ongoing activities included drinking alcohol (10% of the incidents), eating (2%), and physical aggression (6%).

The most favored single location for sexual activity was the bedroom, in 25% of the visual incidents. Other primary sites were the living room (11%), outdoors (10%), a car (9%), at work (3%), in a restaurant (3%), and in a bar (2%). Note, however, that fully 37% of the locations were "other places," indicating a good deal of creativity in the location of this sex activity. Among the other places of note were showers, elevators, cemeteries, staircases, retail stores, and so on.

Concurrent with examining sexual activity in these movies, all incidents of drinking, both alcoholic and nonalcoholic, were identified and all incidents related to drug use were coded. For both, the coders identified if the individual was using the drug or drinking the beverage, or whether the individual was offering, preparing, or selling the substance. Further, for drugs, the substance was identified as marijuana, cocaine, pills, or some other illicit drug; alcoholic beverages were coded as beer, wine, liquor, or some other undefined alcohol; nonalcoholic beverages were tallied without regard for kind. These incidents were not confined to scenes involving sex but were identified wherever they occurred in the movies. Every film had some drinking, with an average of 16 drinking incidents per film. The range was from two incidents in each of three films to 53 incidents in one film, *Spring Break*. A dozen or more drinking incidents were found in nine of the 16 films analyzed. Nine of every 10 drinking incidents involved alcohol.

Ten of the 16 films had zero or a single drug incident, although the per-film average was 3.56. Four films—*Bachelor Party, Class, Revenge of the Nerds*, and *The Wild Life*—accounted for 75% of the drug activities. Two thirds of the drug incidents involved use; marijuana was the most popular drug, involved in 77% of the incidents; the other drugs were evenly divided among the remaining incidents.

Another content area coded was that of the use of profanity by the films' characters. This also was not confined to sexual incidents but covered the entire film. Profanities abounded in this set of movies. There was an average of 45 per film, and the frequencies ranged from 11 to 101. Five key words and their variants accounted for 79% of all the swearing. They were: fuck (found 152 times, 23% of all swearing), shit (146 times, 23%), damn (12%), ass (12%), and hell (9%).

Who swore? Nine times out of 10, the originator was a male, and this was very consistent across the language choices; proportionately, females were more likely to say "damn" than any other option. One male was the intended receiver of these oaths in 49% of the instances, one female in 13%, a group of people 22%, and no one in particular, 15% of the time.

Given this concurrent examination of multiple activities—albeit a central focus on sexual activities—the question arose of the extent of overlap among these activities within the individual films. When you have sex, do you have drinking? Is drug taking accompanied by swearing? Or are these independent events? Only one relationship was statistically significant—the relationship between drinking and using drugs in these films was .48 ($p <$ .05). The presence of sexual activity itself, however, was unrelated to any of these other behaviors.

DISCUSSION

Considerable sex activity is available through the media, but obviously more in some media than in others, and the degree of explicitness is certainly an important differentiating characteristic. The fan of such content need not exert much effort to get what he or she wants—from the bookstore, from the video rental store, from their daytime and primetime broadcast network shows, from their basic and pay cable channels, and by going out to the movies.

Two issues emerge from the magnitude or rate of sexual content on broadcast television. First, comparing the overall per-hour rates with prior studies, the present rates are higher for both daytime and nighttime. For example, the soaps' sex rate is 21% higher than 1982 data and 103% higher than 1980. Two possible explanations cannot be disentangled in this study: There is more sex on a regular basis in the soaps, or there is more sex on a regular basis in the soaps that young adolescents prefer to watch. A second issue relates to the magnitude of viewing or listening to sexual references on television. The per-hour rates described can be extended quite simply: Beginning with prime time and using three acts per hour, 1 hour of viewing per evening on weekdays and 2 hours on weekends (which are low estimates for adolescents), that multiplies to 27 acts per week times 52 weeks, or a minimum of 1,400 per year. Then, for soaps, at least 90 minutes per day for the girls, with four acts per hour times 5 days a week, another 1,000+ acts become part of the yearly content experience. For boys, it may be half that experience from soaps, but their prime-time viewing is heavier. Some prime-time hours (and *all* soaps) feature sex. Thus, what a viewer chooses to watch can greatly affect exposure to sex-related content.

There remains the question of whether what has been coded or defined as sex incidents is appropriate. For example, the inclusion of extended kissing and embraces in several of these studies is questionable. So, those who wish to challenge their inclusion may do so and delete it from a catalog of media sex content. If ignored, then the TV shows most often watched contain *only* 2,000 references to intercourse, prostitution, homosexuality, and so forth on an annual basis. This, by any standard, remains a large number of messages.

Sex is by no means consistently presented in a positive manner on television. When the vast majority of those expressing an attitude about other people's sexual exploits are negative, and when barely half of those participating themselves are positive, the most reasonable hypothesis is that the viewer will be at least ambivalent if not negative—at least about the sexual activity of the television characters.

People talking about sex; that is what commercial television series present primarily. Few models of physical sexual activity appear on television. Of course, testing the proposition that regular viewing of such shows accelerates personal sexual activity has been impeded by the inability of media researchers to query adolescent viewers about their sexual activity; schools are less than eager to participate in such studies.

Moviegoing for adolescents is typically a social activity, in the company of friends of one or both genders. The survey that identified the movies analyzed in this chapter also queried the frequency of moviegoing. Half the youngsters had been out to a movie at least twice in the past 30 days, and 20% of them had been to a movie four or more times in that period. Watching movies in video form was another common occurrence. Clearly, the time spent with movies is not equivalent to that spent with television. An interesting question then is the extent to which differences may accrue from the total time spent with content that contains sex-related materials, and/or from the intensity and magnitude of the individual content experience. All films described, including those on adult and XXX videos contain stronger messages about sexual activity and more concrete models and examples than found on television. One XXX video would seem to provide a far more intense experience than a couple of R-rated or adult films, or many, many hours of television and music videos.

The typical 90-minute R-rated film yields seven times the amount of sexual activity found on commercial broadcast television and nearly that proportion more than found on music videos, and much more of it is visual and explicit. The films' characters are single, young, and quite favorable toward the goings on. For all media, the primary sexual activity is heterosexual intercourse outside of marriage with virtually no discussion or utilization of contraception.

What television suggests, movies and videos do. Perhaps, then, exposure to programming on television that hints at sexual goings on serves best to establish an acceptable mood or tolerance for increased sexual activity or on specific beliefs related to the occurrence of these behaviors, the need for marriage, and so on. Seeing movies may intensify that tolerance and those beliefs and additionally inform as to the conduct and performance of a variety of sexual behaviors.

In concluding, let us construct a series of media effects propositions that more directly reflect the content analytic results. The propositions include the following:

1. More regular viewers of television programs, music videos, movies, and the other media described in this chapter that feature sexual incidents are more likely to be preoccupied with sex. They are more likely to spend more time thinking about sex, talking with peers about sex, to believing that others are more preoccupied with that topic, and that others talk about it more. Sex is likely to be stronger in the hierarchy of things they think are important, to themselves and to others.

2. One can anticipate that heavy users have stronger beliefs that sex is a more regular and popular activity among young people, especially sexual intercourse.

3. More regular users of media sex are more likely to develop or maintain beliefs that sex in various forms happens more frequently. The lesson available is that there is more sex — more premarital, more extramarital, more postmarital, more prostitution, more rape. Perhaps as well, that sex within marriage is rarer.

4. More regular viewers are more likely to think they know more about sex, perhaps that they are better able to counsel others about romance, love, and so on.

5. More regular viewers are more likely to be sanguine about the sanctity of marriage. Themes of divorce, illegitimacy, deception, and general hanky-panky are pervasive.

6. That participants in sexual activities are not negative toward encounters and likely are positive, given that having sex in media portrayals seldom involves consideration of contraception and seldom has negative consequences.

7. The virtually constant accompaniment of music with sexual activity in all video forms raises the question of the import and meaning of that combination.

One further speculation: Regular exposure to successful sex encounters may alter one's self-perception. Those who believe that they have not been having the kind of success they have been viewing or reading about may be less satisfied with their sex life or progress, or perhaps they may more actively seek out opportunities for sexual satisfaction. All these propositions and questions remain open to direct research attention.

As for the question with which we began, just how much sex content is available, the answer is of course as much as you might want. Vast amounts of implicit sexual activity come from our daily television behavior, from the broadcast and cable networks; this is supplemented regularly by far more explicit sex content in the most popular movies available in local theaters. Further enlarged sex diets come from specialized menus available by choice in the bookstores and the video rental stores. All these opportunities for vicarious sex are fairly well documented. What is not is the impact of these experiences on our social, cognitive, and affective orientations toward sex.

ACKNOWLEDGMENT

Valuable assistance in compiling the information for this chapter came from Jeffrey E. Brand, a doctoral student at Michigan State University, where Dr. Greenberg is University Distinguished Professor of Telecommunication and Communication.

REFERENCES

Baxter, R. L., DeRiemer, C., Landini, A., Leslie, L., & Singletary, M. W. (1985). A content analysis of music videos. *Journal of Broadcasting & Electronic Media, 29*(3), 333–340.

Cowan, G., Lee, C., Levy, D., & Snyder, D. (1988). Dominance and inequality in X-rated videocassettes. *Psychology of Women Quarterly, 12*, 299–311.

Greenberg, B. S., Siemicki, M., Dorfman, S., Heeter, C., Stanley, C., Soderman, A., & Linsangan, R. (1993a). *Sex content in r-rated films viewed by adolescents.* In B. S. Greenberg, J. D. Brown, & N. L. Buerkel-Rachfuss (Eds.), *Media, sex and the adolescent.* Cresskill, NJ: Hampton Press.

Greenberg, B. S., Stanley, C., Siemicki, M., Heeter, C., Soderman, A., & Linsangan, R. (1993b). *Sex content on soaps and primetime television series most viewed by adolescents* In B. S. Greenberg, J. D. Brown, & N. L. Buerkel-Rachfuss (Eds.), *Media, sex and the adolescent* (pp. 45–58). Cresskill, NJ: Hampton Press.

Malamuth N. M., & Spinner, B. (1980). A longitudinal content analysis of sexual violence in the best-selling erotic magazines. *The Journal of Sex Research, 16*(3), 226–237.

Matacin, M. L., & Burger, J. M. (1987). A content analysis of sexual themes in *Playboy* cartoons. *Sex Roles, 17*(3/4), 179–186.

Palys, T. S. (1986). Testing the common wisdom: The social content of video pornography. *Canadian Psychology, 27*(1), 22–35.

Peterson, D. L., & Pfost, K. S. (1989). Influence of rock videos on attitudes of violence against women. *Psychological Reports, 64*, 319–322.

Scott, J. E. (1986). An updated longitudinal content analysis of sex references in mass circulation magazines. *Journal of Sex Research, 22*(3), 385–392.

Sherman, B. L., & Dominick, J. R. (1986). Violence and sex in music videos: TV and rock 'n' roll. *Journal of Communication, 36*(1), 79–93.

Smith, D. D. (1976). The social content of pornography. *Journal of Communication, 26*(1), 16–24.

Winick, C. (1985). A content analysis of sexually explicit magazines sold in an adult bookstore. *The Journal of Sex Research, 21*(2), 206–210.

Zillmann, D., & Bryant, J. (1988). Pornography's impact on sexual satisfaction. *Journal of Applied Social Psychology, 18*(5), 438–453.

14

EFFECTS OF MASSIVE EXPOSURE TO SEXUALLY ORIENTED PRIME-TIME TELEVISION PROGRAMMING ON ADOLESCENTS' MORAL JUDGMENT

Jennings Bryant
Steven Carl Rockwell
University of Alabama

Evidence has begun to mount that some of the most durable and important effects of watching television may come in the form of subtle, incremental, cumulative changes in the way we view the world (i.e., in our perceptions of social reality). We like to think of these subtle shifts in the way we think about things as stalagmite effects — cognitive deposits built up almost imperceptibly from the drip-drip-drip of television's electronic limewater.

Today we would like to address one particular type of stalagmite effect, one that is seldom discussed in the scholarly community. That is the potential shifts in *moral judgment* that may come about from watching certain types of television. Moreover, we would like to look at this issue in the context of one of the least discussed and understood audiences for television — young adolescents.

There are some very good reasons why scholars do not talk about moral judgment more than they do; and there are good reasons why we do not focus very much on adolescents as audiences for television. Let us begin with the latter.

Figure 14.1 plots the time Americans spend watching television compared with the time devoted to other daily activities, by age. As you can

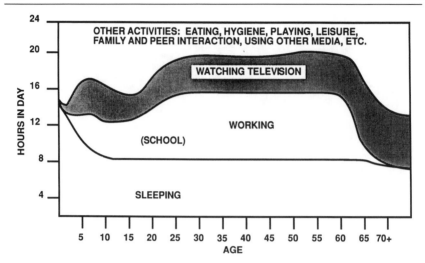

FIG. 14.1.   Diagram of time spent watching television compared to other activities, by age.

readily see, that time interval "between 12 and 20"—the teenage years—is the single period in our lives when we watch television the very least.

As can be seen even more precisely from Fig. 14.2, which reports Nielsen's 1988 estimates of "Weekly Viewing Activity for Women, Men, Teens and Children" (Nielsen Media Research, 1989), during 1988, teenage girls used television 21 hours and 18 minutes per week; teenage boys, 22 hours and 36 minutes. Compare that with the 30 to 40 hours the "twenty-somethings" through the "sixtysomethings" use the medium, and scholars' lack of interest in teenagers' television use can be readily justified.

Just as important, perhaps, is the fact that the proportion of teenagers in

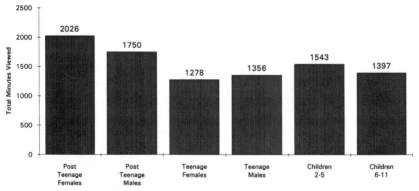

FIG. 14.2.   Number of minutes of television viewed weekly (original data from Nielsen Media Research, November 1988).

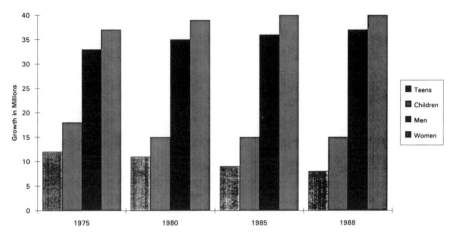

FIG. 14.3. Growth of total persons in TV households (millions).

the audience is continuing to decline. In the *Nielsen Report on Television 1989*, a big deal was made of the fact that teenage viewers have declined from 12% of the television audience in 1920 to 11% in 1980, to 9% in 1985, to 8% in 1988. That is partially a function of the "graying of America" and partially a function of teenagers increased infatuation with other media — their phones and their tunes, for example.

The "good reasons" why scholars have failed to focus much attention on matters like *moral judgment* are less easy to chart, but just as real. A portion of these reasons have to do with the fact that the moral judgment construct is conceptually a bit more slippery than most. But a bigger portion probably has to do with the fact that in some circles moral judgment is somewhat of a taboo subject. Perhaps we believe so strongly in the separation of things civil and things "religious" that issues that may overlap those boundaries make some scholars uncomfortable. These boundary disputes have given us more than one pause to consider whether we were doing the right thing by getting into this area of inquiry. We know that some people are bound to misinterpret our motives, just because of the topic.

Nonetheless, we chose to deal with moral judgment; and we chose to deal with adolescents. Why?

Because the issues involved are so important as to overcome all the valid reasons not to tilt with these particular windmills. Adolescence is a particularly turbulent time in which very insecure people struggle with their self-concepts and their values on a daily basis. More critically for the present study, many teenagers' values appear to be quite frail and very malleable — constantly in a state of flux; continuously seeking some acceptable equilibrium and identity. This is a very vulnerable time — a "make it or break it" time that warrants much more of our scholarly attention than it gets.

Moreover, moral judgmental factors are extremely critical, not only for healthy overall human development, but also for very practical aspects of understanding the mediated entertainment experience that we devote so much of our time to studying. Just to give one example: What little evidence we have in this realm suggests that our enjoyment of television programs is circumscribed by moral judgmental considerations of "what is right," "what is fair," and "what is just." If a producer or director dares to violate our expectations of "what ought to be," the entertainment experience falls flat. Enjoyment goes out the window.

However, in this chapter we focus not on the place of moral judgment in entertainment, but on the effects entertainment fare can have on moral judgment. We have already made the point that, during the formative teenage years, boys' and girls' expectations for "what ought to be" appear to be rather malleable. Although it is doubtful that television plays a dominant role in determining concepts of "what's right," "what's wrong," and the like, the medium is a readily available consultant for teenagers for between 21 to 22 hours per week — far more than the average parent is probably available. Because of this it is highly likely that television contributes at least somewhat to moral development in at least some areas. This should be especially true in those areas about which teenagers want to know a great deal more, about which many of them have very limited personal experiences, and about which parents and caretakers are reluctant to talk. One of the biggest "for instances" may be sex.

As Bradley Greenberg (this volume) demonstrates, quite a bit of the content of prime-time television programming — as well as much of the content of our daytime "soaps" and talk shows — is sexually oriented. And because, according to Nielsen's (1989) estimates, teenagers comprise the same percentage of the television audience at 10:00 p.m. EST (7%) as they do at 8:00 p.m., it seems highly likely that a portion of their "sex education" comes from prime-time programming.

EXPERIMENTAL EXPLORATIONS

In three experimental studies we asked ourselves the question, "What do teenagers learn in terms of moral judgment from prime-time television programming?" More specifically, we asked: "Can the sexually oriented messages of prime-time entertainment change teenagers' moral judgment?" And we asked, "What factors, if any, can mediate any media effects on teenagers' moral judgment?"

EXPERIMENT 1

In the first investigation, which focused on establishing whether there *could be* any media effects on adolescents' moral judgment, we began by screening 120 hours of prime-time television programs from the 1984 to 1987 seasons that we held in our archives. We looked specifically at programming that would be likely to have a lot of sexual content. This amounted primarily to examining the adult-oriented evening serial dramas and related fare popular during the mid to late 1980s. An advantage of such programming was that it was not likely to be very familiar to our young audiences (e.g., "Dynasty," "Dallas," "Falcon Crest," "Knots Landing," "Emerald Point," "Hotel," and the like). Via selecting, editing, and pretesting, we came up with 15 hours of each of three categories of programming content—episodes, or more typically, portions of episodes, which featured (a) sexual relations between unmarried partners, (b) sexual relations between married partners, and (c) nonsexual relations between adults.

The second factor was gender of the research participants. Specifically, the study included 13-and 14-year-old boys and girls. The factorial design employed was a 3 × 2. Procedurally, during a single week, the teenagers watched television in small groups for 3 hours per night for 5 consecutive nights. They were charged with the task of rating the programs they watched at designated points on some spurious items that were designed to mask the real purpose of the study. At least 3 days, but no more than 1 week after the week's viewing had been completed, the research participants returned for a final session. At some point during that session, each subject individually watched 14 brief video vignettes excerpted from commercial network television. The segments ranged in length from 17 sec to 52 sec. Seven of the segments featured a nonsexual transgression or crime, and the other seven featured sexual indiscretions or improprieties. These segments ranged in terms of the severity of the violations from mild to rather severe. To illustrate the sexually oriented fare, the segments ranged from a mild scene from "*Dynasty*" in which Dominique Deveraux accused Blake Carrington of wanting her to go to bed with a mutual acquaintance for material gain, to a much stronger scene from "*Hotel*" in which a wife quietly entered her husband's hotel room and slipped very seductively into bed—to provide hubby with a pleasant surprise. Only she got a not-so-pleasant surprise of her own. Hubby emerged dripping wet from the shower accompanied by his equally wet homosexual lover.

To test the effects of prior exposure to television on the teenagers' prevalent moral judgmental values, after viewing each vignette, each research participant provided ratings on 10-point scales assessing three dimensions of moral judgment: (a) How *bad*, morally speaking, is the indiscretion, impropriety, transgression, or crime that was perpetrated?; (b) how much has the victim—or the victims—been wronged? (c) how much has the victim—or the victims—*suffered*?

This procedure and the dependent measures were adopted wholesale from a pornography impact study that one of us conducted previously with Dolf Zillmann (Bryant, 1985). We also employed several other dependent measures.

What did we find? What, if any, were the carry-over effects on moral judgment of being immersed within one or another television environment for 15 hours? Notice from Fig. 14.4, no gender differences were found. Also, although not seen from this figure, no effects were found for any of the dependent measures depicting nonsexual, criminal, or antisocial behavior. However, for boys and girls alike, massive exposure to prime-time television programming that dwelt on pre, extra, or nonmarital sexual relations caused the young viewers to rate the sexual indiscretions or improprieties depicted in the seven vignettes as significantly *less bad* than their peers in either of the two other viewing conditions rated them.

Likewise, similar effects and the same pattern of mean scores resulted for the question that asked how much the victims had been *wronged*. As can be seen from Fig. 14.5, the differentiation in mean scores is slightly more pronounced for the latter measure than for the former. The same pattern of results was revealed for the question assessing victim suffering. However, the differentiation in mean scores was less pronounced in this instance, and the results failed to achieve acceptable levels of statistical significance.

In the first investigation, then, watching a substantial amount of television programming with rather homogeneous but subtle lessons on moral—or some might say immoral—behavior did "teach" the teenagers a

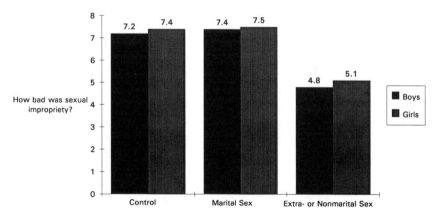

FIG. 14.4.   Study I: Effects on adolescents' moral judgment of massive exposure to sexually oriented television programming by context of sexual relationship and gender.

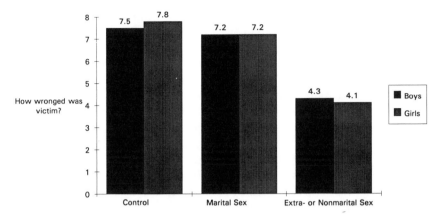

FIG. 14.5. Study I: Effects on adolescents' moral judgment of massive exposure to sexually oriented television programming by context of sexual relationship and gender.

lesson in moral values that they later used to interpret moral judgmental dimensions of other sexually oriented situations and behaviors.

EXPERIMENT 2

Having established via this first study that media exposure can make a difference on moral judgment, we conducted a second study to attempt to replicate and refine these results and to begin to determine those factors, if any, which could mitigate or intervene in those media effects on moral judgment that we had found. The research literature in combination with our own experiences and pretheoretical musings led us to look at two human factors—or individual differences measures—that might be expected to make a difference.

The first individual differences factor we incorporated has been discussed for decades but seldom has been tested directly. It is how *cognitively active* the audience member is in seeking, selecting, receiving, perceiving, processing, and interpreting television's messages. The supposition has been widely made (e.g., Brown, 1991; Bryant & Anderson, 1983) that an active viewing style will lead to more critical media consumption and, therefore, more resistance to attitude change and the like.

In a set of pretests involving hundreds of 13- to 14-year-old boys and girls from Northwest suburban Houston school districts, we attempted to locate a large population of active versus passive viewers. (We were also pretesting for several other factors that are discussed later.) The pretesting took 7 months and included the work of students from two graduate research seminars. Three procedures, ranging from an interview on viewing style to a clinical test of alpha–beta wave blocking, were employed in an attempt to come up with reliable and valid means of testing this construct.

The second human factor incorporated into this experiment was the family communication style that the youngsters experienced at home. It has frequently been alleged and occasionally found that families who establish very open, discussant, participatory lines of communication between all family members create environments in which maturing family members are better equipped to meet the challenges of a rhetorically demanding society – a society in which many public communication messages are designed to manipulate opinions and to persuade viewers and listeners on numerous issues both important and trivial (e.g., Bryant, 1990; Rice & Atkin, 1989; Salmon, 1989; Selnow & Crano, 1987).

We used five tests, ranging from family sociograms to behavioral simulations, to determine whether the teenagers' families tended to communicate in an open or a closed manner. Moreover, we did not stop with the students. For those students whose family communication style seemed either very open or very closed, we completed follow-up surveys with at least one parent or guardian. Ultimately, we found a large pool of teenagers widely differentiated in active versus passive viewing and open versus closed family communication styles.

The 3 × 2 × 2 factorial design we employed used the same procedures as the first study but somewhat different communication-exposure conditions. We retained the condition of exposure to the 15 hours of programming featuring sexual relations between unmarried adults, and we retained the condition featuring exposure to scenes of nonsexual relations between adults. However, we dropped the condition of exposure to scenes of sexual relations between married adults and substituted for it a condition of no exposure to television. The teenagers in this condition met with an experimenter and studied or read books or magazines for 3 hours per night for 5 consecutive nights. We incorporated this nonviewing control in case we had inadvertently created a "treatment" condition via 15 hours of exposure to the nonsexually oriented programming. What did we find? First, as can be seen from Fig. 14.6, the results on the measures assessing media effects on moral judgment were essentially the same as those found in our first study. The earlier results were replicated, and we say no more about them here.

However, if one examines the findings from the condition of heavy viewing of sexually oriented fare and adds the two potentially effect-mitigating human factors, one sees that human factors do make a difference. For ratings of how bad the sexual impropriety depicted in the seven vignettes was, both active viewing and open family communication style mediated the effects of exposure. In fact, a significant three-way interaction indicated that a combination of active viewing and open family communi-

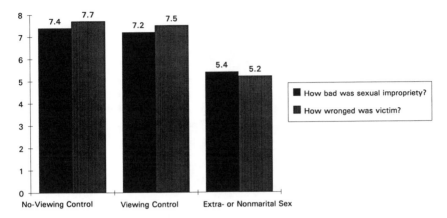

FIG. 14.6. Study II: Effects of massive exposure to sexually oriented television by moral judgmental index on adolescents' moral judgment.

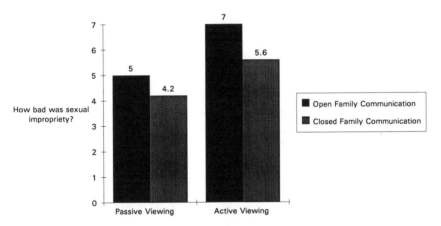

FIG. 14.7. Study II: The mediating effects of family communication and adolescents' cognitive viewing activity on perceived gravity of sexual indiscretions.

cation style completely mitigated any potential message effects. Active viewing teenagers who were from homes in which family members communicated openly apparently were not effected a great deal by being immersed for 15 hours in an alternative value culture. Their moral judgment did not change.

Notice from Fig. 14.8, which charts the ratings of how much the victim was wronged, the only other dependent measure on which significant effects were found, that precisely the same pattern of mean scores resulted. A similar interaction was found also. Once again, active viewing and an open family communication environment apparently provided resistance to cognitive stalagmite formation.

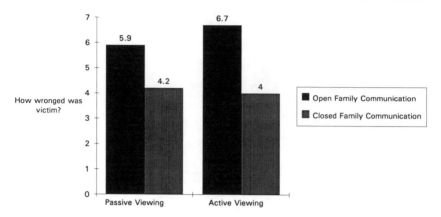

FIG. 14.8.   Study II: The mediating effects of family communication and adolescents'
cognitive viewing activity on perceptions of how severely victim was wronged.

EXPERIMENT 3

The third study utilized two other individual difference factors that we had
tapped in our pretesting. In this instance, we incorporated two "politically
sensitive" factors: (a) whether or not the teenagers came from families with
a *clear, well-defined value* system; and (b) whether the orientation of that
value system was *liberal* versus *conservative*. Again, multimeasure pretests
were used. If testing the adolescents proved promising, we followed up with
confirmatory or disconfirmatory surveys with their parents. The same
media-exposure or nonexposure conditions used in the second study were
employed again, resulting in a 3 × 2 × 2 factorial design.

Once again, the now familiar findings of media effects on moral
judgment were replicated, although as an examination of Fig. 14.9 reveals,
the results were not so robust this time. Why? Probably because we
eliminated so much of the "middle ground" — students from families whose
value systems were only moderately well defined and whose families were
"moderates" in their political and decision-making stances as well.

Figure 14.10 shows, once again, that individual difference factors made
a difference. On the question of "how *bad* were the sexual improprieties?,
"the clearest differentiation in grouped mean scores is between young
teenagers from families with "clear" versus "fuzzy" value systems. Liberal
versus conservative "leanings" tended to made some difference in the other
two conditions, but these mean scores from the condition of exposure to
sexually oriented media messages are not significantly different on the
liberal versus conservative dimensions. Moreover, the only significant
interaction that emerged was a two-way interaction between clarity of the
family value system and the media-exposure condition, further substanti-
ating the importance that coming from a family with a well-defined value
system can have in mitigating media effects.

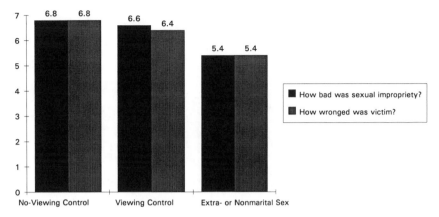

FIG. 14.9. Study III: Effects of massive exposure to sexually oriented television programming by moral judgment index on adolescents' moral judgment.

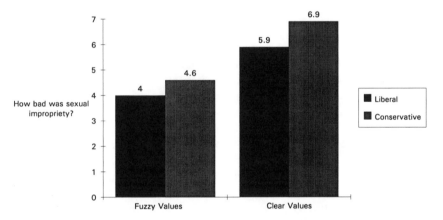

FIG. 14.10. Study III: The mediating effects of clarity of family value system and liberal versus conservative orientation on perceived gravity of sexual indiscretions.

From examining Fig. 14.11, you see the results on the second measure—How severely wronged was the victim?—were almost identical to those assessing the gravity of the sexual improprieties. This, of course, lends further credence to the findings.

DISCUSSION AND CONCLUSIONS

What can we conclude from these three experiments? A great deal, we hope, because these findings form the basis for our position on the role of media effects within the family:

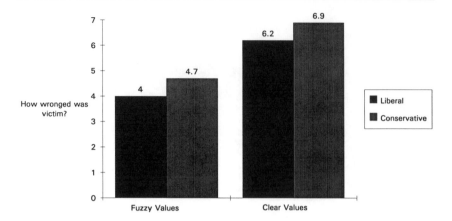

FIG. 14.11. Study III: The mediating effects of clarity of family value systems and liberal versus conservative orientation on perceptions of how severely victim was wronged.

1. For young teenagers, who are one of the most vulnerable groups of family members, heavy exposure to prime-time television programming featuring sexual intimacy between unmarried persons can clearly result in altered *moral judgment*. Because much of television's current sexuality appear's to be comprised of just these kinds of depictions—a supposition clarified in Dr. Greenberg's chapter—we might expect that some young people's moral values are being affected by watching prime-time television.

2. But—and this is a big and important BUT—several individual and family factors can mitigate, if not downright eliminate, any potential unwanted shifts in values that might occur from watching television. Three crucial factors emerged among those we considered: First, having a clear and well-defined family value system—a value system that teenagers can know and use—mediates potentially harmful media effects; the second mitigating factor we found is coming from a family in which free and open discussion of issues is encouraged and practiced. We included in our pretesting the "free and open discussion" of television programming as well as family discussions of issues like media effects. This clearly seemed to make a difference in preventing media effects. Milton (1644, cited in Black & Bryant, 1992) seems to have been both right and prescient when he argued: "Let truth and falsehood grapple. Whoever saw truth put to the worse in a free and open encounter" (p. 530); third, active critical viewing, or the active viewing and analysis of program content, is a most desirable trait for teenagers to have and is to be encouraged. Again, it can make a big difference in mediating the cognitive effects of mass media consumption as far as moral judgment is concerned.

We are sure that many other factors come into play in mitigating media effect on teenagers' moral judgment, but these are all the ones we have examined.

In light of our findings, our final message contains a caveat, a note of hope, and a challenge. The caveat is not to be taken literally, for we conclude that a warning label of sorts could well be put on sexually oriented prime-time television fare: "Teenagers beware. Watching too much television programming featuring premarital, extramarital, or nonmarital sex can be hazardous to your moral health."

The hope: The good news is that the ways families operate can make a difference in terms of establishing more durable modes of moral judgment, even during those malleable teenage years. Individual viewing characteristics can also make a difference: Children and teenagers should be encouraged to view television in an "active" mode.

The challenge: We must be in the business of educating children, teenagers, and their families so that they hold the keys to personal empowerment over media effects. Many if not most unwanted media effects can be controlled; undoubtedly, desirable ones can be optimized as well. If education can make a difference, it must; we must.

REFERENCES

Black, J., & Bryant, J. (1992). *Introduction to mass communication* (3rd ed.). Dubuque, IA: Wm. C. Brown.

Brown, J. (1991). *Television "critical viewing skills" Education: Major media literacy projects in the United States and selected countries.* Hillsdale, NJ: Lawrence Erlbaum Associates.

Bryant, J. (1985, September 11). *Effects of massive exposure to sexually-explicit television fare on adolescents moral judgement.* Testimony presented before the U.S. Attorney General's Commission of Pornography, Houston, TX.

Bryant, J. (1990). *Television and the American family.* Hillsdale, NJ: Lawrence Erlbaum Associates.

Bryant, J., & Anderson, D. (Eds.). (1983). *Children's understanding of television: Research on attention and comprehension.* New York: Academic Press.

Nielsen Media Research. (1989). *Nielsen report on television.* Northbrook, IL: A. C. Nielsen Co.

Rice, R. E., & Atkin, C. K. (1989). *Public communications campaigns* (2nd ed.). Newbury Park, CA: Sage.

Salmon, C. T. (Ed.). (1989). *Information campaigns: Balancing social values and social change.* Newbury Park, CA: Sage.

Selnow, G W., & Crano, W. D. (1987). *Planning, implementing, and educating targeted communication programs: A manual for business communications.* New York: Quorum Books.

Part V

EFFECTS OF EROTICA AND PORNOGRAPHY

15

EROTICA AND FAMILY VALUES

Dolf Zillmann
University of Alabama

The values manifest in erotic entertainment are on a collision course with those pertaining to family as the most fundamental social institution in society. This should be clear to anyone who cares to compare the values in question.

FAMILY IDEALS

Traditionally, family referred to the cohabitational arrangement by a man and a woman who were joined in marriage, who were committed to sexual exclusivity, who produced and raised progeny together, who strived toward common economic goals, and who supported one another through difficult times. Support often extended to parents and grandparents, as well as to grandchildren.

This conception of family seems to have undergone considerable change in recent years (Ahrons & Rodgers, 1987). Family now refers to many cohabitational arrangements of adults that involve children. There appears to be some reluctance to confer family status to childless cohabiting sexual

199

intimates who, mostly for convenience, decided to live together. On the other hand, such status is readily granted to all kinds of contemporary cohabitational arrangements (e.g., to single parents, divorced or otherwise, with their live-in companions).

The definition of what is considered a family may well be vague and change with the mores of the time. What seems to be unchanging in the conceptualization of the family in western cultures, of the American family in particular, concerns not so much its de facto characteristics as its idealized properties. In other words, we have adjusted our descriptive criteria, but we have adhered to our values concerning the so-called nuclear family.

Let me enumerate what appear to be the most significant, persisting, highly valued features of the family:

1. The male–female pair, capable of reproduction and nurturance of offspring, constitutes the nucleus of the family.
2. The pair commits itself to cohabitation for an unlimited period of time, potentially for life.
3. The pair intends to have and eventually has children.
4. The pair is committed to caring for the children.
5. The pair is committed to supporting the children to mental, emotional, moral, and economic independence.
6. The pair pursues common economic objectives for the future.
7. The pair accepts sexual exclusivity.
8. The pair accepts that numerous gratifications within the family require, and depend on, the continual investment of time and effort.
9. The pair furthermore accepts the resistance of temptations that would place the family in disharmony and create a propensity for friction and violent action.

By all counts, then, family is not a social aggregate in which members can pursue gratifications on impulse and in disregard of the interests of other members. We are free to form a family; but once we have formed it, we are bound by a multitude of considerations and regulations (White, 1987). Our freedom is curtailed—in the interest of the welfare of the family. Parenting, whatever its intrinsic and delayed gratifications may be, is a commitment that translates into responsibilities, obligations, investments, and un-counted compromises. Hedonistically speaking, parenting in the traditional family context is obviously not a winning formula.

The societal significance of the nuclear family is independent of hedo-nistic considerations. This significance squarely lies in what the family is capable of producing: healthy, intellectually and morally mature, and emotionally well-adjusted offspring. We have firmly adhered to the belief that the parenting of healthy progeny is best accomplished in the nurturant environment of the nuclear family, and that this social arrangement is superior to alternatives. In sociological lingo, the nuclear family is deemed an *optimal child-rearing structure.*

This is not to say that the family concept guarantees positive results. If the parental commitment is lacking, no formal social arrangement will create the needed nurturant environment. *Parental commitment to family and the nurturance of progeny* is the crucial component. It is the component that we have cause to value as highly as we do.

FAMILY REALITIES

It is no secret that parental commitment has notably deteriorated in recent years, especially in particular sections of the population. The American family seems in disarray (Select Committee on Children, Youth, and Families, 1983). Although getting married has lost little of its popularity, and despite the best of intentions by those entering into matrimony, the formed union does not last as long as it did in earlier times (Cherlin, 1981; Rodgers & Thornton, 1985; U.S. Bureau of Census, 1987). In some sections of the population, only a tiny minority of the children grow up in the nurturant environment provided by both parents (Alwin, 1984; Hofferth, 1985). Marriage seems to have become an arrangement of convenience that is readily abandoned (Weitzman, 1985). As a result, a large proportion of children are raised by single parents. Or they are raised by an admixture of natural and stepparents, or simply by either mothers or fathers with their live-in companions (Thornton, 1988; Thornton & Freedman, 1982). Under these conditions, parental commitment is often deficient. The result is growing child neglect (Finkelhor, 1986; Gelles, 1974; Gil, 1973). Increasingly, children are perceived as burdens, impairing careers and preventing access to a multitude of immediate gratifications (White, 1987). Resentment toward children tends to replace the inclination to care for them; and the propensity for hostility toward children, as well as for child abuse of any conceivable kind, appears to grow steadily. Recent assessments of such collapse of caring show the abuse of children in defunct families to have reached staggering proportions (Pagelow, 1984; Shupe, Stacey, & Hazlewood, 1987). Spouse abuse is similarly rampant (Dobash & Dobash, 1979; Dutton, 1987; Gelles, 1979).

What causes this deterioration of parental commitment? Social scientists are quick to point out that there may be no single cause, but a multitude of factors—such as economic conditions, changing sexual mores, and a new egocentricity—that act in concert. Although this is in all probability true, it should not deter the search for single factors capable of influencing the changing dispositions toward child rearing and the family context in which it is to take place. Granted that other influences may exist, what, in and of itself (as well as in concert with other forces), could affect, for instance, the desire to have and raise children, judgments of the viability of marriage as a social institution, the evaluation of infidelity, and the perception of the nature of sexuality?

EROTIC PROMISES

Having explored some of the effects of prolonged exposure to erotic entertainment, my collaborator, Jennings Bryant, and I thought that pornography carries a message that might prove capable of influencing the indicated beliefs and dispositions. Why? Because pornography's message is entirely antithetical to marriage and child care with their freedom-curtailing commitments. Pornographic sexuality is sexuality without procreational purpose. It is totally recreational—projecting fun to be had by anyone who, for the moment, cares to play.

We (Zillmann & Bryant, 1988b) have emphasized that:

> pornographic scripts dwell on sexual engagements of parties who have just met, who are in no way attached or committed to one another, and who will part shortly, never to meet again. Not by accident, the parties involved accept no curtailing rules for their social and sexual conduct, enjoy sexual stimulation for what it is, and do so at no social or emotional expense. Sexual gratification in pornography is not a function of emotional attachment, of kindness, of caring, and especially not of continuance of the relationship, as such continuance would translate into responsibilities, curtailments, and costs. (p. 521)

Systematic analyses of the contents of pornography (Brosius, 1992; Brosius, Staab, & Weaver, 1991; Palys, 1984; Prince, 1990) substantiate this specification. The findings of these analyses may be summarized as follows:

1. Pornography depicts sexual engagements among persons who have just met. These persons are strangers by definition. The sexual engagements are not precipitated by efforts on the part of the participants to gain knowledge about one another. There is no indication that the various parties involved will ever meet again. Essentially, then, strangers meet to have sex and thereafter part as strangers.

2. With considerable regularity, pornography depicts consecutive sexual engagements by featured persons with different partners. This further underscores the impersonality of pornographic sex and the "substitutability of bodies."

3. Whatever the sexual activities that are being portrayed in pornography, all are shown to produce extreme euphoria in all persons who participate in them.

Pornography thus projects ready access to immediate sexual gratifications. It projects that the greatest sexual pleasures are fully attainable in transitory relationships. More importantly here, it projects that these pleasures can be experienced without freedom-curtailing emotional involvement or commitment to other human beings.

VALUES ON A COLLISION COURSE

To the extent that the implicit values are adopted, it should become most undesirable to commit oneself to another person in an enduring, intimate, sexual relationship. Such a relationship, as we have argued, calls for compromise, if not sacrifice. If sexual gratifications are expected to be as high in impersonal relationships as in commitment-marked lasting ones, perhaps even higher, the former is, hedonistically speaking, preferable to the latter. Analogously, it should become most undesirable to commit oneself to parenting, essentially for the same reasons.

Could the consumption of pornography have such deleterious effects on values concerning intimate relationships, marriage, family, and progeny? We decided to conduct an investigation to find answers to these questions (Zillmann & Bryant, 1988b).

PORNOGRAPHY'S INFLUENCE

The research paradigm we used was much the same as that of our earlier work on the rape-trivializing effect of pornography (Zillmann & Bryant, 1982, 1984). Both male and female subjects were exposed to either commonly available, nonviolent pornography or innocuous entertainment fare devoid of sexual content. The subjects consumed the materials in hourly sessions in 6 consecutive weeks. As most earlier work had been done with college students only, efforts were made to expand the generalizability of findings by representing nonstudents in addition to students. All presentations came off color and sound videocassettes that were acquired from rental stores. The pornographic material was the latest available. It was pre-examined to assure that none of the depicted behaviors were violent or coercive or could be construed in these terms.

By way of overview: Male and female college students and male and female nonstudent adults were repeatedly exposed to either nonviolent pornography or innocuous material, and effects of such exposure were determined thereafter. More specifically, 1 week after the exposure treatment the subjects returned once more to take part in ostensibly unrelated research on the American family and aspects of personal happiness. They responded to an especially constructed Value-of-Marriage Survey and additionally completed an especially constructed Inventory of Personal Happiness.

Our earlier work (Zillmann & Bryant, 1982, 1984) had shown that the perception of the popularity of particular sexual practices is greatly influenced by prolonged consumption of pornography. The subsequent investigation sought to extend our knowledge of such perceptual effects. It focused on perceptions relevant to living with sexual partners, on marriage, and on the family. The survey then turned to attitudes and behavioral dispositions concerning these matters. A set of questions addressed marriage and divorce specifically. Finally, the survey assessed the subjects' desire to have children.

Perception of Faithfulness and Promiscuity

Figure 15.1 summarizes the perceptual changes that were brought about by prolonged consumption of pornography. The left and middle columns show the extent to which the sexual promiscuity of men and of women is perceived as natural. As can be seen, male promiscuity and, especially female promiscuity, were deemed more natural—and accordingly, more acceptable or less objectionable—after prolonged exposure to pornography than without such exposure. The columns to the right show a related consequence of exposure: The perception of faithfulness of sexual intimates. If promiscuity is presumed natural, it stands to reason not to expect that partners are highly faithful to one another. Prolonged exposure to pornography thus should prompt a decline in expected faithfulness, and it did so. All these effects, as well as those yet to be reported, were found for males and females and students and nonstudent adults alike.

Attitudes About Faithfulness and Promiscuity

Perceptions pertain mostly to the sexuality of others. Attitudes to dispositions, in contrast, are personally committal. Dispositions entail our judg-

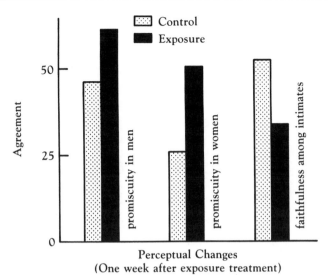

FIG. 15.1.   Perception of others' sociosexual behavior as a function of prolonged exposure to pornography (from Zillmann & Bryant, 1986b).

ment of what is good and bad for us, what we condone and oppose, and what we ultimately want and try to avoid. Figure 15.2, accordingly, shows the extent to which subjects accepted views pertaining to their own behaviors. The left columns of the figure show that prolonged exposure to pornography fostered greater acceptance of sexual engagements prior to marriage and with partners outside of marriage. The middle columns show the same effect in more general terms: Nonexclusive sexual intimacy was accepted to a much higher degree. Interestingly, this greater acceptance does not merely mean that persons, after prolonged consumption of pornography, were more intent on claiming for themselves the freedom manifest in not being someone's exclusive partner; they also became more tolerant of their intimate partners' indiscretions. This dispositional effect, then, is two-pronged: Prolonged consumption of pornography fosters rejection of the notion that sexual relationships be exclusive for self and for one's intimate partner. It is important here to point out that pornography did not, as had been expected, instill distrust by heightening apprehensions about the possible infidelity of intimate partners. Instead, pornography promoted tolerance for such infidelity—or put less positively, pornography trivialized the consequences of these indiscretions for sexual intimates.

Beliefs About Sexual Repression

In Fig. 15.2, the columns to the right show another related phenomenon and a likely reason for the increasing tolerance of sexual indiscretions by

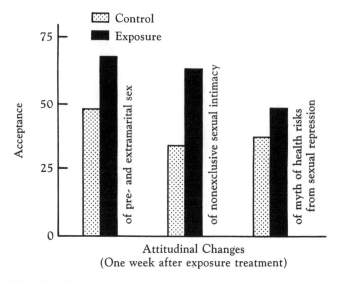

FIG. 15.2. Dispositions toward pre- and extramarital sex, nonexclusivity of sexual relations, and health risks from sexual repression as a function of prolonged exposure to pornography (from Zillmann & Bryant, 1986b).

intimate partners. Prolonged consumption of pornography promoted greater acceptance of the myth of health risks from sexual repression. Pornography apparently manages to convince people that unrestrained sexuality is wholesome and healthy; and moreover, that any sexual restraint poses health risks.

Our survey then turned to marriage, divorce, and progeny, specifically.

Beliefs About the Institution of Marriage

Two key questions dealt with marriage. The first one asked: "Do you feel that the institution of marriage is essential to the well-functioning of society?" The prolonged consumption of pornography had a marked effect on the answers. Whereas 60% of the subjects in the control condition responded affirmatively, only 38.8% of those having been exposed to pornography did so. The second question asked: "Do you believe that the institution of marriage will eventually become obsolete and be abandoned in modern society?" In the control group, only 15% thought so. In the group exposed to pornography this percentage more than doubled, rising to 36.2%. These effects, somewhat surprisingly, were parallel for men and women and for students and nonstudent adults. Prolonged consumption of common pornography thus was found to make the institution of marriage appear less significant for society, as well as altogether less viable in the future.

Beliefs About Divorce

Dispositions toward the dissolution of marriage were assessed in reactions to a list of potential grounds for divorce. The findings show that "being beaten by spouse" tends to be considered sufficient grounds by many respondents (73.8%). However, the evaluation of spouse beating was not influenced by pornography consumption. Evaluation of the "occasional infidelity of spouse," in contrast, was influenced: The percentage of 70 in the control group dropped to 50 in the exposure group. Exposure to pornography made "sexual disinterest by spouse" a stronger reason for divorce: 45% in the control group versus 61.2% in the exposure group. On the other hand, exposure was of no consequence for "incompatible leisure interests" and "disagreement on religious issues." "Frequent infidelity" showed the tendency reported for "occasional infidelity": a drop from 81.2% to 63.8%. "Unacceptable sexual requests" became a less acceptable reason after exposure: 55%, compared with 83.8% in the control group. For this particular case, a gender difference was observed: Females (81.2%) thought it to be a stronger reason than did males (57.5%). After prolonged consumption of pornography, the "desire for additional lovers" diminished as a reason for the dissolution of marriage: Compared to 77.5% in the control group, only 55% of the respondents in the exposure group considered it cause for dissolution. Finally, "spouse having homosexual affairs," which without pornography consumption proved the strongest reason for divorce at 92.5% — proving stronger than spouse beating (73.8%), spouse's sexual disinterest (72.5%), or spouse's frequent infidelity (69.4%) — fell to 68.8% in the exposure group.

The pattern emerging from these effects is this: Prolonged consumption of pornography is of no consequence for divorce reasons that are unrelated to sex. The consideration of all sex-related grounds for divorce, in contrast, is greatly influenced by exposure to pornography. Specifically, deficient sexual interest and deficient sexual initiative become more acceptable grounds for divorce, whereas various sexual indiscretions become less acceptable reasons for the discontinuance of an intimate relationship.

Desire for Progeny

The desire for progeny was assessed by simply asking the subjects whether or not they wanted to have natural nonadopted children; and if yes, by asking how many boys and how many girls they would want to have.

The effect of prolonged exposure to pornography on the reactions to these queries was most astounding. As can be seen from Fig. 15.3, exposure to pornography reduced the desire to have children, and it did so in a uniform fashion. Male and female respondents, students and nonstudent adults alike, wanted fewer children on the average. The desire to have male offspring dropped 31%. The desire for female offspring, being lower overall, dropped by about twice that margin: by 61%, to be precise. This reduction proved specific to gender. Male respondents expressed little desire for female offspring altogether. It is the desire of females for offspring of their own kind that, after consumption of pornography, shrank to one third of its normal strength. The columns to the far right in Fig. 15.3 display this surprisingly strong effect.

Taken together, the findings seem to support the contention that prolonged consumption of pornography makes having children and raising a family appear an unnecessary inconvenience — presumably because pornography continually projects easy access to superlative sexual gratifications, these gratifications being attainable without emotional investment, without social confinements, without economic obligations, and without sacrifices in time and effort. It should be clear, however, that such reasoning explains only the overall reduction in reproductive desire. It leaves unexplained the discrimination against female offspring by women. Exactly what, within pornography, inspires this own-gender discrimination remains unclear. One can only speculate that there must be something grossly demeaning to women in women's portrayal in common pornogra-

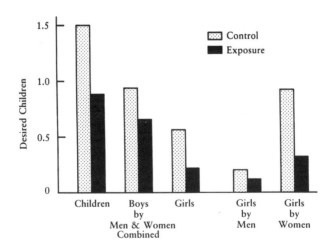

(One week after exposure treatment)

FIG. 15.3.   Reproductive desire of men and women, specific to gender of progeny, as a function of prolonged exposure to pornography (from Zillmann & Bryant, 1986b).

phy, and that this portrayal creates the discrimination against women by women that expresses itself in their diminished desire for female offspring.

Supplementary Influences

Note that all the perceptual and dispositional changes we have reported are entirely in line with independent, sociological assessments of changing attitudes toward family issues in the United States. Thornton (1989) recently reviewed the pertinent evidence and concluded that the findings document "an important weakening of the normative imperative to marry, to remain married, to have children," and "to restrict intimate relations to marriage" (p. 873). He also pointed out that the most striking changes in family attitudes and values were observed in the 1960s and 1970s. It is perhaps more than coincidental that pornography has gone public and became a household item during this period (Brown & Bryant, 1989; Bryant & Brown, 1989). Because the embrace of pornography also coincided with growing support for civil liberties generally, one might argue that the changing attitudes toward family and marriage merely reflect a stronger endorsement of civil liberties and that, moreover, the acceptance of pornography as a form of entertainment similarly reflects these general trends and is part and parcel of it. However, the demonstration that the dispositional changes under consideration manifest themselves after prolonged exposure to pornography challenges such an interpretation. Pornography consumption, in and of itself, is apparently capable of altering family dispositions. It therefore must be considered a causal factor capable of contributing to the changes that have been observed nationally and, more broadly, in the western world. This is not to say that pornography is the sole cause, nor that it is the most important causal factor in a potentially large number of contributing factors. The magnitude of pornography's contribution, relative to other factors, remains to be determined. But to repeat: Prolonged consumption of commonly available pornography is undeniably a contributing factor in the changing dispositions toward sexual relationships, marriage, and progeny.

Sexual Dissatisfaction

I indicated earlier that our investigation also addressed personal happiness: satisfaction with life in general and with sex in particular. Our inventory, accordingly, mixed queries about accomplishments in college or in business, about same-gender friendships, and about family relations with queries about sexual satisfaction and satisfaction with sexual partners (Zillmann & Bryant, 1988a). Figure 15.4 summarizes the findings. The columns to the

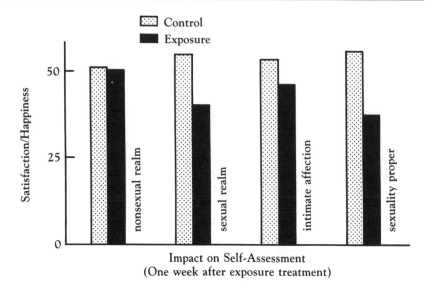

FIG. 15.4.   Sexual satisfaction as a function of prolonged exposure to pornography
(from Zillmann & Bryant, 1986a).

far left show that prolonged consumption of pornography was without
appreciable effect on happiness outside the sexual realm. In contrast, as can
be seen from the second group of columns, pornography consumption
greatly diminished sexual satisfaction. Inspection of the affective and
sensual components of sexual satisfaction (see the right-hand side of Fig.
15.4) makes it clear that happiness had declined on both counts. The
strongest decline was observed for satisfaction with the sexual behavior of
partners specifically. Thus, whereas discontent with the emotional commitment of intimate partners grew, discontent with such matters as partners'
physical appearance, partners' sexual performances, and partners' willingness to explore novel avenues of sexual gratification grew most strongly.
These effects were again observed for men and women, students and
nonstudent adults alike.

The findings document a dilemma for pornography consumers. Presumably, pornography is initially consumed because of curiosity and in hopes of
finding something that could enhance the consumer's own sexual gratifications. But as it is routinely consumed for immediate gratification, the
"pornotopia" (See, 1980) exhibited in it eventually invites comparisons:
Consumers compare what they have, by way of sexual intimacy, with what
pornography tells them they might and should have. As pornography
features beautiful bodies in youthful sexual interactions during which they
continually express nothing short of ecstasy, consumers of such entertainment are readily left with the impression that "others got more" and that

whatever they themselves have in their intimate relationships is less than it could be. In all probability, it is this implicit comparison of the consumer's own lot with the utopia of pornography that fosters and intensifies sexual dissatisfaction.

If, as proposed, initial sexual dissatisfaction drives exposure to pornography, a vicious circle suggests itself: Those who are already somewhat dissatisfied are more strongly drawn to pornography than are others; as a result of greater consumption, their dissatisfaction grows more strongly, drawing them deeper into consumption, which makes them even more dissatisfied, and so on.

Shifting Sexual Interests

There are alternative and complementary mechanisms. Research has shown that sexual arousal (Howard, Reifler, & Liptzin, 1971) and accompanying excitedness (Zillmann & Bryant, 1982) diminish with repeated exposure to sexual scenes. As exposure to commonly shown sexual activities leaves consumers relatively unexcited, they are likely to seek out pornography that features novel and potentially less common sexual acts. Such a shift toward a stronger interest in less common sexual practices — as, for instance, in bestiality and sadomasochism — has in fact been demonstrated (Zillmann & Bryant, 1986).

It has also been observed (Marshall, Seidman, & Barbaree, 1990) that exposure to commonly available, nonviolent pornography tends to reduce men's inhibitions to get sexually excited by exposure to rape scenarios or rape fantasies. Together with reports that, on occasion, pornography-inspired sexual fantasies are converted into action — sometimes coercive, and possibly violent action (Russell, 1984; Silbert & Pines, 1984), such observations lead to the projection that prolonged consumption of commonly available nonviolent or violent pornography contributes to coercive sexuality among intimates, within the family in particular. Inhibitions lacking, the conflicts that sexual discontent is likely to produce, may all too often escalate to the violent behaviors that mar the American family (Dobash & Dobash, 1978; Lincoln & Straus, 1985; Pagelow, 1984). Additionally, if accounts of the influence of pornography on the increasingly sadistic treatment of prostitutes ("Freier sind," 1992) are any indication, the large majority of women should expect more pornography-inspired abusive violent sexual action from their intimate male partners.

EPILOGUE

Needless to say, these are projections based on scarce data. No one has compellingly demonstrated, and in a free society no one will be able to do so, that pornography contributes directly to the deterioration of sexually intimate relationships and to violence in these relationships. What we know is that prolonged exposure to pornography is capable of altering dispositions toward such relationships. The conversion of dispositions into actions is suggested by numerous observations, but it has by no means been demonstrated beyond reasonable doubt.

The remaining uncertainty concerning the effects in question is likely to be exploited by those who promote pornography as an essential part of sexual liberation. Claims that pornography has "no effects" will continue, no doubt. So will allegations that all research demonstrations are flawed and not to be trusted. Meanwhile, as changing dispositions will eventually express themselves in actions, as we have reason to believe they will, we are bound to witness the continuing influence of pornography, apparently secured by the first amendment, on the erosion of the nuclear family in America and elsewhere.

REFERENCES

Ahrons, C. R., & Rodgers, R. (1987). *Divorced families: A multidisciplinary view*. New York: Norton.

Alwin, D. F. (1984). Trends in parental socialization values: Detroit, 1958 to 1983. *American Journal of Sociology, 90* 359-382.

Brosius, H. (1992). Sex and Pornographie in den Massenmedien: Eine Analyse ihrer Inhalte, ihrer Nutzung und ihrer Wirkung. In R. Frohlich (Ed.), *Der andere Blick: Aktuelles zur Massenkommunikation aus weiblicher Sicht* (pp. 139-158). Bochum: Brockmeyer.

Brosius, H., Staab, J., & Weaver, J. B. (1991, May). *Exploring the social "reality" of contemporary pornography*. Paper presented at the International Communication Association meeting, Chicago.

Brown, D., & Bryant, J. (1989). The manifest content of pornography. In D. Zillmann & J. Bryant (Eds.), *Pornography: Research advances and policy considerations* (pp. 3-24). Hillsdale, NJ: Lawrence Erlbaum Associates.

Bryant, J., & Brown, D. (1989). Uses of pornography. In D. Zillmann & J. Bryant (Eds.), *Pornography: Research advances and policy considerations* (pp. 25-55). Hillsdale, NJ: Lawrence Erlbaum Associates.

Cherlin, A. J. (1981). *Marriage, divorce, remarriage*. Cambridge, MA: Harvard University Press.

Dobash, R. E., & Dobash, R. P. (1978). Wives: The "appropriate" victims of marital violence. *Victimology, 2*(3/4), 426-442.

Dobash, R. E., & Dobash, R. P. (1979). *Violence against wives: A case against patriarchy*. New York: Free Press.

Dutton, D.G. (1987). Wife assault: Social psychological contributions to criminal justice policy. In S. Oskamp (Ed.), *Applied Social Psychology Annual. 7: Family processes and problems: Social psychological aspects* (pp. 238-261). Newbury Park, CA: Sage.

Finkelhor, D. (1986). *A sourcebook on child sexual abuse*. Beverly Hills, CA: Sage.

Freier sind heimliche Sadisten. (1992). *Der Spiegel, 31,* 168-170.

Gelles, R. J. (1974). *The violent home*. Beverly Hills, CA:Sage.

Gelles, R. J. (1979). *Family violence*. Beverly Hills, CA: Sage.

Gil, D. G. (1973). *Violence against children: Physical child abuse in the United States*. Cambridge, MA: Harvard University Press.

Hofferth, S. L. (1985). Updating children's life course. *Journal of Marriage and the Family, 47*, 93-115.

Howard, J. L., Reifler, C. B., & Liptzin, M. B. (1971). Effects of exposure to pornography. In *Technical Report of The Commission on Obscenity and Pornography* (Vol. 8, pp. 97-132). Washington, DC: U.S. Government Printing Office.

Lincoln, A. J., & Straus, M. A. (1985). *Crime and the family*. Springfield, IL: Charles C. Thomas.

Marshall, W. L., Seidman, B. T., & Barbaree, H. E. (1990). *The effects of prior exposure to rape stimuli on patterns of erectile responding to consenting and forced sex in normal males*. Unpublished manuscript, Queen's University, Kingston, Ontario.

Pagelow, M. D. (1984). *Family violence*. New York: Praeger.

Palys, T. S. (1984, June). *A content analysis of sexually explicit videos in British Columbia* (Working papers on pornography and prostitution, Research Report No. 15). Ottawa, Canada: Department of Justice.

Prince, S. (1990). Power and pain: Content analysis and the ideology of pornography. *Journal of Film and Video 42*(2), 31-41.

Rodgers, W. L., & Thornton, A. (1985). Changing patterns of first marriage in the United States. *Demography, 22*, 265-279.

Russell, D. E. H. (1984). *Sexual exploitation: Rape, child sexual abuse, and workplace harassment*. Beverly Hills, CA: Sage.

See, C. (1980, December 28). Angry women and brutal men. *The New York Times Book Review*, pp. 123-124.

Select Committee on Children, Youth, and Families. (1983). *U.S. children and their families: Current conditions and recent trends*. Washington, DC: U.S. Government Printing Office.

Shupe, A., Stacey, W. A., & Hazlewood, L. R. (1987). *Violent men, violent couples*. Lexington, MA: Lexington Books.

Silbert, M., & Pines, A. M. (1984). Pornography and sexual abuse of women. *Sex Roles, 10*(11-12), 857-867.

Thornton, A. (1988). Cohabitation and marriage in the 1980s. *Demography, 25*, 497-508.

Thornton, A. (1989). Changing attitudes toward family issues in the United States. *Journal of Marriage and the Family, 51*, 873-893.

Thornton, A., & Freedman, D. S. (1982). Changing attitudes toward marriage and single life. *Family Planning Perspectives, 14*, 297-303.

U.S. Bureau of the Census. (1987). *Statistical Abstract of the United States, 1988*. Washington, DC: Superintendent of Documents.

Weitzman, L. J. (1985). *The divorce revolution: The unexpected social and economic consequences for women and children in America*. New York: Free Press.

White, L. (1987). Freedom versus constraint. *Journal of Family Issues, 8*, 468-470.

Zillmann, D., & Bryant, J. (1982). Pornography, sexual callousness, and the trivialization of rape. *Journal of Communication, 32*(4), 10-21.

Zillmann, D., & Bryant, J. (1984). Effects of massive exposure to pornography. In N. M. Malamuth & E. Donnerstein (Eds.), *Pornography and sexual aggression* (pp. 115-138). Orlando: Academic Press.

Zillmann, D., & Bryant, J. (1986). Shifting preferences in pornography consumption. *Communication Research, 13*, 560-578.

Zillmann, D., & Bryant, J. (1988a). Pornography's impact on sexual satisfaction. *Journal of Applied Social Psychology, 18*, 438-453.

Zillmann, D., & Bryant, J. (1988b). Effects of prolonged consumption of pornography on family values. *Journal of Family Issues, 9*(4), 518-544.

16

PORNOGRAPHY AND SEXUAL CALLOUSNESS: THE PERCEPTUAL AND BEHAVIORAL CONSEQUENCES OF EXPOSURE TO PORNOGRAPHY

James B. Weaver, III
Auburn University

Over the last two decades the status of sexually explicit mass media (i.e., erotica and pornography) in the entertainment marketplace has been radically transformed and expanded (cf. Weaver, 1991, 1992). According to Hebditch and Anning (1988), production and distribution of such materials have rapidly evolved from "a seedy and illicit cottage industry to a stable and well-refined, mass-production business employing the latest know-how" and yielding annual worldwide revenues in excess of $5 billion (p. 3). Spurred by new communication technologies—especially the domestication of videotape recorders—the marketplace for pornography has metamorphosed from one tailored to a few elite connoisseurs into a mass market providing an affordable form of entertainment to all consumers (cf. Zillmann & Bryant, 1989).

Awareness of the prolific availability and tremendous popularity of pornographic fare has fueled substantial public scrutiny of and debate over such materials (cf. Attorney General's Commission on Pornography, 1986; Lederer, 1980; Zillmann & Bryant, 1989). Two distinct and yet inseparable concerns, issues that have been the focus of discussion for some time (cf. Kendrick, 1987), are the basic contentions in this controversy. One involves interpretation of the content characteristics of pornography. The other concern deals with the potential perceptual and behavioral consequences of viewing such materials.

PROJECTED EFFECTS OF PORNOGRAPHY CONSUMPTION

Various ideas have been advanced to explain the basic interaction between the content of pornographic fare and the consequences of exposure (cf. Weaver, 1991, 1992). Common to most of these perspectives is the tenet (Fisher, 1986) that "merely observing a model engaging in sexual behavior (on film, in written material, or wherever) may affect our sexual beliefs, expectancies, and fantasies" and, consequently, our sexual behaviors (p. 143; also see Check & Malamuth, 1985). The perspectives differ dramatically, however, in the nature and extent of the responses projected following exposure to pornography.

One thesis, labeled the *sexual communication model* (Malamuth & Billings, 1986), maintains that pornographic materials are simply entertaining communications that pertain to sexual behavior and have no negative consequences. Advocates of this viewpoint (Gagnon, 1977; Stoller, 1976; Wilson, 1978) contend that such materials perform a positive function by serving as important educational and/or therapeutic aids that according to Goldstein (1984), encourage "sexual pleasure and sexual abandon" and help eradicate "puritanical attitudes about sex that have long dominated our society" (p. 32). Accordingly, consumption of pornographic fare is projected to have positive rather than adverse consequences.

A recent qualification of this idea, referred to as the *violence desensitization model*, proposes that only pornography involving blatant portrayals of women as victims of coercion, aggression, and violence influence asocial attitudes and behaviors toward women. Specifically, advocates of this thesis (Donnerstein, Linz, & Penrod, 1987) maintain that the typical pornographic presentation "does not foster negative attitudes or behaviors *unless* it is combined with images of violence" (jacket).

Propositions such as these have been rejected by many analysts, however. In fact, advocates from diverse social and political orientations (e.g., feminists, family, and community organizations) have converged in proposing that exposure to pornography fosters detrimental perceptions of female sexuality, a misogynous cultural climate, and promotes intergender violence (cf. Weaver, 1987). Several variations of this *sexual callousness model* (Zillmann & Weaver, 1989) have been articulated (e.g., Attorney General's Commission on Pornography, 1986; Check & Malamuth, 1985; Kendrick, 1987), including one advanced by the Commission on Obscenity and Pornography (1970) that stated:

It is often asserted that a distinguishing characteristic of sexually explicit materials is the degrading and demeaning portrayal of the role and status of the human female. It has been argued that erotic materials describe the female as a mere sexual object to be exploited and manipulated sexually.

One presumed consequence of such portrayals is that erotica transmits an inaccurate and uninformed conception of sexuality, and that the viewer or user will (a) develop a calloused and manipulative orientation toward women and (b) engage in behavior in which affection and sexuality are not well integrated. (pp. 239–240).

Although the 1970 Commission on Obscenity and Pornography concluded, based on exiguous data, that such concerns were "probably unwarranted" (p. 240), more recent analysts have commended the insightfulness of this basic proposition (cf. Garry, 1978; Zillmann & Weaver, 1989).

Feminist commentators, for example, have been particularly outspoken in their efforts to elaborate this viewpoint. They maintain that pornography does typically depict women as promiscuous and sexually hyperactive and contend that this characterization disparages and demeans women by portraying them (Diamond, 1985) as "malleable, obsessed with sex, and willing to engage in any sexual act with any available partner" (p. 42). Brownmiller (1984) argued that exposure to this "dangerously distorted picture of female sexuality" (p. 34), produces adverse perceptions of women—such as a general "loss-of-respect" for women as persons—and, ultimately, results in asocial behavioral consequences ranging from sexual discrimination to rape (cf. Garry, 1978; Lederer, 1980; Russell, 1988).

PERTINENT RESEARCH FINDINGS

What are the predominant content themes of contemporary pornography and what, if any, consequences result from consumption of these sexually explicit materials? This question has fostered a huge volume of research that provides a rich foundation for developing our understanding of the pornography phenomenon. At the same time, however, investigators have demonstrated obtrusive eclecticism in the ways they have conceptually and operationally defined sexually explicit materials, in the responses they have observed following exposure to such materials, and in the interpretations they have accorded their results. This fact has lead many analysts to proclaim caveat emptor (i.e., "let the buyer beware") to consumers of this literature because an incautious or poorly informed review of the aggregate findings can easily yield a complex, seemingly contradictory image (e.g., Copp, 1983; Howitt, 1989; Page, 1989; Zillmann, 1989b).

With this in mind, and in an effort to promote simplification and synthesis, this summary concentrates first on research documenting the content features of pornography. Then, using this content-based framework, several pertinent investigations illustrating the perceptual and behavioral consequences resulting from exposure to pornography are detailed.

Content Characteristics of Pornography

The bulk of the pornographic material available worldwide depicts *standard-fare nonviolent* themes. This "mainstream" category of pornography, according to Hebditch and Anning (1988), accounts for "more than 90 per cent of the world production of still photographs and video/film sequences of heterosexual acts of intercourse" (p. 7). Such productions customarily feature a uniquely "macho or masculinized" orientation that evolves around a seemingly obsessive "preoccupation with sexual activity to the exclusion of all other facets of human social behavior" (p. 15). Pornographic fare typically features, for instance, heterosexual intercourse in innumerable circumstances and "as a matter of routine—lesbianism, group sex, anal intercourse, oral–genital contact and visible ejaculation" (p. 7), whereas depictions of other basic aspects of human sexuality—such as communication between sexual partners, expressions of affection or emotion (except fear and lust), and concerns about the consequences of sexual activities—are minimized (Brosius, Weaver, & Staab, 1993; Prince, 1990; Rimmer, 1986). Furthermore, within this context, women are normatively portrayed as eagerly soliciting, and responding with hysterical euphoria, to any of a variety of sexual encounters (Palys, 1986). The predominant theme of standard-fare pornography, in other words, spotlights the sexual desires and prowess of men, whereas consistently and persistently portraying women as sexually promiscuous and obsequious (Brosius, Weaver, & Staab, 1993).

The availability of pornography involving *coercive and/or violent* themes, productions that were initially the focus of considerable critical attention, appears limited (cf. Brown & Bryant, 1989). Research suggests that materials in this category typically portray women in a manner consistent with the cultural myth that women enjoy being raped (Cowan, Lee, Levy, & Snyder, 1988). In this "rape myth" scenario, the woman's initial reactions of distress during rape are quickly transformed into sexual arousal and, ultimately, enjoyment.

Only a few sexually explicit materials involve *idealized sexual themes*. Productions in this category, which are referred to by some as "erotica" (e.g., Lawrence, 1936; Steinem, 1980), present more compassionate, egalitarian portrayals of sexuality by focusing on the social and relational aspects of heterosexual coital activities.

Perceptual Consequences of Pornography

Considerable research evidence shows that exposure to pornography facilitates the formation and reinforcement of inappropriate or undesirable perceptions of women in both sexual and nonsexual contexts (cf. Weaver, 1991, 1992; Zillmann, 1989a). Foremost among these investigations is the work of Zillmann and Bryant (1982, 1988a, 1988b). In a series of studies, these researchers observed numerous persistent changes in perceptions concerning sexuality and sexual behavior after repeatedly exposing (i.e., six 1-hour weekly sessions) volunteers to pornography. These include the trivialization of rape as a criminal offense, exaggerated perceptions of the prevalence of most sexual practices, increased callousness toward female sexuality and concerns, dissatisfaction with sexual relationships, and diminished caring for and trust in intimate partners. Similarly, Buchman (1988) found that repeated exposure to pornography promoted callous perceptions of the extent of suffering experienced by child victims of sexual abuse and trivialized the sexual abuse of females, whether adults or children, as a criminal transgression.

Research examining the perceptual consequences of exposure to pornography involving coercive and/or violent themes reveals that exposure to unambiguous "rape myth" scenarios consistently produces adverse effects on observers' perceptions of women, in general, and of rape victims, in particular. Exposure to realistic rape depictions (i.e., the victim expresses abhorrence throughout her assault), on the other hand, yields essentially no negative effects (cf. Malamuth, 1984).

Several recent studies comparing the perceptual consequences following consumption of both sexually explicit (X-rated) and suggestive (R-rated) materials portraying the standard nonviolent pornographic theme, sexual coercion and/or violence, and idealized sexuality have also revealed strong negative shifts in perceptions of female sexuality and victims of sexual assaults (cf. Weaver, 1991, 1992; Zillmann, 1989a). For instance, Weaver (1987; also see Zillmann & Weaver, 1989) found that exposure to depictions of both sexual and coercive and/or violent media depictions can induce adverse shifts in perceptions of women and dispositions about the punishment of a convicted rapist. The most striking finding was that, for male viewers, exposure to sexual themes strongly influenced perceptions of the "sexual receptivity or permissiveness" of otherwise sexually discriminating females. This effect was not observed following exposure to sexually coercive and/or violent themes. Women responded quite differently. They did not perceive more permissiveness in these females after viewing the sexual themes. However, they did tend to perceive greater permissiveness after viewing scenes of coercive and/or violent sex.

On the other hand, perceptions of rape as a criminal offense — measured in the sentencing of a rapist—were trivialized for both male and female consumers by the exposure treatments. Specifically, those who viewed portrayals of women as sexually promiscuous proved the most lenient toward a rapist. Furthermore, additional analyses revealed that, the more strongly the exposure treatments influenced perceptions of women as sexually permissive and promiscuous, the greater the trivialization of rape as a criminal offense.

Behavioral Consequences of Pornography

Taken together, the research evidence highlights the fact that exposure to commonly available sexually explicit materials can foster and reinforce negative perceptions of women in both sexual and nonsexual contexts. In other words, the data at hand (Commission on Obscenity and Pornography, 1970) show that consumers of pornography do "develop a calloused and manipulative orientation toward women" (p. 239). But the question remains whether such perceptual shifts bring about corresponding calloused and manipulative behaviors.

Before addressing this issue, it is necessary to recognize that research examining the behavioral consequences of exposure to pornography has been deemed by some critics as insufficient to inform the current debate. Specifically, it is argued that anything less than compelling proof of a causal connection between the consumption of pornography and the enactment of sexually violent behaviors is wanting (cf. Brannigan, 1987; Howitt, 1989). However, it must be understood that, given ethical considerations, evidence sufficiently definitive to satisfy this rigorous mandate will not be forthcoming. Obviously, any research activity employing the enactment of sexually abusive behaviors as a dependent measure cannot be sanctioned. Consequently, we *must* rely on the available research to develop our understanding of the behavioral consequences of exposure to pornography; realizing that such data, with several acknowledged limitations, are much better than conventional wisdom, guessing, or ignorance (cf. Zillmann, 1989b).

Given these considerations, what can be learned from the available research evidence? Two facts are readily apparent: first, that a substantial and robust correlation emerges between the availability of pornography and the incidence of sexually abusive behaviors across a variety of natural settings; and, equally important, that in several controlled circumstances exposure to sexually explicit materials has caused men to target aggressive and/or manipulative behaviors against women.

Evidence of the link between the availability of sexually explicit materials and the occurrence of criminal sexual offenses is provided by several investigations (cf. Baron & Straus, 1984; Court, 1984). Initially, data from a study in Denmark revealed a negative association between the availability of sexually explicit materials and the incidence of sexual offenses reported to police (Kutchinsky, 1973); that is, increased circulation of such materials appeared linked to a significant drop in sexual offenses, particularly rape and child molestation. This trend was interpreted as suggesting that unrestricted distribution of sexually explicit materials provided a "safety valve" for deviant sexual behaviors. Subsequent critiques have, however, outlined several shortcomings of the Danish study that severely challenge this conclusion (cf. Court, 1984). More importantly, recent explorations of this issue have demonstrated a positive relationship between the incidence of sexual offenses and the availability of sexually explicit materials. In an examination of data collected from various countries, for example, Court (1984) provided substantial evidence that variations in the availability of pornography corresponds positively with changes in the reported occurrences of rape. Extensive data from the United States have yielded even more detailed results (cf. Baron & Straus, 1984, 1987; Jaffee & Straus, 1987; Scott & Schwalm, 1988). Scott and Schwalm (1988) found, for instance, a quite significant positive relationship between the incidence of rape and per capita sales of sexually explicit magazines (e.g., *Playboy* and *Penthouse*), that withstood statistical control for many demographic factors plus the general circulation rates of nonerotic magazines (e.g., *Newsweek*). Baron and Straus (1987) examined similar data using a structural equation model that provided substantial control for both demographic characteristics and other variables believed to mediate the incidence of rape. From this elaborate model emerged strong evidence of a very robust, direct relationship between the circulation rate of sex magazines and rape rates.

Other survey research highlights the fact that women often suffer sexually abusive treatment apparently instigated by exposure to sexually explicit materials. Russell (1984), for example, questioned a representative sample of the adult females in San Francisco and found that approximately 10% reported "upsetting sexual experiences with people who tried to get them to do something sexual they'd seen in pornography" (p. 124). Further, Russell noted that there may have been several other "upsetting sexual experiences in which the women were unaware that the men's desires came from pornography" (p. 124) that her questionnaire did not ascertain. Similarly, the Committee on Sexual Offences Against Children and Youths (1984) concluded that the "findings of two (Canadian) national surveys — population and police — indicate that, for a number of persons, pornography had served as a stimulus to committing sexual assaults against children" (p. 1283).

Recent clinical research further illustrates the potential role of sexually explicit materials in the commission of sex related criminal offenses (cf.

Marshall, 1989; Silbert & Pines, 1984). For instance, working with a sample of sex offenders in a voluntary outpatient environment, Marshall (1988) found that child molesters and rapists frequently used sexually explicit materials incitefully both immediately prior to and during sexual assaults. In addition, Marshall discovered that, when compared with two different control groups, offenders reported substantially greater use of sexually explicit materials, and that such use was significantly related to the chronicity of sexual offenders' assaults. Other investigations highlight the apparent pivotal impact of exposure to sexually explicit materials in the development of deviant sexual interests (e.g., Abel, 1985); interests that appear to exert a strong negative influence on subsequent sexual behaviors (Davis & Braucht, 1973; Propper, 1970).

Viewed together, these findings strongly implicate a direct link between exposure to sexually explicit materials and the occurrence of criminal sexual offenses. Despite the recurrent pattern of results, however, the limitations inherent to correlational data must be recognized and the findings interpreted with appropriate caution. Specifically, although increasingly improbable given the weight of evidence, it is possible that the observed relationships actually result from the intervention of other, as yet, unidentified factors. Furthermore, it is impossible, given these correlational data, to determine the causal direction of the link between exposure to sexually explicit materials and the incidence of sexually abusive and/or sexually violent behaviors. Both limitations have been overcome, however, by experimental research.

More direct evidence of the adverse behavioral effects of exposure to sexually explicit materials is provided by studies using experimental paradigms that offer considerable control of intervening factors and permit determination of causality (cf. Malamuth & Donnerstein, 1984). Indeed, the fact that exposure to nonviolent sexually explicit materials can cause aggressive behaviors, at least under some circumstances, is well established (cf. Sapolsky, 1984; Zillmann, 1984). Consistent with considerations derived from physiological excitation-transfer theory (Zillmann, 1978, 1979)—which projects that any activity or stimulus that elevates physiological arousal can accentuate subsequent behaviors—research has repeatedly demonstrated that elevated physiological excitedness (e.g., sexual arousal) induced by exposure to standard-fare, nonviolent, sexually explicit materials can intensify aggressive behaviors directed at both male and female targets. Further, the capacity of sexually explicit materials to enhance aggressive responses generally appears limited to circumstances in which the viewer is provoked prior to exposure by the individual against whom their aggression is targeted (cf. Zillmann, 1984).

However, investigations involving informative extensions of these generalizations have provided valuable insights for understanding the behavioral consequences of viewing pornography. In a study by Leonard and Taylor (1983), for example, male subjects were paired with a female confederate and exposed to a slide presentation featuring persons engaged in explicitly depicted precoital and coital heterosexual behaviors or nonsexual, neutral behaviors (control condition). Of equal importance, three different manipulations of the social situation were enacted by the female confederate during presentation of the sexually explicit slides. In what was termed the *permissive cues* condition, the female made apparently spontaneous positive comments such as "that looks like fun" and "I'd like to try that." In a *nonpermissive cues* condition the female made negative, disapproving comments such as "this is disgusting" and "oh, that's awful." And, in a *no cues* condition the female made no comments. Following the exposure treatment, the subjects participated in a multiple-trial reaction-time task. On the first trial, the subject chose a level of shock without knowledge of the confederate's intentions (i.e., no provocation). Then in subsequent trials the subject responded to inappropriately intense electrical shocks he received at the hands of the female confederate (i.e., provocation). For all trials, the shock intensity selected by the subject served as the measure of aggression.

Leonard and Taylor (1983) found that men in the *permissive cues* condition—where the female displayed eager sexual openness—had a significantly more aggressive response than their counterparts in the other two conditions. This pattern was apparent even in the first trial, which was devoid of prior aggressive provocation by the female confederate, and aggressiveness was further enhanced by the provocation of subsequent trials. Recognizing that these effects could not be explained entirely by excitation-transfer considerations, Leonard and Taylor (1983) speculated that, because of her sexually permissive and promiscuous behavior, subjects formed callous perceptions of the female confederate that disinhibited aggressive responsiveness (cf. Check & Malamuth, 1985).

This explanation also appears applicable to the findings of investigations exploring the aggression facilitating impact of sexually explicit materials involving coercive and/or violent themes. Research shows, for example, that exposure to rape myth depictions (i.e., portrayals consistent with the cultural myth that women enjoy being raped) can intensify both provoked and nonprovoked aggressive reactions against women, but not against male targets (cf. Donnerstein, 1983, 1984; Zillmann, 1984).

CONCLUSIONS

The fact that exposure to pornography can activate sexually callous perceptions of women and promote manipulative and, in some instances, aggressive behaviors is highlighted clearly by the research evidence. Enhanced perceptual and behavioral callousness toward women is most apparent following consumption of materials that unambiguously portray women as sexually promiscuous and indiscriminating—a depiction that dominates modern pornography. Adverse consequences resulting from consumption of coercive and/or violent pornography—especially portrayals in which women are shown tolerating, if not enjoying, abusive sexual activities—appear equally substantial.

The nature and extent of the observed responses to pornography, taken together, appear most consistent with the projections of the sexual callousness model (Zillmann & Weaver, 1989) whereas contradicting the alternative viewpoints. For instance, the fact that many viewers extract callousness-promoting information from pornography is clearly inconsistent with the idea that such materials yield only positive consequences. Similarly, the fact that consumption of pornography devoid of violence can produce significant asocial perceptual responses presents a serious challenge to the Donnerstein and Linz (1986) ideology "it is not sex, but violence" (p. 56).

Consideration of the pragmatic implications of the evidence at hand suggests, first of all, that sexually explicit mass media messages may be, as others have projected (Russell, 1988), a potent catalyst for sexually abusive behaviors such as rape. Exposure to pornography, remember, results in both a "loss-of-respect" for female sexual autonomy *and* the disinhibition of men in the expression of aggression against women. Extensive research evidence shows that these two factors are prominent interwoven components in the perceptual profiles of sexually abusive and aggressive individuals (cf. Costin, 1985; Kanin, 1985; Rapaport & Burkhart, 1984).

A second implication concerns the extent to which pornography-induced misogynic perceptions negatively influence the welfare of women in everyday, nonsexual circumstances. Many writers (e.g., Garry, 1978; Lederer, 1980) have suggested that the most damaging consequences of the essentially unrestricted availability of sexually explicit materials are evident in the ill treatment of women (e.g., employment discrimination, economic exploitation, etc.) simply because of their gender. Although empirical evidence addressing this issue is lacking, the occurrence of such effects seems, at least to some degree, probable given that pornographic productions typically portray women in a manner consistent with a nexus of adversarial sex-role beliefs that permeate most Western cultures (cf. Belk & Snell, 1986; Garry, 1978).

Finally, there is reason to suspect that pornography—with its seemingly factual, documentary-style presentation of sexual behaviors—has usurped most other socialization agents to become a primary institution of sexual indoctrination in many societies (Zillmann & Weaver, 1989). Research shows, for example, that many young people in North America become consumers of sexually explicit materials during preadolescence (Bryant & Brown, 1989). Clearly, in light of the research findings, the desirability of pornography as a rudimentary "educator" about sex must be contemplated.

REFERENCES

Abel, G. G. (1985, September). *Use of pornography and erotica by sex offenders.* Paper presented to the United States Attorney General's Commission on Pornography, Houston, TX.

Attorney General's Commission on Pornography. (1986). *Final Report.* Washington, DC.: U. S. Government Printing Office.

Baron, L., & Straus, M. A. (1984). Sexual stratification, pornography, and rape in the United States. In N. M. Malamuth & E. Donnerstein (Eds.), *Pornography and sexual aggression* (pp. 185-209). Orlando: Academic Press.

Baron, L., & Straus, M. A. (1987). Four theories of rape: A macrosociological analysis. *Social Problems, 34,* 467-489.

Belk, S. S., & Snell, W. E., Jr. (1986). Beliefs about women: Components and correlates. *Personality and Social Psychology Bulletin, 12,* 403-413.

Brannigan, A. (1987). Pornography and behavior: Alternative explanations. *Journal of Communication, 37*(3), 185-192.

Brosius, H., Weaver, J., & Staab, J. (1993). Exploring the social and sexual "reality" of contemporary pornography. *The Journal of Sex Research, 30,* 161-172.

Brown, D., & Bryant, J. (1989). The manifest content of pornography. In D. Zillmann & J. Bryant (Eds.), *Pornography: Research advances and policy considerations* (pp. 3-24). Hillsdale, NJ:Lawrence Erlbaum Associates.

Brownmiller, S. (1984, November). The place of pornography: Packaging eros for a violent age (Comments to a Forum held at the New School for Social Research in New York City moderated by L. H. Lapham). *Harper's,* pp. 31-39, 42-45.

Bryant, J., & Brown, D. (1989). Uses of pornography. In D. Zillmann & J. Bryant (Eds.), *Pornography: Research advances and policy considerations* (pp. 25-55). Hillsdale, NJ: Lawrence Erlbaum Associates.

Buchman, J. G. (1988). *Effects of repeated exposure to nonviolent erotica on attitudes about sexual child abuse.* Unpublished doctoral dissertation, Indiana University, Bloomington.

Check, J. V. P., & Malamuth, N. M. (1985). Pornography and sexual aggression: A social learning theory analysis. In M. L. McLaughlin (Ed.), *Communication yearbook* (Vol. 9, pp. 181-213). Beverly Hills, CA: Sage.

Commission on Obscenity and Pornography (1970). *Report of the Commission on Obscenity and Pornography.* New York: Bantam Books.

Committee on Sexual Offences Against Children and Youths (1984). *Sexual offences against children.* Ottawa: Canadian Government Publishing Centre.

Copp, D. (1983). Pornography and censorship: An introductory essay. In D. Copp & S. Wendell (Eds.), *Pornography and censorship* (pp. 15-41). Buffalo, NY: Prometheus Books.

Costin, F. (1985). Beliefs about rape and women's social roles. *Archives of Sexual Behavior, 14,* 319-325.

Court, J. H. (1984). Sex and violence: A ripple effect. In N. M. Malamuth & E. Donnerstein (Eds.), *Pornography and sexual aggression* (pp. 143-172). Orlando: Academic Press.

Cowan, G., Lee, C., Levy, D., & Snyder, D. (1988). Dominance and inequality in x-rated videocassettes. *Psychology of Women Quarterly, 12,* 299-311.

Davis, K. E., & Braucht, G. N. (1973). Exposure to pornography, character, and sexual deviance: A retrospective survey. *Journal of Social Issues, 29,* 183–196.

Diamond, S. (1985). Pornography: Image and reality. In V. Burstyn (Ed.), *Women against censorship* (pp. 40–57). Vancouver, BC: Douglas & McIntyre.

Donnerstein, E. (1983). Erotica and human aggression. In R. Geen & E. Donnerstein (Eds.), *Aggression: Theoretical and empirical reviews* (Vol. 2, pp. 127–154). New York: Academic Press.

Donnerstein, E. (1984). Pornography: Its effect on violence against women. In N. M. Malamuth & E. Donnerstein (Eds.), *Pornography and sexual aggression* (pp. 53–81). Orlando: Academic Press.

Donnerstein, E., & Linz, D. G. (1986, December). The question of pornography. *Psychology Today,* pp. 56–59.

Donnerstein, E., Linz, D., & Penrod, S. (1987). *The question of pornography.* New York: Macmillan.

Fisher, W. A. (1986). A psychological approach to human sexuality: The sexual behavior sequence. In D. Byrne & K. Kelley (Eds.), *Alternative approaches to the study of sexual behavior* (pp. 131–171). Hillsdale, NJ: Lawrence Erlbaum Associates.

Gagnon, J. H. (1977). *Human sexualities.* Glenview, IL: Scott, Foresman.

Garry, A. (1978). Pornography and respect for women. *Social Theory and Practice, 4,* 395–422.

Goldstein, A. (1984, November). The place of pornography: Packaging eros for a violent age (Comments to a Forum held at the New School for Social Research in New York City moderated by L. H. Lapham). *Harper's,* pp. 31–39, 42–45.

Hebditch, D., & Anning, N. (1988). *Porn gold: Inside the pornography business.* London: Faber & Faber.

Howitt, D. (1989). Pornography: The recent debate. In G. Cumberbatch & D. Howitt (Eds.), *A measure of uncertainty: The effects of mass media* (pp. 61–80). London: Libbey.

Jaffee, D., & Straus, M. A. (1987). Sexual climate and reported rape: A state-level analysis. *Archives of Sexual Behavior, 16,* 107–123.

Kanin, E. J. (1985). Date rapists: Differential sexual socialization and relative deprivation. *Archives of Sexual Behavior, 14,* 219–231.

Kendrick, W. (1987). *The secret museum: Pornography in modern culture.* New York: Viking.

Kutchinsky, B. (1973). Eroticism without censorship. *International Journal of Criminology and Penology, 1,* 217–225.

Lawrence, D. H. (1936). Pornography and obscenity. In E. D. McDonald (Ed.), *Phoenix: The posthumous papers of D. H. Lawrence* (pp. 170–187). New York: Viking.

Lederer, L. (1980), *Take back the night: Women on pornography.* New York: William Morrow.

Leonard, K. E., & Taylor, S. P. (1983). Exposure to pornography, permissive and nonpermissive cues, and male aggression toward females.*Motivation and Emotion, 7,* 291–299.

Malamuth, N. M. (1984). Aggression against women: Cultural and individual causes. In N. M. Malamuth & E. Donnerstein (Eds.), *Pornography and sexual aggression* (pp. 17–52). Orlando: Academic Press.

Malamuth, N. M., & Billings, V. (1986). The functions and effects of pornography: Sexual communications versus the feminist models in light of research findings. In J. Bryant & D. Zillmann (Eds.), *Perspectives on media effects* (pp. 83–108). Hillsdale, NJ: Lawrence Erlbaum Associates.

Malamuth, N. M., & Donnerstein, E. (1984). *Pornography and sexual aggression.* Orlando: Academic Press.

Marshall, W. L. (1988). The use of sexually explicit stimuli by rapists, child molesters, and nonoffenders. *Journal of Sex Research, 25,* 267–288.

Marshall, W. L. (1989). Pornography and sex offenders. In D. Zillmann & J. Bryant (Eds.), *Pornography: Research advances and policy considerations* (pp. 185–214). Hillsdale, NJ: Lawrence Erlbaum Associates.

Page, S. (1989). Misrepresentation of pornography research:Psychology's role. *American Psychologist, 44*, 578–580.

Palys, T. S. (1986). Testing the common wisdom: The social content of video pornography. *Canadian Psychology, 27*(1), 22–35.

Prince, S. (1990). Power and pain: Content analysis and the ideology of pornography. *Journal of Film and Video, 42* (2), 31–41.

Propper, M. (1970). Exposure to sexually oriented materials among young male prison offenders. *Technical Reports of the Commission on Obscenity and Pornography* (Vol. 9, pp. 313–404). Washington, DC: U. S. Government Printing Office.

Rapaport, K., & Burkhart, B. R. (1984). Personality and attitudinal characteristics of sexually coercive college males. *Journal of Abnormal Psychology, 93*, 216–221.

Rimmer, R. H. (1986). *The X-rated videotape guide.* New York: Harmony.

Russell, D. E. H. (1984). *Sexual exploitation: Rape, child sexual abuse, and workplace harassment.* Beverly Hills, CA: Sage.

Russell, D. E. H. (1988). Pornography and rape: A causal model. *Political Psychology, 9*, 41–73.

Sapolsky, B. S. (1984). Arousal, affect, and the aggression-moderating effect of erotica. In N. M. Malamuth & E. Donnerstein (Eds.), *Pornography and sexual aggression* (pp. 85–113). Orlando: Academic Press.

Scott, J. E., & Schwalm, L. A. (1988). Rape rates and the circulation of adult magazines. *Journal of Sex Research, 24*, 241–250.

Silbert, M. H., & Pines, A. M. (1984). Pornography and sexual abuse of women. *Sex Roles, 10*, 857–868.

Special Committee on Pornography and Prostitution (1985). *Report of the Special Committee on Pornography and Prostitution.* Ottawa: Canadian Government Publishing Centre.

Steinem, G. (1980). Erotica and pornography: A clear and present difference. In L. Lederer (Ed.), *Take back the night: Women on pornography* (pp. 35–39). New York: William Morrow.

Stoller, R. (1976). Sexual excitement. *Archives of General Psychiatry, 33*, 899–909.

Weaver, J. B. (1987). *Effects of portrayals of female sexuality and violence against women on perceptions of women* (Unpublished doctoral dissertation, Indiana University, Blooming-ton, 1988). *Dissertation Abstracts International 48* (10), 2482-A (University Microfilms No. DA8727475)

Weaver, J. (1991). Responding to erotica: Perceptual processes and dispositional implications. In J. Bryant & D. Zillmann (Eds.), *Responding to the screen: Reception and reaction processes* (pp. 329–354). Hillsdale, NJ: Lawrence Erlbaum Associates.

Weaver, J. (1992). The perceptual and behavioural consequences of exposure to pornography: The social science and psychological research evidence. In C. Itzin (Ed.), *Pornography: Women, violence & civil liberties* (pp. 284–309). Oxford University Press.

Wilson, W. C. (1978). Can pornography contribute to the prevention of sexual problems? In C. B. Qualls, J. P. Wincze, & D. H. Barlow (Eds.), *The prevention of sexual disorders: Issues and approaches* (pp. 159–179). New York: Plenum Press.

Zillmann, D. (1978). Attribution and misattribution of excitatory reactions. In J. H. Harvey, W. J. Ickes, & R. F. Kidd (Eds.), *New directions in attribution research* (Vol. 2, pp. 335–368). Hillsdale, NJ: Lawrence Erlbaum Associates.

Zillmann, D. (1979). *Hostility and aggression.* Hillsdale, NJ: Lawrence Erlbaum Associates.

Zillmann, D. (1984). *Connections between sex and aggression.* Hillsdale, NJ: Lawrence Erlbaum Associates.

Zillmann, D. (1989a). Effects of prolonged consumption of pornography. In D. Zillmann & J. Bryant (Eds.), *Pornography: Research advances and policy considerations* (pp. 127–157). Hillsdale, NJ: Lawrence Erlbaum Associates.

Zillmann, D. (1989b). Pornography research and public policy. In D. Zillmann & J. Bryant (Eds.), *Pornography: Research advances and policy considerations* (pp. 387–403). Hillsdale, NJ: Lawrence Erlbaum Associates.

Zillmann, D., & Bryant, J. (1982). Pornography, sexual callousness, and the trivialization of rape. *Journal of Communication, 32*(4), 10–21.

Zillmann, D., & Bryant, J. (1988a). Effects of prolonged consumption of pornography on family values. *Journal of Family Issues, 9*, 518–544.

Zillmann, D., & Bryant, J. (1988b). Pornography's impact on sexual satisfaction. *Journal of Applied Social Psychology, 18*, 438–453.

Zillmann, D., & Bryant, J. (1989). *Pornography: Research advances and policy considerations*. Hillsdale, NJ: Lawrence Erlbaum Associates.

Zillmann, D., & Weaver, J. B. (1989). Pornography and men's sexual callousness toward women. In D. Zillmann & J. Bryant (Eds.), *Pornography: Research advances and policy considerations* (pp. 95–125). Hillsdale, NJ: Lawrence Erlbaum Associates.

17

PORNOGRAPHY EFFECTS: EMPIRICAL AND CLINICAL EVIDENCE

Victor B. Cline
University of Utah

Whether pornography has any significant harmful effects on consumers continues to be a very controversial issue, not only for "average citizens" but also for behavioral scientists. This is not surprising in light of two national commissions—in the last two decades—coming to diametrically opposite conclusions about this matter.

Some social commentators claim that pornography is mainly a form of entertainment, possibly educational, sometimes sexually arousing—but essentially harmless. Or at least there is no good scientific evidence of harm. Others claim more dire consequences and give as examples recent cases played up by the media of sex murderers who have claimed that pornography "made them do it."

To ascertain something about pornography's effects, we first need to define it. The word *pornography* is a "lay term" used in common parlance to usually mean "graphic and explicit depictions of sexual activity." Whereas *obscenity* is a legal term that comes to us from the U.S. Supreme Court's definition (rendered in 1973, *Miller v. California*). Here for something to be found *legally* obscene, a jury (representing a cross section of the community) must find *three* things wrong with it: (a) It must appeal to a prurient (sick, morbid, shameful, or lustful) interest in sex; (b) it must be patently offensive (e.g., go beyond contemporary community standards with regards to depictions of sexual content or activity); (c) taken as a whole it must lack serious literary, artistic, political, or scientific value.

The material has to fail *all three tests* before it can be found obscene in the eyes of the law and any penalties proscribed. This means that something could be regarded as "pornographic" but still not be legally obscene, such as explicit sex films used to teach medical students about human sexuality or even a film or book with high artistic and/or literary value that had explicit sexual content.

Thus, the Supreme Court has protected a wide variety of sexual matter in movies, books, magazines, art displays, and in other formats from being censored or prohibited for adults, although there is a more strict or conservative standard with respect to minors. Under the "Miller test," however, "hardcore" and child pornography can be prohibited and penalties proscribed, if the community wishes. In some communities, however, although obscenity statutes are on the books, these statutes are not rigidly enforced, allowing for legally obscene material to be available in adult bookstores or even neighborhood video rental outlets.

PORNOGRAPHY HAS AN EFFECT — BUT WHAT KIND?

There is a belief strongly held by some Americans that pornography (or obscenity), whereas it may be vulgar and tasteless, is still essentially harmless and has no real effect on the viewer and can certainly do no real harm.

However, for someone to suggest that pornography cannot have an effect (including a harmful one) is to deny the whole notion of education generally or suggest that people are not effected by what they read and see. If you say that a pornographic book or film cannot effect you, then you also have to say that Karl Marx's Das Kapital, the Bible, the Koran, or advertising also have no effects on their readers or viewers, and that is nonsense. But, of course, books and other media do have an effect on their consumers. Consider a single book by Ralph Nader, *Unsafe at any Speed.* It set in motion a whole series of events leading to legislation that is now undoubtedly saving thousands of lives yearly on the highway, and which put General Motor's Corvair out of business.

Shrewd businessmen would not spend over $10 billion a year on television advertising if their visual–verbal messages and imagery did not motivate people to buy deodorant, Chevies, or Pampers. But then for those who do admit that it may have some effect, the key question is what kind of effect?

Its Educative Impact

At the very least, pornography educates. However, if you were to regard pornography as a form of sex education, you would have to label most of it as *mis*education, as false, and as misleading information about human sexuality, especially female sexual nature and response. Also, much pornography models "unhealthy" or even antisocial kinds of sexual activity such as sadomasochism, abuse, humiliation of the female, involvement of minors, incest, group sex, voyeurism, exhibitionism, bestiality, and so on. Thus, if we examine just its educative impact, it presents us with some concerns.

Anthropologist Gilbert Bartell in his study of 280 American couples involved in mate swapping and group sex found that it was primarily books and pornographic films that provided the stimulus, model, or "instruction manual" that prompted the men to push their wives and girl friends into having homosexual sex — as a "turn on" for the men. But the end results from this type of "sex education" turned out disastrous for the men, reported Bartell (Bartell, 1971).

Clinics Use Sex Films to Change Sexual Behavior and Attitudes

Many hundreds of sex-counseling clinics in the United States daily make use of explicit sexual pictures, films, books, and videos to change couples' sexual behavior, beliefs, and attitudes. Other centers use graphic sex films to recondition the sexual behavior of sex offenders. However, these are as carefully selected and prescribed as a physician would in writing a prescription for a particular drug to treat a specific illness or infection. No responsible doctor would ever send a patient to a pharmacy and say, "Take anything available on the shelf." And no responsible sex therapist would ever say to a patient who had a specific focused sexual problem, "Go down to the adult bookstore and help yourself to whatever you find there."

You cannot logically argue that the kind of change that goes on in a sex-counseling clinic can go only one way (just make people healthy). It can go the other way too. The possibility certainly exists that some pornography can harm people by suggesting through modeling and imitative learning (as well as through accidental conditioning processes) inappropriate, unhealthy, or illegal kinds of sexual activity — which some suggestible viewers may later act out. We also have a great deal of information gained from studies of and treating sex offenders, suggesting that pornography is often used by them as a facilitator in not only acquiring their own deviation but also as a device to break down the resistance and inhibitions of their victims or targets of molestation, especially where these are children or juveniles (Burgess, 1984; Carnes, 1984).

Why Sex Education in the Schools?

Or consider also the spread of sex education instruction throughout schools in the United States. The assumption is that you can change attitudes and behavior about sex through some form of teaching and instruction. If you assume that this is so (still a controversial issue among researchers), then you have to admit to the possibility that films, magazines, and books that model rape and the dehumanization of females in sexual scenes are another powerful form of sex education and thus educate too.

Anyone who has seen much pornography knows that most of it is made by men for male consumption, is extremely sexist, gives a great deal of misinformation about human sexuality, and that most of it is devoid of love, relationship, responsibility, mentions nothing about the risks of sexually transmitted diseases, and for the most part dehumanizes both male and female participants. Much pornography falsely represents sex, and some of it is very hostile to the females who are often denigrated and humiliated.

National Poll of Mental Health Workers

In a national poll of mental health professionals (Lipkin & Carns, 1970), 254 psychotherapists reported that they had come across cases in their clinical practices where pornography was found to be an instigator or contributor to a sex crime, personality disturbance, or antisocial act. Another 324 psychotherapists reported suspecting such a relationship to exist. Although a larger number of other professionals responding to the survey had not found such relationships in their clinical practice, the response of the 578 psychotherapists that did find such a harmful relationship (or suspected same) certainly cannot be casually dismissed or disregarded, especially when a health hazard is involved.

Pornography Effects: Data from Clinical Case Studies

In reviewing the literature on the effects of pornography, there is a variety of evidence suggesting risk and the possibility of harm from being immersed in repeated exposure to pornography. These data come from three sources: (a) *experimental laboratory-type studies*, (b) *field studies*, and (c) *clinical case history data* from the offices of professional health-care personnel treating individuals with sexual dysfunctions or paraphilias, as well as clergy and attorneys who counsel or provide services to sexually troubled individuals. Also, in this category is the evidence provided by sexual addicts affiliated with such national support groups as "Sexaholics Anonymous," or in treatment at such centers as the "Institute for Behavioral Medicine" at Golden Valley, Minnesota.

I am a clinical psychologist. I have treated over many years approximately 300 sex addicts, sex offenders, or other individuals (96% male) with sexual illnesses. This includes many types of unwanted compulsive sexual acting out plus such things as child molestation, exhibitionism, voyeurism, sadomasochism, fetishism, rape, and so forth. With only several exceptions, pornography has been a major or minor contributor or facilitator in the acquisition of their deviation or sexual addiction.

However, regardless of the nature of the deviation, I found a four-factor syndrome common to nearly all my clients with almost no exceptions, especially in their early involvement with pornography.

The first thing that happened was an *addiction* effect. They got hooked. Once involved in obscene materials they kept coming back for more and still more. The material seemed to provide a very powerful sexual stimulant or aphrodisiac effect followed by sexual release most often through masturbation. The pornography provided very exciting and powerful fantasies that they frequently recalled to mind and elaborated on in their fantasies. One of my patients, even for $1,000, could not stay away from pornography for 90 days, he was so deeply addicted. And in his case he desperately wanted to stop his dependency on this material because of its negative effect on his marriage as well as on his personal behavior.

Second, there was an *escalation effect*. With the passage of time they required more explicit, rougher, more deviant, and "kinky" kinds of sexual material to get their "highs" and "sexual turn ons." It was reminiscent of those individuals afflicted with drug addictions. Over time, there is nearly always an increasing need for more of the stimulant to get the same effect as one got initially. If their wives or girl friends were involved with them, they eventually pushed their partners into doing increasingly bizarre and deviant sexual activities. In many cases this resulted in a rupture in the relationship when the woman refused to go further — often leading to much conflict, separation, or divorce.

Being married or being in relationships with a willing sexual partner did not solve their problem. Their addiction and escalation was mainly to the powerful sexual imagery in their minds. They often preferred this, accompanied by masturbation, to sexual intercourse itself. This nearly always diminished their capacity to love and express affection to their partner in their intimate relations. The fantasy was all powerful, much to the chagrin and disappointment of their partner. Their sex drive had been diverted to a degree away from their spouse. And the spouse could easily sense and tell this and often felt very lonely and rejected. I have had a number of couple clients where the wife tearfully reported that her husband preferred to masturbate to pornography than make love to her.

The third thing that happened was *desensitization*. Material (in books, magazine, or film-videos) that was originally perceived as shocking, taboo breaking, illegal, repulsive, or immoral — although still sexually arousing — in time came to be seen as acceptable and commonplace. The sexual activity they witnessed (no matter how antisocial or deviant) became legitimized. There was increasingly a sense that "everybody does it," and this gave them permission to also do it — even though, possibly, illegal and contrary to their previous moral beliefs and personal standards.

The fourth thing that occurred was an increasing tendency to *act out sexually* the behaviors viewed in the pornography that they had been repeatedly exposed to — including compulsive promiscuity, exhibitionism, group sex, voyeurism, frequenting massage parlors, having sex with minor children, rape, inflicting pain on themselves or partner during sex, and so on. This behavior frequently grew into a sexual addiction that they found themselves locked into and unable to change or reverse — no matter what the negative consequences in their life.

Many examples of negative effects from pornography use come from the private or clinical practice of psychotherapists, physicians, counselors, attorneys, and ministers. Here we come face to face with real people who are in some kind of significant trouble or pain. A few examples might illustrate this.

The 46-year-old deputy mayor of the city of Los Angeles attended a West L.A. porn theater one afternoon a few years ago. While watching the sex film he became so aroused that he started to sexually assault or molest a patron sitting next to him. The individual turned out to be an undercover city vice-squad officer. The deputy mayor was arrested, booked, and found guilty in a subsequent trial. This distinguished public servant left office shamed and humiliated, his career in shambles.

A 36-year-old married, college-educated, professional man, who was very successful financially, had an addiction to pornography, masturbation, and frequenting massage parlors where he had paid sex. He had an excellent marriage, four children, and was very active in his church, where he assumed important positions of responsibility. Although he felt guilty about his engagement in illicit sex, which was contrary to his religious ethic and personal values, and had the potential of seriously disturbing his marriage if found out, he compulsively continued to do that which at a rational level he did not want to do. His problem came to light when he infected his wife with a venereal disease. This created many serious and disturbing consequences in his life and marriage.

A 30-year-old single male, religiously active and very committed to his faith, had a history of pornography addiction. He was too shy and backward to ask adult females on dates. So he developed intimate relationships with his 4-and 7-year-old nieces and their girl friends that culminated in his repeatedly sexually molesting them. The modeling of explicit sexual activity in the pornography that he consumed helped fuel his sexual interest in these children. Because of his guilt over what he was doing, he eventually sought professional help. However, his state had a "disclosure law" that required that he be reported to state officials for his sexual abuse of these children. Because of his cooperative attitude and the fact that he sought treatment on his own, he was placed on probation, received long-term psychotherapy, and is now living a more normal life.

EARLIER EMPIRICAL STUDIES ON PORNO EFFECTS

If we look at field and laboratory studies on pornography's effects, we might cite evidence going back to the 1970 Presidential Commission on Obscenity and Pornography Report, all of whose technical reports I carefully reviewed and later wrote a book about (Cline, 1974).

In a sophisticated commission-financed study of seven different populations of subjects comprising 365 people, Davis and Braucht (1971) assessed the relationship between exposure to pornography and moral character, deviance in the home and neighborhood, and sex behavior. In their study, impressive in its rigorous methodology and statistical treatment, they concluded that: "One finds exposure to pornography is the strongest predictor of sexual deviance among the early age of exposure subjects"(p. 205).

Davis and Braucht also found that there was a "positive relationship between sexual deviance and exposure to pornography at all ages of exposure: In the early age of exposure (to pornography) subgroup, the amount of exposure was significantly correlated with a willingness to engage in group sexual relations . . . 'serious' sexual deviance; and there were trends for the number of both high school heterosexual partners and total homosexual partners to be positively related to (pornographic) exposure" (pp. 206–213). This suggests that pornography may act as a facilitator or accelerator of youthful promiscuity—which could raise health concerns relative to the acquisition and spread of AIDS, herpes, and other sexually transmitted diseases as well as sexual addictions.

Correlation alone never demonstrates a causal relationship—however, it does sometimes permit a reasonable hypothesis. Because the researchers had partialed out the contribution of other key variables in this study, the possibility of causation (of harm via pornography exposure) was highly suggested.

In a study by Propper (1971) of 476 reformatory inmates, he repeatedly noted a relationship between high exposure to pornography and sexually promiscuous and deviant behavior, as well as affiliation with groups high in criminal activity and sex deviancy. In another study by Walker (1971) it was found that 39% of the sex offenders interviewed indicated that "pornography had something to do with their committing the sex offense that they were convicted of." Whereas one must be cautious in interpreting these results, they again raise the possibility of negative outcomes from exposure to pornography.

The Michigan State Police Study.   Still another type of evidence comes from a study conducted by Pope (1983) with the Michigan State Police, who found that, of 38,000 cases of sexual assault on file in Michigan, 41% involved pornography exposure just prior to the act or during the act.

Sex Offenders Use of Pornography.   In another study by Marshall (1983), almost half the rapists that he studied used consenting sex pornography to arouse themselves preparatory to seeking out a victim to rape.

Conditioning into Deviancy with Pornography: The Rachman Studies

Other powerful cause–effect data come from the conditioning laboratories of investigators such as Dr. Stanley Rachman (1968), who demonstrated that, with the use of highly erotic pictures, sexual deviations could be created in live subjects in a laboratory setting. He was actually able to condition (repeatedly) 100% of his male subjects into a sexual deviancy (fetishism).

Additionally, the work of McGuire (1965) suggests that exposure to special sexual experiences (which could include witnessing pornography) and then masturbating to the fantasy of this exposure can sometimes later lead to participation in deviant sexual acts.

The massive literature on therapy for sex deviates suggests that their sexual orientation can sometimes be changed (reconditioned) with the use of explicit sex films as a therapeutic tool (Marquis, 1970). If these data are valid, then one must also allow for the possibility that deliberate or accidental exposure to pornography or deviant real-life sex experiences can also facilitate the conditioning of individuals into sexual aberrations.

All Sex Deviations are Learned Behavior.   The best evidence to date suggests that all sexual deviations are learned. None are inherited. As

McGuire explained it, as a man repeatedly masturbates to a vivid sexual fantasy as his exclusive outlet (introduced by pornography or maybe a real-life experience), the pleasurable experiences endow the deviant fantasy (rape, molesting children, injuring one's partner while having sex, etc.) with increasing erotic value. The orgasm experienced then provides the critical reinforcing event for the conditioning of the fantasy preceding or accompanying the act (McGuire, 1965).

Other related studies by Evans (1968) and Jackson (1969) support this thesis. They found that deviant masturbatory fantasy very significantly affected the habit strength of the subject's sexual deviation. McGuire indicated that any type of sexual deviation can be acquired in this way, that it may include several unrelated deviations in one individual and cannot be eliminated even by massive feelings of guilt. His paper cited many case histories to illustrate this type of conditioning.

McGaugh's Research on Memory.   The work of psychologist James L. McGaugh (1983) at the University of California, Irvine, needs mention here. His findings (oversimplifying considerably) suggested that memories of experiences that occurred at times of emotional arousal (which could include sexual arousal) get locked into the brain by an adrenal gland hormone, epinephrine, and are difficult to erase. This may partly explain pornography's addicting effect. Powerful sexually arousing memories of experiences from the past keep intruding themselves back on the mind's memory screen serving to stimulate and erotically arouse the viewer. If he masturbates to these fantasies, he reinforces the linkage between sexual arousal and orgasm with the particular scene repeatedly rehearsed in his mind.

One might quickly see the risks involved with large numbers of males being exposed to the following film. This 8 mm motion picture film marketed out of Los Angeles depicts two Girl Scouts in their green uniforms selling cookies from door to door. At one residence they are invited in by a mature, sexually aggressive adult male, who proceeds to seduce them and subject them to a number of unusual and extremely explicit sexual acts, all shown in greatest detail. The girls are depicted as eagerly enjoying this sexual orgy. This film is what is usually termed hardcore pornography. This is the kind of pornographic stimulus film that the male viewer can play again and again, either in the privacy of his home or in his mind for his sexual pleasure.

If the research of Rachman, McGuire, McGaugh, and hundreds of other investigators in the area of human learning has any meaning at all, it would suggest that such a film could be dangerous and could potentially condition some male viewers into having reoccurring sexual fantasies (vividly imprinted into the brain by the epinephrine), which they might repeatedly masturbate to and then later be tempted to act out as sexual advances toward female minors — especially if they were in Girl Scout uniforms.

Regularly Masturbating to Pornography is a Common Pathway to Self-Inflicted Sexual Illness. In my treatment of hundreds of primarily male patients I consistently find that they are vulnerable to the effects of masturbatory conditioning with the consequence of sexual ill health.

In my experience as a sexual therapist, many individuals who regularly masturbate to pornography become at risk, in time, of acquiring a sexual addiction or paraphilia and/or disturb a bonded relationship with a spouse or intimate partner. A common side effect is that it also reduces their capacity to love (e.g., it results in a marked dissociation of sex from friendship, affection, caring, and other normal healthy emotions and traits that help marital relationships). Their sexual side becomes in a sense dehumanized. Many of them develop an "alien ego state," whose core is antisocial lust devoid of most values. In time, the "high" obtained from masturbating to pornography becomes more important than real-life relationships.

It has been commonly thought by health educators that masturbation has negligible consequences, other than reducing sexual tension. Although this may be generally true, one exception may be in the area of repeatedly masturbating to deviant pornography imagery (either as memories in the mind or as explicit pornographic stimuli), which risks (via conditioning) the acquiring of sexual addictions and/or other sexual pathology.

It makes no difference if one is an eminent physician, attorney, minister, athlete, corporate executive, college president, unskilled laborer or an average 15-year-old boy. In fact, in my experience the brighter the man is, the more vulnerable he is — possibly because of a greater capacity to fantasize. The process of masturbatory conditioning is inexorable and does not spontaneously remiss. The course of this illness may be slow and is nearly always hidden from view (it's usually a secret part of the man's life). Like a cancer, it keeps growing and spreading, and rarely ever reverses itself. It is also very difficult to treat and heal. Denial on the part of the male addict and refusal to confront the problem is typical and predictable. And this almost always leads to marital or couple disharmony, sometimes divorce and sometimes the breaking up of other intimate family relationships.

The Research on Aggressive Pornography (Porno-Violence)

Aggressive sexual crimes against women are a very serious and escalating problem in the United States. Recent Senate Judiciary Committee hearings concluded that rape has increased four times as fast as the overall crime rate over the last decade. And, in fact, the United States leads the world in rape statistics, with a rape rate four times that of Germany, 13 times as much as England, and 20 times as much as Japan ("The Mind of the Rapist," 1990, pp. 51–52).

In recent years there has been a considerable body of research on aggressive pornography—a lot of it found in hard-R-rated films. Many of these are also broadcast on cable TV. The typical film shows nude females or females in sexually arousing situations and postures being raped, tortured, or murdered. The results of this research suggest the possibility of conditioning male viewers into associating sexual arousal with inflicting injury, rape, humiliation, or torture on females. Where these films are available on videotapes (which most are), these can be repeatedly viewed in the privacy of one's residence and masturbated to with the associated risks of negative or antisocial conditioning noted before.

Malamuth and Donnerstein (1984) noted: "Certain forms of pornography (aggressive) can affect aggressive attitudes toward women and can desensitize an individual's perception of rape. These attitudes and perceptions are furthermore directly related to actual aggressive behavior against women." p. 54 or "These results suggest, again, that aggressive pornography does increase aggression against women" (p. 67). In films where the woman is depicted as saying that she enjoys being raped, they found an increased male acceptance of interpersonal violence against women, and it tended to increase the male's acceptance of rape myths (such as believing that women enjoy rape). These authors concluded that "There can be relatively long-term anti-social effects of movies that portray sexual violence as having positive consequences" (e.g., the woman indicated she enjoyed being raped, or when she said "no" she really meant "yes" when being sexually assaulted) (p. 34).

The literature on aggressive pornography is rather impressive in its consistency in suggesting a variety of harms or possibility of antisocial outcomes from exposure to this material. This is not too unexpected after 40 years of research on film, and TV violence coming to essentially the same conclusion (Rubinstein, 1983).

In research by Neil Malamuth and associates where college males were exposed to sexually violent pornography—such as rape and other forms of sexual violence—two thirds of the male subjects following exposure indicated an increased willingness to force a woman into sex acts if they were assured of not being caught or punished. In similar research by Malamuth & Feshback (1978), 51% of "normal" UCLA males indicated the likelihood of emulating a sadomasochistic rape (seen in porn material they had been exposed to) if they were assured of not getting caught (Malamuth, 1981).

The 10-member panel of the Attorney General's Commission on Pornography (1986) concluded *unanimously* after reviewing a great volume of clinical and experimental research that "Substantial exposure to sexually violent materials (violent pornography) . . . bears a causal relationship to antisocial acts of sexual violence . . ." and "There is a causal relationship between exposure to sexually violent materials and an increase in aggressive behavior directed towards women" (p. 324). They also commented, "The evidence from formal or informal studies of self-reports of offenders themselves supports the conclusions that the causal connection we identify relates to actual sexual offenses" (p. 326).

The Effects of "Nonviolent" Pornography

The issue that has caught the attention lately of some behavioral scientists doing work in this area is whether it is the violence or the sex that is doing most of the "harm" when it is fused together in so-called aggressive pornography or porno-violence. Or some will say, "Just eliminate the violence – the sex is OK."

If we look at *nonviolent pornography* totally devoid of violence, we might well ask what about its effects? First, we might indicate several examples of *non*violent pornography that most therapists as well as ordinary citizens would not regard as healthy models of sexual behavior: (a) *child pornography*; (b) *incest type porn* (e.g., mother seducing son, daughter seducing father, older brother seducing younger sister, etc.); (c) *sex with animals*; (d) *group sex* (e.g., 3 on 1, group mate swapping, etc.); (e) *sex that humiliates and denigrates women* and their sex role in man–woman relationships (but without overt violence); (f) *pornography such as that involving the eager Girl Scout teenagers having 2 on 1 sex with the adult male*; and (g) *obscene films that present a massive amount of misinformation or gross distortions about human sexuality*. All the preceding, whereas lacking violence, still have the potential of having negative effects on some viewers because they model unhealthy sex-role behavior or give false information about human sexuality. Additionally nonviolent pornography can contribute to acquiring a sexual addiction.

The Attorney General's Commission on Pornography (cited earlier), in further reviewing the research on pornographic materials that whereas *not violent* but did involve degradation, domination, subordination, and humiliation (of women), concluded: "Substantial exposure to materials of this type bears some casual relationship to the level of sexual violence, sexual coercion, or unwanted sexual aggression in the population so exposed . . . as well as the incidence of various non-violent forms of discrimination against or subordination of women in our society" (pp. 333–334).

Additionally, there exists empirical research on the effects of straight adult *non*violent pornography by researchers Zillmann and Bryant (1984). This research suggested that when experimental subjects are exposed to repeated presentations of hardcore *nonviolent* adult pornography over a 6-week period they: (a) develop an increased callousness toward women; (b) tend to trivialize rape as a criminal offense – to some it was no longer a crime at all; (c) develop distorted perceptions about sexuality; (d) develop an appetite for more deviant, bizarre, or violent types of pornography (escalation). Normal sex no longer seemed to "do the job"; (e) devalue the importance of monogamy and lack confidence in marriage as either a viable or lasting institution; and (f) come to view nonmonogamous relationships as normal and natural behavior.

In a further study reported to the commission by Bryant (1985), 600 American males and females of junior high age and above were interviewed about their "out in real-life involvement with pornography." He found that 91% of the males and 82% of the females admitted having been exposed to X-rated hardcore pornography. Two thirds of the males and 40% of the females reported wanting to try out some of the sexual behaviors they had witnessed. And 25% of the males and 15% of the females admitted actually *doing* some of the things sexually they had seen in the pornography *within a few days after exposure*. This clearly suggests the modeling effect or "imitative learning" effect as well as "triggering effect" that even nonviolent pornography has on human sexual behavior in some individuals.

Additionally, it was found that massive (e.g., 6 weeks) exposure to nonaggressive pornography was able to change the attitudes and feelings of their subjects in the direction of making sexual improprieties and transgressions seem *less bad*. The victims of such transgressions were perceived to *suffer less* and be *less severely wronged*. In other words, they had become to some degree desensitized to the breaking of sexual taboos as a result of the pornography exposure.

Bryant commented:

> "If the values which permeate the content of most hardcore pornography are examined, what is found is an almost total suspension of the sorts of moral judgement that have been espoused in the value systems of most civilized cultures. Forget trust. Forget family. Forget commitment. Forget love. Forget marriage. Here in this world of ultimate physical hedonism, anything goes. If we take seriously the social science research literature in areas such as social learning or cultivation effects, we should expect that the heavy consumer of hardcore pornography should acquire some of these values which are so markedly different from those of our mainstream society, especially if the consumer does not have a well-developed value system of his or her own."

And, of course, this is just what Dr. Bryant found in his research reported previously.

Dial-A-Porn

With the sponsorship of the U.S. Dept. of Justice, I was commissioned to conduct a pilot field study on the effects of Dial-A-Porn on children. In

January 1985 I interviewed a number of children (mostly preteens or early teens) and their parents who had become involved with this type of pornography.

When one makes a Dial-A-Porn call, it is usually answered by a very sexy seductive-sounding female (actually a recording) who talks directly to the caller about how badly she wants to have sex with him now. With panting voice she then tells him in specific detail all the things she wants to do to him sexually. There may be a second young woman on the line, and they may talk about having sex together as well as with the caller or others. They may mention having a sex marathon (dozens of partners) with all the explicit details.

In some cases bondage is part of the scenario (having sex while gagged, handcuffed, and leashed at the neck), suggesting that sex is better if it "hurts so good — don't stop." Sex with animals is also included as well as group sex (3, 4, or 5 men on 1 girl), rape, inviting a married male to have sex with the "baby sitter," a school teacher having sex with her students, inviting the caller to urinate in the woman's face, degrading the woman as a slut and trash while having sex with her, as well as inviting beatings, torture, and general physical abuse as part of the sexual activity.

The messages keep changing every hour or so, and new phone numbers are given out in order to encourage call backs.

Any youngster of any age can call these porno lines and get these messages from nearly any place in the country. All they need is a phone number to call. And these numbers are very easy to come by (on the playground of nearly every school in America as well as ads in most men's magazines). If parents put a "block" on their phone to prevent these calls, the children merely find another phone to use.

With every one of the children we studied we found an "addiction effect." In every case, without exception, the children (girls as well as boys) became hooked on this sex by phone and kept going back for more and still more. They did not cease until found out. None of them. In some cases more than 300 long distance calls were made by particular children. Disclosure usually occurred when the parents later received an enormous phone bill. This alerted them that something was amiss. Only after investigation (often having to call the number that was printed on the phone bill) did the parents become aware of what their children were calling and listening to. There was always a major confrontation. The children were usually made to pay the long distance phone costs as well as given a variety of chastisements, lectures, and/or punishments.

Where both parents worked or where there was a single working parent in the home meant that they had to leave behind "latch key children" who were not monitored or supervised for a number of hours during the day. This created a very difficult problem in controlling phone use. In the case of one one-parent family, the young son still continues to make Dial-A-Porn calls, and the distraught mother has found no way to get him to stop. Threats, physical abuse, nothing has worked.

I found that nearly all the children had clear memories of a great deal of the content of the calls they heard, even with a time lag of 1 or 2 years. I also found that, almost without exception, the children felt guilty, embarrassed, and ashamed about their involvement with Dial-A-Porn. In nearly all cases there were some problems and tensions generated in the parent–child and family relationships because of their making these calls.

I have also interviewed some children where, as a result of their hearing these kinds of Dial-A-Porn messages, they engaged in sexual assaults on other children. One 12-year-old boy in Hayward, California listened to Dial-A-Porn for nearly 2 hours between church meetings one Sunday afternoon in the chapel. Some time later he sexually assaulted a 4-year-old girl in his mother's day care center. He had never been exposed to pornography before. He had never acted out sexually before and was not a behavior problem in the home. He had never heard or knew of oral sex before listening to Dial-A-Porn. And this was how he assaulted the girl, forcing oral sex on her in direct imitation of what he had heard on the phone. I later interviewed a number of children in Michigan where similar sexual assaults occurred, males in their early teens "raping" younger females as a result of listening to Dial-A-Porn. All these children might be considered victims—the abusers as well as the abused.

The National Center on Child Abuse and Neglect reported (1988) that the incidence of child sexual abuse reports have tripled in the last 6 years in the United States. This has not happened in a vacuum or for no reason. In my clinical judgment, at least part of this can be attributed to the influence of Dial-A-Porn—as a "how to" manual, especially where older children are sexually abusing younger ones. Federal legislation has been introduced to restrict Dial-A-Porn; but how effective it will be remains to be seen.

If Pornography is in the Home, Children Find It

I find a spill-over effect where pornography used by adults very frequently gets into the hands of children living in the home *or neighborhood* where adults are using it. This can cause very negative outcomes.

Example. A mother brought her pregnant 13-year-old daughter to my office. The girl and her 14-year-old boyfriend had discovered the father's secret cache of pornography and had imitated the sexual acts portrayed in those materials. The ensuing consequences, including abortion and divorce, were very traumatic for the whole family as well as for both youngsters.

Example. From my private practice: Two brothers, ages 9 and 10, stumbled across their parents' X-rated videotapes and secretly played them for many months while their parents were at work. They later forced two younger siblings and a neighbor boy to view the videotapes, stripped all three children naked, forced dirt, sticks, and small rocks into their rectums, forced them to engage in oral and anal sex, and threatened to shoot them with a BB gun if they told. This abuse continued for nearly a year before finally being discovered when one of the younger abused children could no longer tolerate it and gained the courage to report it.

Example. Reported to the U.S. Attorney General's Pornography Commission, their Final Report (1986): "My daughters also had an experience with an 11-year-old neighbor boy . . . porno pictures that he had were shown to the girls and to the other children on the block. Later that day, he invited my daughters into his house to play video games, but then tried to imitate the sex acts in the photos with my eleven year old daughter as his partner; my other daughter witnessed the incident" (p. 785).

Example. A mother's testimony to the U.S. Attorney General's Commission on Pornography, their Final Report (1986): "My son was murdered on August 6, 1981, by the greed and avarice of the publishers of *Hustler* magazine. My son read the article "Orgasm of Death," set up the sexual experiment depicted therein, followed the explicit instructions of the article, and ended up dead. He would still be alive today were he not enticed and incited into this action by *Hustler* magazine's "How to do it" August 1981 article, an article which was found at his feet and which directly caused his death" (p. 797).

The Effects of the "Rape Myth" on Pornography Consumers

In a study by Mills College sociologist, Diana Russell (1982), it was found that the depiction and dissemination of the "rape myth" (e.g., that most women really enjoy having sex forced on them) was a significant element in reducing inhibitions to the use of violence, habituating both males and females to the idea of rape, and also accepting sexual aberrance as "normal" behavior. She found that once the seeds of deviant behavior were planted in the male fantasy, the men she studied were inclined to act out their fantasies. She found that both the fantasies that were acted out, as well as the mere conceptualization of these deviant fantasies as viable behaviors, led to considerable conflict and suffering on the part of both males and females, particularly in their sexual relationships with intimate partners.

Is Pornography as a Form of "Speech" Protected by the "First Amendment?"

No. There are additionally many other kinds of speech and expression also not protected by the U.S. Constitution's First Amendment such as slander, libel, false advertising, conspiracy, yelling "FIRE" in the crowded theatre, as well as pornography. The relevant statutes were designed to protect the public interest – enacted using democratic processes and procedures that can always be revoked or modified if the elected legislatures choose to do so.

The U.S. Supreme Court of has repeatedly held that those laws controlling obscenity are constitutionally valid: "This much has been categorically settled by the Court, that obscene material is unprotected by the First Amendment" (*Miller v. California*, 413 U.S. 15, 1973). "We hold that obscenity is not within the area of constitutionally protected speech or press" (*Roth v. United States*, 354 U.S. 476, 1957); see Schauer [1976] for information regarding these two cases).

Conclusion

It should be emphasized that in this brief chapter it is not possible to review any more than a few representative studies and summarize some of the trends of current as well as past research on pornography's effects, focusing especially on the harm issue. But these should still be sufficient to give the reader a sense of the field and answer for him or herself the question of pornography's potential to change or influence sexual attitudes and behavior in adults as well as children.

Whereas a few people may still argue that there is no proof that pornography can harm anyone, there now exists – as this chapter suggests – a number of experimental, field, and clinical studies that give contrary evidence. From my own personal experience, I daily treat in my clinical practice both children and adults who have been unequivocally and repeatedly injured by exposure to pornography, where the cumulated evidence demonstrates a cause–effect relationship between such exposure and harm.

However, in fairness, it should be emphasized that, as with using alcohol or even some of the highly addictive drugs, not everyone exposed will become alcoholic or addictive, at least in the early stages of use. But there are risks, and there seems little doubt that there are at least some people – even those who are initially healthy – who can be eventually harmed through repeated exposure to pornography.

In a free society some individuals may choose to immerse themselves in a pornographic milieu, just as some people may choose to drink or smoke excessively or use toxic drugs. In such cases these individuals should be made fully cognizant of the health hazards involved so that they can make informed decisions. This kind of knowledge is especially important for parents to have, because many sexual and pornographic addictions begin in middle childhood or early adolescence, often without the parents awareness or the children themselves having a sufficient understanding of the risks involved.

REFERENCES

Bartell, G. (1971). *Group sex* (pp. 215–216). New York: New American Library.

Bryant T, J. (1985) *Reports to the U.S. Attorney General Commission on Pornography.* Houston, TX.

Burgess, A. (1984). Pornography-victims and perpetrators. In D. Scott (Ed.), *Symposium on media violence and pornography: Proceedings resource book and research guide* (pp. 173–183). Toronto: Media Action Group.

Carnes, P. (1984). *Out of the shadows: Understanding sexual addiction.* Minneapolis: Compcare Publications.

Cline, V. (1974). *Where do you draw the line: Explorations in media violence, pornography and censorship,* Provo, UT: BYU Press.

Davis, K. E., & Braucht, G. N. (1971). *The Commission's Technical Reports* (Vol. VII). Washington, DC: U.S. Government Printing Office.

Evans, D. R. (1968). Masturbatory fantasy and sexual deviation. *Behavioral Research & Therapy, 6,* 17.

Jackson, B. Y. (1969). A case of voyeurism treated by counter conditioning. *Behavior Research & Therapy 7,* 133.

Lipkin, M., & Carns, D. E. (1970, Winter). *University of Chicago Division of Biological Sciences and Pritzker School of Medicine Reports.*

Malamuth, N. (1981). Rape fantasies as a function of exposure to violent-sexual stimuli. *Archives of Sexual Behavior, 10,*34–37.

Malamuth, N., & Donnerstein, E. (1984). *Pornography and sexual aggression.* New York: Academic Press.

Malamuth, N., & Feshboch, S. (1978). Sex and aggression: Proving the link. *Psychology Today,* 111–122.

National Center on child abuse and Neglect (1988). *Study findings: Study of the national incidence and prevalence of child abuse and neglect* Washington, DC: U.S. Department of Health and Human Services.

Marquis, J. N. (1970). Orgasmic reconditioning: Changing sexual object choice through controlling masturbation fantasies. *Journal of Behavior Therapy & Experimental Psychiatry, 1,* 263–271.

Marshall, W. (1983). *A report on the use of pornography by sexual offenders.* Ottawa, Canada: Federal Dept. of Justice.

McGaugh, J. L. (1983). Preserving the presence of the past. *American Psychologist, 38,* 161.

McGuire, R. J. (1965). Sexual deviations as conditioned behavior: A hypothesis. *Behavior Research Therapy, 2,* 185.

The mind of the rapist. (1990, July 23). *Newsweek,* pp. 51–52.

Pope, D. (1983, June 3). New weapon against obscenity. *Paducah Sun-Democrat.*

Propper, M. (1971). *Technical Reports of the Commission on Obscenity and Pornography.* Washington, DC: U.S. Government Printing Office.

Rachman, S. (1968). Experimentally induced 'sexual fetishism': A replication and development. *Psychological Record, 18,* 25.

Rubinstein, E. A. (1983). Television and behavior, *American Psychologist, 38,* 830.

Russell, D. (1982). *Rape and marriage,* Beverly Hills, CA: Sage.

Schauer, F. (1976) *The law of obscenity.* Washington, DC: Bureau of National Affairs.

U.S. Dept. of Justice. (1986). *Attorney General's Commission on Pornography* (final report, pp. 324–326, 333–334). Washington, DC: U.S. Government Printing Office.

Walker, C. E. (1971). *Technical Reports of the Commission on Obscenity and Pornography.* Washington, DC: U.S. Government Printing Office.

Zillmann, D., & Bryant, J. (1984). *Symposium on media violence and pornography.* Toronto: Media Action Group.

18

PORNOGRAPHY ADDICTION AND COMPULSIVE SEXUAL BEHAVIOR

M. Douglas Reed
Emerson A. North Hospital Life Way Unit and Xavier University

C an behavior such as the excessive viewing of pornography constitute an addiction? Clinical evidence says "yes." Clinicians and researchers have recognized that sexual addiction, including addiction to the use of pornography, is a clinically identifiable illness (Carnes, 1990; Coleman, 1990a). This chapter provides clinical evidence that the use of pornography can be instrumental in the development of compulsive, dependent, and addictive sexual behavior. The use of pornography can be both a cause and a symptom of behavior that serves to arouse or sedate individuals, dependent on their neurochemistry and conditioning. *Any kind of pornography* is potentially addictive, as it serves the purpose desired by the user, to either provide escape from internal discomfort or to produce pleasure. Not everyone who uses pornography is addicted, but thousands are. Diagnostic criteria focus around how the use of pornography relates to and affects the individual's ability to cope with life. Donovan (1988) stated: "The person becomes addicted to an experience, and addiction for an individual may take on a number of different objects" (p. 10).

Operant conditioning principles determine whether pornography usage, or other mood-altering behavior, *causes* addiction (or other deviant behavior such as aggression) or *reinforces* addictive behavior (or aggression).

Clinicians and researchers have found that the relationship dynamic between media viewing and subsequent antisocial behavior is *bidirectional* (cf. Carter, 1986; Eron, 1987; Friedrich-Cofer & Huston, 1986; Goldstein, Kant, & Harman, 1974; Malamuth, 1984; Marshall, 1988; Murrin & Laws, 1990; Rosenberg, 1989). Some believe that the relationship is, or can be, *causal* (Bergman, 1982; Donovan, 1988; Marshall, 1988, 1989; Marshall & Barbaree, 1990; Milkman & Sunderwirth, 1987; Robertson, 1990).

Genetic inheritance, psychodynamics, sociocultural factors, environmental factors, and pure chance all play a role in determining the behavior a person will choose (Lord, 1990). It has been demonstrated that addictions can occur in the absence of ingested drugs (which produce increasing tolerance with repeated use and withdrawal symptoms with cessation; Donovan, 1988). There are addictions to behaviors and even to memories (fantasies) of behaviors. This makes out of date the earlier narrow definition of addiction; it no longer matches the research or clinical evidence. Whereas all addictions involve both compulsion and dependence, there are dependencies and compulsions that are not addictions (see Table 18.1).

Two research tracks have converged, leading to our current awareness that behavior, as well as drugs, can be addictive. First, according to Donovan (1988), practitioners observed that clients who engaged excessively in activities such as drinking, gambling, eating, drug use, and sexual behavior presented "very similar descriptions of the phenomenology of their disorders" (p. 5). There are common features across *all* addictive behaviors. Solomon's (1980) "opponent-process" theory of addiction proposed that any behavioral excess could lead to dependence on the behavior to feel normal. His model of acquired motivation parsimoniously accounts for major phenotypic characteristics of both pharmacologically and nonpharmacologically motivated behaviors (Carnes, 1991).

All kinds of pornography are prevalent in these clinical cases of addiction, including material described in experimental research as erotica, soft core, degrading, nonviolent, aggressive, and violent. Marshall (1989) pointed out, however, that "the more explicit the images are, the stronger their influence will be" (p. 10).

Second, researchers made amazing discoveries about the neurochemistry of the brain, exemplified by the 1974 discovery of enkephalins: pain-killing molecules that are produced naturally in the brain (Carnes, 1991). By 1977, the National Science Foundation had identified sex addiction as a priority research area in the general field of addiction. There was greater scientific awareness that addiction could exist within the body's own chemistry (Wise, 1988). Carnes (1991) learned from his research that "one of the more destructive parts of sex addiction is that you literally carry your own source of supply . . . being able to get high on your own brain chemicals" (p. 30).

TABLE 18.1
Addiction to Pornography A = C + D

Addiction (A) includes elements of compulsive behavior (C) and dependent behavior (D). Addictive disorder is expressed as A = C + D. This combination of: escape from internal discomfort, and gratification, involves both compulsion and dependence; both negative reinforcement and positive reinforcement. If the use of pornography functions both to help alleviate uncomfortable feelings and to produce pleasurable feelings, it can be engaged in addictively.

For a pornography user to have an addictive disorder, there must be a set of relationships between the pornography use pattern and certain other processes or life events. It is not the type of pornography used, its frequency, or its social acceptability that determine whether the pattern of use qualifies as an addictive disorder. It is how this behavior pattern relates to and affects the individual's life.

In our clinical judgement, addiction to pornography use is a self-induced pathological relationship with a mood-altering experience, leading to social problems. It meets certain clinical diagnostic criteria, which are common to all other addictions:

1. Recurrent failure to resist impulses to use pornography or engage in its related activities, such as masturbation.
2. A buildup of emotional tension immediately prior to use.
3. Pleasure or relief at the time of engaging in pornography use.
4. A feeling of giving in, or a lack of control while engaging the pattern of pornography use.
5. Some of these symptoms usually will have occurred for at least one month, or will have occurred repeatedly over a longer period of time.
6. At least 5 of the following 9 criteria are usually present:
   a. Frequent obsession or preoccupation with pornography use, or with activity that is preparatory to the behavior, such as going where pornography is available;
   b. Using pornography, buying it, masturbating, or other acting out behavior, to a greater extent or over a longer period than intended;
   c. Efforts to reduce, control, or stop using the pornography or its related activity. These are often accompanied by discarding caches or collections of material, only to repurchase again and again;
   d. A great deal of time spent (1) in activities necessary for using pornography (getting ready); (2) actually using the pornography, almost always as fantasy material accompanied by masturbation or orgasm; and (3) recovering from its effects (physical injury, for example, or the emotional shame, and/or degradation that is usually felt);
   e. Frequent engaging in pornography use when expected to fulfill occupational, academic, domestic, or social obligations (such as leaving work early, extending lunch hours, arranging trips to places where preferred pornography is readily available; etc.);
   f. Important occupational, social, or leisure activities are given up or reduced because of pornography use. Often this behavior causes the user to desire being alone, or to stay up late watching videos instead of sleeping, etc.;
   g. Continuation of the behavior despite knowledge of having a persistent or recurrent social, financial, psychological, or physical problem that is caused or made worse by the behavior;
   h. Tolerance and escalation; need to increase the intensity of the pornography, or frequency of its use, in order to achieve the desired effect. There is a diminished effect with continued use of pornography of the same intensity; and
   i. Irritability or tension build-up if unable to engage in pornography use or related activities.

(continued)

TABLE 18.1 *(continued)*

$$A = \quad C \quad + \quad D$$

Addiction =	Compulsion: Negative Reinforcement	+	Dependency: Positive Reinforcement
	Avoidance of unpleasurable aversive internal state (e.g. anxiety, grief, rage)	+	Attempt to create a pleasurable internal state via gratification of needs (basic or derived)

Addiction is a process whereby a behavior, that can function both to provide pleasure and provide escape from internal discomfort, is employed in a pattern characterized by:

(1) recurrent failure to control the behavior (powerlessness)

(2) continuation of the behavior despite significant negative consequences (unmanageability).

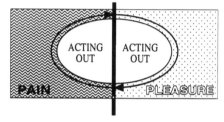

"Drugs, in fact, are involved—in the form of naturally occurring peptides such as endorphins that govern the electrochemical interactions within the brain. These peptides parallel the molecular construction of opiates like morphine, but they are many times more powerful" (p. 22). Addictive sexual behavior—including the pathological use of standard fare nonviolent pornography—has now been integrated into the general field of addiction and addictionology.

It is noteworthy clinically that the public awareness of the destructive nature of addictive sexual behavior increased concurrently with: (a) the professional awareness that the disorder created serious medical and psychological problems, and (b) with the proliferation of sexually explicit media (hardcore pornography) following the report of the 1970 Presidential Commission (Reed, 1990).

PORNOGRAPHY ADDICTION, CLINICAL PATTERNS, AND DIAGNOSTIC CRITERIA

I have provided a list of diagnostic criteria and a conceptual framework that incorporates the widely accepted clinical patterns of this illness (cf. Goodman, 1989). In Table 18.1, A = C + D shows that addiction is comprised of compulsive[1] and dependent behavior, over which the person feels

---

[1]The *DSM-III-R* points out that "some activities,such as eating (e.g., Eating Disorders), sexual behavior (e.g., Paraphilias), gambling (e.g., Pathological Gambling), or drinking (e.g.,

powerless, and which causes his or her life to be out of balance or unmanageable.

Pornography addiction is a complex self-induced pathological relationship with a mood-altering experience, leading to social problems. It is a disordered condition—an illness. The *experience* associated with the addictive use of pornography is powerful because it is both a positive reinforcer and a negative reinforcer. The behavior produces salient alterations in mood because there are structural functional biological changes.

Donovan (1988) defined addiction—including sexual addiction—as: "a complex progressive behavior pattern having biological, psychological, sociological, and behavioral components. What sets this behavior pattern apart from others is the individual's overwhelmingly pathological involvement in or attachment to it, subjective compulsion to continue it, and reduced ability to exert personal control over it" (p. 5).

Clinical examples of addictive behaviors are: (a) "viewing pornography" and "masturbating" (Coleman, 1988, p. 191); (b) "sex, promiscuity, sexual conquest, chronic sex-excitement behavior, use of pornography and other sexually addictive behavior" (Robertson, 1990, p. 17); (c) "any behavior that causes intense excitement and, pleasure . . . such as sexual assault, fantasies of rape, and depictions of rape in pornography" (Herman, 1990, pp. 178-179); (d) "TV-watching, overeating, masturbating while gazing at pictures of women, and looking at girlie magazines" (Milkman & Sunderwirth, 1987, pp. 50-51); and (e) "sexual behavior" (Goodman, 1990, p. 10).

There are four common elements in the clinical evidence for sexual addiction that relate to the initiation or development of the addiction, and its maintenance or escalation. These four elements determine and reflect the way individuals learn to cope with stress and to obtain gratification. They are (a) cyclic mood swings, (b) analgesic fix, (c) damaging consequences, and (e) an etiology typified by a dysfunctional, shame-bound family-of-origin (Carnes, 1983; Coleman, 1990b; Donovan, 1988; Milkman & Sunderwirth, 1987).

Pornography had damaging consequences for participants in each of three research groups[2] studied by Carnes (1989): It was a self-reported "problem" behavior for 53% of the persons in Group 1, 30% in Group 2

Alcohol Dependence or Abuse), when engaged in excessively may be referred to as "compulsive." However, the activities are not true compulsions because the person *derives pleasure* from the particular activity and may wish to resist it only because of its secondary deleterious consequences" (p. 246).

[2]"Levels" ranged from one to three in social "acceptance," (e.g., masturbation at level one to rape at level three). The problem behaviors are clearly progressive. Pornography usage for persons at the "illegal" levels (i.e., Levels 2 and 3) was certainly not innocent fun; it was associated with prosecutable offenses. This counters marketing claims by the pornography industry that their product is "entertainment" and is "victimless" sex (Reed, 1990).

and 20% in Group 3. Pornography usage was correlated significantly with masturbation, prostitution, and bestiality in Level 1, with voyeurism in Level 2, and with child molestation in Level 3 (p. 206).

A later survey by Carnes (1991) of recovering sex addicts "showed that pornography and voyeurism were also very highly related" (p. 57). So also were pornography and prostitution (Carnes, 1989, p. 207). Examples of visual sex that caused them serious social consequences were (Carnes, 1991):

> Patronizing adult bookstores, using pornography for masturbation or acting-out behavior, and keeping collections of pornography at home or at work. Among the 932 sex addicts surveyed, 90% of the men and 77% of the women reported pornography as significant to their addiction. . . . For some, the costs were staggering. Among those whose acting out was primarily visual in nature, it is not unusual to hear reports of pornography collections with cumulative costs in six figures. (p. 57)

SEX ADDICTION AS A CLINICAL CLASSIFICATION

The term *sexual addiction* is used in the *Diagnostic and Statistical Manual of Mental Disorders* (see American Psychiatric Association, 1987, *DSM-III-R*) as an example of Other Sexual Disorder Not Otherwise Specified (not elsewhere classified) 302.90, "distress about a pattern of repeated sexual conquests or other form of nonparaphilic sexual addiction, involving a succession of people who exist only as things to be used" (p. 296). The clinical frequency or prevalence of sexual addiction, paraphilias, and sexual disorders numbers thousands of persons, and is "far higher than indicated by statistics from clinical facilities" (*DSM-III-R*, p. 281).

BEHAVIOR ORIENTATION AND DISPOSITION

An individual's behavioral orientation is an important part of the addiction mechanism and is consistent with his or her characteristic ways of dealing with stress. It is determined also by whether the individual seeks to increase stimulation and personal energy, to withdraw from it, or to alternatively seek it and withdraw from it. These are "addictive states" identified by Milkman and Sunderwirth (1987). It is important to note clinically that *any kind* of pornography can serve to accomplish the user's desired or preferred mood state by altering neurotransmission patterns (Milkman & Sunderwirth, 1987, p. 12). Long-term behavior patterns that produce preferred mood states or temperaments are what clinicians refer to as dispositions. Pornography use can produce, maintain, or facilitate change in dispositions, over time, by altering one's neurochemistry. The two basic types of behavioral orientation are excitatory-*arousal* orientation and inhibitory-*satiation* orientation. These are demonstrated in Fig. 18.1, which shows how the experience of pornography use causes addiction.

Milkman and Sunderwirth (1987) described another behavior orientation: a variation of the satiation and arousal orientations. This type of addict uses fantasy-*imagination* as the preferred way of dealing with the world. Other researchers (e.g., Langevin, 1990; Robertson, 1990; Wise, 1988) have discovered that, in addition to producing different patterns of neurotransmission, the three types of addiction seem to involve different parts of the brain. Mood shifts appear to be influenced by the limbic system located near the middle of the brain. The limbic system appears to play a major role in pleasurable sensations connected with altered levels of arousal produced by exposure to pornography, for example. The convoluted outer brain known as the cerebral cortex is an important determinant of mental *content*, shown to be instrumental in both rape myth pornography and in certain arousing "permissive cues" in nonviolent pornography (Weaver, 1987). Excessive activity in the cortex of the right hemisphere may help explain the uncontrolled imagery found in the fantasies of cocaine users, mystics, and schizophrenics. Similar cortical activity in the left hemisphere may be responsible for feelings. We do not know precisely how pornography use affects these specific areas of the brain; more research is needed. Carnes (1991) stated: "Of the over 300 chemicals involved in the chemistry of the brain, we have a working understanding of only about 60" (p. 32).

Milkman and Sunderwirth (1987) cited studies by Liebowitz on the importance in romantic attraction of the peptide called Phenylethylamine (PEA), which is critical to the chemistry of courtship. Its molecular structure parallels that of amphetamines and creates a high-arousal state. PEA and sexual arousal are highly affected by the presence of fear, risk, and danger. This may be part of the neurochemical "residue" described by Zillmann in his research on "excitation transfer," modified by himself and Sapolsky (1984). PEA is probably but one of the many brain chemicals that exist in the chemistry of sexuality and love. Milkman and Sunderwirth (1987) said: "Consistent with Liebowitz's theory of neurochemical adaptations, sex addicts report the need for continuous escalation in the intensity of their sexual encounters"(pp. 47–50). This clinical evidence provides support for laboratory findings on "habituation," by Zillmann (1989). Figure 18.1 shows how this works neurochemically. Eysenck (1984) accurately projected this progression in usage of pornography that is demonstrated by the clinical evidence: "In real life, it is much more likely that people graduate through a series of slightly erotic to more erotic to pornographic to hard-core pornography presentations, becoming desensitized more and more at each state" (p. 314).

Arousal/Activation Orientation

1. User desires activation and arousal; has learned pornography-use patterns which excite, change user's mood.

2. Excitatory neurotransmitters are released from neuron one and fit into receptor sites on neuron two. Enkephalin sites are not occupied. Inhibitory neurotransmitters are not released.

3. Numerous occupied receptor sites on neuron two increase membrane sensitivity and rate of neurotransmission.

4. ATP is converted to cyclic AMP; user's mood is elevated.

5. Optimum feeling is obtained when neurotransmitters are retained in synapse, with minimal reuptake of excitatory neurotransmitters.

6. Enzyme levels decline through chronic overstimulation. Tolerance develops. There is escalation of amount of pornography use required to achieve the previous mood effect, discomfort.

7. Attempts to abstain from use cause withdrawal effects.

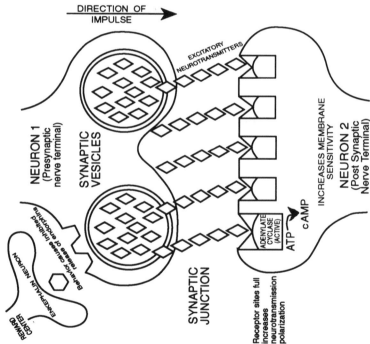

DIRECTION OF IMPULSE

EXCITATORY NEUROTRANSMITTERS

NEURON 1 (Presynaptic nerve terminal)

SYNAPTIC VESICLES

REWARD CENTER

ENKEPHALIN NEURON

Behavior cause of release of inhibited endorphins

SYNAPTIC JUNCTION

Receptor sites full increases neurotransmission polarization

ADENYLATE CYCLASE (ACTIVE)

ATP

cAMP

INCREASES MEMBRANE SENSITIVITY

NEURON 2 (Post Synaptic Nerve Terminal)

256

Sedation/Inhibition Orientation

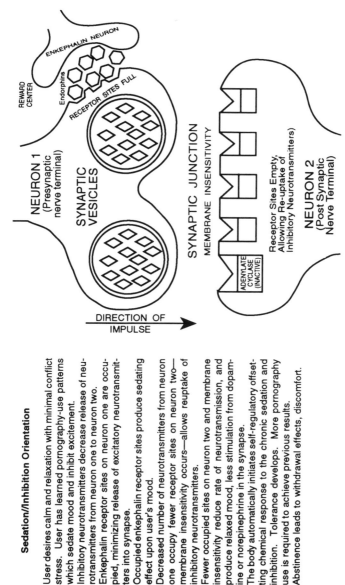

1. User desires calm and relaxation with minimal conflict stress. User has learned pornography-use patterns which sedate mood and inhibit excitement.

2. Inhibitory neurotransmitters decrease release of neurotransmitters from neuron one to neuron two.

3. Enkephalin receptor sites on neuron one are occupied, minimizing release of excitatory neurotransmitters into synapse.

4. Occupied enkephalin receptor sites produce sedating effect upon user's mood.

5. Decreased number of neurotransmitters from neuron one occupy fewer receptor sites on neuron two—membrane insensitivity occurs—allows reuptake of inhibitory neurotransmitters.

6. Fewer occupied sites on neuron two and membrane insensitivity reduce rate of neurotransmission, and produce relaxed mood, less stimulation from dopamine or norepinephrine in the synapse.

7. The body automatically initiates self-regulatory offsetting chemical response to the chronic sedation and inhibition. Tolerance develops. More pornography use is required to achieve previous results.

8. Abstinence leads to withdrawal effects, discomfort.

FIG. 18.1. Addiction Behavior A = C + D (© 1992 M. Douglas Reed, PhD).

257

Psychological Pornography Addiction is Physiological Addiction

The effect of the mental functions are integrated with the physical in the modern "biopsychosocial" model of addiction (Donovan, 1988, p. 7). Milkman and Sunderwirth (1987) stated: "Often we hear the comment that something is psychologically and not physiologically addicting. Such a distinction is artificial and has no place in a sophisticated discussion on addiction. This distinction implies that the central nervous system (psychological addiction) is somehow separate from the rest of the body's functions (physiological addiction) — sheer nonsense" (p. 71). Goodman (1990) added: "It is generally accepted that there is an essential unity between psychological processes and physiological processes, that every psychological process is equivalent to or correlated with some physiological process. Thus, it is not meaningful to speak of dependence or distress that is psychological, but not physiological" (p. 6).

Psychological addiction to pornography use is also physiological addiction; it is as distressing to a person as is drug addiction.

Paraphilias and Pornography

There is a category of compulsive–addictive mental illness that is related to sexually deviant behavior called paraphilias. They are characterized by recurrent, intense, sexual urges. There are eight of these *major* sexual disorders (deviations) and literally dozens of other minor ones, based on how often they occur in our society. These are described in Table 18.2. Pornography use is related to all of them: causing, maintaining, or exacerbating these illnesses.

Pornography plays a large role in the paraphilias, although not all paraphiliacs are addicted. According to the *DSM-III-R* (American Psychiatric Association, 1987):

> Specific paraphilic imagery is selectively focused on and sought out by people with one or more paraphilias. The person may selectively view, read, purchase, or collect photographs, films, and textual depictions focusing on his preferred type of paraphilic stimulus. . . . Judging from the large commercial market in paraphilic pornography and paraphernalia, the prevalence in the community is believed to be far higher than that indicated by statistics from clinical facilities. Because of the highly repetitive nature of paraphilic behavior, a large percentage of the population has been victimized by people with paraphilias. (p. 281)

TABLE 18.2
Paraphilias and Pornography

Paraphilias	Typical Behavior [Recurrent, intense, sexual urges, and sexually arousing fantasies]
1. Pedophilia	Sexual activity with a prepubescent child. Those attracted to girls usually prefer 8–10 years old. Those attracted to boys usually prefer slightly older children. Nothing is more important to pedophiles than their pornography collections. Pornography is used in a repetitive cyle of abuse.
2. Fetishism	The use of nonliving objects, such as bras, women's underpants, stockings, shoes, etc. Pornography magazines (pictures) have clinically been demonstrated to serve as a fetish.
3. Sexual Masochism	The act of being humiliated, beaten, bound, or otherwise made to suffer. Most people with this disorder increase the severity of the acts over time, or during stress. One variation, *infantilism* is a desire to be treated as a helpless infant and clothed in diapers. Many media ads suggesting that one "baby oneself" feed this illness. Another, *hypoxyphilia*, or autoerotic asphysixia, involves sexual arousal by oxygen deprivation. It was fostered by a pornographic magazine and is considered to have caused hundreds of deaths.
4. Sexual Sadism	Acts in which the psychological or physical suffering (including humiliation) of the victim is sexually exciting. Usually the severity of the sadistic acts increases over time. This illness is joked about by the media, but it is no joke to real victims. Pornography fuels this disorder.
5. Transvestic Fetishism	Cross-dressing, from occasional solitary wearing of female clothes to extensive involvement in a transvestic subculture. There is substantial pornography related to this disorder.
6. Voyeurism	The act of observing unsuspecting people, usually strangers, who are either naked, in the process of disrobing, or engaging in sexual activity. Usually no sexual activity is sought with the person being viewed. Pornography fuels this paraphilia, as it does fetishism, because it always portrays the stimulus desired by the voyeur. Looking at pornography constitutes voyeurism for some persons.
7. Frotteurism	Touching (Toucherism) and rubbing (Frotteurism) against a nonconsenting person. It is the touching, not the coercive nature of the act, that is sexually exciting. Some men are stimulated by pornography to engage in this illegal behavior.
8. Exhibitionism	The exposure of one's genitals to a stranger, sometimes masturbating while exposing. Some men fantasize with pornography that they are getting the reaction they want from the person in the pornography.

Note: There are numerous examples of other paraphilia that are encouraged by pornography. Here are a few:

1. Partialism: Exclusive focus on part of the body, such as breasts, buttocks, vaginas, etc. More than half of the commercial pornography objectifies and focuses on some part of the body. The graphic closeups in hard core pornography feed this disorder.
2. Urophilia: Focus on urinating, which pornography calls "wet sports."
3. Zoophilia: Sex with animals.
4. Klismaphilia: Enemas, preparatory to anal intercourse, or as an arousing act alone.
5. Telephone scatalogia: Phone lewdness. Dial-a-porn is the perpetration of this illness.

Sears and Dietz (1987) found that approximately 13% of all pornography produced focuses on the major paraphilic illnesses (pp. 19–21). If "partialism" pornography is counted, about *half* the pornography produced fuels one or more of the paraphilias.

Abel and Rouleau's (1990) study of nonincarcerated paraphiliacs revealed that:

> of the 53.6% of 561 adult offenders reporting the onset of deviant sex interest prior to age 18, each reported two different paraphilias and an average commission of 380.2 sex offenses by the time he reached adulthood. Similar information from adolescent sex offenders [younger than 18] revealed that each adolescent offender had 1.9 paraphilias and had committed an average of 6.8 sex offenses, with child molestation or rape represented by 54.1% of his deviant sex acts. (p. 13)

These numbers showed Abel and Rouleau (1990) that the majority of sexual assaulters develop deviant sexual interest prior to age 18, a time when adolescents report more frequent exposure to pornography than adults, or any other age group (Reed, 1990). Abel and Rouleau (1990) asserted: "Histories from offenders clearly indicate that one individual can have multiple paraphilic interests throughout his lifetime. Some sex offenders [paraphiliacs] have as many as 10 categories of paraphilic interest throughout their lifetime"(p. 14). The data concerning paraphilias point to the role of pornography in the *development* and the *maintenance* of these addictive and compulsive behaviors.

The use of pornography by pedophiles is particularly disturbing. People with pedophilia generally report an attraction to children of a particular age range. Some pedophiles (exclusive, preferential, or predatory type) are sexually attracted only to prepubescent children, whereas others (nonexclusive or situational type) are sometimes attracted to older adolescents. According to the *DSM-III-R* (American Psychiatric Association, 1987), people with this mental disorder who compulsively or addictively act on their urges with children "may limit their activity to undressing the child and looking, exposing themselves, masturbating in the presence of the child, or touching and fondling of the child. Others, however, perform fellatio or cunnilingus on the child or penetrate the child's vagina, mouth, or anus with their fingers, foreign objects, or penis, and use varying degrees of force to achieve these ends"(p. 284).

These activities are commonly explained with excuses or rationalizations (*DSM-III-R*, 1987): that the illegal activities have "educational value" for the child; that the child derives "sexual pleasure" from them; or that the child was "sexually provocative"—excuses and "themes that are also common in pedophilic pornography" (p. 284).

Pedophiles use standard fare nonviolent adult pornography, pseudo-child pornography (in which "actresses" are dressed to appear youthful), and child pornography, to seduce targeted children (Lanning & Burgess, 1989). Then they usually take pictures or make videos of the children, once the children have been compromised sexually. Thereby the pedophile perpetuates a cycle of abuse. Nonviolent pornography in the hands of a pedophile leads to violence and abuse. The explicit sexual material in the hands of child molesters becomes their curriculum of seduction—they "teach" from it and entrap their victims. Lanning and Burgess (1989) wrote that pornographic pictures taken of the seduced children represent "a permanent record of the sexual abuse" (p. 238).

Rape is a Paraphilia

Clinical interviews of rapists provide support for classifying rape as a paraphilia, according to Abel and Rouleau (1990), because many individuals report having recurrent, repetitive, and compulsive urges and fantasies to commit rape. The cycle of ongoing urges, attempts to control them, breakdown of those attempts, and recurrence of the sex crime is alarmingly similar to the clinical picture presented by exhibitionists, voyeurs, pedophiles, and other traditionally recognized categories of paraphiliacs. Abel and Rouleau (1990) found that nonincarcerated rapists they studied had averaged *seven* rapes.

Not all rapists are addicted. Rapists who are addicted to the pathological mood-changing experience of raping (like other addicts) do not discontinue that deviant behavior. They repeatedly return to that behavior until caught and imprisoned and, once released from jail, are highly likely to rape again.

Abel and Rouleau (1990) stated: "Further support for rape as a paraphilia comes from the age of onset of interest in rape and rape's association with other common paraphilias. Fifty percent of individuals who rape have the onset of this deviant interest by age 21, which is similar to the early onset of arousal in other paraphilias"(p. 19).

The fantasy life of rapists, sadists, and masochists is fueled by pornography and is of particular concern. The chronic behaviors emanating from their fantasies usually increase in potential injuriousness—especially during periods of stress (*DSM-III-R*, 1987 p. 286).

Researchers (e.g., Check & Guloien, 1989; Malamuth, 1984) have attested to the harm of pornography that depicts rape as pleasurable for the victim: the "rape myth" pornography. Clinicians agree: Pornography fuels aggressive and violent behavior in rapists, sadists, and masochists (Marshall, 1989; Murrin & Laws, 1990; Rosenberg, 1989).

Predisposing Normal Persons to Antisocial Attitudes and Behavior

Rape myth pornography also affects "normal" nonpsychotic men with little or no self-reported likelihood of committing rape (low LR), as well as nonpsychotic men with high-reported likelihood of committing rape (high LR). Malamuth (1984) found[3] that when exposed to pornography portraying the rape myth, normal men were sexually aroused to a level near that of men (i.e., high-LR men) who have attitudes and arousal typical of rapists (pp. 25–26). Normal men are thereby predisposed to become sexually aroused to previously non arousing pornography. Marshall (1989) said: "Perhaps the only difference, if any, between normals and rapists is simply that the normals can, with practice, exert greater control over responding to forced sex" (pp. 192–193).

Carnes (1989) believed the connection he discovered (in his research on sex addicts) between pornography and prostitution includes the objectification of women. Darke (1990) added: "The most blatant misogynist practices are those which objectify women and portray them as commodities for male use. The conditions that render pornography acceptable, and rape myths believable, ultimately breed sexual violence" (p. 68). The objectification of women noted by Carnes and Darke is consistent with the *DSM-III-R* (1987) description of "sexual addiction" cited earlier: "a pattern of sexual conquests of people who exist as things to be used" (p. 286). Zillmann and Weaver (1989) poignantly described the "ubiquity of callous sexual dispositions and behaviors in pornography. . . . encouraging male dispositions of [imagined] entitlement" (p. 107).

Pornography and Sex Offenders (Paraphilic and NonParaphilic)

Not all sex addicts become sex offenders, but many of them do. Some are incarcerated—most are not. We noted earlier the connection of pornography with the paraphilias. We reported also the large number of sex offenses committed by nonincarcerated paraphiliacs. It is important to note that only 15% of the known sex offenders are, in fact, incarcerated—85% are "on the street" with their recurrent, intense urges to act out. Marshall

---

[3]The penile tumescence measure for normal men who were exposed to the rape myth pornography *increased* over levels obtained when they witnessed consenting sex. This was not emphasized by Malamuth. Apart from the differences in the *change* in penile tumescence between high- and low- LR subjects, both arrived at similar arousal levels after exposure to rape myth pornography (i.e., just over 38mm for high- LR subjects and just under 37mm for low- LR subjects).

(1989) asserted: "The duration of paraphilias is associated with increasingly greater use of pornography" (p. 194). The clinical evidence concerning the role of pornography in the lives of incarcerated sex offenders can reasonably be said to be characteristic of nonincarcerated sex offenders as well (Abel & Rouleau, 1990); it is summarized in Table 18.3.

PORNOGRAPHY'S ROLE IN THE DEVELOPMENT AND MAINTENANCE OF DEVIANT INTERESTS IN SEX OFFENDERS

According to Rosenberg (1989), most sex-offender treatment and research specialists believe that "the use of sexual media is clearly associated with

TABLE 18.3
Role of Pornography in the Lives of Incarcerated Sex Offenders

1. Compared to nonoffenders, adult masturbatory activity in response to pornography is more common in sex offenders. (Murrin & Laws, 1990, p. 88)
2. Compared to nonoffenders, sex offenders show a greater desire to own pornography; and report owning more; and reported a greater desire to procure pornography for themselves in adolescence (Murrin & Laws, 1990, p. 88)
3. Compared to normals, rapists are 15 times as likely to have been exposed to explicit pornography during ages 6–10 (Goldstein, Kant, & Harman, 1974).
4. One third of the rapists and nonfamilial child molesters reported exposure to explicit pornography during pubescence (Marshall, 1989, p. 206).
5. High-frequency masturbation behavior patterns predict general pornography use. More pedophiles than rapists are high-frequency masturbators. When they masturbate, they fantasize about raping or child molesting (Marshall, 1989, p. 207).
6. Sex offenders with high-frequency rates of masturbation are more likely to be current users of pornography. It plays a more important role in the life of pedophiles than to rapists (Marshall, 1988).
7. More than one third of the rapists and child molesters had been incited by the use of hard-core sexual stimuli (depicting both aggressive and consenting sex) to commit an offense (Marshall, 1989, p. 207).
8. Exposure to pornography prior to age 14 years predicted greater involvement in deviant sexual practices (Davis & Braucht, 1970, p. 7).
9. Chronic offenders are more likely to be pornography users (Abel, Mittelman, & Becker, 1985; cited in Marshall, 1989).
10. Over half the rapists who were current users of consenting sex pornography claimed they used it to stimulate fantasies of rape (Marshall, 1989, p. 207). Explicit materials elicit a greater arousal in rapists than does nonexplicit pornography (Marshall, 1989, p. 190).
11. Child molesters and rapists reported use of pornography prior to and during their offenses (Marshall, 1989, p. 205).
12. Rapists and child molesters deliberately use pornography as part of their preoffense preparation to commit an offense, after incitement. The extensive use of pornography serves as an escalating factor in their rape and assault cycles (Blanchard, 1989, p. 54; Marshall, 1989).
13. Rapists justify their deviant actions by viewing pornography which appears to sanction the behavior (Silbert, 1989); so do child molesters (DSM-III-R).

sexually aggressive behavior" (p. 33). Some believe that it *can cause addiction* or compulsive sexual behavior, and almost all believe that it facilitates, maintains, or reinforces it (Rosenberg, 1989, p. 33).

This is particularly true (a) if the pornography is arousing; (b) if it is coupled with masturbation and subsequent organism; (c) when alternative nondeviant fantasies are unavailable; (d) if the pornographic stimuli occurs during puberty and the 10 to 24 months afterwards (the crucial period for the development of enduring sexual propensities (Marshall & Barbaree, 1990, p. 259); and (e) if the child (at the onset of adolescence) has little or no previous sexual experience to draw on (Rosenberg, 1990, pp. 33-35).

CONDITIONING OF ADDICTIONS AND SEXUAL DEVIATIONS

Classical and operant conditioning, as well as social learning principles, can be demonstrated in acquisition and maintenance of normal sexual behavior (cf. Eysenck, 1984). Several researchers (Laws & Marshall, 1990) have demonstrated that "sexually deviant interests are learned through the same mechanisms by which conventional sexuality is learned" (p. 227). Marshall and Barbaree (1990) stated: "In the case of sexual offending we believe that the contribution of biological factors is minimal once learning has established patterns of behavior" (p. 259).

Sexual deviance, like any human behavior, is the result of orderly and understandable processes and is consequently modifiable. Laws and Marshall (1990) demonstrated convincingly the conditioning principles of deviant sexual preference and behavior: acquisition, maintenance, and extinction. Pornography, as a reinforcer at these critical learning points, causes conditioned pairings of behavior and moods. These clinical findings underscore Eysenck's (1984) observations about Pavlovian conditioning and Seligman's concept of biological "preparedness" for conditioning: that there is "a very extensive literature on these processes" (pp. 310-311).

NONVIOLENT PORNOGRAPHY AND NORMAL VIEWERS

In the absence of any addiction, pornography use can be highly conditioned and highly resistant to extinction or abstinence, once conditioned, because of its arousal effect. The harm of both standard-fare nonviolent pornography and aggressive pornography to nonaddicted, nonpsychotic pornography users has been well documented in the professional literature (e.g., Check & Guloien, 1989, pp. 160, 178-179; *Final Report of the Attorney*

General's Commission on Pornography, 1986; Lyons, Anderson, & Larson, 1990; Mulvey & Haugaard, 1986; Zillmann, 1989, pp. 153–155; Zillmann & Bryant, 1988, pp. 438–453).

IMPLICATIONS

Research on the mediating effects of pornography needs to be based on what we know about neurobiochemical processes in humans. The "uses" of pornography are more specific to the individual consumer's biopsychosocial needs than previously known and potentially are as important as the kind of pornography viewed. The concept of sexual assault as a potentially addictive behavior, for example, has major implications for treatment and social rehabilitation of detected offenders, only 15% of whom are incarcerated. Although Marshall, Laws, and Barbaree (1990) believed that "sexual offending is not a sickness or disease" (p. 390), Blanchard (1989) correctly pointed out that for sex offenders who are *addicted* it is an illness, however: "Among sexually addicted offender populations, pornography plays a contributing role in the ritualized sexual patterns that accompany any assaultiveness" (p. 56). Pornography to addicted sex offenders is as dangerous as matches and gasoline to an arsonist.

To consider that the neurotransmitters that are activated by pornography use may trigger similar neural pathways as cocaine or heroin (Milkman & Sunderwirth, 1987) is staggering, given the natural allure and ready availability of pornography. We know that nicotine and caffeine can reactivate detoxed cocaine users (Milkman & Sunderwirth, 1987, pp. 72, 97). What if nonviolent pornography use, in stimulating sexual arousal, also stimulates aggression? It appears to in rapists. Marshall and Barbaree (1990) cited biological research that "aggression and sex appear to be mediated by the same neural substrates; the neural networks within the midbrain structures appear to be remarkably similar for sex and aggression" (p. 259).

The clinical evidence refutes the contention of Donnerstein, Linz, and Penrod (1987) that it is portrayals of the violence, not the sex, that are harmful. The erroneous contention sets the stage for incarcerated sex offenders — who use consenting pornography in their sex crimes — to feed on that material (at taxpayer expense) *while in prison* and act out their fantasies once they leave. The clinical evidence consistently contradicts the near-reckless speculation of Donnerstein et al. (1987) that "rape-myth acceptance among subjects exposed to violent pornography might well decline naturally with the passage of time" (p. 187). Rapists, child molesters, and addicts do not "return to baseline levels of hostility and aggression toward women, or even dip below baseline [levels] once given time to reflect" (p. 187). They repeat the fantasies and behaviors progressively. That claim and others made by Donnerstein research have been severely criticized (Reed, 1989).

It is important to know that pornography can serve as a fetish where pictures replace people (Bergman, 1982; Rachman & Hodgson, 1968). Children and adults have been conditioned to develop fetishes of pornography. Knowing the power of compulsive—addictive behavior when paired with a fetish (pornography), we can see the difficulty in breaking the addiction.

Virtually all the paraphilias have onset in childhood or adolescence when psychological and physiological changes are at their peak. That is the time for major harm from dysfunctional families, as well. Studies show that children under 17 report more frequent exposure to pornography than other age groups (Reed, 1990).

We note that in the research by Check and Guloien (1989) a difference of only one or two "deviant or psychotic" beliefs (out of 20 on Eysenck's Psychoticism Scale) changed the pornography viewers' classification from *low* psychoticism (low P) to *high* psychoticism (high P). The evidence seems clear that pornography changes attitudes enough to entice a viewer to adopt one or more deviant beliefs.

Pornography use conditions and predisposes persons—especially younger persons—to objectify women and adopt other deviant beliefs, such as (Goodchilds & Zellman, 1984) "it is okay" under certain conditions "for a guy to hold a girl down and force her to have sexual intercourse." (p. 241). Not all those deviant beliefs will lead to aggressive sexual acting out, but it increases the probability.

If our society wants to curtail dysfunctional sexual compulsions and addictions, it would seem imperative to curtail the production and distribution of pornography materials that feed such addictions. Materials capable of fostering compulsion to rape, sexual violence, sadism, and asocial paraphilias should be legally curtailed, as is child pornography.

REFERENCES

Abel, G. C., & Rouleau, J. L. (1990). The nature and extent of sexual assault. In W. L. Marshall, D. R. Laws, & H. E. Barbaree (Eds.), *Handbook of sexual assault: Issues, theories, and treatment of the offender* (pp. 9–21). New York: Plenum Press.

American Psychiatric Association. (1987). *Diagnostic and statistical manual of mental disorders* (3rd ed., rev.). Washington, DC: American Psychiatric Association.

Bergman, J. (1982). The influence of pornography on sexual development: Three case histories. *Family therapy* (Vol. IX, No. 3). New York: Libra.

Blanchard, G. (1989). *Sex offender treatment: A psychoeducational model.* Golden Valley, MN: Golden Valley Institute for Behavioral Medicine.

Carnes, P. J. (1983). *Out of the shadows: Understanding sexual addiction*. Minneapolis: Comp Care.

Carnes, P. J. (1989). *Contrary to love: Helping the sexual addict*. Minneapolis: Comp Care.

Carnes, P. J. (1990). Sexual addiction: Progress, criticism, challenges. *American Journal of Preventive Psychiatry and Neurology, 2*(3), 1-8.

Carnes, P. J. (1991). *Don't call it love*. New York: Bantam.

Carter, D. L., Prentky, R., Knight, R. A., Vanderveer, P., & Boucher, R. (1986). *Use of pornography in the criminal and developmental histories of sexual offenders*. Unpublished manuscript, Massachusetts Treatment Center, Research Dept., Bridgewater, MA.

Check, J. V. P., & Guloien, T. H. (1989). Reported proclivity for coercive sex following repeated exposure to sexually violent pornography,nonviolent dehumanizing pornography, and erotica. In D. Zillmann & J. Bryant (Eds.), *Pornography: Research advances and policy considerations* (pp. 159-184). Hillsdale, NJ: Lawrence Erlbaum Associates.

Coleman, E. J. (1988). Sexual compulsivity: Definition, etiology, and treatment considerations. In E. Coleman (Ed.), *Chemical dependency and intimacy dysfunction* (pp. 189-204). New York: Haworth Press.

Coleman, E. J. (1990a). *Compulsive sexual behavior*. Minneapolis: Minnesota Medical Foundation.

Coleman, E. J. (1990b). The obsessive–compulsive model for describing compulsive sexual behavior. *American Journal of Preventive Psychiatry and Neurology, 2*(3), 9-14

Collins-Dooley, L. B. (1991). The behavioral and psychological correlates among drug, food, and sexual addictions. *American Journal of Preventive Psychiatry and Neurology, 2*(3), 42-44

Darke, J. L. (1990). Sexual aggression. In W. L. Marshall, D. R. Laws, & H. E. Barbaree (Eds.), *Handbook of sexual assault: Issues, theories, and treatment of the offender* (pp. 55-72). New York: Plenum Press.

Darke, J. L., Marshall, W. L., & Earls, C. M. (1982, April). *Humiliation and rape: A preliminary inquiry*. Paper presented at the fourth National Conference on the Evaluation and Treatment of Sexual Aggressors. Denver, CO.

Davis, K. E., & Braucht, G. N. (1970). Exposure to pornography, character and sexual deviance. *In Technical Reports of the Commission on Obscenity and Pornography* (Vol. 7). Washington, DC: U. S. Government Printing Office.

Donovan, D. M. (1988). Assessment of addictive behaviors: Implications of an emerging biophychosocial model. In D. M. Donovan & G. A. Marlatt (Eds.), *Assessment of addictive behaviors*. New York: Guilford Press.

Donnerstein, E., Linz, D., & Penrod, S. (1987). Is it the sex or is it the violence? *In the question of pornography* (pp. 108-136). New York: The Free Press.

Eron, L. D. (1987, May). The development of aggressive behavior from the perspective of a developing behaviorism. *American Psychologist*.

Eysenck, H. (1984). Sex, violence, and the media; Where do we stand now? In N. Malamuth & E. Donnerstein (Eds.), *Pornography and aggression* (pp. 305-318). Orlando: Academic Press.

Final Report of the Attorney General's Commission on Pornography. (1986). Nashville, TN: Rutledge Hill Press.

Friedrich-Cofer, L., & Huston, A. C. (1986). Television violence and aggression: The debate continues. *Psychological Bulletin 100*(3), 364-371.

Goldstein, M. J., Kant, H. S., & Harman, J. J. (1974). *Pornography and sexual deviance*. Berkeley: University of California Press.

Goodchilds, J. D., & Zellman, G. L. (1984). Sexual signaling and sexual aggression in adolescent relationships. In N. M. Malamuth & E. Donnerstein (Eds.), *Pornography and sexual aggression* (pp. 233-243). Orlando: Academic Press.

Goodman, A. (1989). Addiction defined: Diagnostic criteria for addictive disorder. *American Journal of Preventive Psychiatry and Neurology, 2* (1), 12–15.

Goodman, A. (1990). *Sexual addiction: Designation and treatment.* St. Paul, MN: Paul Minnesota Institute of Psychiatry.

Herman, J. L. (1990). Sex offenders: A feminist perspective. In W. L. Marshall, D. R. Laws, & H. E. Barbaree (Eds.), *Handbook of sexual asault: Issues, theories, and treatment of the offender* (pp. 177–194). New York: Plenum Press.

Langevin, R. (1990). Sexual anomalies and the brain. In W. L. Marshall, D. R. Laws, & H. E. Barbaree (Eds.), *Handbook of sexual assault: Issues, theories, and treatment of the offender* (pp. 257–275). New York: Plenum Press.

Lanning, K., & Burgess, A. (1989). Child pornography and sex rings. In D. Zillmann & J. Bryant (Eds.), *Pornography: Research advances and policy considerations* (pp. 235–255). Hillsdale, NJ: Lawrence Erlbaum Associates.

Laws, D. R., & Marshall, W. L. (1990). A conditioning theory of the etiology and maintenance of deviant sexual preference and behavior. In W. L. Marshall, D. R. Laws, & H. E. Barbaree (Eds.), *Handbook of sexual assault: Issues, theories, and treatment of the offender* (pp. 209–229). New York: Plenum Press.

Lord, W. H. (1990, May 20–22). Sexual addiction: Psyche? Soma? Neurobiochemical perspective on sex/love addiction. *National Conference on Sexual Compulsivity/Addiction.* Minneapolis: University of Minnesota Continuing Education and Extension.

Lyons, J. S., Anderson, R. L., & Larson, D. B. (1990). *A systematic analysis of the social science research on the effects of violent and non-violent pornography.* Pittsburgh: Conference on Media and the Family.

Malamuth, N. M. (1984). Aggression against women: Cultural and individual causes. In N. M. Malamuth & E. Donnerstein (Eds.), *Pornography and sexual aggression* (pp. 19–52). Orlando: Academic Press.

Marshall, W. L. (1988). The use of explicit sexual stimuli by rapists, child molesters and nonoffender males. *Journal of Sex Research, 25,* 267–288.

Marshall, W. L. (1989). Pornography and sex offenders. In D. Zillmann & J. Bryant (Eds.), *Pornography: Research advances and policy considerations* (pp. 185–214). Hillsdale, NJ: Lawrence Erlbaum Associates.

Marshall, W. L., & Barbaree, H. E. (1990). An integrated theory. In W. L. Marshall, D. R. Laws, & H. E. Barbaree (Eds.), *Handbook of sexual assault: Issues, theories, and treatment of the offender* (pp. 257–275). New York: Plenum Press.

Marshall, W. L., Laws, D. R., & Barbaree, H. E. (1990). Present status and future directions. In W. L. Marshall, D. R. Laws, & H. E. Barbaree (Eds.), *Handbook of sexual assault: Issues, theories, and treatment of the offender* (pp. 389–395). New York: Plenum Press.

Milkman, H., & Sunderwirth, S. (1987). *Craving for ecstasy: The consciousness and chemistry of escape.* Lexington, MA: Lexington Books.

Milkman, H., & Sunderwirth, S. (1990, May 20–22). Craving for ecstasy. *National Conference on Sexual Compulsivity/Addiction.* Minneapolis: University of Minnesota Continuing Education and Extension.

Milkman, H., Weiner, S. E., & Sunderwirth, S. (1983). Addiction relapse. *Advances in Alcohol and Substance Abuse, 3,* 119–134.

Mulvey, E. P., & Haugaard, J. L. (1986). *Report of the Surgeon General's Workshop on Pornography and Public Health.* U.S. Dept. of Health and Human Services. Washington DC: U.S. Govt Printing Office.

Murrin, M. R., & Laws, D. R. (1990). The influence of pornography on sexual crimes. In W. L. Marshall, D. R. Laws, & H. E. Barbaree (Eds.), *Handbook of sexual assault: Issues, theories, and treatment of the offender* (pp. 73–91). New York: Plenum Press.

Rachman, S., & Hodgson, R. (1968). Experimentally induced 'sexual fetishism': Replication and development. *Psychological Record, 18,* 25–27.

Reed, M. D. (1989). Review of research on the effects of sexually indecent materials of concern to the Federal Communications Commission. *In reply comments to notice of inquiry: Enforcement of prohibitions against broadcast indecency in 18 U.S.C.* (Section 1464, (pp. 43–49). [Before the Federal Communications Commission H. Robert Showers MM Docket No. 89-494 (1989)].

Reed, M. D. (1990) *Research on pornography:The evidence of harm.* Cincinnati, OH: National Coalition Against Pornography.

Robertson, J. C. (1990). Sex addiction as a disease: A neurobehavioral model. *American Journal of Preventive Psychiatry and Neurology, 2*(3), 15–18.

Rosenberg, J. (1989). *Fuel on the fire: An inquiry into pornography and sexual aggression in a free society.* Orwell, VT: The Safer Society Press.

Sapolsky, B. (1984). Arousal, affect, and the aggression — moderating effect of erotica. In N. M. Malamuth & E. Donnerstein (Eds.), *Pornography and sexual aggression* (pp. 84–114). Orlando: Academic Press.

Sears, A., & Dietz, P. (1987). Pornography and obscenity sold in adult bookstores: A survey of 5,132 books, magazines, and films in four American cities. *University of Michigan Journal of Law Reform, 21,* 7–46.

Silbert, M. H. (1989). The effects on juveniles of being used for pornography and prostitution. In D. Zillmann & J. Bryant (Eds.), *Pornography: Research advances and policy considerations* (pp. 215-235). Hillsdale, NJ: Lawrence Erlbaum Associates.

Solomon, R. L. (1980). The opponent process theory of acquired motivation: The costs and benefits of pain. *American Psychologist, 35,* 691–712.

Weaver, J. (1987). *Effects of portrayals of female sexuality and violence against women on perceptions of women.* Unpublished doctoral dissertation, Indiana University.

Wise, R. A. (1988). The neurobiology of craving: Implications for the understanding and treatment of addiction. *Journal of Abnormal Psychology, 97*(2), 118–132.

Zillmann, D. (1989). Effects of prolonged consumption of pornography. In D. Zillmann & J. Bryant (Eds.), *Pornography:Research advances and policy considerations* (pp. 127-157). Hillsdale, NJ: Lawrence Erlbaum Associates.

Zillmann, D., & Bryant, J. (1988). Pornography's impact on sexual satisfaction. *Journal of Applied Social Psychology 8,* 438–453.

Zillmann, D., & Weaver, J. (1989). Pornography and men's sexual callousness toward women. In D. Zillmann & J. Bryant (Eds.), *Pornography: Research advances and policy considerations* (pp. 95-125). Hillsdale, NJ: Lawrence Erlbaum Associates.

19

A Systematic Review of the Effects of Aggressive and Nonaggressive Pornography

John S. Lyons
Rachel L. Anderson
Northwestern University Medical School

David B. Larson
National Institute of Mental Health

Since the 1960s, research on the effects of exposure to sexually explicit materials has been a field of inquiry within the social sciences. Social science research has become a controversial part of federal policy-advising commissions on pornography for two decades. In 1970, the Presidential Commission on Obscenity and Pornography found insufficient evidence that exposure to explicit sexual materials played a significant role in the causation of delinquent or criminal behavior. However, the social science literature on which these claims were based was widely criticized for a failure to include materials of a sexually violent or aggressive nature and a failure to investigate specific effects on violence against women.

In 1986 the Meese Commission reached conflicting conclusions supporting restrictions of pornographic materials, due in part to the changing nature of the content of commercially available pornography and its increased availability (Brown & Bryant, 1989). However, the report bred considerable controversy as some thought the contentions made were not supported by the empirical evidence (Donnerstein, Linz, & Penrod 1987).

The Commission Reports are but two of the markers in the debate over sexually explicit materials. The debate over pornography has involved many communities and groups with various orientations. Despite orientation, a reason for concern remains an issue of harm; potential behavioral–attitudinal harm produced by viewing erotica and/or aggressive sexual depictions.

This review takes a systematic approach to study the empirical literature in pornography. By carefully identifying articles for inclusion and classifying these articles using a reliable coding scheme, this chapter attempts to provide an overview of the methods and findings of experimental social science research in pornography. The replicability of this review strategy thus mitigates against the controversial results of earlier attempts to synthesize research on the effects of pornography (Baretta, Larson, Lyons, & Zorc 1990).

METHOD

Definition of Terms

In this report pornography is defined as any material that is predominately sexually explicit and intended primarily for the purpose of sexual arousal (Attorney General's Commission on Pornography, 1986). Further, for the present analysis, pornography is categorized as either aggressive or nonaggressive. Aggressive sexual materials contain images of sexual coercion in which physical force is used or implied *usually* against a woman in order to obtain certain sexual acts, as in scenes of rape and other forms of sexual assault (Donnerstein, Linz, Penrod, 1987, italics added).

Procedure

The process of identifying articles for inclusion in this study involved a five-part strategy. First, a computerized literature search was undertaken in which the words "pornography," "erotica," "sexually explicit" were used as keywords in searches of titles and abstracts in PSYCHLIT and MEDLINE literature databases. However, because it has been demonstrated that this process is not sufficient (Baretta et al., 1990), four additional steps were undertaken. In the second step, the reference sections of the computer-identified studies were reviewed and new studies identified. This iterative process continued until no new studies were identified.

The third step consisted of identifying all primary authors and undertaking a name search to identify other works by these authors. Next, the journals with the most articles identified were systematically reviewed for additional studies. Finally, identified references were shared with a number of experts in the field of pornography research and additional studies were identified.

The preceding strategy identified 152 empirical studies published in peer-reviewed scientific journals of the effects of pornography from 1971 to

1991. Only peer-reviewed studies were included as both a replicable sampling frame and a quality control. Although not a standard review strategy in psychological research, this form of article inclusion is a common practice in systematic reviews in other fields (Larson et al., 1989; Lyons et al., 1990; Mulrow, 1989; Pilmer & Light, 1985). Whereas a number of original studies on the effects of pornography have been published as dissertations and book chapters and some relevant research never published, one should concep-tualize the present sample as a representative sample of existing research rather than an exhaustive one. Two concerns guide the decision to focus only on articles in peer-reviewed journals. First, this strategies allows maximal replicability—any reviewer has equal access to the identified articles. Book chapters (particularly if the book is out of print) and unpublished manu-scripts are not nearly as easily identifiable or retrievable. Second, peer review, although by no means infallible, is an important hallmark of the process of scientific communication (Mulrow, 1989). Given the relative rigors of the peer-review process, these articles probably represent the highest quality scientific research that addresses the topic.

Studies were divided by research strategy; cross-sectional (one time ex-posure) versus prospective (repeated measures or follow-up over time), na-ture of pornography; aggressive versus nonaggressive as determined by stim-uli, and nature of dependent variable; rape–aggression toward women versus all others. Further, studies were classified by results based on evidence of effects on any of the following three dimensions: sexual arousal, attitudes, and behavior. The definitions used for classification of results are as follows: (a) positive—pornographic stimuli produced a statistically significant effect, (b) negative—pornographic stimuli produced no statistically significant ef-fects, (c) mixed—evidence of both positive and negative.

The reliability of this classification scheme was tested by having two raters (RLA and JSL) rate 10 studies independently. Inter-rater reliability of classifications was .97, calculated using Kappa. This high reliability is consistent with other systematic reviews of the scientific literature (Lyons et al., 1990).

Eighty-one studies published in peer-reviewed journals that utilized audio or visual pornographic stimuli were used in the final analysis. Nonexperimental studies that measured attitudes and behaviors using surveys or questionnaires but did not experimentally manipulate exposure to sexually explicit material (31), content reviews (10), those that contained unspecified stimuli (4), or the focus was measurement (5), effects of debriefing (2), or pedophilia (1) were excluded from analysis. Also excluded were those studies whose outcome was unrelated to effects of pornographic materials. In these studies, the stimuli used were to show a preference for specific sexual content, or the main focus was a comparison–contrast between groups (i.e., gender 18). Table 19.1 contains a list of all studies included in the review with some of their characteristics.

TABLE 19.1
Summary of Pornography

Researchers	Subjects	Research Strategy	Pornographic Stimuli	Dependent Measures	Major Findings	Relationship
Abel, Barlow, Blanchard, & Guild (1977) Experiment 1	M20 rapists nonrapists	Cross-sectional	Audiotape -heterosexual activity -rape	Physiological and self-report sexual arousal	Based on erection measures, rapists were separated from nonrapists in that the former developed erections to rape descriptions while the latter did not. Peak arousal occured with victims whose age the rapist had reported was most erotic to them.	Positive causal
Experiment 2	M9 rapists	Cross-sectional	Audiotape -nonsexual aggression -rape	Physiological and self-report sexual arousal		
Experiment 3	M9 rapists	Cross-sectional	Audiotape -rape	Physiological and self-report sexual arousal		
Baron (1974a)	M36 college students	Cross-sectional	Pictures -nudity	Shock duration and intensity delivered to a male confederate	Aggression was reduced by minimal as well as moderate levels of sexual arousal.	Negative causal
Baron (1974b)	M40 college students	Cross-sectional	Pictures -nudity	Shock intensity delivered to a male confederate	Heightened sexual arousal was effective in inhibiting subsequent aggression by subjects who were angered.	Negative causal
Baron & Bell (1977)	M86 college	Cross-sectional	Pictures and passages -nudity -heterosexual activity	Shock intensity and duration administered to a male confederate	Exposure to mild erotic stimuli inhibited later aggression, while exposure to more arousing sexual materials neither facilitated nor inhibited such behavior.	Negative causal
Baron (1979)	F45 college students	Cross-sectional	Pictures -nudity -heterosexual activity	Shock intensity delivered to a female confederate	Aggression by previously angered individuals was inhibited by exposure to mild erotic stimuli, but actually enhanced by exposure to more arousing materials.	Mixed causal

274

Study	Design	Stimulus	Measure	Findings	Conclusion
Baxter, Barbaree, & Marshall (1986)	M60 rapists M41 college students	Prospective	Audiotape -consent varying amounts of consent -rape varying amounts of violence	Physiological reports of sexual arousal	Nonrapists and rapists showed less arousal to rape episodes than to consenting episodes. Rapists' weakest responses were to the most violent rape scene.	Negative causal
Brown, Amoroso, Ware, Pruesse, & Pilkey (1973)	M40 college students	Cross-sectional	Slides ranging from fully dressed to heterosexual activity	Self report of pornographic contents and viewing time	Viewing time decreased when subjects were observed by an audience. When alone viewing times increased as the slides were rated more pornographic.	Positive causal
Brown, Amoroso, & Ware (1976)	M56 college students	Prospective	Slides -heterosexual activity	Self-reports of sexual behavior one week following exposure	Self reports of sexual behavior revealed no increase from the week preceding slide viewing to the week following exposure. A temporary increase in sexual outlets was observed the same day the slides were viewed, disappearing the next day.	Mixed causal
Brown (1979)	M30 college F30 students	Cross-sectional	Slides -heterosexual activity -homosexual activity -group sex -transvestitism	Viewing time, pornographic ratings, evaluative ratings and activity-factor ratings	Females viewing times gradually increased whereas males viewing times first increased and then decreased for the high pornographic slides.	Positive causal

(continued)

275

TABLE 19.1 (continued)

Researchers	Subjects	Research Strategy	Pornographic Stimuli	Dependent Measures	Major Findings	Relationship
Byrne, Fisher, Lamberth, & Mitchell (1974)	M31 married F32 couples one partner of each pair was a college student	Cross-sectional	Pictoral or Verbal -heterosexual activity -homosexual activity -autosexual activity	Affect and evaluative responses	Positive and negative affective responses were associated with pornography judgments and with restrictiveness opinions for males, for females only negative affective responses were associated with these two response measures.	Mixed causal
Centi & Malamuth (1984)	M69 recruited from a university	Prospective	Written and pictoral depiction (pre-exposure) -rape/nonrape Films, passages and pictures (exposure) -heterosexual activity -group activity -sexual violence	Physiological and self-report arousal	Repeated exposure to sexually aggressive or nonaggressive pornography resulted in satiation in sexual arousal to rape themes for those who prior to any exposure had shown high levels of arousal to rape.	Positive causal
Check & Malamuth (1983)	M/F 289 college students	Prospective	Stories -consenting -acquaintance rape -stranger rape	Sexual arousal, perception of the reactions of the women in the story and self-reported likelihood of raping	High sex role stereotyping individuals showed high levels of arousal to rape (especially acquaintance rape). Forty-four percent of men indicated some likelihood of raping when assured of anonymity.	Positive causal

276

Study	Sample	Design	Stimulus	Measure	Findings	
Donnerstein, Donnerstein, & Evans (1975)	M81 college students	Cross-sectional	Pictures -nudity -implied sexual activity	Shock duration and intensity to a male confederate	Mildly erotic pictures presented after instigation of affect reduced aggression; mildly and highly erotic pictures presented before instigation of affect increased aggression.	Mixed causal
Donnerstein & Barrett (1978)	M72 college students	Cross-sectional	Films -neutral -heterosexual activity	Shock administered to a male or female confederate	Previously angered subjects showed an increase in aggression following the viewing of erotic films, however, no differential aggression was observed toward females as a function of film exposure.	Positive causal
Donnerstein & Hallam (1978)	M60 college students	Cross-sectional	Films -heterosexual activity -aggression	Shock administered to a male or female confederate	Both the aggressive and the erotic films immediately increased aggression to both males and females; after a ten minute delay the aggressive film increased aggression to males, while the erotic film increased aggression to females.	Positive causal

(continued)

TABLE 19.1 (continued)

Researchers	Subjects	Research Strategy	Pornographic Stimuli	Dependent Measures	Major Findings	Relationship
Donnerstein (1980)	M120 college students	Cross-sectional	Films -heterosexual activity -rape	Intensity of shock to a male or female confederate	The aggressive erotic film was effective in increasing aggression and it produced the highest increase in aggression against a female. Angered subjects revealed a larger increase in arousal over nonangered subjects. Arousal was higher for aggressive-erotic film when a female instead of a male was the target.	Positive causal
Donnerstein & Berkowitz (1981) Experiment 1	M80 college students	Cross-sectional	Films -heterosexual activity -rape negative/positive outcome	Intensity of shock to a male or female confederate	Aggressive-erotic films (victim enjoyed or reacted negatively) increased aggression to a female confederate. There were no increases in aggression toward males as a function of film exposure.	Positive causal
Experiment 2	M80 college students	Prospective	Films -heterosexual activity -rape negative/positive outcome	Intensity of shock to a female confederate	Angered males were more aggressive toward the female after viewing either aggressive or positive erotic film, but only the positive-outcome aggressive film increased aggression in nonangered subjects.	Positive causal
Eccles, Marshall, & Barbaree (1988)	M15 college students	Prospective	Videotapes -heterosexual activity -homosexual activity	Physiological measures of arousal	A significant decrease was found in arousal both within and across sessions.	Negative causal

278

Study	Sample	Design	Stimulus	Measures	Findings	Direction
Fehr & Schulman (1978)	F13 college students	Cross-sectional	Passages -sexually tones	Pleasurable/ unpleasurable response ratings and physiological responses	Sexually pleasurable, as opposed to sexually aversive was more sexually stimulating, less anxiety and guilt provoking, and less disgusting, but equally well portrayed and interesting.	Positive causal
Fisher & Byrne (1978) Experiment 1	M30 college F32 students	Cross-sectional	Film -heterosexual activity affectionate unemotional	Self-report sexual arousal, affect, evaluate responses	Males and females were not differentially responsive to the love or lust themes, however, both experienced sexual arousal.	Positive causal
Experiment 2	M36 married F36 couples (one partner was a college student)	Cross-sectional	Film -heterosexual activity affectionate unemotional casual sex	Self-report sexual arousal, affect, evaluative responses	Replicated experiment 1 and indicated that both males and females were more sexually aroused by casual sex theme that by love or lust theme.	Positive causal
Fisher & Byrne (1978)	M31 college F31 students	Cross-sectional	Film -heterosexual activity	Film evaluation and sexual activity subsequent to exposure	Those rating film as pornographic reported a greater increase in sexual activity subsequent to exposure than those who did not rate the film as pornographic.	Positive causal

(continued)

TABLE 19.1 (continued)

Researchers	Subjects	Research Strategy	Pornographic Stimuli	Dependent Measures	Major Findings	Relationship
George & Marlatt (1986)	M64 college students	Cross-sectional	Slides -violent beatings -violent-erotic bondage -erotica	Verbal aggression toward male confederate, sexual arousal and viewing time	Alcohol expectancy increased viewing times for the non-neutral slides and overrode the impact of alcohol content. Viewing times were greatest for violent erotic slides. Anger provocation increased verbal aggressiveness and reduced slide viewing. Alcohol expectancy increased self-report arousal.	Mixed causal
Griffitt & Kaiser (1978)	M40 F40 college students	Cross-sectional	Slides -erotic -non-erotic	Affect as a condition as sex-guilt	High sex-guilt made fewer choice responses leading to erotica than low sex-guilt, and females made fewer erotica-producing choices than males. High sex-guilt and females were less positive in affective reactions to erotica than low sex-guilt and males.	Positive causal
Jaffe, Malamuth, Feingold, & Feshbach (1974)	M44 F47 college students	Cross-sectional	Passage -erotic	Intensity of shock to a male or female confederate	Sexually aroused males and females delivered more intense shocks than nonaroused subjects regardless of the gender of the confederate or experimenter.	Positive causal

280

| Kelley (1985a) | M30 college F30 students | Cross-sectional | Film -heterosexual activity | Number of trials of a paired-associates learning task, number of errors before reaching criterion and affect scores | When the list consisted of competitive word pairs, persons with positive sexual attitudes required more trials and made more errors before criterion was reached, only after viewing an erotic film. Their non-competitional performance was facilitated after viewing the erotic relative to the nonerotic film. | Positive causal |
| Kelley (1985b) | M135 college F129 students | Cross-sectional | Films -aggressive -sexually aggressive rape -heterosexual activity | Affect, sexual arousal, and helping, hostility and attraction attitudes | Males extended the least help to experimenter following the aggressive film and expressed more positive affect than females. Erotophilic males expressed slightly less hostility toward a female than a male experimenter. Erotophiles expressed more positive attitudes toward women and men after viewing either the rape film shown by a male experimenter or the erotic film shown by a female experimenter. | Negative causal |

281

(continued)

TABLE 19.1 (continued)

Researchers	Subjects	Research Strategy	Pornographic Stimuli	Dependent Measures	Major Findings	Relationship
Kelly (1985c)	M185 college F185 students	Cross-sectional	Slides -autosexual activity -heterosexual activity	Affective and self-report sexual arousal, and authoritarianism	Males expressed more positive affect and higher sexual arousal. Those with higher sex guilt expressed less positive affect about the stimuli. Authoritarianism was negatively related to positive feelings about same-sex slides. Females with low positive feelings about the heterosexual and same-sex masturbation slides accepted less responsibility for slide watching and expressed more dislike of the experimenter.	Positive causal
Kelley & Musialowski (1986)	M28 college F28 students	Prospective	Films -heterosexual activity	Affect, self-report sexual arousal and concern about the stimulus	Self-rated responses showed that negative affect increased with film repetition and returned to original levels with the introduction of novelty. Males became more aroused and concerned by novelty consisting of different actors. Females became more aroused and concerned by the same actors performing different acts.	Positive causal

Study	Sample	Design	Stimuli	Measure	Findings	Direction
Kercher & Walker (1973)	M56 rapists/ nonsex crimes	Cross-sectional	Slides -heterosexual activity -sadomasochism (male dominant)	Evaluation of erotic stimuli and physiological arousal	Rapists evaluated the erotic stimuli more negatively than nonrapists.	Negative causal
Lang, Searles, Lauerman, & Adesso (1980)	M72 college students	Cross-sectional	Slides -content varied from individual, partially clothed females to heterosexual activity	Recorded time viewing slides	Individual differences in sexual guilt mediated the effect of alcohol expectancy cognitions on behaviors relating to sexual stimuli.	Positive causal
Leonard & Taylor (1983)	M40 college students	cross-sectional	Slides -heterosexual activity	Electic shock to a female confederate who made either permissive, non-permissive or no comment on erotic slides	Erotic slides with permissive comments increased aggression over other conditions.	Positive causal
Linz, Donnerstein, & Penrod (1988)	M156 college students	Prospective	Films -portraying women as sexual objects -sexually explicit and degrading to women -violent	Affect and film evaluation and attitudes about rape in stranger/acquaintance trial	Sexually violent material became less anxiety provoking and depressing with prolonged exposure. These films also produced a tendency of less sympathy to the victim of rape portrayed in a trial. Those exposed to sexually degrading films reported seeing less violence with continued exposure, and found less degradation to women after prolonged exposure.	Positive causal

(continued)

TABLE 19.1 (continued)

Researchers	Subjects	Research Strategy	Pornographic Stimuli	Dependent Measures	Major Findings	Relationship
Love, Sloan, & Schmidt (1976)	M35 college students	Cross-sectional	Slides partial nudity to heterosexual activity	Obscenity ratings and viewing time	Viewing time of the low sex guilt group increased linearly as a function of increasing pornographic content.	Positive causal
Malamuth & Check (1980a)	M77 college F66 students	Cross-sectional	Passages -consent/no consent -pain/no pain -arousal/disgust	Self-report self arousal, perception of sexual portrayals regarding women's willingness, pain and pleasure	Portrayals depicting a woman as experiencing sexual arousal rather than disgust, irrespective of whether rape or consent was depicted produced more sexual arousal. Males reported more sexual arousal than females.	Positive causal
Malamuth, Haber, & Feshbach (1980)	M53 college F38 students	Cross-sectional	Passages -rape victim arousal heterosexual activity	Reaction to rape depiction: sexual arousal, perception of victim and assailant	Males exposed to aggressive pornography and low aggression-anxious were more sexually aroused to rape depictions and more punitive toward rapists, however perceived the victim experiencing less pain, trauma and resisting less (the opposite was found for males high and females low in aggression-anxiety). Fifty-one percent of males indicated some likelihood of raping if assured of not being punished.	Positive causal

284

Study	Sample	Design	Method/Cues	Measures	Findings	Direction
Malamuth & Check (1980b)	M75 college students	Cross-sectional	Audiotape -rape arousal/disgust Questionnaire -perceptions of an audiotaped rape-criterion story (presented to all groups)	Physiological and self-reports of sexual arousal, perceptions of rape	The rape arousal story was more arousing than rape-disgust story. Exposure to rape-arousal produced more arousal to to rape-criterion story than exposure to rape-disgust. Rape-arousal subjects rated woman as experiencing less trauma in rape-criterion. Finally, 69% of men stated some likelihood of rape when assured of not being punished. This was found to correlate with callous attitudes to rape and with self-report sexual arousal to aggressive sexuality.	Positive causal
Malamuth, Heim, & Feshbach (1980) Experiment 1	M135 college F159 students	Cross-sectional	Passage -rape/nonrape -pain/no pain -planned/unplanned -aggressive cues	Self-report of sexual arousal. Ten descriptors of various moods (boredom, anxiety, embarrassment)	Themes portaying sexual assault are less sexually arousing than mutually consenting depictions. Those exposed to mutually consenting depictions felt more positive, less angry and less offended.	Positive causal

(continued)

285

TABLE 19.1 (continued)

Researchers	Subjects	Research Strategy	Pornographic Stimuli	Dependent Measures	Major Findings	Relationship
Experiment 2	F68 college	Cross-sectional	Passage -rape/nonrape -pain/no pain -planned/unplanned -aggressive cues	Self-report of sexual arousal. The descriptors of various moods (boredom, anxiety, embarrassment)	Males reported arousal when the victim experienced orgasm and pain. Females reported arousal when the victim experienced orgasm and no pain.	Positive causal
Malamuth (1981)	M29 college students	Prospective	Slides with audio stimuli -rape -mutual consent	Physiological and self-reports of arousal and content of created sexual fantasies	Those exposed to rape version, irrespective of their sexual classification, created more violent sexual fantasies than those exposed to the mutually consenting version.	Positive causal
Malamuth (1983)	M42 41 college students 1 former student	Prospective	Stories -consenting -rape	Levels of aversive noise administered to female and reported desire to harm her	Factors associated with real-world aggression against women successfully predicted men's laboratory aggression against a female.	Positive causal
Malamuth & Check (1983)	M145 college students	Prospective	Audiotape -consent/no consent -pain/no pain -arousal/disgust	Physiological and self-report of sexual arousal	Arousal to rape depictions is not an isolated response but is associated with other measures of aggressive tendencies (likelihood of rape, power motivation). When disgust and non-consent were present both low and high likelihood of rape were less aroused, however, there was greater arousal when the woman was perceived as sexually aroused.	Mixed causal

286

Study	Sample	Design	Stimuli	Measures	Results	Conclusion
Malamuth & Check (1985)	M145 college students	Cross-sectional	Audiotaped stories -rape/consent consent/nonsent pain/no pain arousal/disgust	General beliefs in rape myths	Media depictions suggesting that rape results in the victim's arousal can contribute to men's beliefs in a similar rape myth. Men with higher inclinations to aggress against women are particularly likely to be affected by media deictions of rape myths.	Positive causal
Malamuth, Check, & Briere (1986) Experiment 1	M37 college F43 students	Cross-sectional	Stories -nonaggressive nonsexual -aggressive nonsexual -nonaggressive sexual -aggressive sexual	Self-report measure of sexual arousal, perception of woman's willingness, pain and pleasure	Males and females reported more sexual arousal in response to sexually explicit nonaggressive than aggressive sexual depictions. Women in the aggressive sexual depictions were seen as more willing and experiencing less pain than those in nonsexual aggressive depictions.	Positive causal
Experiment 2	M359 college students	Cross-sectional	Tape-recorded passages -nonaggressive nonsexual -aggressive nonsexual -nonaggressive sexual -aggressive sexual	Physiological and self-report measures of sexual arousal, likelihood of force and measures that test less sensitivity toward women	The high arousal from force group reported more sexual arousal by aggressive than nonaggressive sexually explicit portrayals; the opposite was found for the no and moderate arousal group. Likelihood of force was correlated to self-report arousal.	Positive causal

(continued)

TABLE 19.1 (continued)

Researchers	Subjects	Research Strategy	Pornographic Stimuli	Dependent Measures	Major Findings	Relationship
Malamuth (1986)	M155 80% college students 20% non-students	Prospective	Stories -mutual consent -rape	Self-reported sexual aggression	Predictor factors: sexual arousal in response to aggression, dominance as a motive for sexual acts, hostility toward women, attitudes accepting of violence against women, and sexual experience, related to sexual aggression. A better prediction of sexual aggression was achieved by a combination of these factors than by any one singularly.	Positive causal
Malamuth & Centi (1986)	M42 41 college students 1 former student	Prospective	Films, written and pictoral depictions -sexually nonviolent -sexually violent	Behavioral effects	Exposure to aggressive or nonaggressive pornographic stimuli was not found to affect laboratory aggression against women.	Negative causal
Mann, Sidman, & Starr (1973)	M/F 166 public population	Prospective	Films -heterosexual activity -homosexual activity -sadomasichism	Measures of behavior and attitudinal change	Couples viewing erotic films reported more sexual activity on film nights and became more tolerant of legal exhibition of erotic films. No stable changes in sexual behavior occurred.	Mixed causal
Mann, Berkowitz, Sidman, Starr, & West (1974)	M/F 136 married couples	Prospective	Films -heterosexual activity -homosexual activity -whipping -nonerotic	Measures of sexual activity	Sexual films stimulated sexual activity on movie viewing nights, however, the movies became less effective elicitors of sexual reaction with the successive presentations. There was no evidence that the sexual movies produced a disinhibition effect or produced new learning.	Positive causal

Mayerson & Taylor (1987)	F96 college students	Cross-sectional	Stories -consent/no consent -arousal/no arousal	Attitudes about rape and interpersonal violence	Reading any story generally led to changes in self-esteem and greater acceptance of rape myths and interpersonal violence. High sex role stereotyping reported lower self-esteem and more tolerance of rape and other violence.	Positive causal
Meyer (1972)	M48 college students	Cross-sectional	Films -violent -heterosexual activity	Number of shocks administered to a male confederate	Angered subjects viewing violence returned more shocks than any other group. Angered subjects viewing the sexually arousing film returned more shocks than those viewing nonviolent or no film.	Positive causal
Mosher (1973)	M194 college F183 students	Prospective	Films -heterosexual activity	Film reaction -affective -physiological Behavioral response -24 hour -two week	Females, high sex-guilt and less sexually experienced rated the films as more pornographic, disgusting and offensive. No evidence that explicit sexual films had negative effects on those who viewed them.	Negative causal

(continued)

TABLE 19.1 (continued)

Researchers	Subjects	Research Strategy	Pornographic Stimuli	Dependent Measures	Major Findings	Relationship
Padgett, Brislin-Slutz, & Neal (1989) Experiment 3	M27 college F39 students	Prospective	Films -erotica	Self-reported pornography viewing and measurement of attitude toward women	Erotica did not enhance negative attitudes toward women.	Negative causal
Quinsey, Chaplin, & Varney (1981)	M50 rapists, nonsex offender patients of a mental health care center and non-patient volunteers	Cross-sectional	Audiotape -nonsexual neutral -heterosexual activity consent -rape -nonsexual violence	Physiological measures of sexual arousal	Rapists responded more to the rape narratives than the non-sex offender patients and the community members with normal instructions, but not more than the altered instructions group (this group was told that they may become sexually aroused to the descriptions of sexual situations.	Positive causal
Quinsey & Chaplin (1984)	M30 sexual offenders and non-offenders from a mental health center, community members	Cross-sectional	Audiotape -hetero-social stories -heterosexual activity woman active/passive -rape active/passive enjoy/suffer	Physiological measures	Non-sex offenders responded most to the consenting sex narratives and least to the stories in which the victim suffered. Rapists responses did not vary over the various categories of con-senting and nonconsenting stories, however, rapists responded more to the rape scenes than the nonrapists.	Positive causal

290

Quinsey, Chaplin, & Upfold (1984)	M40 rapists, non-sex offenders from a psychiatric institute, and community members	Cross-sectional	Audiotape -heterosexual activity -rape -nonsexual violence -bondage consent/ nonconsent	Physiological measures of sexual arousal	Rapists were more sexually aroused to rape descriptions and less to consenting sex than controls. Rapists were sexually aroused by depictions of nonsexual violence. No differences were found between rapists and controls in responsiveness to spanking and bondage stories.	Positive causal
Ramirez, Bryant, & Zillmann (1982)	M72 college students	Cross-sectional	Slides -nudity -heterosexual activity	Evaluation of the stimulus properties of the visual material and evaluation of the two experimenters	Exposure to pleasant but nonarousing materials reduced hostile behavior under conditions of mild provocation, but no effect under conditions of severe provocation. Exposure to explicit erotica increased hostile behavior regardless of degree of provocation.	Positive causal
Reed & Reed (1972)	M/F 212 college students	Cross-sectional	Readings and pictures -erotic content	Reaction responses to erotic stimuli -positive -neutral -negative	Males accounted for the most of the positive responses to erotic stimuli; females favored neutral or negative responses. Group responses modified the minority definition and attitude toward pornography.	Mixed causal

(continued)

291

TABLE 19.1 (continued)

Researchers	Subjects	Research Strategy	Pornographic Stimuli	Dependent Measures	Major Findings	Relationship
Sapolsky & Zillmann (1981) Experiment 1	M120 college students	Cross-sectional	Film -nudity -heterosexual activity	Retaliatory behavior toward a male and excitatory and affective reactions	The hostile behavior of provoked males was enhanced by strongly arousing but moderately disturbing erotica.	Positive causal
Experiment 2	M60 college students	Cross-sectional	Film -heterosexual activity	Retaliatory behavior and excitatory and affective reactions toward a female		
Schaefer & Colgan (1977)	M8	Prospective	Passage heterosexual activity followed by either nonpornographic material or ejaculation	Penile response	Decreased reaction to sexual stimuli may be caused by extinction rather than non-satisfaction. Men with immediate sexual gratification showed greater response to pornography over time.	Positive causal
Schill, Evans, Monroe, & Drain (1975)	M48 college students	Cross-sectional	Magazine -erotic pictures	Viewing time	High-guilt viewed magazines longer when exposed to a positive or negative comment as opposed to a neutral comment. Low-guilt viewing time was longer when exposed to negative comment.	Positive causal
Schill, Van Tuinen, & Doty (1980) Experiment 1	M42 college students	Cross-sectional	Passages -heterosexual activity -group sex -seduction	Arousal and feelings ratings	High and low sex guilt initially reported a moderate level of sexual arousal which declined with repeated exposure.	Positive causal

(continued)

Experiment 2	M40 college students	Cross-sectional	Passage -same passage for 8 trials	Arousal and feelings ratings	Over time subjects felt less entertained, less anxious and more bored.	Positive causal
Stauffer & Frost (1976)	M50 college F50 students	Cross-sectional	Features in sexually oriented magazines and a nonsexual magazine (letter to the editor, film review, centerfold)	Interest ratings of individual features	Men gave higher interest ratings, were more sexually stimulated and felt more positively than females after viewing the sexually oriented material.	Positive causal
Wallace & Wehmer (1971)	M40 college students	Prospective	Pictures -nudity -heterosexual activity -homosexual activity -sadomasochism	Attitudes change regarding moral values, human behavior, erotic materials and censorship practices	Exposure to erotic pictures did not cause a change in attitudes toward pornography, in attitudes toward censorship, and did not cause a change in moral values.	Negative causal
Weaver, Masland, & Zillmann (1984)	M46 college students	Cross-sectional	Pictures -nude women attractive unattractive	Reported physical appeal and sexual satisfaction with mate	Preexposure to attractive females suppressed mates' appeal while preexposure to unattractive females enhanced appeal. After exposure to attractive females, mates' aesthetic value fell below assessments made after exposure to unattractive females.	Positive causal

TABLE 19.1 (continued)

Researchers	Subjects	Research Strategy	Pornographic Stimuli	Dependent Measures	Major Findings	Relationship
White (1979)	M95 college students	Cross-sectional	Slides -heterosexual activity -homosexual activity	Intensity and duration of shocks to a male confederate	Exposure to affectively positive erotic stimuli reduced retaliatory behavior by angered males. Exposure to erotic stimuli that were reported to be disgusting and unpleasant slightly enhanced subsequent aggressive behavior.	Mixed causal
Wishnoff (1978)	F45 college students	Prospective	Videotapes -nonexplicit -explicit -heterosexual activity	Responses of sexual anxiety, preferred sexual behavior and manifest anxiety	Exposure to sexual stimuli reduced sexual anxiety and increased ratings of likelihood of engaging in a greater variety of sexual behavior under appropriate circumstances.	Negative causal
Wydra, Marshall, Earls, & Barbaree (1983) Experiment 1	M50 rapists nonrapists normal	Cross-sectional	Audiotape -heterosexual activity -consent -rape -physical assaults	Responses to inappropriate sexual actions	Rapists do not differ from other men in their ability to exert control over their arousal, and in their ability to identify inappropriate cues to arousal.	Negative causal
Experiment 2	M20 rapists normals	Cross-sectional	Audiotape -consent/rape	Physiological arousal responses		
Zillmann, Hoyt, & Day (1974)	M60 college students	Cross-sectional	Films -aggressive prize-fight -violent -heterosexual activity	Intensity of noxious noise delivered to male confederate	The effect of the erotic communication yielded more intense aggressiveness, whereas the aggressive or violent communication did not.	Positive causal

Zillmann & Sapolsky (1977)	M66 college students	Cross-sectional	Slides -nonerotic -mildly erotic nudity -highly erotic heterosexual activity	Annoyance, retaliatory behavior against a male and excitatory potential (heart rate and blood pressure)	Provoked subjects expressed greater annoyance after being exposed to erotica, however, exposure to erotica had no effect on unprovoked subjects. Under conditions of provocation, annoyance in both erotica conditions was less than in the nonerotica condition; there was no difference in retaliatory behavior. The excitatory potential of the erotica proved to be minimal.	Mixed causal
Zillmann, Bryant, Comisky, & Medoff (1981)	M74 college students	Cross-sectional	Pictures and Films -non-erotic -nudity -heterosexual activity -bestiality -sadomasochism	Obnoxious noise and written reprisal to a male confederate	Erotica high in excitatory potential and negative hedonic valence were found to increase aggression. Exposure to non-arousing and pleasing erotica or non-erotica resulted in similar levels of aggression.	Positive causal
Zillmann, Bryant, & Carveth (1981)	M40 college students	Cross-sectional	Pictures -nudity Films -bestiality -sadomasochism	Measure of excessive pressure on male confederate's arm.	Exposure to arousing, displeasing erotica, regardless of the degree of apparent aggressiveness involved, was found to increase retaliatory aggression.	Positive causal

(continued)

TABLE 19.1 (continued)

Researchers	Subjects	Research Strategy	Pornographic Stimuli	Dependent Measures	Major Findings	Relationship
Zillmann & Bryant (1982)	M80 college F80 students	Prospective	Films -heterosexual activity	Habituation effects and perceptions of sexuality, dispositions concerning sex and gender and reaction to a simulated rape trial	Under controlled conditions, massive exposure to pornography resulted in a loss of compassion toward women as rape victims and toward women in general. Exposure also produced distorted assessments of sexuality in society.	Positive causal
Zillmann & Bryant (1986)	M80 student/ F80 non-student	Prospective	Films per week for six weeks -non-violent pornography	Time of selective exposure to portrayals of less commonly practiced sexual activities	Exposure to nonaggressive pornography aroused an interest in pornography that portrays less commonly practiced sexual activities.	Positive causal
Zillmann & Bryant (1988)	M/F 160 college students non-students	Prospective	Videotapes -heterosexual activity	Responses to the Inventory of Personal Happiness scale	After consumption of pornography less satisfaction with intimate partners was reported; specifically with affection, physical appearance, sexual curiosity and sexual performance.	Positive causal

RESULTS

Samples and Sample Frames

The average samples size for all studies was 81 (*S.D.* = 79, range 8 to 377). Fifty-one studies (63%) were male subjects only, 5 studies (6%) were female subjects only, and 25 studies (31%) sampled both men and women. The vast majority of studies consisted of solely college student samples (*n* = 63, 78%). An additional 4 studies (5%) used college students as a comparison sample. Ten studies (12%) had a sample of convicted rapists, of these eight had some comparison group. Three studies (4%) sampled married couples; in two studies, one partner was a college student. One study was a community sample (1%), and one study did not specify its sample (1%).

Almost all studies had no defined sample frame (*n* = 79, 98%), whereas two studies (2%) used random samples.

Type of Stimuli

Forty-seven studies (58%) presented visual stimuli: films (*n* = 24), pictures (*n* = 7), slides (*n* = 13), picture and film (*n* = 2), and slide with audio (*n* = 1). Fourteen studies (17%) used written passages as the stimuli. Fourteen studies (17%) used audiotaped passages as the stimuli. Six additional (7%) studies used mixed media: four used pictures and passages, one used film, pictures, and written passages, and one used picture or verbal stimuli.

There was a significant relationship between type of stimuli and evidence of causal effects (X = 6.47, *p* < .04). All 14 studies (100%) that used written passages only as stimuli reported positive evidence of causal effects. Nine of 13 studies using audiotapes reported positive causal effects, three reported negative findings, one mixed. Finally, 33 of 50 (66%) of studies using visual stimuli reported positive evidence of causal effects.

Amount of Exposure

Sixty-five studies (81%) specified the amount of experimental exposure to pornographic stimuli in terms of minutes (it was assumed that a "feature length film" was 60 minutes in duration). Some studies had exposure to materials in a pre-experimental phase, but this exposure was not counted. The range of exposure time for all studies was from 2 minutes to 420 minutes. There were two modal exposure times—4 minutes and 10 minutes. The average exposure time was 51.8 minutes; however, only six studies provided more than 1 hour of exposure to pornographic materials.

Sixteen studies (19%) described the amount of exposure in terms of the number of pictures or slides viewed. The range for these studies were 6 to 84. The median number of slides–pictures viewed was 17. The average was 19.8.

Fourteen studies (17%) described the amount of exposure in terms of numbers of stories read. Eight of these studies used only 1 story (or passage from a story). Three studies used 3 stories, two used 6 and one study used 11 stories. (The discrepancy in total number of types of stimuli is due to studies containing more than one type of pornographic presentation; e.g., written passage and film, therefore, all were included.)

There was no relationship between amount of exposure and evidence of causal effects over all studies.

Aggressive Versus Nonaggressive Stimuli

Table 19.2 breaks out studies with aggressive versus nonaggressive stimuli showing evidence of causal effects of exposure to pornography. Fifty-seven studies (70%) had clear evidence of such effects. An additional 10 studies (12%) had mixed results; in the majority of cases this was due to an effect immediately after exposure that dissipated over time.

Table 19.3 compares studies of rape–aggression toward women as the

TABLE 19.2
Comparison of Studies Containing Aggressive Sexual Stimuli Versus Nonaggressive

	Positive	Mixed	Negative
Prospective Studies			
Aggressive	8	2	3
Nonaggressive	5	1	4
Cross-sectional Studies			
Aggressive	19	1	4
Nonaggressive	25	6	3
All Studies			
Aggressive	25	3	7
Nonaggressive	32	7	7

TABLE 19.3
Studies in Which Rape Aggressive Attitudes and Behaviors Toward Women was a Dependent Variable

Based on Nonrapist Population Rape/Aggression was a Dependent Variable			
	Positive	Mixed	Negative
Aggressive-Prospective	7	1	1
Aggressive-Cross-sectional	9	0	2
Nonaggressive-Prospective	1	0	1
Nonaggressive-Cross-sectional	5	1	0
Rape/Aggression was not a Dependent Variable			
	Positive	Mixed	Negative
Aggressive-Prospective	1	1	1
Aggressive-Cross-sectional	3	2	0
Nonaggressive-Prospective	4	1	3
Nonaggressive-Cross-sectional	20	4	3

dependent variable to all other studies. Only the studies using nonrapist samples were included in this analysis to address the question of whether exposure to pornography increases in aggression in the general population. It is likely that the rapist samples differ substantively from college students and other community samples on a variety of dimensions. Twenty-two of 28 (78.6%) studies using rape myth–aggression toward women as a dependent measure reported positive evidence of causal effects. There was a trend for more consistent evidence of causal effects compared to all other studies (Fishers' Exact, $p < .08$).

When this analysis was repeated for studies using aggression against men as the dependent measure (Table 19.4), 9 of 18 studies (50%) reported positive evidence of causal effects. (None of the 18 studied effects long term.) Comparing studies measuring aggression toward women to those measuring aggression toward men as dependent variables, there was more positive evidence of causal effects for studies using aggression toward women–rape myth as a dependent measure (Fishers' Exact, $p < .05$).

Analyzing all studies in terms of stimuli and dependent variables, 15 of the 17 studies that used aggressive stimuli and aggression toward women––rape myth as dependent variables reported causal effects of exposure, one study was negative, and one reported mixed evidence. This was a significantly higher proportion of effects than for studies using nonaggressive stimuli in which 6 of 12 studies had evidence of causal effects (Fisher's Exact, $p < .04$). Therefore, it appears that among those studies that used

TABLE 19.4
Studies in Which Aggressive Behaviors Toward Men was a Dependent Variable

Based on Nonrapist Population
Aggression was a Dependent Variable

	Positive	Mixed	Negative
Aggressive-Prospective	0	0	0
Aggressive-Cross-sectional	3	1	2
Nonaggressive-Prospective	0	0	0
Nonaggressive-Cross-sectional	6	3	3

Aggression was not a Dependent Variable

	Positive	Mixed	Negative
Aggressive-Prospective	8	2	2
Aggressive-Cross-sectional	9	1	0
Nonaggressive-Prospective	5	1	4
Nonaggressive-Cross-sectional	19	2	0

aggressive sexual stimuli, effects of aggression toward women and/or rape myth attitudes were greatest.

Of the studies that used aggression toward women–rape myth as a dependent variable, studies that reported positive evidence of causal effects had shorter exposure times than those that reported mixed or negative evidence ($t = 2.03$, $df = 16$, $p < .06$).

Study of Rapist Populations

Researchers have studied the effects of aggressive sexual materials on rapist populations in order to better understand the basis for the rapist's aggressive behavior and as a tool for needed prediction of such behaviors. Although an attempt has been made to see if deviant sexual arousal may explain or cause deviant sexual acts, limitations remain.

Much of the research to date has focused on the arousal patterns of the rapist to various scenes depicting sexual violence and has shown mixed results. It has been suggested that some men engage in aggressive sex because they are maximally aroused by nonconsent or violent sex, and they prefer such types of sexual behaviors (Baxter, Barbaree, & Marshall, 1986). Findings by Quinsey and associates have been consistent with this theory. Measuring physiological responses to audio aggressive sexual stimulation,

Quinsey et al. reported that rapists showed greater sexual arousal to rape depictions than to scenes of consenting sex as compared to controls (Quinsey & Chaplin, 1984; Quinsey, Chaplin, & Upfold, 1984; Quinsey, Chaplin, & Varney, 1981). Inconsistent with this theory of sexual aggression are findings by Abel, Barlow, Blanchard, and Guild (1977). These researchers also exposed rapists to audiotaped aggressive pornography and measured physiological arousal. Although rapists were equally aroused to rape and consenting sex whereas nonrapists were less aroused by rape, rapists did not show a preference for rape. Additional studies have shown that rapists and nonrapists are similar in their arousal patterns to rape and consent scenes; rapists show similar or less arousal to rape depictions compared to nonrapists (Baxter et al., 1986; Wydra, Marshall, Earls, & Barbaree, 1983), and both were similar in their ability to discern the inappropriateness of certain sexual cues (Wydra et al., 1983).

There are limitations to this body of literature that must be considered before making any conclusions. The subjects employed came from variable environments: penitentiaries, psychiatric institutions, and public and private evaluation services for sexual deviation, making generalizability among this population difficult. Additionally, aggressive behaviors toward women were not directly measured. Perhaps measures similar to those employed with the nonrapist population, provocation, shock administration, and measures of lessened sensitivity toward women, would clarify the relationship between pornography and aggression motivation in the rapist population.

Discussion

Experimental studies of effects of pornography reveal that exposure to sexually explicit nonviolent materials resulted in mixed effects. Whereas there is evidence that behavioral effects occur after short-term exposure to erotica, effects appear to dissipate over time (Brown, Amoroso, & Ware, 1976). Studies measuring arousal (Eccles, Marshall, & Barbaree, 1988; Schaefer & Coglan, 1977) and attitudinal (Padgett, Brislin-Slutz, & Neal, 1989; Zillmann & Bryant, 1982, 1986, 1988) effects due to nonaggressive sexual materials also revealed mixed result, including satiation effects, callousness toward women, and lessened sensitivity toward rape victims.

Two studies measuring arousal are particularly noteworthy. When measuring penile response (Eccles et al., 1988), after exposing subjects to films depicting heterosexual and homosexual activities, a decrease in arousal both within and across sessions was found. Schaefer and Colgan (1977) found opposite results. In this study of eight males, a passage describing heterosexual activity was followed by either nonpornographic material or ejaculation. Men experiencing immediate sexual gratification showed greater penile response to nonviolent pornography over time. This study employed a very small sample but is the only study that has explicitly observed the effects of pornography under conditions of sexual gratification. The use of sexual gratification as an independent variable may be beneficial for future study of the effects of nonaggressive and aggressive pornography.

Often pornographic materials are consumed in association with sexual gratification (e.g., Carter, Prentky, Knight, Vanderveer, & Boucher, 1987). The viewing of pornography is associated with masturbation or some interactional sexual encounter. Of the more than 8,000 subjects studied in the reviewed investigations, only two experienced any form of sexual gratification as a measured variable (Schafer & Coglan, 1977). The effects from the two subjects were strong enough to provide statistical significance in a comparison with the six other subjects – evidence of a large effect size.

There is substantial reason to suspect that sexual gratification is a potentially powerful reinforcer of the consumption of pornography and thus may also have a significant impact on the effects of this exposure. There is a clinical literature that has demonstrated that masturbatory fantasies are important in the etiology and clinical manifestations of sexual deviance (MacCulloch, Snowden, Wood, & Mills, 1983). There is also evidence that masturbatory fantasy can be altered through pairing masturbation with exposure to specific sexually explicit materials (Goldfried & Davison, 1977). Thus, the potential importance of pairing exposure to pornography with sexual stimulation and gratification is dramatic.

When categorizing all studies using rape–aggression toward women as a dependent variable, there was a trend toward these studies reporting evidence for causal effects. Seventy-eight percent of these studies provided consistent evidence that exposure to pornography had negative effects on attitudes or behavior toward women. In particular, when aggressive sexual stimuli was studied for its effects on aggressive behaviors–attitudes toward women, the evidence for causal effects is greatest. Effects were seen in arousal (Check & Malamuth, 1983; Malamuth & Check, 1980b), negative attitudes (Linz, Donnerstein, & Penrod, 1988; Malamuth, Heim, & Feshbach, 1980; Mayerson & Taylor, 1987; Zillmann & Bryant, 1982), and aggressive behaviors (Donnerstein, 1980; Donnerstein & Berkowitz, 1981) toward women. Effects on attitude reveal that after exposure to pornography men judged rape victims to be less injured, resisting less, and experiencing less trauma. Further, when assured of anonymity, about half the men surveyed expressed some likelihood of raping (from 27% to a high of 69%). This self-report likelihood of rape is correlated with sexual arousal to rape stimuli, callous attitudes toward rape, and self-reported sexual arousal toward aggressive sexual stimuli (Malamuth, 1986; Malamuth & Check, 1980b). Baron and Staus (1989) found a significant positive relationship between the circulation rates of adult magazines and rape rates; the present findings are consistent with these.

Exposure to sexually explicit rape scenes that portray a positive outcome (scenes in which the rape victim became aroused) rather than negative outcomes (rape victim experiences disgust) produced higher levels of arousal (Malamuth & Check, 1980b), contributed to men's beliefs in a similar rape myth (Malamuth & Check, 1985), produced an increase in the self-reported likelihood of rape (Malamuth, 1981), and increased aggression in some subjects (Donnerstein & Berkowitz, 1981).

Interestingly, the effects of pornography and aggression do not appear to be specific to men. Research studying the aggressive effects of women against other women has shown evidence that, when presented with either aggressive or nonaggressive pornographic stimuli, women have aggressed against other women (Baron, 1979). Additionally, the trivialization of rape and rape myths by women subjects were present after exposure to sexual materials (Malamuth, Check, & Briere, 1986; Zillmann & Bryant, 1982).

A related question is whether exposure to various types of pornographic materials would have similar effects on aggressive behavior toward males and females. It appears that exposure to aggressive stimuli is most likely to lead to aggression toward women compared to aggression toward men. Donnerstein and Berkowitz (1981) showed that aggressive–erotic films (victim enjoyed or reacted negatively) increased aggression to a female confederate, whereas there was no increased aggression toward a male as a function of film exposure. Donnerstein (1980) reported similar results concerning a female confederate. As aggression was highest after viewing the aggressive–erotic film when paired with a female, subjects paired with a male confederate in both the erotic and aggressive–erotic conditions showed increased aggression beyond the neutral film. Finally, using male and female targets, Donnerstein and Hallam (1978) exposed college males to a film depicting heterosexual activity or an aggressive film. Both the aggressive and the erotic films immediately increased aggression to males and females. After a 10-minute delay, the aggressive film increased aggression to males, whereas the erotic film increased aggression to females.

Baron (1979) suggested that exposure to sexual imagery that evokes patterns of affect and arousal responses in males and females will lead to comparable levels of subsequent aggression. However, the specific characteristics of the stimuli (thematic content) that stimulates positive, negative, ambivalent, and neutral responses may differ greatly for males and females (White, 1979). It may be the extent to which one identifies with content of the stimuli that produces intensity of responses leading to dissimilar and varying reactions toward males and females; and perhaps such a process is present regarding aggressive pornography. The typical rape scenario is the victimization of a female eventually experiencing arousal. As past research suggests, exposure to such a portrayal contributed to belief in rape myth (Malamuth & Check, 1985) and produced an increase in self-report likelihood or raping (Malamuth, 1981), which may lead to an acceptance of violence against women and callous attitudes toward rape (Malamuth, 1986; Malamuth & Check, 1980), thus leading to an acceptance of the "common" rape scenario. Additionally, it may be easier for the male to place a female in the role of victim rather than himself or another male. Acceptance and personal distance from victim identification may make it easier to accept sexual violence against women and contribute to the degree and prevalence of aggressive behaviors toward women reported in the literature.

Although this study could be conceptualized as a form of meta-analysis, it is not one by the traditional definition (Glass, McGaw, & Smith, 1981). The present systematic analysis uses the presence of statistical significance in an experimental design as evidence for a potential causal effect (Cook & Campbell, 1979). Thus, the effect size for each study is adjusted by the degrees of freedom (sample size) into a significance level. Meta-analysis traditionally combines unadjusted effect sizes and then tests whether or not the literature-wide average effect size is different from zero.

There are several reasons why a traditional meta-analysis is not optimal for the present review. First, estimation of a per-study effect size requires a level of detail regarding study data that is not consistently available, particularly for older studies. This results in the exclusion of some studies. Second, average effect size gives added weight to studies with inordinately large effects. Large effects are particularly common in small studies. Thus, traditional meta-analysis can be subject to overestimates (the mean is an overestimate when a distribution is skewed) or estimates that give greater importance to smaller studies. The present review looks at the consistency of effects instead, giving equal weight to each study. Third, each of the studies included involved multiple outcome measures, some of these measured over multiple intervals. Decisions on which time frame to use for effect size estimation would be inordinately complicated introducing the potential for misleading results. Finally, the interpretation of an average effect size is complicated. Beyond saying that it is significantly different from zero, little else is learned. For example, the literature-wide effect size of psychotherapy was estimated to be 0.27 (Glass et al., 1981). Without some frame of reference, this number provides little knowledge.

The present synthesis of findings demonstrates that well beyond chance studies of the effects of pornography reliably and consistently report causal effects. The consistency of these findings is particularly pronounced for aggressive, sexually explicit stimuli and for stimuli present in written form.

These findings must be considered within the context of the methodological flaws inherent in this literature. First, the samples tended to be ones of convenience: nonrandom samples of college males. One might reasonably posit that the high level of education of these individuals might buffer against negative effects of exposure. Second, in most cases exposure time was minimal. It is unlikely that a 10-minute viewing of pornographic materials is generalizable to how sexually explicit products are actually consumed. The issue of exposure time is also worthy of further note. It would be reasonable to propose that, if there are effects of a little exposure, there should be bigger effects with more exposure. However, it appears that the opposite may be more likely to be true; that is, the more exposure the less the effect. This is consistent with the satiation effect model of exposure that states that boredom or habituation reduce the effects of pornographic stimuli with increased exposure. Unfortunately, the absence of any studies that address this hypothesis within the context of sexual gratification is very problematic. Viewing sexually explicit materials for an extended period may hold the attention of a few individuals. However, viewing these materials as they are paired with sexual stimulation and gratification might have very different effects.

The findings regarding type of media are also noteworthy. It appears that written stories have the most consistent effects followed by audiotapes and then visual stimuli. The implications these findings have for understanding the impact of "phone-sex" services is provocative. One can only speculate as to the mechanism of this effect, but it is tempting to postulate that written and audio stimuli allow for greater latitude in personalizing sexual fantasies.

CONCLUSIONS

Despite methodological shortcomings, the empirical research on the effects of aggressive pornography shows, with fairly impressive consistency, that exposure to these materials has a negative effect on attitudes toward women and perceived likelihood to rape. Although there are a number of methodological shortcomings in this literature, most are likely to lead to an underestimation of the causal effects of exposure to pornography. Despite this, the vast majority of studies demonstrates consistent short-term effects.

It is clear from the literature that not everyone exposed to aggressive pornography develops negative attitudes toward women, becomes a rapist, or experiences any harm. However, there is sufficient evidence for concern that some individuals may be at risk for harmful effects that could be attributable to the consumption of sexually explicit pornographic materials.

Acknowledgment

The authors would like to acknowledge H. Robert Showers for his assistance in the conceptualization of this chapter.

References

Abel, G. G., Barlow, D. H., Blanchard, E. B., & Guild, D. (1977). The components of rapists' sexual arousal. *Archives of General Psychiatry, 34*, 895–903.

Attorney General's Commission on Pornography. (1986). *Final report of the Attorney General's Commission on Pornography.* Nashville, TN: Rutledge Hill Press.

Bareta, J. C., Larson, D. B., Lyons, J. S., Zorc, J (1990). A comparison of a MEDLARS and systematic review of the consultation-liaison literature. *American Journal of Psychiatry, 147*, 1040–1042.

Baron, R. A. (1974a). The aggression inhibiting influence of of heightened sexual arousal. *Journal of Personality and Social Psychology, 30*, 318–322.

Baron, R. A. (1974b). Sexual arousal and physical aggression: The inhibiting influence of "cheesecake" and nudes. *Bulletin of the Psychonomic Society, 3*, 337–339.

Baron, R. A., & Bell, P. A. (1977). Sexual arousal and aggression by males: Effects of type of erotic stimuli and prior provocation. *Journal of Personality and Social Psychology, 35*, 79–87.

Baron, L, & Straus, M.A. (1989). *Four theories of rape in America society. A state-level analysis.* New Haven, CT: Yale University Press.

Baron, R. A. (1979). Heightened sexual arousal and physical aggression: An extension to females. *Journal of Research in Personality, 13*, 91–102.

Baxter, D. J., Barbaree, H. E., & Marshall, W. L. (1986). Sexual responses to consenting and forced sex in a large sample of rapists and nonrapists. *Behavior Research and Theory, 24*(1), 513–520.

Brown, M. (1979). Viewing time of pornography. *Journal of Psychology, 102*, 83–95.

Brown, M., Amoroso, D. M., & Ware, E. E. (1976). Behavioral effects of viewing pornography. *The Journal of Social Psychology, 98*, 235–245.

Brown, M., Amoroso, D. M., Ware, E. E., Pruesse, M., & Pilkey, D.W. (1973). Factors affecting viewing time of pornography. *Journal of Social Psychology, 90*, 125–135.

Brown, D., & Bryant, J. (1989). The manifest content of pornography. In D. Zillmann & J. Bryant (Eds.), *Pornography: Research advances and policy considerations.* Hillsdale, NJ: Lawrence Erlbaum Associates.

Byrne, D., Fisher, J. D., Lamberth, J., & Mitchell, H. E. (1974). Evaluations of erotica: Facts or feelings. *Journal of Personality and Social Psychology, 29*(1), 111–116.

Carter, D. L., Prentky, R. A., Knight, R. A., Vanderveer, P. L., & Boucher, R. J. (1987). Use of pornography in the criminal and developmental histories of sexual offenders. *Journal of Interpersonal Violence, 2*, 196–211.

Ceniti, J., & Malamuth, N. M. (1984). Effects of repeated exposure to sexually violent or nonviolent stimuli on sexual arousal to rape and nonrape depictions. *Behavioral Research and Therapy, 22*(5), 535–548.

Check, J. V. P., & Malamuth, N. M. (1983). Sex role stereotyping and reactions to depictions of stranger versus acquaintance rape. *Journal of Personality and Social Psychology, 45*, 344–356.

Cook, T., & Campbell, D. T. (1979). *Quasi-experimentation. Design & analysis issues for field setting.* New York: Houghton, Miflin.

Donnerstein, E. (1980). Aggressive erotica and violence against women. *Journal of Personality and Social Psychology*, *19*, 269–277.

Donnerstein, E., & Barrett, G. (1978). Effects of erotic stimuli on male aggression toward females. *Journal of Personality and Social Psychology*, *36*, 180–188.

Donnerstein, E., & Berkowitz, L. (1981). Victim reactions in aggressive erotic films as a factor in violence against women. *Journal of Personality and Social Psychology*, *41*, 710–724.

Donnerstein, E., Donnerstein, M., & Evans, R. (1975). Erotic stimuli and aggression: Facilitation or inhibition. *Journal of Personality and Social Psychology*, *32*(2), 237–244.

Donnerstein, E., & Hallam, J. (1978). Facilitating effects of erotica on aggression against women. *Journal of Personality and Social Psychology*, *36*, 1270–1277.

Donnerstein, E., Linz, D., & Penrod, S. (1987). *The question of pornography*. New York: Free Press.

Eccles, A., Marshall, W. L., & Barbaree, H. E. (1988). The vulnerability of erectile measures to repeated assessments. *Behavior Research and Therapy*, *26*(2), 179–183.

Fehr, F. S., & Schulman, M. (1978). Female self-report and automatic responses to sexually pleasurable and sexually aversive readings. *Archives of Sexual Behavior*, *7*, 443–453.

Fisher, W. A., & Byrne, D. (1978a, October–December). Individual differences in affective, evaluative, and behavioral responses to an erotic film. *Journal of Applied Social Psychology*, *8*, 355–365.

Fisher, W. A., & Byrne, D. (1978b). Sex differences in response to erotica? Love versus lust. *Journal of Personality and Social Psychology*, *36*, 177–125.

George, W. H., & Marlatt, G. A. (1986). The effects of alcohol and anger on interest in violence, erotica, and deviance. *Journal of Abnormal Psychology*, *95*(2), 150–158.

Glass, G. V., McGaw, B., & Smith, M. L. (1981). *Meta-analysis is social research*. Beverly Hills, CA: Sage.

Goldfried, I., & Davison, A. (1977). *Behavior therapy*. Englewood Cliffs, NJ: Prentice-Hall.

Griffitt, W., & Kaiser, D. L. (1978). Affect, sex guilt, gender, and the rewarding–punishing effects of erotic stimuli. *Journal of Personality and Social Psychology*, *36*, 850–858.

Jaffe, Y., Malamuth, N., Feingold, J., & Feshbach, S. (1974). Sexual arousal and behavioral aggression. *Journal of Personality and Social Psychology*, *30*, 759–764.

Kelley, K. (1985a) The effects of sexual and/or aggressive film exposure on helping, hostility, and attitudes about the sexes. *Journal of Research in Personality*, *19*, 472–483.

Kelley, K. (1985b). Sexual attitudes as determinants of the motivational properties of exposure to erotica. *Personality and Individual Differences*, *6*, 391–393.

Kelley, K. (1985c). Sex, sex guilt, and authoritarianism: Differences in responses to explicit heterosexual and masturbatory slides. *Journal of Sex Research*, *21*, 68–85.

Kelley, K., & Musialowski, D. (1986). Repeated exposure to sexually explicit stimuli: Novelty, sex, and sexual attitudes. *Archives of Sexual Behavior*, *15*, 487–498.

Kercher, G. A., & Walker C. E. (1973). Reactions of convicted rapists to sexually explicit stimuli. *Journal of Abnormal Psychology*, *81*, 46–50.

Lang, A. R., Searles, J., Lauerman, R., & Adesso, V. (1980). Expectancy, alcohol, and sex guilt as determinants of interest in and reaction to sexual stimuli. *Journal of Abnormal Psychology*, *89*, 644–653.

Larson, D. B., Lyons, J. S., Hohmann, A. A., Beardsley, R. S., Huckeba, W., Rabins, P. V., Lebowitz, D. B. (1989). A systematic review of nursing home research in three psychiatric journals: 1966-1985. *International Journal of Geriatric Psychiatry*, *4*, 129–134.

Larson, D. B., Sherrill, K. A., Lyons, J. S., Craigie, F. C., Thielman, S. B., Greenwold, M. A., Larson S. S. (1990). Associations between dimensions of religious commitment and mental health reported in the *American Journal of Psychiatry* and *Archives of General Psychiatry*: 1978-1989. *American Journal of Psychiatry*, *149*, 557–559.

Leonard, K. E., & Taylor, S. P. (1983). Exposure to pornography, permissive and non-permissive cues, and male aggression toward females. *Motivation and Emotion, 7*(3) 291–299.

Linz, D. G., Donnerstein, E., & Penrod, S. (1988). Effects of long-term exposure to violent and sexually degrading depictions of women. *Journal of Personality and Social Psychology, 55,* 758–768.

Love, R. E., Sloan, L. R., & Schmidt, M. J. (1976). Viewing pornography and sex guilt: The priggish, the prudent, and the profligate. *Journal of Consulting and Clinical Psychology, 44,* 624–629.

Lyons, J. S., Larson, D. B., Bareta, J. C., Liu, I., Anderson, R. L., & Sparks, C. H. (1990). A systematic analysis of the quantity of AIDS publications and the quality of research methods in three general medical journals. *Evaluation and Program Planning, 13,* 73–77.

MacCulloch, M. J., Snowden, P. R., Wood, P. J. W., & Mills, H. E. (1983). Sadistic fantasy, sadistic behaviour, and offending.*British Journal of Psychiatry, 143,* 20–29.

Malamuth, N. M. (1981). Rape fantasies as a function of exposure to violent sexual stimuli. *Archives of Sexual Behavior, 10,* 33–47.

Malamuth, N. M. (1983). Factors associated with rape as predictors of laboratory aggression against women. *Journal of Personality and Social Psychology, 45,* 432–442.

Malamuth, N. M. (1986). Predictors of naturalistic sexual aggression. *Journal of Personality and Social, 50*(5), 953–962.

Malamuth, N. M., & Centi, J. (1986). Repeated exposure to violent and nonviolent pornography: Likelihood of raping ratings and laboratory aggression against women. *Aggressive Behavior, 12,* 129–137.

Malamuth, N. M., & Check, J. V. P. (1980a). Sexual arousal to rape and consenting depiction: The importance of the woman's arousal. *Journal of Abnormal Psychology, 89*(6), 763–766.

Malamuth, N. M., & Check, J. V. P. (1980b). Penile tumescence and perceptual responses to rape as a function of victim's perceived reactions. *Journal of Applied Social Psychology, 10,* 528–547.

Malamuth, N. M., & Check, J. V. P. (1983). Sexual arousal to rape depictions: Individual differences. *Journal of Abnormal Psychology, 92,* 55–67.

Malamuth, N. M., & Check, J. V. P. (1985). The effects of aggressive pornography on beliefs in rape myths: Individual differences. *Journal of Research in Personality, 19,* 299–320.

Malamuth, N. M., Check, J. V. P., & Briere, J. (1986). Sexual arousal in response to aggression: Idiological, aggressive, and sexual correlates. *Journal of Personality and Social Psychology, 50,* 330–340.

Malamuth, N. M., Haber, S., & Feshbach, S. (1980). Testing hypotheses regarding rape: Exposure to sexual violence, sex differences, and the "normality" of rapists. *Journal of Research in Personality, 14,* 121–137.

Malamuth, N. M., Heim, M., & Feshbach, S. (1980). Sexual responsiveness of college students to rape depictions: Inhibitory and disinhibitory effects. *Journal of Personality and Social Psychology, 38,* 399–408.

Mann, J., Berkowitz, L., Sidman J., Starr S., & West, S. (1974). Satiation of the transient stimulating effect of erotic films. *Journal of Personality and Social Psychology, 30,* 729–735.

Mann, J., Sidman, J., & Starr, S. (1973). Evaluating social consequences of erotic films: An experimental approach. *Journal of Social Issues, 29,* 113–131.

Mayerson, S. E., & Taylor, D. A. (1987). The effects of rape myth pornography on women's attitudes and the mediating role of sex role stereotyping. *Sex Roles, 17* (5/6), 321–338.

Meyer, T. P. (1962). The effects of sexually arousing and violent films on aggressive behavior. *Journal of Sex Research, 8,* 324–331.

Mosher, D. L. (1973). Sex differences, sex experience, sex guilt, and explicitly sexual films. *Journal of Social Issues, 29,* 95–112.

Mulrow, C. (1987). Needed: review articles with more scientific rigor. *Archives of Internal Medicine, 106*, 470–471.

Padgett, V. R., Brislin-Slutz, J., & Neal, J. A. (1989). Pornography, erotica, and attitudes toward women: The effects of repeated exposure. *Journal of Sex Research, 26*(4), 479–491.

Quinsey, V. L., & Chaplin, T. C. (1984). Stimulus control of rapists' and non-sex offenders' sexual arousal. *Behavioral Assessment, 6*, 169–176.

Quinsey, V. L., Chaplin, T. C., & Upfold, D. (1984). Sexual arousal to nonsexual violence and sadomasochistic themes among rapists and non-sex-offenders. *Journal of Consulting and Clinical Psychology, 52*, 651–657.

Quinsey, V. L., Chaplin, T. C., & Varney, G. (1981). A comparison of rapists' and non-sex offenders' sexual preference for mutually consenting sex, rape, and physical abuse of women. *Behavioral Assessment, 3*, 127–135.

Ramirez, J., Bryant, J., & Zillmann, D. (1982). Effects of erotica on retaliatory behavior as a function of level of prior provocation. *Journal of Personality and Social Psychology, 43*, 971–978.

Reed, J. P., & Reed, R. (1972). P.R.U.D.E.S. *Journal of Sex Research, 8*, 237–246.

Sapolsky, B. S., & Zillmann, D. (1981). The effect of soft-core and hard-core erotica on provoked and unprovoked hostile behavior. *Journal of Sex Research, 17*, 319–343.

Schaefer, H. H., & Coglan, A. H. (1977). The effect of pornography on penile tumescence as a function of reinforcement and novelty. *Behavior Therapy, 8*, 938–946.

Schill, T., Evans, R., Monroe, S., & Drain, D. (1975). Effects of approval or disapproval on reading behavior of high-and low-guilt subjects. *Journal of Consulting and Clinical Psychology, 43*, 104.

Schill, T., Van Tuinen, M., & Doty, D. (1980). Repeated exposure to pornography and arousal levels of subjects varying in guilt. *Psychological Reports, 46*, 467–471.

Stauffer, J., & Frost, R. (1976). Male and female interest in sexually-oriented magazines. *Journal of Communication*, 25–30.

Wallace, D. H., & Wehmer, G. (1971). Pornography and attitude change. *Journal of Sex Research, 7*, 116–125.

Weaver, J. B., Masland, J. L., & Zillmann, D. (1984). Effect of erotica on young men's aesthetic perception of their female sexual partners. *Perceptual and Motor Skills, 58*, 929–930.

White, L. A. (1979). Erotica and aggression: The influence of sexual arousal, positive affect, and negative affect on aggressive behavior. *Journal of Personality and social Psychology, 37*, 591–601.

Wishnoff, R. (1978). Modeling effects of explicit and nonexplicit sexual stimuli on the sexual anxiety and behavior of women. *Archives of Sexual Behavior, 7*, 455–461.

Wydra, A., Marshall, W. L., Earls, C. M., & Barbaree, H. E. (1983). Identification of cues and control of sexual arousal by rapists. *Behavior Research and Therapy, 21*, 469–476.

Young, M. (1979). Sexual attitudes and behavior of female readers and non-readers of erotic literature. *Psychological Reports, 45*, 932–934.

Zillmann, D., & Bryant, J (1982). *Journal of Communication, 32*, 10–21.

Zillmann, D., & Bryant, J. (1986). Shifting preferences in pornography consumption. *Communication Research, 13*(4), 560–578.

Zillmann, D., & Bryant, J. (1988). Pornography's impact on sexual satisfaction. *Journal of Applied Social Psychology, 18*, 438–453.

Zillmann, D., Bryant, J., & Carveth, R. A. (1981). The effect of erotica featuring sadomasochism and bestiality on motivated intermale aggression. *Personality and Social Psychology Bulletin, 7*(1), 153–159.

Zillmann, D., Bryant, J., Comisky, P. W., & Medoff, N. J. (1981). Excitation and hedonic valence in the effect of erotica on motivated intermale aggression. *European Journal of Social Psychology, 11*, 233–252.

Zillmann, D., Hoyt, J. L., & Day, K. (1974). Strength and duration of the effect of aggressive, violent, and erotic communications on subsequent aggressive behavior. *Communication Research, 1*(3), 286–306.

Zillmann, D., & Sapolsky, B. S. (1977). What mediates the effect of mild erotica on annoyance and hostile behavior in males? *Journal of Personality and Social Psychology, 35,* 587–596.

Part VI

SOCIAL AWARENESS AND PUBLIC POLICY

20

CHILD PORNOGRAPHY IN EROTIC MAGAZINES, SOCIAL AWARENESS, AND SELF-CENSORSHIP

Judith A. Reisman
Institute For Media Education Arlington, Virginia

Although it is understood that accepted scientific research findings can dramatically affect legislative, judicial, and individual conduct, it is less recognized that even hotly contested social-science research findings can also quietly affect changes in conduct by the agents under scrutiny.

The American people are unusual among the world's population for many reasons, one of which is their ability to successfully lobby the extant power structure or businesses for social change. American "special interest" and consumer groups garner funds and political "clout" to protect whales and dolphins, to leverage for their own pro or antireligious views, to urge medical preference for AIDS or breast cancer research, to end or increase privileges for the tobacco, liquor, and marijuana industries, and so on.

The Supreme Court of Canada unanimously ruled in February 1992 that pornography harms women and is generally no longer acceptable in that Northern clime (*New York Times*, February 28, 1992, B7). Here in the United States, family rights' groups are joining with other environmental lobbyists to campaign for the strengthening of laws on "second-hand pornography effects" as well as for tougher penalties for sex offenses, illegal drug use, and other criminal acts. Whereas government prosecution and imprisonment is surely a crime deterrent, few people are aware that good social-science research can facilitate self-correction in some borderline industries that elude legal penalties.

In 1984, with a trained staff and several skilled peer consultants, I undertook the role of principal investigator for a Department of Justice-funded analysis of the three largest selling "soft" pornography magazines in the United States of America. The findings, *Images of Children, Crime and Violence in "Playboy," "Penthouse" and "Hustler"* (Reisman, 1989), identified these influential magazines as having mainstreamed child pornography[1] into our nation for three decades since (1954) *Playboy's* first full year of publication.

With findings of child pornography and glamorized rape in *Playboy, Penthouse*, and *Hustler*, the research effort sustained an onerous legislative, academic, and press firestorm during and following project closure in 1985. The two key senators who had battled to terminate the research project were found to have shared an undisclosed "conflict of interest" regarding pornography magazines. Senator Arlen Specter received funds from a pornography profiteer (*Washington Times*, March 18, 1992), and Senator Howard Metzenbaum accredited *Penthouse* by a generous interview (*Penthouse*, November 1982).

On the academic front, I had been very puzzled as to why my host institution, The American University, had been so hostile, allowing brazen efforts to undermine our research on child pornography. When a key research opponent, American University's psychology chairman, Dr. Elliot McGinnies, was arrested for sexually abusing a child in his trailer at a nudist colony (*The Washington Post*, September 19, 1986), things seemed clearer. All the more so when this University's president, Dr. Richard Berendzen, was found with child pornography after his own arrest for child sex-related offenses (*The Washington Post*, September 23, 1990).

By 1992 the Department of Juvenile Justice and Delinquency Prevention expressed its thanks for the rigor and accuracy of the methodology and the usefulness of the report on *"Images of Children, Crime and Violence in Playboy, Penthouse and Hustler."* (Reisman, 1989).[2] Whereas the academic community, the press, and federal agencies had disdained our findings, the

---

[1]*Pornography* is defined here using the Attorney General's Commission on Pornography (1986) definition as "material [which is] sexually explicit and intended primarily for the purpose of sexual arousal" (see esp. p. 2). *Child pornography* refers to any imagery or language that exploits/uses children in a sexual context.

[2]See the official September 13, 1991 letter from Department of Justice, Office of Juvenile Justice and Delinquency Prevention (OJJDP) Administrator Alfred Regnery—that OJJDP "Images" research product was fully peer approved and was a product of correct and appropriate scientific methodology—fraudulent mass media and sex industry claims to the contrary.

magazines themselves busily initiated self-censorship. For, the magazine data were presented in two U.S. Supreme Court child pornography cases (*Osbone v. OH*, 1990 and *Oakes v. MA*, 1989), were cited in at least one child sex abuse conviction (*California v. Tinsely*, 1990), as well as by Southland 7-11 Corporation in their letter of April 10, 1986, when they determined to divest from sales of *Playboy and Penthouse*.

Content-Analysis Revelations

The study findings were certainly more damaging than expected. Sexual and violent scenes involving children were a magazine genre motif. After narrowing the "child" criterion, instead of the original 9,000 "children," 6,004 child images (persons under 18) were found in *Playboy, Penthouse,* and *Hustler*, on average nine times per issue with most of these in sexual or violent scenes. Of the child themes, a surprising 29% involved scenes with nude or genital displays, 20% genital activity, 16% included a sexual encounter with an adult, 10% force, 10% killing or maiming, 6% *pink* (the pornographic term for exposing the internal lips of the vaginal walls), and 4% sex with animals or objects.

From 1954 to 1984 *Playboy*[3] averaged 8 child images per issue (5% of their total imagery), *Penthouse* 6 child images per issue (4% of their total imagery), and *Hustler* 14 child images per issue (12% of their total imagery). The child themes were juxtaposed with almost 15,000 images of crime and violence, laced within 45,000 frames of female breasts and female genitalia. Thematically, adult sex with small girls and boys—even uncles, dads, grandfathers, moms, aunts—was modeled in *all* magazines as fun, harmless, and even beneficial to the child victims.

Another unanticipated finding involved pernicious sexual consequences. Although the magazines editorially suggested they fulfilled a need for sex education, marriage was modeled as repugnant while wives (fat–ugly) were commonly cartooned as copulating with the family dog or other beast—in all three publications. Moreover, sexual harassment in the workplace, out-of-wedlock pregnancy and rape of women and children were uniformly cartooned as humorous. Whereas sex with same-age and older children was rare in the magazines (60 cases) when compared to sex with adults (over 1,000 cases), venereal disease (10 cases), AIDS, herpes, syphilis, gonorrhea scenes were entirely negligible.

---

[3]Although *Playboy* began publication in December 1953, the first child pornography (images of children sexually associated with adults) appeared at first as a series of cartoons in 1954.

Self-Censorship in Action

As would be anticipated, *Playboy, Penthouse*, and *Hustler* publishers were cognizant that a candid analysis of their product would yield the preceding data on media toxicity. Hence, immediately following the announcement of the plans for this research project, agencies and individuals economically tied to *Playboy* and *Penthouse* (Reisman, 1990)[4] initiated vigorous objections to the study as both government waste and a threat to free speech.

Despite our child pornography research findings, to my knowledge, the sex industry fully retains its free speech. Nonetheless, having said this, *Playboy, Penthouse*, and *Hustler* concerns regarding the impact of these data on their product sales were prudent.

Typical of the sex industry, *Playboy* publisher, Hugh Hefner, had long censored negative remarks about his magazine. One of Hefner's many deferential biographers reprinted the publisher's memo to his editorial staff (Reisman, 1991):

> In the future, pick the Letters To The Editor on the basis of their interest value. Do not feel obliged a la TIME MAGAZINE to give both sides and to include a lot of stuff that is negative about the magazine. We assume that most of our readers dig us so we don't have to include lots of letters calling us homosexuals or sex nuts. . . . Pick the letters, as I said, for . . . what they continually do to build the image of the magazine. (p. 64)

An examination of the "Letters" columns confirms Hefner's censorship policy. Although many pornography victims (see the Attorney General's Commission on Pornography, July 1986) have testified to *Playboy's* role in their victimization, no such serious grievances of incest, rape, or wifely humiliation appear among the magazine "Letters." This December 1985 "Letter To The Editor" excerpt, then, is a sign that *Playboy* received too many of the following communiqués to ignore:

> I am enclosing an article I just read in *The NewPaper* (Providence, Rhode Island). It seems to be saying that *Playboy*, as well as *Penthouse* and *Hustler*, regularly publishes pornographic cartoons of children. I have been reading PLAYBOY for years and know that to be untrue. . . . I think your magazine should force those folks to print a retraction.

---

[4]In Reisman (1990), I address the June 5, 1986 Gray and Company letter written to the Media Coalition. Gray, a highly placed Washington, DC public relations firm with extensive ties to the Department of Justice and the White House, wrote to the Media Coalition, a media conglomerate funded by the *Playboy* Foundation, proposing at a cost of up to "$900,000 during the first year" for "discrediting the organizations and individuals who have begun to seriously disrupt" sales of pornography (p. 4). On the evidence, the Reisman project was chosen for such a "discrediting" campaign. See especially Trento (1992) for this expose.

Playboy's December 1985 reply was, that the research to which the reader referred was the "Reisman" study:

To which we say. . . . If other magazines are publishing cartoons of "gang rapes of children, fathers sexually abusing daughters, benevolent or father figures raping or murdering young girls," PLAYBOY never has, never will. Our readers know that. And lying with statistics is still lying. (p. 16)

Playboy did not seek a "retraction," for on the graphic evidence, each year for 30 years, publisher Hefner personally culled about 400 cartoons from roughly 200,000 submissions. Until very recently the *Playboy* publisher selected all the magazine cartoons (Reisman, 1991). Thus he mindfully selected and published the monthly child cartoons that included "gang rapes of children" and sexual abuse by benevolent father (and mother) figures."[5]

The distribution of the Executive Summary, with its graphic anthology of child pornography examples in *Playboy, Penthouse*, and *Hustler*, troubled many of the magazine consumers who saw the 24-page précis. In February 1986, *Playboy* finally reprinted one of what appear to have been many negative "Letters to the Editor"—this one allegedly from a Kentucky doctor who had subscribed to PLAYBOY "for several years." Although he did not consciously recall seeing child pornography, apparently something nagged at his subconscious memory, for the doctor concluded with a plea to the publication:

Please comment on this Justice Department study and its validity, if any. I'm opposed to cartoons involving child pornography per se, but I'd have canceled my subscription to Playboy long ago if I had considered it to be a conduit for such cartoons.

Playboy did not answer Fuson's direct question about "cartoons involving child pornography per se." Instead, the editor simply said:

It wouldn't be news if the other magazines published such cartoons, so we're included in the "top three" just to get the public's attention. . . . It's also convenient, unfortunately, to refer to all "adult" magazines as Playboys. (p. 44)

Two years later, in a *New York City Tribune* article (March 30, 1988), page 1 carried an article entitled, "Child-Sex Cartoons and Photographs Common in Adult Magazines, Study Says." *Playboy's* general counsel and

---

[5]Although this volume could not include the original cartoons and photographs included in Reisman (1989), those desiring a copy of the report can contact the author.

past chairman of the Media Coalition, Burton Joseph, was reported as stating that pornographic child pictures in *Playboy* are "extremely rare and occurred mostly in older issues." While he admitted that *Playboy* does run cartoons with children being sexually molested, he said they were meant to be "commentaries of societies' defects." Joseph also faulted Reisman's study for overcounting incidents of child-related cartoons in *Playboy*. He said Reisman counted each panel of a several-page long comic strip as a separate cartoon, thus inflating the numbers.

On "Oprah Winfrey," and elsewhere, Joseph also asserted as before, that our research counted every panel of "Little Annie Fannie" and thus obtained high numbers of child pornography in his magazine.[6] However, Joseph had allegedly read our report and thus would know that no comic strips or comic strip characters (e.g., "Little Annie Fannie") were included in our research methodology—due only to time limitations.

Bequeathed: Thirty Years of Child Pornography "Humor"

The idea that children could be happily sexual with adults first appeared in a May 1954 *Playboy* cartoon. By November 1954 the *Playboy* publisher felt sufficiently secure about his constituency to have one of his more popular artists, "Cole," cartoon the following:

> The scene: A woman's bedroom. A nude toddler, something less than two-years old, stands before a bed. The tot, pulling his tiny clown toy behind him, is grinning widely as he holds out a shiny coin to his nude mom-sis (or other kin) who sits, bored on her bed. A giant cash register is her headboard, and an hour-glass is prominently displayed on her bedstand. The woman is eying the little boy with her finger poised on the "NO SALE" sign of the cash register. The title of the cartoon is "The Pro" and we viewer-participants— millions wholly unfamiliar with the normal behavior and development of children—are left to wonder whether the smiling baby has just been sexually serviced or if he is just offering to pay for the sex he clearly desires.

These are cruel lies about the sexuality of innocent little tots, toddlers just beginning to talk and walk, boys who would still be nursing from a bottle, babes who sweetly sleep with stuffed animals, kiss their teddy bears "good-night," and who play with their little toy cars for hours.

Such "jokes" about little boys seeking (incestuous) sex with adult women were shortly followed by similarly callous lies sexualizing small girls who are allegedly unharmed by adult rapists. By November 1972 *Playboy* found an

---

[6]See Reisman (1989) regarding *Playboy* denial of child pornography cartoons and/or photos or illustrations in its own publications as well as press clippings in December 1985.

artist, Bill Lee, who would pose a 2-year-old girl soliciting sex from an adult man.

> Scene: Outdoor, blank background. A man holds a candy cane out to a tiny, hair-bowed girl who says "No, thank you, nice man, I don't want to go for a ride in your car. Why don't we just go to my place and ball?"

September 1969 *Playboy's* Hugh Hefner found Marty Murphy, who cartooned a great deal of the child pornography for *Playboy*.

> The scene: A girls' schoolbus is stopped on the side of the road. A policeman is walking toward his motorcycle as he is pulling up his pants. The activity in the schoolbus reveals that the officer has just had sex with all of the little girls and the teenagers on the schoolbus. The half-nude head mistress, who apparently also had sex with the officer, sits at the wheel and angrily remarks to the children as they put on their dresses that even after they all had sex with him, she was worried the officer would "give us a ticket *anyway!*"

In February 1971 incest began to appear more regularly as child sex abuse "humor."

> Scene: A middle-class living room. *Playboy's* "Cole" drew an old man fantasizing his naked granddaughter posing for him.

In March 1972 *Playboy* continued to desensitize its readers—media participants—with a full-color, full-page, elegantly designed "Ffolkers" child pornography cartoon. Ffolkers used a traditionist's artistic style to market his child pornography—adult assaults with "old fashioned" costumes and frilly decor.

> Scene: An upper-middle class child's well-appointed, Victorian-style bedroom. A small naked girl of about 6 or 8 years (cartooned with typically *Playboy* exaggerated breasts) is in bed with an enormous teddy bear twice her size. An upscale, middle-age dad–kin is pulling off his pants to have sex with the child, when she smilingly warns that "Teddy" says she must charge $40 for the sex.

In March 1978 *Playboy*-Ffolkes provided a full-color, full-page "Child Magnet" cartoon, exploiting a key feature in what we called "The Culture of Childhood," the child's fairy tale.

> Scene: The "Yellow Brick Road." A prepubescent, half-nude Dorothy of the Wizard of Oz is sprawled on the road with her blouse ripped open and her (*Playboy*) exaggerated breasts exposed. Dorothy has just been raped by her

happy "Wizard" surrogate family protectors—the Lion, the Straw Man, and the Tin Man. The three Wizard child rapists are whistling off into the distance having left the child on the ground,complaining to an unresponsive policeman about her assault, saying, "That's them officer!"

In May 1974 the Hefner–Ffolkes' "happy incest" theme continued to desensitize *Playboy* reader–participants.

Scene: An old man's bedroom. Another naked little girl of roughly 8 years is in bed with an old man. The curly-top "Shirley Temple" child (with exaggerated breasts) is talking to her mom on the phone. She says she and grinning "Uncle William" are playing a game of "consequences."

This is typical of the magazines' "child entrapment" themes that often have a "clever" adult male who tricks a child into sex by saying this will cure her hiccups, fix a headache, as her "consequence" for losing her game, and so on.

Eight years later, November 1982, cartoonist Bill Lee of *Penthouse* humorized another adult rape of children.

Scene: A hotel bedroom. A nude child of about 6 years, in bed with a nude corpulent man, is also talking to her mom on the phone. The child abuse theme is now political (anti-conservative) as the child tells mom she just met this man and he is a "leader of the Moral Majority on Capitol Hill."

The November 1982 political child sex abuse theme is repeated several pages earlier in a man-rapes-boy cartoon.

Scene: Abstract background. A young boy is cartooned being (orally) sodomized by a politician. The boy's parents sent him to Washington to learn, but he says he did not realize he would be "dessert." The elderly adult offender's face—busily buried in the boy's crotch—is invisible to the viewer.

The same November 1982 *Penthouse* issue that humorized rape of both a girl and a boy in two separate cartoons also featured an apparently paid interview with *Penthouse* supporter Senator Howard Metzenbaum (D-OH), alongside a full-page, full-color portrait of the Senator. Three years later, Metzenbaum—a lawyer—instead of recusing himself from involvement in our *Playboy–Penthouse* study, concealed his *Penthouse* relationship and interests and tried to legislatively halt our proposed study as a waste of taxpayers money.

Playboy and *Penthouse*, upon the announcement of our research project, began internal housecleaning—purging the child abuse and rape photos and cartoons they had ritualized since magazine inception (Reisman, 1989). Cartoonists documented as specializing in child–adult sex scenes (e.g., *Playboy's* Buck Brown, Jack Dempsey,Ffolkes, Mal, and *Penthouse's* Bill Lee and Revilo),[7] suddenly began cartooning adult subject matter — with "funny" child abuse and rapes now few and far between.

It should be noted that *Hustler* child molestation counts in Ventura, California, March 1990. In personal correspondence (March 28, 1990 from Det. Sgt. Anthony Harper III, Simi Valley, California) the prosecutor stated that he had used the Reisman research "as a reference source for putting together his closing arguments, and for his cross examination of Mr. Tinsley" (Tinsley, like *Playboy* chief counsel, Burton Joseph, had claimed his child pornography cartoons were really social commentary). Tinsley's young victim was his daughter. She testified that Tinsley's "Chester the Molester" cartoons were an ongoing record of 5 years of her incestuous victimization.

At the time this article goes to press, after 2 years in prison, the Court of Appeals ruled that Tinsley should be released because the prosecution should not have shown the jury Tinsley's child sex abuse art, as these cartoons clearly "inflamed" the "passions" of the jury. Daniel Lungren, Attorney General of the State of California, has challenged the Court of Appeals, and the case appears to be moving toward a higher court.

A point that Dwaine Tinsley establishes is that an artists' product generally reflects the values and often even the conduct of said artist — and that of his vender. Hence, one must be able to first imagine and then enjoy the idea of raping children in order to make this artistic statement, or in order to market such "humor" as ones' product (see Reisman, 1991, for a fuller discussion of this issue).

It should be noted that "even" *Playboy* exploited children in *photos* with men. For example, in November 1971 a *Playboy* photo posed a naked child asleep. Clutching her Raggedy Ann doll with bobby-sox and hair bows as her only "clothes," consumers were sexually cued to "Come on Strong, Big Daddy" for the "cuddly type above . . . digs forceful father figures." In a *Playboy* November 1976 photograph, a man raped a half-nude "Retarded Numphette." In August 1975 a naked teenager was chained to the metal post of a bed, sexually provoking the consumer, awaiting to be "punished" by her "family." In November 1980 *Playboy* printed a photo of a father about to (orally) sodomize his nightgowned daughter, and one of the last child sex exploitation photos was a July 1985 waist-to-toes photostory surrounding a naked knocked-kneed, "Young Girl" . . . [and her] "Rubber Ducky."[8]

---

[7]See the "Child Cartoonists" listing taken from Reisman (1989, p. 155).
[8]Most of these examples may be found in Reisman (1989).

Monitoring Child Pornography After 1985

The pornography industry worked to cripple legislative efforts to initiate age 21 as the age of consent for pornographic posing.[9] Similarly, a "reporting" component for age 18 is now being fought by the sex industry,[10] as is the "Pornography Victims Compensation Act" currently proposed by Senator Mitch McConnell (R-KY). That the industry requires youth is a given. Therefore, as our research forced *Playboy, Penthouse,* and *Hustler* into self-censorship, it was likely child images would be worked into the visual motifs in more devious and insurgent ways.

Post-1985 *Playboy, Penthouse,* and *Hustler* photos were found to include cosmetically airbrushed, long-legged, and genitally shaved (child) women posed alongside a text that, "recalls" the women as a "child." Or, women were posed reliving alleged teenage bobby-sox sexual adventures in nude photostories, and so forth. Having largely censored children from Playmate biographies, post our 1985 research, the September 1991 *Playboy* just resurrected 'The-Playmate-Child' (a "Sixth-Grade" photo) that the art editor juxtaposed next to the (naked) child as 'Playmate-Grown-Up' in the "Playmate Data Sheet." This same issue reintroduced the spectre of *Playboy* cartooning the child and statutory rape trickery (getting the victim drunk), which was also suspended post-1985.

> The scene: An outdoor picnic. A couple sits beneath a green-leafed tree. A pony-tailed, wide-eyed, bobby-socked girl—clasps her legs together as her companion, a man in shorts and sunglasses holds a bottle out to the girl saying: "I know you are young and inexperienced, but you can trust me to be sensitive and understanding. Tequila?" (p. 155. The cartoonist's name resembles "Kihi Saat").

The New Zealand Indecency Tribunal 1988–1989

A content analysis of *Penthouse* USA magazine (1988–1989) presented to the New Zealand Indecency Tribunal (November 1990)[11] confirmed the

---

[9]Although the Attorney General's Commission on Pornography (1986) strongly urged that 21 be the age of consent for pornography modeling, this was somehow translated to age 18 before the document got to the floor of Congress. This would seem to be a fine research project on whether special interests are impacting our pornography laws in unethical ways.

[10]Immediately upon the passage of the "reporting" requirement for pornography models, *Playboy* and other publications ran editorials, both in print and on television, against requiring pornographers to prove the age of the models posing for them.

[11]See the *New Zealand Indecent Publications Act* (1963, No. 22, pp. 2, 7). This paper was presented in New Zealand in 1991 by Dr. John Court to address the ways in which *Penthouse* impacts upon juvenile viewers-participants.

Penthouse pedophile self-censorship policy since 1985. (As noted, *Hustler* was not monitored post-1985.) On the positive side, our 1988–1989 *Penthouse* study found a near elimination of "real" child pornography imagery. On the negative side, we find a systematic use of sadosexual crime and violence designed for juvenile and adult patrons. Sadosexual magazine images are increasingly "spiced" by ever-larger, bulgingly freakish silicone-breasted women performing pseudo-lesbian acts—with close-ups of shiny red tongues (pseudo-lesbian)—exploring the (pseudo-child pudenda) shaved genitalia.

For consumers, a key child abuse concern should be the "body part" activity of these magazines. By making bare, hairless genitalia, and cameoing a magnified naked pudenda being sexually manipulated by a "partner," juvenile and adult male and female consumers intuitively "see" and are thus frequently aroused by a blowup of a little girl's sexualized pudenda. Adding *Playboy* and *Penthouse*'s glamorized sadistic imagery to its child genitalia model suggests additional problems for children and society.

Just as the September 1991 *Playboy* marketed a "Playmate" child alongside its sexually freighted Playmate "biography," the December 1988 *Penthouse* also marketed a naked Tiny Tim—cartooned as the family-*Penthouse* Christmas dinner. An example of testing readers for their limits of child abuse humor was this *Penthouse* Christmas cartoon "joke" about cannibalizing Tiny Tim.

> The scene: The family's Victorian dining room. Dad, mom, and the children—in full color—are smilingly seated around the table, Tiny Tim's crutches laid across his empty stool. The boy is decapitated, trussed, and dressed as a nude dinner "roast," his naked buttocks thrust up on the serving plate, his little body garnished with grapes and apples. His family members clutch their knives and forks in preparation for dining on Tiny Tim's bare buttocks for Christmas. In his final religious attack, the anonymous *Penthouse* artist–author has Tim's father bless the family's cannibal feast on his handicapped son by saying: " . . . And God bless Tiny Tim." (p. 210)

CONCLUSION

August 24, 1990 *The Washington Post* reported in "Ratings: A Matter of Seconds" on two films to be judged "X" or "R" based only on "two camera angles during one love scene, for a total of about 36 seconds. . . . 38 frames, totaling about ½ seconds." The scholarly research on visual stimulation confirms the empirical observations of the movie raters regarding the potency of a half-second image received by the brain of adults, juveniles, and children. (If "every second, 100 million messages bombard the brain carrying information from the body's senses," only the most stimulating, the most exciting, threatening, shameful messages will penetrate into one's brain.)[12] The addictive nature of the pornographic media may be seen in its recent incursion into network TV.

Beginning in January 1991, the *Playboy* world has emerged as "Peep TV"—pornographic depictions in network TV "talk shows," afternoon "soap" dramas, evening "miniseries" dramas, primetime dramas, and, more subtly, in evening situation comedies. Since then, talk show hosts Oprah Winfrey, Phil Donahue, Geraldo Rivera, Sally Jesse Raphael, Jennie Jones, and others, have all appeared as what could be called the old time carnival "shills" beckoning the viewer-participants in to watch their daily sexual exhibitions of pornography models, "S&M" sadistic sex movie clips, sex "toy" displays, nude dancers, transvestites, prostitutes, strippers, and sundry other sexual deviants. The socialization of voyeurism among millions of adult and juvenile media viewer-participants could be seen as the inevitable outcome of mainstreaming pornography print media via *Playboy* and *Penthouse*, and so on. (Indeed, "Peep TV" appears to be a purposeful attempt to undermine the nation's legal recourse to "community standards" vis-à-vis prohibitions against obscenity.)

Considering the excitation-stimulation features of provocative sexual images, both the scholarly research and empirical data suggest that we must take very seriously the rating of magazine "frames" that may be innocent "humor" or pornography. It is especially important that we consider carefully both the access of children to pornography and the treatment of children *in all* pornography. Massive youthful exposure to mainstream pornography (*Playboy, Penthouse*, and *Hustler*) as well as its offshoot—sadistic sexual films, MTVs, and videos—establishes the gravity of reexamining pornographic "entertainment" as emotional and cognitive education for both juvenile and adult publics.

The academic community is generally naive about how industries, including the sex industry, commonly will employ a broad variety of techniques to sway scholarly, mass media, legislative, and even federal treatment of academic findings. News stories that simultaneously appeared nationwide were part of a carefully staged campaign to undermine public confidence in our research findings on "Images of Children, Crime and Violence in *Playboy, Penthouse* and *Hustler*." An impartial academic and

---

[12]Although this citation is taken from Pinchot (1984, pp. 122–123), it is argued here that much of the objective, measurable data on pornography effects may be found in current brain studies including hemispheric stratification as well as the psychopharmacological findings on endogenous drug production. Much of the information that is basic in these fields needs to be imported into the communication field and applied to problems in television violence and pornography research (see Reisman, 1992).

legislative investigation of the attack and suppression of other valid research that was costly to powerful special interests would be of value to science and society.

The value of the reported research may be found in the impact it has had on the industry under investigation. Despite the economic power behind the offensive against our peer-approved report on child pornography and violence in these mainstream magazines, fear of consumer awareness documentably forced *Playboy* and *Penthouse* to *temporarily* clean up their products, hastily self-censoring their more blatant *visual* child pornography, rape, and violence productions.

Based on the recent effort to return these magazines to local stores, and the slow infiltration of the child pornography and sadosexual contents back into the materials, *Playboy, Penthouse*, and *Hustler* self-monitoring may not be the long-range answer to the environmental hazards of erotic–pornographic exploitation. Certainly, the unanimous decision of the Canadian Supreme Court to classify all pornography as harm to women and thus as obscenity, suggests a movement in the West toward proscription. If scientifically accurate data were able to bypass the media gatekeepers and thus gain access to the polity—the public and their democratic representatives—such an open and fair dialog would go far toward controlling and even eliminating the "toxic" entertainment media in their most malignant forms.

REFERENCES

Attorney General's Commission on pornography. (1986, July). *Summary of the Final Report of the Attorney General's Commission on Pornography*. Cincinnati, OH:National Coalition Against Pornography.

Reisman, J. A. (1989). *Images of children, crime and violence in "Playboy," "Penthouse" and "Hustler."* Lafayette, LA: Huntington House.

Reisman, J. A. (1990). *Public policy implications of sex industrial power*. Unpublished manuscript.

Reisman, J. A. (1991). *"Soft porn" plays hardball*. Lafayette, LA: Huntington House.

Reisman, J. A. (1992). *X & R rated media and the harm factor*. Testimony presented to the Australian Parliament Inquiry, Australia.

Trento, S. (1992). *The power house*. New York: St. Martin's Press.

Pinchot, R. (Ed.). (1984). *The human body: The brain*. New York: Torstar Books.

21

RESEARCH, PUBLIC POLICY, AND LAW: COMBINATION FOR CHANGE

Robert Showers
National Law Center for Children and Families, Fairfax, VA

TRENDS IN RESEARCH ON THE EFFECTS OF PORNOGRAPHY

Rarely can scientific results of research be effectively explained and understood in ways to influence law and public policy directly on controversial social issues. However, research has increasingly been utilized successfully to affect public opinion and law changes in the area of pornography, sexual exploitation, and violence in the media.

Initially, scientific research was put forward by the 1970 Commission on Pornography to justify their recommendations to legalize virtually all pornography and violent depictions in all media (*Report*, 1970). Research allegedly found that such pornography had either *no adverse effects*, or a *cathartic impact* on attitudes and behavior (*Report*, 1970; Zillmann, 1989).[1]

However, by the late 1970s and early 1980s, the Report's conclusions, which were overwhelmingly rejected by Congress and the President, were

---

[1] From the outset, it was clear that its verdict of "no ill effects" was based on few and tentative findings, many of which were lately generated by the Commission itself to justify its biased conclusions.

being questioned in some sections of the scientific community (Cline, 1974; see also Donnerstein, 1983, 1988; Malamuth, 1981, 1984; Zillmann & Bryant, 1982). In 1986, a new Pornography Commission concluded: "In both clinical and experimental settings, exposure to sexually violent materials has indicated an increase in the likelihood of aggression. More specifically, the research . . . shows a causal relationship between exposure to material of this type and aggressive behavior towards women" (*Final Report of the Attorney General*, 1986, p. 39)

Later, two dozen leading researchers, gathered by the U.S. Surgeon General and including many critics of the Pornography Report like Professors Malamuth and Donnerstein, reached five "consensus" conclusions:

1. Children and adolescents who participate in the production of pornography experience adverse and enduring effects.

2. Prolonged use of pornography increases the belief that less common sexual practices are common.

3. Pornography that portrays sexual aggression as pleasurable for the victim increases the acceptance of the use of coercion in sexual relations.

4. Acceptance of coercive sexuality appears to be related to sexual aggression.

5. Exposure to violent pornography increases punitive behavior toward women even if only short-term exposure in laboratory settings (*Final Report of the Surgeon General*, 1986).

How have these very different research conclusions from 1970 and 1986 affected public policy and law in the 1980s, and more importantly how could this research trend have an impact on pornography and sexually violent material and its distribution in the 1990s? The evidence affecting public policy falls into three general categories: (a) general anecdotal evidence (b) law enforcement data and (c) scientific research (field, laboratory, or clinical) — all of which have significant value and impact on law and public policy.

GENERAL ANECDOTAL EVIDENCE

First, a dramatic change in the *content of pornography* over the last 20 years was illustrated by the 1986 Commission's findings and a 1982 Harvard Medical School content analysis that revealed that "mainstream" pornography freely available on the open market in the 1980s was virtually unavailable in 1970 (Dietz, 1988; *Final Report of the Attorney General*,

1986). For example, in 1970, the vast majority of "hardcore" pornography featured a nude woman posing alone, whereas only a small percentage today contains such imagery, and less than 10% of today's pornography depicts vaginal intercourse between one man and one woman (Dietz, 1988; *Final Report of Attorney General*, 1986; *Final Report of Surgeon General*, 1986).

Today, the most prevalent themes in hardcore pornographic material focus on sexually deviant or violent behavior, including child sexual abuse, bondage, torture, rape, incest, group sex, sex with animals, excretory functions, lesbian, homosexual, and transsexual activity, and a wide variety of violent and degrading sexual practices, which can only be described as extremely "unsafe." Exploitation, degradation, victimization, and humiliation — especially of women and children — pervade current hardcore pornography (*Final Report of the Attorney General*, 1986).

Second, the largest age category of pornography consumers appears to be children age 12 to 17 (*Final Report of the Attorney General*, 1986; *Final Report of the Surgeon General*, 1986; *Presidential*, 1970). Although the total effect on children is unknown, the 1970 Presidential Commission on Pornography, the Surgeon General's Report, and the 1986 Commission on Pornography all concluded that pornography could have a serious, harmful, and lasting adverse effect on the attitudes and behavior of a child (*Final Report of the Attorney General*, 1986; *Final Report of the Surgeon General*, 1986; *Presidential*, 1970).

Third, pornography in the United States has become a large and very profitable commercial enterprise. Annual revenues from its production, distribution, and sale are now estimated between $7 and $10 billion, with organized criminal networks controlling the vast majority of its profits (*Attorney General's Organized*, 1986). The dramatic increase in distribution, accompanied by the exploitative, violent, and deviant changes in content, appear to parallel the unprecedented increase in rape (526% increase since 1980) and child molestation (175% increase since 1980) (*Lifetime*, 1987). Conversely, when pornography is removed from the open market, rape rates significantly decrease long term even when rape rates in surrounding areas are increasing during the same period[2] (American Family, 1989). For example, states of the highest incidence of pornography magazines also have the highest per capita incidence of rape. (Baron & Strauss, 1984; Court, 1977; Scott & Schwalm, 1989).

Fourth, many public health officials have linked pornography consumption and adverse public health consequences because of anonymous sexual

---

[2]Oklahoma City experienced a 26% decrease in rapes after removing over 100 hard-core pornography outlets, whereas the entire state had a 21% increase in rape during the same period.

activity in adult bookstores and the promotion of unsafe sex by such material. According to Dr. James Mason (1986), Assistant Secretary for Health, Department of Health and Human Services:

> It doesn't matter what one (sexually transmitted disease) of these we talk about, they are out of control because the nation's behavior is out of control and I can't help but believe that an indulgent society that permits pornography in media that is seen casually by youth and adults, is a significant contributor to the epidemic of sexually transmitted diseases in our country. (Video Interview, Religious Alliance Against Pornography, "Together we can make a difference in the fight against pornography," 1986, on file with the National Law Center for Children and Families).

Fifth, victim testimony about the connection of pornography to rape, child molestation, murder, family breakup or violence, and other sexual dysfunctions is now widely reported in books, newspapers, and on television and radio ("Porn Victims," 1992; Schafley, 1987).

LAW ENFORCEMENT DATA

Law enforcement agencies have collected data showing that people convicted of serial murders, sex crimes, and child molestation often used pornography. For example, a recent FBI study of 36 serial murders revealed that 81% reported significant pornography consumption, making pornography one of the most common profile characteristics of serial murders and rapists (Hazelwood, 1985). A Michigan state police survey of 42,000 sex crimes discovered that 42% of all sex crimes involve pornography either immediately prior to or during the commission of the act (Pope, 1987). The rates of child molestation have dramatically increased over the last few years, and, according to present crime trends, one in three females and one in seven males will be sexually molested before the age of 18 (Rabin, 1984). Sex crimes are frequent in neighborhoods with pornography businesses.

According to the U.S. Department of Justice, law enforcement statistics have reported that pornography's clientele have a frightening degree of correspondence with the police's list of sex criminals and violent assaults. Indeed, empirically verifiable connections have been established between pornography and violent sex-related crimes, including rape of women and child molestation (National Task Force, 1987; Karms, 1992; Showers, 1988).

SCIENTIFIC RESEARCH

Although research on this subject has been sparse and its methodology often questionable, a recent systematic review found that the best research on pornography found harmful effects (Lyons & Larsen, 1990). However, due to three major obstacles, this harm finding appears to be only the "tip of the iceberg." The three apparent shortcomings are that such scientific studies: (a) do not study subjects who are most vulnerable and most affected — teenagers and sexual deviants; (b) have not used materials that might produce the most adverse effects (hardcore and violent pornography); and (c) fail to study exposure in the most potentially dangerous real-life setting (i.e., heavy doses for long terms with masturbation) (Lyons & Larsen, 1990).

Significantly, the trend in research on pornographic and violent depictions appears to be uncovering more evidence of harm (see chapter 5).

SEX OFFENDERS

Eighty-six percent of convicted rapists in one study admitted to regular use of pornography, with 57% admitting imitation of pornography seen in the commission of sexual crimes. (Marshall, 1988). A 1983 field study of convicted child molesters indicated that 87% of those who molest girls, and 77% of those who molest boys, admitted use of pornography (a) to stimulate themselves, (b) to lower the inhibitions of their child victims, and (c) to teach the child to model the activity in real-life sexual encounters (Marshall, 1983).

NONVIOLENT, DEGRADING PORNOGRAPHY

In a 1981 study conducted by Zillmann and Bryant, an experimental group of males and females were exposed to nonviolent, hardcore pornography once a week for 6 consecutive weeks, while a control group watched films with innocuous content such as nature films. Three weeks later, the groups who watched pornography had noticeably different and prejudiced opinions from the control group (Zillmann & Bryant, 1982). They overestimated the popularity of less common sexual practices, were more tolerant toward behaviors deemed deviant by others, trivialized rape as a criminal offense, and reacted to pornography with less repulsion (Zillmann & Bryant, 1984).

Weaver (1991) found that exposure to pornography devoid of violence seemed to heighten, not lower, effects of trivialization of rape and beliefs that women want to be raped (Weaver, 1987, 1991). Buchman (1988) extended the study of effects of prolonged exposure to nonviolent pornography on attitudes about sexual abuse of children. Sexual coercion was deemed a lesser crime with less punishment required after extended consumption of pornography. Most importantly, extended exposure to pornography led to trivialization of rape of adults, and tolerance for the usually rather nonviolent sexual abuse of children (Buchman).

Malamuth and Check found that pornography that described the woman experiencing sexual arousal—whether being raped or consenting—aroused respondents more than when the woman did not like it or felt disgust (Malamuth & Check, 1983). Even critics Linz, Donnerstein, and Penrod (Linz, Donnerstein, & Penrod, 1987) found in their 1987 studies that:

> The 1986 Commission maintained that there was a causal relationship between exposure to sexually violent pornography and negative changes in certain attitudes towards and perceptions of women as well as increased aggression towards women. THIS IS AN ACCURATE STATEMENT as long as we are referring to the results of laboratory studies examining sexually violent images. (p. 949)

In a recent laboratory experiment, male college students and nonstudents were randomly assigned to various experimental conditions (Check & Guloien, 1989). Participants exposed to sexually violent pornography reported a greater likelihood of raping than subjects in the no-exposure group. Further, more than twice as many men indicated a likelihood of raping after exposure to nonviolent, dehumanizing pornography than after no exposure (Check & Guloien, 1989). All such studies have limitations, but the clear trend appears to indicate that real-life pornography consumption involving such conditions as prolonged exposure for months or years by teenagers or sexually deviant males, with masturbation, involving exclusively hardcore pornography, may have considerable *negative impact*.

POLICY CHANGES IN THE 1980s

The hearings for the 1986 Commission on Pornography and its Final Report were primary factors contributing to the growing public awareness and to the federal government's decision to launch a major initiative against illegal pornography and child exploitation through the National Obscenity Enforcement Task Force (now called Child Exploitation and Obscenity Section). This federal initiative, which included a national law center, federal, state, and local training, legislative assistance, and "how to publications" for prosecutors and investigators, created a dramatic increase in federal prosecutions of obscenity and child pornography and comprehensive changes to the federal and state laws (see Table 21.1).

Echoing the Department of Justice's determination that obscenity and child pornography would be two of the top criminal justice priorities in the

TABLE 21.1
Federal Prosecutions from 1983 Through 1989

	1983	1986	1987	1988	1989
Obscenity	0	10	78	37	120
Child exploitation	3	147	249	150	255

Justice Department, President Bush in his October 1991 White House Address called the prosecution of obscenity and child pornography top priority in his administration (*President*, 1991).

Prior to 1982, child pornography was adjudicated under the strict three-part obscenity definition that made prosecution of this material difficult. Among other things, research led both the U.S. Supreme Court in 1982 and later Congress in 1984 to conclude that child pornography must be a separate, distinct, criminal offense with a lower standard of proof because of its harm to the child victim: "The prevention of sexual exploitation and abuse of children constitute a government objective of surpassing importance" (*Ferber v. New York*, 1982, p. 1123).

Recently, in a U.S. Supreme Court decision concerning whether the criminalization of the mere private possession of child pornography was constitutional, the Court held in *Osborne v. Ohio*, 1989 and *Osborne v. Ohio*, 1990 that the harm to children from pornography far outweighed any minimal privilege that a possessor may have. In a key brief filed with the Court, the following summary of argument was:

> Scientific research and law enforcement studies further reveal an indisputable link between child pornography and child exploitation, as well as a severe harm suffered by children from child pornography. Evidence overwhelmingly supports the conclusion that child pornography primarily exists for the use and consumption by pedophiles and child molesters. Removal of all incentive for the production and distribution of child pornography, which is the ability to sell or distribute the pornography to a customer or possessor, is essential to dry up the circular chain of child pornography. Therefore, criminalizing possession of child pornography is paramount to curtail the harm to children, to break the cycle of child victimization and to dry up the market for child pornography. (*Osborne v. Ohio*, 1989, p. 3)

Research was also utilized in a recent Supreme Court case, *Maryland v. Craig* (*Maryland v. Craig*, 1990) which allowed videotaped or closed circuit testimony of the child abuse victim witness in a case against the molester because of the significant harm that might be experienced in the courtroom.

Law enforcement data concerning the connection between pornography and sexual crimes, as well as control of the industry by organized crime, led to the passage of RICO laws with the base offense of obscenity and child pornography. In two Supreme Court cases, *Ft. Wayne Books* and recently *Pryba*, the U.S. Supreme Court found that it is fully constitutional to make obscenity (and child pornography) one of the base offenses in proving the criminal enterprise under the powerful racketeering laws that permit asset forfeiture and increased jail terms (*Fort Wayne Books*, 1989; *United States v. Pryba*, 1990).

Public opinion about the secondary effects of pornography establishments has led to a multitude of local regulations of sexually oriented businesses such as laws for zoning and licensing, public nuisance, removal of peep show door booths, and sex supermarket ordinances. The U.S. Supreme Court in at least two cases, *Renton* and *Arcara Books* (*Arcara v. Cloud Books, Inc.*, 1986; *Playtime Theaters v. Renton*, 1986) has recently found that secondary effects and evidence of harm were sufficient reasons to zone adult establishments, permit removal of peep show door booths, and close pornography outlets because of sexual activity in such outlets.

Finally, investigative techniques on child molesters have been significantly altered based on the research that pedophiles and molesters often consume and use child and adult pornography in the commission of their criminal behavior against children. Thus, questions such as "Did the molester show you any videos or pictures or did he take pictures of you?" are often asked of the abused child. Further, search warrants prior to or concomitant with arrest are generally issued if there is probable cause to believe that pornography exists in the home of the molester. When pornography is found, it often constitutes powerful evidence in difficult child molestation trials that otherwise rely on child testimony (Showers & Malpas, 1992).

Although the 1980s have seen a dramatic shift in public policy, law enforcement techniques, and laws concerning the regulation of pornography due to the research that has been uncovered and publicized concerning the adverse effects and harm of pornography, the 1990s may show an even more dramatic trend.

TRENDS IN PUBLIC POLICY AND LAW FOR THE 1990s

Legislators, prosecutors, public opinion, city officials, and the courts are more often asking whether "pornography harms real victims" or "is it a victimless crime involving harmless entertainment?" If research, broadly defined, continues to show that pornography harms real victims in both the short-term and the long-term, public policy and law will continue to evolve toward regulation in all media. Whereas any predictions are always subject to crystal ball gazing, the trends in the 1980s lead to some predictions in the 1990s if research, public policy, and law continue to be integrated in the area of pornography and sexual exploitation. There are strong indications that there will be major changes in at least eight critical areas.

Broadcasting and cable will be more closely regulated due to the harm of pornography to children and the pervasive presence of children in the audience in the 1990s. Already the FCC has proposed a 24-hour ban on broadcast indecency due to three reasons: (a) pervasiveness of children in the late night hours, (b) harm to children from indecent broadcasting, and (c) new technology making it difficult, if not impossible, to prevent access to children (*Action for Children's Television v. FCC*, 1988; 1991; 1992; *Indecent*, 1991).

"Safe-harbor" periods are indefensible in light of the broadcast data showing large numbers of children in late night broadcast audiences and are further discredited by evidence showing a higher ratio of children to adults in the broadcast audience during late night or early morning hours than at other times. "Time channeling" alternatives endorsed by broadcasters would in fact "narrowcast indecent programming to the very audience in need of protection — children."

Telephone pornography, called dial-a-porn, will be virtually eliminated due to the harm to children and their potential imitation in committing sex crimes against other children. Obscene dial-a-porn was banned under the Child Protection and Obscenity Enforcement Act of 1988 and upheld under a recent U.S. Supreme Court decision of *Sable v. FCC* (1989). In July of 1990, indecent telephone communication was severely restricted by the FCC primarily based on numerous official comments outlining the research and harm to children from indecent telephone communications (*Religious*, 1990). In fact, the FCC received comments that highlighted recent cases of sexual molestation of children by children who listen to dial-a-porn. The more subtle, but equally devastating, effects on children from dial-a-porn could be: (a) the degrading and dangerous imagery of sex, (b) the possibility of compulsive–addictive behavior related to exposure to dial-a-porn, (c) the trivialization of sexual violence, and (d) the perpetuation of the rape myth to immature and impressionable children. Thus, many legal commentators believe that research may persuade the high court to uphold the strict regulation of indecent dial-a-porn and broadcasting (*Religious*, 1990)

The further discovery of secondary adverse effects of pornography in the 1990s may cause, along with other factors, *adult bookstores and X-rated theaters to virtually disappear from the landscape in America*. Whereas at one time there were more pornography outlets than McDonalds restaurants in America, numerous local regulations against pornography and public health concerns may drive the more egregious distribution centers of hardcore pornography and videotapes (i.e., adult bookstores and X-rated theaters) out of business.

Proliferation of violence in the media and the concomitant studies of the effect of graphic visual violence on children have led at least two states to attempt to *control "violence for violence sake" in video and movie theater films under the harmful to minors statutes* (*Media Violence*). These statutes in Missouri and Tennessee are presently undergoing court challenges to their constitutionality. If research continues to show that graphic violence can lead to negative changes in attitudes and behavior, including the commission of violent crimes, many other states and the FCC may attempt to regulate violence in the media under the harmful to minors laws.

Another predicted area of change in the 1990s is that *pornography victims legislation*, both federal and state, will provide for compensation to victims of rape and child molestation when pornography has been a catalyst or primary incitement to commit such crimes (Poor Victim, 1992). Because the harm of pornography to minors is unquestioned, *harmful matter per se* laws may be passed to prevent any pornographic material from being distributed or shown to minors.

Finally, one of the most notable changes that may occur in the 1990s is to apply an *obscene per se standard*, and not the three-part *Miller* test for obscenity, *to all hardcore pornography or to some more egregious categories of adult pornography*. Some forms of pornography may be considered "obscene per se" because of demonstrated harm to victims or society, using the same rationale as that used by the Supreme Court for child pornography (Taylor). If research demonstrates that some forms of adult pornography produce harmful effects similar to those of child pornography, it might influence public opinion, legislators, and courts to conclude that other categories of pornography are obscene per se. Some viable candidates are (a) pseudo child pornography (adults dressed like children), (b) sexual violence, (c) unsafe sex acts, and (d) deviant sexual acts.

Legislatures, courts, and the public may ask two primary questions: (a) How serious are the negative effects of such pornography; and (b) does such pornography produce any positive results? Moreover, if the harm from pornography is documented, *possession* of illegal pornography will be made criminal in nature to stop the market that promotes and incites child molestation and rape.

Research can provide answers that can influence law and public policy in the 1990s. Clearly, pornography and sexual exploitation are no longer only moral or religious issues but are now matters of public health and safety.

CONCLUSION

Results of scientific research have rarely translated into changes in public policy and law. However, in the 1980s research on pornography and sexual exploitation was integrated effectively into legal and political arguments. Broadly defined, such research includes general anecdotal evidence, law enforcement data, and scientific field and laboratory research. The impacts include: (a) dramatic changes in federal law enforcement initiatives; (b) child pornography becoming a separate, distinct crime from adult obscenity; (c) criminalizing possession of child pornography; (d) legal protection of child abuse victim–witness testimony; (e) altering child molestation investigation techniques; and (f) numerous local regulations of sexually oriented businesses due to adverse secondary effects.

New research continues to show the correlations between pornography and sexual crime and to highlight the adverse short-term and long-term impact of pornography and its related exploitation on children and women. If such important research continues, there will be a continued necessity to translate such findings to affect public policy, public opinion, and law. Thus, the 1990s may see dramatic changes: broadcast pornography and violence closely regulated; dial-a-porn and sex lines virtually eliminated; "adult" bookstores and X-rated theaters disappear; pornography victims legislation and lawsuits; graphic violence on all media strictly controlled to prevent child access; and "obscene per se" and "harmful matter per se" laws being passed in obvious areas of harmful pornography.

Successful research effectively explained drives change in public opinion that directly affected public policy and law in the 1980s and will continue to do so in the 1990s. The great challenge for researchers, lawyers, and policymakers is to integrate research, public policy, and law to protect America's most precious resources, our children and family for the next century.

REFERENCES

Action for Children's Television v. FCC, (Act I) 852 F.2d 1332 (D. C. Cir. 1988).
Action for Children's Television v. FCC, (Act II) 932 F.2d 1504 (1991).
Action for Children's Television v. FCC, (Act III) 117 L.Ed. 2d 507, cert denied (March 2, 1992).
American Family Association. (1989). *Pornography: A report.* Tupelo, MS: Author.
Arcara v. Cloud Books, Inc., 478 U.S. 697 (1986).
Attorney General's Organized Crime Report in California. (1986).
Baron, L., & Strauss, M. A. (1984). Pornography and rape in America. In N. M. Malamuth & E. Donnerstein (Eds.), *Pornography and sexual aggression* (pp. 185–209). New York: Academic Press.
Buchman, J. G. (1988). *Effects of repeated exposure to non-violent erotica on attitudes about sexual child abuse.* Unpublished doctoral dissertation, Indiana University, Bloomington.
Check, J. V. P., & Guloien, T. H. (1989). Reported proclivity for coercive sex following repeated exposure to sexually violent pornography, non-violent pornography and erotica. In D. Zillmann (Ed.), *Pornography: Research advances and policy considerations* (pp. 159–184). Hillsdale, NJ: Lawrence Erlbaum Associates.

Cline, V. B. (1974). *Where do you draw the line*. Salt Lake City, UT: Brigham Young University Press.

Court, J. H. (1977). Pornography and sex crimes. *International Journal of Criminology and Penology, 5*(2), 129–157.

Dietz, P. (1988). Pornography imagery and prevalence of paraphilia. *American Journal of Psychiatry, 139*, 1493–1495.

Donnerstein, E. (1983). Erotica and human aggression. In R. Geen & E. Donnerstein (Eds.), *Aggression: Theoretical and empirical reviews* (Vol. 2, pp. 127–154). New York: Academic Press.

Donnerstein, E. (1988). Pornography and violence against women. *Annals of New York Academy of Sciences, 347*, 277–288.

Donnerstein, E., Linz, D., & Penrod, S. (1987). *The question of pornography: Research findings and policy implications*. New York: Free Press.

Ferber v. New York, 458 U.S. 747, 757 (1982).

Final Report of the Attorney General's Commission on Pornography. (1986). Nashville, TN: Rutledge Hill Press.

Final Report of the Surgeon General's Workshop on Pornography and Public Health. (1986). Washington, DC: U.S. Government Printing Office.

Fort Wayne Books, 489 US 46 (1989).

Harms of pornography. (1992). Fact sheet. Alexandria, VA: National Law Center for Children and Families.

Hazelwood, R. (1985, August). *The men who murdered*. FBI law enforcement bulletin.

Indecent broadcasting. (1991). Report of FCC.

Lifetime likelihood of victimization. (1987). Washington, DC: U.S. Government Printing Office. U.S. Department of Justice.

Linz, D., Donnerstein, E., & Penrod, S. (1987). The findings and recommendations of the Attorney General's Commission on Pornography: Do the psychological "facts" fit the political fury? *American Psychologist, 42*, 946–953.

Lyons, J., & Larsen, D. (1990, November). *A systematic analysis of the social science research on the effects of violent and non-violent pornography*. Paper presented at the NFF Symposium, Pittsburgh, PA.

Malamuth, N. M. (1981). Rape proclivity among males. *Journal of Social Issues 37*(4), 138–157.

Malamuth, N. M. (1984). Aggression against women: Cultural and individual causes. In N. M. Malamuth & E. Donnerstein (Eds.), *Pornography and sexual aggression* (pp. 19–52). New York: Academic Press.

Malamuth, N. M., & Check, J. V. P. (1983). Sexual arousal to rape depictions: Individual differences. *Journal of Abnormal Psychology, 92*, 55–67.

Marshall, W. (1983). *Report on the use of pornography by sexual offenders*. Report to the Department of Justice, Ottowa, Canada: Government publication.

Marshall, W. (1988). Use of sexually explicit stimuli by rapists, child molesters and non-offenders. *Journal of Sex Research, 25*, 267–288.

Maryland v. Craig, 497 U.S. 111 L.Ed. 2nd 666, 1990.

Mason, J. (1989, October). *The harm of pornography*. Paper presented to the Religious Alliance Against Pornography, Washington, DC.

Media violence: The verdict is in. See supra Chapter 10.

National Task Force on Child Exploitation and Pornography created. (1987, Feb 21). U.S. Department of Justice press release.

Osborne v. Ohio, N. 88-5986 (October Term 1989). Amici brief of National Coalition Against Pornography, Concerned Women for America, Focus on the Family, et al. at 3.

Osborne v. Ohio, (1990). 495 U.S., 108 S. Ct. 1691.

Playtime Theaters v. Renton, 475 US 41 (1986).

Pope, D. (1987, September 16). *Hearing on women, violence and the law.* Testimony before the Select Committee on Children, Youth and Family.

Porn Victim Compensation Act, S. 1521 (1992) sponsors J. McConnell (Kentucky) and Grassley (Iowa).

Porn victims need this bill. (1992, April 21). *USA Today,* p. 10A.

President Bush's public comments to Religious Alliance Against Pornography, October, 1991.

Presidential commission report on pornography, Technical reports Vol. VI. (1970).

Rabin, J. (1984). Testimony before the Subcommittee on Juvenile Justice, Judiciary Committee, U.S. Senate.

Religious Alliance Against Pornography. (1986). *Together we can make a difference in the fight against pornography.* Video on file at National Law Center for Children and Families, Fairfax, VA.

Religious Alliance Against Pornography in the regulation of telephone Dial-a-Porn. F. C. C. Comments. (1990).

Report of the Commission on Obscenity and Pornography. (1970). Washington, DC: U.S. Government Printing Office.

Sable Communication of California v. F. C. C. 492 U.S. 115 (1989).

Schafley, P. (1987). Victim testimony before the pornography commission.

Scott, J. E., & Schwalm, L. A. (1989). Rape rates and the circulation rates of adult magazines. *Journal of Sex Research, 77,* 203–204.

Showers, R. (1988). Myths and misconceptions of pornography. Brochure published by *Christian Legal Society.*

Showers, R., & Malpas, G. (1992). *Child sexual exploitation and child pornography* (in publication National Center for Missing and Exploited Children). See F. C. C. Decision in.

Taylor, B. *Obscenity, Per Se,* Mich L. J.

United States v. Pryba, 1990.

Weaver, J. B. (1987). *Effects of portrayals of female sexuality and violence against women on perceptions of women.* Unpublished doctoral dissertation, Indiana University, Bloomington.

Weaver, J. B. (1991). Responding to erotica: Perceptual processes and dispositional implications. In J. Bryant & D. Zillmann (Eds.), *Responding to the screen: Reception and reaction processes* (pp. 329–354). Hillsdale, NJ: Lawrence Erlbaum Associates.

Zillmann, D., & Bryant, J. (1982). Pornography, sexual callousness, and the trivialization of rape. *Journal of Communication, 32*(4), 10–21.

Zillmann, D. & Bryant, J. (1984). Effects of massive exposure to pornography. In N. M. Malamuth & E. Donnerstein (Eds.), *Pornography and sexual aggression* (pp. 115–138). New York: Academic Press.

Zillmann, D., & Bryant, J. (1989). Pornography: *Research advances and policy considerations.* Hillsdale, NJ: Lawrence Erlbaum Associates.

Author Index

341

SUBJECT INDEX